A volume in the
DOUGLASS SERIES IN EDUCATION,
edited by HARL R. DOUGLASS, Ph.D.,
DIRECTOR OF THE COLLEGE OF EDUCATION,
UNIVERSITY OF COLORADO

VOLUMES IN

DOUGLASS SERIES IN EDUCATION

ADMINISTRATIVE LEADERSHIP

in the

ELEMENTARY SCHOOL

By

HANNE J. HICKS

PROFESSOR OF EDUCATION
INDIANA UNIVERSITY

THE RONALD PRESS COMPANY · NEW YORK

Library of Congress Catalog Card Number: 56–6264

PRINTED IN THE UNITED STATES OF AMERICA

To the memory of
MARTHA

PREFACE

This book is dedicated to clarifying and strengthening the modern concept of educational leadership in the elementary school of today. Intended primarily as a textbook for courses in elementary school administration, its content covers all the major facets of the elementary school program and answers the "why," "what," and "how." It should also prove useful as a source book for seminar groups, in which a compact treatment of the organization and processes of the elementary school is desired, and to individuals interested in improving the quality of educational leadership.

The pattern of organization is a consistent one. Each of the seven Parts deals with one of the major concerns of leadership as applied to the development of better American schools. They have been formulated from the valued observations of seasoned educators, from the immense store of research on elementary education, and from convictions which have grown out of the experience of the author throughout his professional career as an elementary school teacher, elementary school principal and supervisor, state curriculum supervisor, and as a teacher of college courses in elementary school administration and supervision.

The systematic pattern of organization of the book will, it is hoped, enhance its usefulness as a textbook. Each chapter contains a chart depicting the significant relationships brought out in the chapter. Each chapter is developed around a thorough discussion of these basic relationships which, when considered as a whole, represent a comprehensive program for the progress of modern elementary education. The emphasis is on improvement rather than on the ideal situation—on translating theory into practice. At the conclusion of each chapter, specific "action suggestions" are listed, which increase the book's usefulness to the student and to principals and supervisors with varying degrees of in-service experience, as they evaluate and fulfill their responsibilities as educational leaders.

The author is indebted to many associates and graduate students at Indiana University for their direct and indirect contributions to the content and preparation of the manuscript. Grateful acknowledgment is also made to numerous publishers and organizations for permission to use quotations from their publications. Particular appreciation is extended to Gerry Howard, who prepared the charts, and to the author's wife, Laurie, who worked overtime in the final preparation of the manuscript.

HANNE J. HICKS

December, 1955

CONTENTS

PART I

The Role of the Educational Leader

PART II

Purposes and Functions of the School

PART III

Improving the Organization and Management of the School

PART IV

Improving the Curriculum of the School

PART V

Improving the Services of the School

PART VI

Improving Professional Relationships in the School

PART VII

Evaluating the Effectiveness of the School

FIGURES

PART I

THE ROLE OF THE EDUCATIONAL LEADER

Chapter 1

BASIC FUNCTIONS OF
EDUCATIONAL LEADERSHIP

*No man is good enough to govern another without the other's
consent—Abraham Lincoln*

The fortunes of men, throughout the ages, have been determined
largely by their leaders. The dreams and aspirations of each generation
have sought substance in those occupying positions of responsibility. At
the same time, however, even the necessities of mankind have been
denied by the tyrannical assumption of power by unscrupulous leaders.
The success or failure of man's quest for both freedom and security has
seemed to rest largely on the motives, wisdom, and efforts of those to
whom he has entrusted leadership. The role of leadership, then, may be
one of society's most effective instruments for advancement, or one of
its most destructive enemies. And a basic element of the democratic way
of life is a concept of leadership which demands that leaders serve as well
as direct. The successful development of democracy as a system of group
living has depended greatly upon the attitudes of leaders toward
their functions.

The level of civilization enjoyed at any particular time in history is
an indication of the quality of leadership experienced in preceding generations. However, it must be recognized that the quality of leadership
enjoyed or endured bears both cause and effect relationship to the conditions found during any period. On the one hand, the effectiveness of
the agencies of society is directly related to the quality of its leadership;
on the other, the peculiar demands and conditions of each period determine to a large degree the character of the leaders it produces.

The necessity for effective and enlightened leadership is not limited
to any particular facet of enterprise. It is true that political leaders, by
virtue of broad responsibilities and continuous publicity, often bask in an
aura not enjoyed by leaders in other fields. However, many of the advances of civilization may be attributed directly to wise leadership in
such fields as business, labor, religion, science, and education.

3

The role of the leader in education is particularly important. Society has created schools as basic instruments for producing the kind of citizens it desires. It has then placed the direction and operation of these schools largely in the hands of educational leaders. Such a leader becomes more than a professional technician or specialist. He is actually an engineer of humankind, upon whom rests much of the responsibility for the perpetuation and refinement of the society in which he functions.[1]

He is in a strategic position to influence constructively the lives and well-being of his contemporaries and of posterity. His ideas are spread widely by the efforts of his associates, and his greatest rewards are the achievements and successes of those who come after him. The educational leader is in a position to study and evaluate the past, to contribute to the organization of the present, and to build the human bases upon which the structures of future civilization depend. It would be difficult to conceive a role which involves greater challenges or nobler ends.

While serving in the improvement of the lot of man, education itself has benefited from the continuous refinement of its own processes. In this internal development, educational leadership has been exercised in many different ways. It obviously has been present in such aspects of education as research, administration, curriculum study and improvement, and in the scientific movement in education. These and many other facets of educational endeavor are clearly marked by the enthusiasm and specialized competence of persons in positions of leadership. It may be contended, with considerable justification, that the contributions of effective leadership have simultaneously affected the end products of the educational process, the process, and the leadership function itself.

NATURE OF EDUCATIONAL LEADERSHIP

Leadership undertakes the achievement of the goals which members of a group establish for themselves on the basis of some common concern. Indeed, genuinely effective leadership not only contributes to the realization of such goals but frequently may also serve in the formulation and clarification of group objectives. At the same time, the processes of leadership must guarantee that the rights, privileges, and contributions of the individual (or the few) will not be ignored for the sake of the purposes of the many.

In the evolution of educational leadership, two distinct types of leaders have emerged. One is the *status leader,* usually a person whose official responsibilities arise out of the nature of his position. These responsi-

---

[1] The masculine pronoun is used here and throughout succeeding chapters in its generic sense to denote teachers or principals of both sexes.

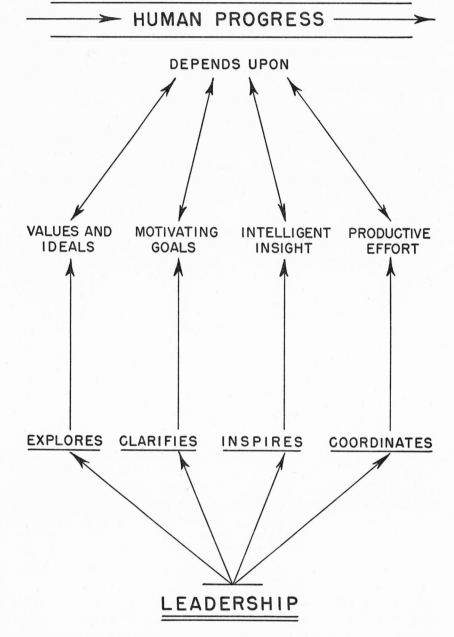

Figure 1

Leadership and Progress

bilities, usually broad and long range in nature, are placed upon such a leader by virtue of his selection by members of his group or organization. The positions of such leaders are usually related to the *structure* of the educational enterprise. Superintendents of schools, directors of instruction, supervisors, and principals are status leaders typical of the current structure of American schools.

Another type is *the contributing leader,* concerned with the solution of those educational problems which often extend across the lines established by the administrative structure of the schools. The intelligent operation of education today seems to demand that the leadership function be sufficiently diffused to utilize effectively the specialized knowledge and talents of all members of a group or staff. This means a sharing of the role of leader so that it may be shifted from one person to another in terms of the nature of the problem to be considered and the specialized competencies possessed by various members of the group.

The successful maintenance and continuous improvement of the school program require the recognition and effective utilization of both concepts of leadership. The emphasis currently being placed on the role of the contributing leader, though fully justified, cannot diminish or eliminate the necessity for good status leaders. In fact, each type of leadership supports and strengthens the other if both are democratically conceived and utilized.

Two basic considerations make the role of the status leader in education important. First, he often is in control of many essential factors of the educational situation in which he and his associates work. Furthermore, the presence of the status leader lends continuity and stability to the educational process which could not be enjoyed under a scheme of constantly shifting leadership. In view of these two vital functions, this volume analyzes critically the role of the status leader in the elementary school—particularly the elementary school principal—and suggests some of the theoretically sound and practical means whereby such a role may be assumed with optimum effectiveness.

Some Basic Principles of Educational Leadership

Genuinely effective educational leadership requires knowledge of the principles of administration and evaluation of its practices.

1. *Genuine leadership places greater value on coordination than on conformity.* This implies the right of each member of a group to be himself and to make his unique contribution to the group effort. The application of this principle negates the expectation that each member will contribute equally and in identical manner to the common cause. Con-

formity is a tool of authoritarianism, and a reverence for blind submission to some uniform pattern of action seems to have little, if any, place in the democratic process. On the contrary, competent leadership will be characterized by proper encouragement of individual effort and by thoughtful means for merging wholly different contributions into a productive kind of teamwork.

2. *Effective leadership is usually reflected in the successes of persons other than the leader himself.* Self-aggrandizement is not the prime motivation in the life of the truly great educational leader. Rather, he is stimulated by the achievements of his associates and is pleased by the recognition of their individual and collective successes. Since the very concept of democratic leadership is based on the idea of helping people help themselves, it is in the ultimate achievement of others that wise leadership finds fruition.

A primary concern of real leadership is to capitalize fully on the strengths of individuals who comprise the educational team. When all members of a group appear to be growing rapidly or enjoying unusual success in their work, one may be sure that wholesome and effective leadership is operating.

3. *Real leadership employs the same sort of techniques in human relations that it seeks to develop in others.* The best single approach to the development of democratic attitudes and practices in teachers in the classroom is the demonstrated use of such attitudes and practices by the educational leader himself. Democracy is not an idea that can be transmitted best through verbal means; it appears to be understood best when the evidence of its application is present and recognized.

The qualities of graciousness and consideration likewise seem to beget themselves in others when emphasized in the attitudes and actions of administrative leaders. In most recent analytical studies of teachers' reactions to their leaders the "human" quality appears high on the list of desired attributes. In short, it may be said that the most direct way to create in staff members a genuine consciousness of the value of being "human" in personal and professional relationships is for the leader himself to exemplify this quality.

Objectivity is also a necessary element of good leadership. Many decisions can be made wisely only after all the evidence is gathered and evaluated. Leadership based on whim is certainly destined to be ineffective. Leadership, on the other hand, which utilizes the scientific approach in the solution of problems gradually builds for itself the justified respect of all persons involved. In fact, each member of the educational team is much more likely to utilize the same approach to the solution of his problems once he has seen its efficacy demonstrated.

Professional imagination and the spirit of experimentation are other qualities of effective leadership. Only through such approaches can the demands of changing conditions, general or local, be met with reasonable facility. Adaptability is certainly one of the essential components of fruitful leadership, and the wise leader should not hesitate to employ approaches and techniques that offer the greatest opportunity for his educational policies to be realized.

4. *Effective leadership must be related to goals.* By its very definition, leadership implies action or movement toward a specific goal. By the same reasoning, then, it becomes one of the chief functions of leadership to assist in the achievement of goals. However, the responsibilities of leadership go much farther. In addition to helping a group accomplish its pre-established goals, leadership also encompasses activities designed to formulate, clarify, and evaluate goals, or to discover those previously unrecognized. Certainly, one of the basic roles of the educational leader is the clear formulation and understanding of purposes and the cooperative development of efficient means for their realization.

5. *Effective leadership must be considered a means rather than an end.* In the democratic process, emphasis must be placed on both the individual and the collective welfare of the members of a group and on the maintenance of an appropriate balance between the two. Leadership should be a means whereby the welfare and progress both of individuals and the group may be protected and advanced simultaneously. Democracy involves the concept that leaders spring from a group to serve the purposes of the group and of those who compose it. Only in totalitarian schemes of human regulation do the purposes and will of the leader become those also of the group. Only under totalitarian conditions does leadership become an end in itself. It is obvious that such a concept of leadership is incompatible with the spirit of democracy and thus with an educational process designed to promote the democratic way of life.

6. *Effective leadership depends upon both the motives and competencies of those who serve as leaders.* Although the processes of leadership rest heavily upon the technical and human skills of the leader, they depend to an equal extent on the values which motivate the leader. Just as electricity may be used to operate an electric chair for the destruction of life or to furnish power for lighting a hospital where the chief object is the saving of life, so the powers of leadership may be applied to either constructive or destructive social purposes according to the dominating motives of the leader. Leadership based on a stock of highly refined competencies is profitable in so far as it is directed into socially and ethically constructive channels consistent with soundly established goals. Actually, a highly developed set of administrative and

social skills may serve as a real hazard to democratic education in the hands of the leader with questionable motivating interests.

7. *Effective leadership includes in its processes the participation of all persons with rightful stakes in the educational program.* Genuine leadership utilizes profitably the contributions of all persons directly associated with the program it seeks to stimulate. In the development, operation, and evaluation of the educational program, teachers, children, parents, nonteaching staff members, specialists, and laymen all have vital roles to play. The leader with insight will discover ways of incorporating these contributions into the educational process for which he assumes status responsibility. One of the most basic functions of administrative leadership is certainly that of encouraging the participation of all who have a contribution to make and, in turn, of providing machinery for the coordination of such contributions into a meaningful, unified, and productive effort.

8. *Effective leadership involves the development of a policy continuum sufficiently flexible to serve as a guide in specific cases and sufficiently strong to sustain the efforts of a program through periods of emergency or crisis.* It is not a valid function of constructive leadership to anticipate every decision that must be made in the operation of the school program and to provide ready-made solutions in advance for such cases. Rather it is the function of leadership to work for the development of general policies which can serve as guides when applied to given situations. Such policies should be directive, without being restrictive, and adaptable. They certainly should bear some relationship to common sense, logic, expediency, and the prevailing purposes of the school program.

It should be pointed out that, just as there is danger in attempting to operate a school program without established policy, it is equally hazardous to try to develop a separate policy for each different problem that arises in the course of a school day or year. It is impossible, in fact, to do so. Such an effort usually results in overorganization without commensurate benefits. Furthermore, it usually results also in diminishing initiative on the part of individual staff members.

9. *Effective leadership involves the continued search for common denominators of human communication and action.* Wherever various members of a group are engaged in a common enterprise such as providing a good instructional program for children, it is too much to expect that there will be perfect agreement or complete cooperation at all times. Even if such a state of affairs were possible within the limits of human nature, it is doubtful if it would provide the most desirable setting for the program. The effective leader cannot hope to find or create a com-

munity free from conflicting ideas and varying attitudes. He should expect to discover common grounds of experience upon which communication may be achieved and understanding improved. Such a leader will be quick to concede minor points of contention in order to secure the cooperative attitude of a group member at a point where major principles and policies are at stake. Instead of emphasizing differences of opinion, such a leader will seek and give recognition to actual and potential points of agreement.

Effective leadership creates an atmosphere in which no stigma is attached to honest difference of opinion, whether it exists between staff members or between a member and the administrative leader. The continued suggestion, confirmed by the practices of the administrative leader himself, that decisions should be made on the basis of *objective* and *complete* information usually does much to eliminate the more clamorous and unjustifiable dissenting views.

10. *Effective leadership regards working associates as co-workers rather than as mere followers.* The application of this principle places the emphasis on cooperative effort rather than on the command-execution type of organization. It presupposes that members of the group will understand the job to be done and will have the opportunity to make varied and unique, though not necessarily identical, contributions in carrying the work forward. Though the administrative leader has certain responsibilities not borne by his associates, this does not provide any justifiable basis for a superior-subordinate relationship with members of his staff.

11. *Effective leadership is concerned with development rather than dictation.* This is a corollary to the preceding principle. Dictation implies blind obedience; development involves thoughtful and often deliberative approaches to problems. It must be admitted that sometimes orders must be given and enforced; but the processes of education, involving as they do the complexities of human growth and behavior, do not appear to lend themselves readily to a regular diet of authoritarian tactics. Another characteristic of sound educational leadership is its concern for the *operator* as well as the *operation*. An effective school program should result not only in the development of the learners but in the continued growth of teachers and parents as well. Little staff development can occur through carrying out the dictates of an autocratic leader, but much growth can take place as members engage in the cooperative building of a truly fine instructional program for the children of a community.

12. *Effective leadership is sparked by, and appears to generate in others, a strong faith in education as a basic means for human improvement.* The attitudes and activities of the truly great educational leader

radiate a proud consciousness of the social and spiritual significance of his job. He is aware of the faith represented by the cumulative investment in public education, and in that faith he finds great challenge. He recognizes that the outcomes of his constructive leadership will be increased manyfold in the lives of those who come after him. A responsibility of such magnitude evokes in the conscientious leader the feeling of both pride and humility—but each leaves him glad to be a part of such a vital social process.

The enthusiasm of the effective educational leader is often contagious. Sooner or later, it is usually caught by his associates. To them he transmits his own zeal for the job to be done, his own energetic approach to it, and his own pride in its importance. This constitutes real motivation and is the essence of genuine leadership.

The Functions of the Administrative Leader

The administrative leader in the elementary school has both an opportunity and a responsibility for influencing the quality of the educational program. Practically his every professional act bears either direct or indirect relationship to the instructional program of the school. Furthermore, the influence of the administrative leader is often extended into the home and community life of children. As a person, such a leader can make significant contributions to the strength of the educational program. Furthermore, these contributions can be multiplied in effectiveness many times through the subsequent efforts of his co-workers. It may be well to suggest here at least three forms through which such leadership can find expression.

Professional Perspective.—A vital element of productive leadership is the ability to illuminate. Through enlightenment it becomes possible to look beyond the status quo to potentiality. Most of the advances of civilization have resulted from individual willingness and ability to scan the horizons of possibility. Indeed, it is obvious that many of the real advances in education have stemmed directly from such exploration by educational leaders.

The alert elementary school principal, as a leader, spends a considerable amount of his time and energy on the frontiers of education. From such activity, he gains increased breadth of perspective, which will help him to develop ways of directing forward the activities of the professional group. There is an old story about a man who asked one of his elders how to train a dog. The answer was: There is just one basic requisite—one must know more than the dog. While no literal analogy is suggested between such advice and the effective exercise of leadership in the elementary school, it is true that the leader must seek the broadest possible perspective on education before attempting to help others to progress.

In addition to its contribution to the guidance and development of the educational program, professional perspective may well discover new approaches through which increased educational facility may be realized. Through good use of professional vision and imagination, the principal may help a staff stake out for itself new goals and discover for itself improved ways of realizing them.

The emphasis here has been placed deliberately on the projected vision of the leader. It should be noted, however, that true perspective also includes the critical survey of the *past* and the *present*. Out of the past comes the cumulative experience which offers a base for refinement of educational practice. Out of the current situation must be derived the resources for the maintenance of the present program and for building improved programs of the future.

The professional perspective of the administrative leader should be directed toward at least three purposes. The first of these is the *discovery and continuous re-evaluation of objectives*. Probably the most revealing evidence of a good school program is that each participating member has a clear concept of the purposes toward which the school is directing its energies. Further evidence of quality is an awareness of the staff that changing conditions sometimes necessitate a corresponding change in purpose. One of the greatest tasks of the administrative leader is to demonstrate and to encourage a consideration of this necessity. Schools simultaneously provide a program for the development of the capacities of individuals and for carrying out the purposes of the society in which they live. The search for clear and sound objectives must continuously reflect an awareness of both facets.

A second purpose served by professional perspective is the *critical survey of resources*. The leader develops a knowledge of all types of resources which might be useful to the educational program. Furthermore, he seeks kinds of resources hitherto untapped but potentially useful in education. Through an extension of resources, the program can be constantly enriched and vitalized. Investigation of these potentialities will take the leader into contact with newer methods and materials of instruction, and into the community to view it as an educational laboratory.

The resources of the school program are chiefly facilities and people. The principal, in his role as leader, can work with his staff in appraising facilities—plant, instructional materials, and equipment—and in determining how effectively their use contributes to the achievement of the objectives of the school. In addition, the principal has responsibility for leadership through the best possible utilization of the professional resources of the staff and through investigation of the possibility of using various members of the community in the program of the school.

A third purpose which professional perspective may serve is the *revelation of the findings of research in education.* The leader with perspective respects research as a means for professional improvement. This respect is usually reflected in an effort to keep abreast of research findings, to use available opportunities for sharing these findings with others, and to encourage the research attitude on the part of co-workers and learners.

The outcomes of research can be helpful to the administrator in many ways. Much research has been directed toward child development in recent years, and the resulting findings have served to suggest means for improving the structure of the modern school program. Research in the psychological bases of learning has done much to eliminate the wasteful learning exercises prevalent some years ago; research has also done much to replace them with learning experiences more in keeping with sound learning principles. In a similar manner, much has been found regarding the comparative effectiveness of various teaching methods and the comparative usefulness of various types of instructional materials. A thorough knowledge of educational research related to elementary education bolsters the position and status of the principal as a leader of his staff and as an interpreter of the school program in the community, and is essential equipment for the effective administrator.

Coordination.—Administration is not an end in itself. Its justification lies in the contribution it makes to the effectiveness of learning and teaching. Since unity is essential to an effectual school program, a criterion for judging administration is the extent to which it is able to integrate the individual activities of members of the staff into a meaningful and efficient pattern of operation. Prerequisite to such integration is the recognition that teachers, as well as children, legitimately and often advantageously, may have individual differences.

Adequate coordination of individual contributions necessitates a concern for maintaining a wholesome balance between the resources of each member of the group and the demands that are placed upon him. This consideration is not only a necessity for reasonable mental health but also goes far in establishing the proper atmosphere for the vocational efficiency of professional workers.

A certain amount of coordination in the allocation and utilization of educational supplies and equipment is necessary to a smooth-working school. While much of the effectiveness in the use of materials comes from business-like management, real leadership is often a factor in creating the cooperative attitudes necessary for the efficient sharing of facilities.

Another mark of modern administrative leadership is the manner in which it is able to synthesize sound educational theory with the practical and localized expediencies of the day-to-day operation of the school. Such leadership brings into the machinery of the program the best that is known about education and yet is able to make the intelligent adaptations necessary in each particular case. This, too, requires a high level of coordination on the part of the leader.

The proper merging of the varying and often conflicting goals and ideas of individuals into a consensus or a plan of action is another of the great professional challenges confronting the administrator. Respect for expressed individual opinions, along with an objective approach to the solution of problems, can do much to guarantee positive outcomes for efforts at coordination in this field of human relations. The same sort of coordinative effort usually pays dividends in developing optimum interaction between school and community.

By way of summary it should be noted, then, that one of the greatest concerns of responsible administrative leadership is the adequate coordination of resources in the formulation of educational purposes; the planning, development, organization, and evaluation of learning experiences; and the interpreting of the school program to the community and beyond.

Motivation.—It has been pointed out earlier that one of the services of leadership lies in the area of helping members of a group arrive at intelligent decisions regarding the *nature of the job to be done* through education. It was suggested that such professional analyses could be achieved at least partially through the professional perspective of the leader. The idea of the need for coordinative effort and planning in *getting the job done* was also advanced. Certainly the importance of both of these aspects of leadership should not be underestimated. However, they do not encompass the complete picture of genuine leadership.

The power of individual or group enterprise lies in the motivation which sparks the effort. A powerful locomotive may possess a searching headlight to peer into the distance and warn of possible obstacles. It may be built of finest parts, skillfully coordinated into a unified machine, carefully oiled and ready to carry its cargo on its way. However, it is not until human will and purpose are applied to the throttle that constructive action results. In a similar manner, all the essential elements for a good educational program may be present without producing the desired results. Only when all concerned *want to get the job done* can the educational effort produce the spark essential to maximum power.

The over-all quality of the educational program may be measured by the extent to which it offers opportunity for success among its practitioners and its consumers. The same scale can be applied equally well to the quality of the leadership which prevails at any given time. Motivation comes from hope of success; it is diminished by the feeling of failure or inadequacy. The wise administrator recognizes this fact and appreciates its implications. Therefore, he seeks to exert a type of leadership that will (1) create the atmosphere and working conditions under which success is recognized as being possible to achieve with reasonable effort by each individual co-worker; and (2) give proper recognition where recognition is due. Nothing serves as a greater motivating force than the probability of receiving credit and recognition for one's efforts.

Levels of Administrative Leadership

Absolute competence does not exist in the field of educational administration. Administrative leaders, like other workers, have some strengths and some weaknesses. Some are specialists in a particular aspect of administration; others appear to be equipped with wholly different types of competency. At any rate, over-all competence has numerous components and thus is difficult to define or evaluate with any degree of confidence. However, critical observation and analysis of kinds of leadership exercised by numerous educational leaders in the elementary school reveal several levels of competence at which administrators operate.

The Level of Continuing Status.—Some school administrators seem satisfied if they are able to perpetuate the conditions they find in a school at the time of their own appointment. Indeed, it frequently taxes the energy and ingenuity of the administrator just to maintain the constructive features of the school program in the face of the everyday problems which arise. It is easy for such an administrator to lapse into a form of professional complacency which gives little thought to improvement. In such cases, he usually becomes embroiled in the affairs and routines of each day, gradually evolving into an executive officer rather than assuming the role of leadership in its truest sense.

The Level of Informed Leadership.—As previously indicated, the elementary school principal usually can improve the quality of his performance by extending his information about his job. Through research reports and literature, much helpful knowledge can be gained about such aspects of the job as child development, measurement and evaluation in the educational process, personnel and guidance techniques, and improved instructional materials and facilities. Visits to other schools, advanced professional study, and participation in professional associations are other types of activities which help to extend the principal's knowledge. By supplementing existing practice through applications of the best information available, the principal can raise his professional level of operation well above the mere concern for the status quo.

The Level of Constructive Adaptation.—There comes the time when the skills and information possessed by the typical administrator seem insufficient to cope with the problems that arise. It becomes necessary to seek additional information that will be useful in administering the program. This information becomes useful, however, only to the extent that it can be adapted to existing situations and needs. Rarely can an educational technique which is completely effective in one situation be wholly and successfully transplanted to another situation without some modification or adaptation. The leader who engages in the perpetual search for the best professional information available, and who then possesses the imagination necessary for using it to improve his own school program, is learning to operate at a relatively high level of leadership.

The Level of Creative Leadership.—Professional enthusiasm, stimulating experience, and advanced educational preparation occasionally combine in the development of the creative leader. Such a person, of course, is well informed. In addition, he is able to capitalize on the discoveries and knowledge of others in the performance of his duties. But when these are still insufficient, he has the drive, the zeal, and the professional know-how to construct the means of his own salvation and that of the program for which he assumes responsibility. This is the essence of creative leadership. It involves knowledge, wisdom, and courage. It is dedicated to the belief that, once educators can develop a high level of understanding, they are in the best possible position to create the means of getting the educational task done.

Action Suggestions for the Principal

1. Attempt to become conversant with the literature which describes and analyzes the historical development of leadership functions under different political systems and varying philosophies.

2. Know, or learn, the major theses of the chief prevailing philosophies of education.

3. Utilize the leadership abilities of members of the professional staff in deciding policy matters and in such areas of activity as school improvement, curriculum development or revision, or the establishment of new school services.

4. Refrain from assuming sole responsibility for policy decisions.

5. Share with contributing leaders the authority necessary for carrying out their responsibilities.

6. Use staff meetings to come to a consensus regarding the purposes of the school.

7. Study ways in which individual strengths of staff members may be utilized and incorporated into the total educational effort of the school.

8. Recognize and give full credit for the individual and group accomplishments of members of the staff.

9. Demonstrate a desire for truth, pursuing all constructive means for its discovery, encouraging others to do likewise.

10. Possess and demonstrate a genuine faith in the democratic process and in its basic tenets.

11. Attempt to make staff assignments in terms of special interests and competencies of people—refrain from attempting to make all conform to a pattern.

12. Help all members of the school family to succeed in their particular responsibilities.

13. Permit staff members the privilege of disagreement or criticism.

14. Look for the best in others—ascribe honorable motives to others until there is evidence to the contrary.

15. Demonstrate the kinds of attitudes toward staff members that one expects them to employ in their daily associations with others.

16. Encourage experimentation and the expression of creative ideas by members of the staff.

17. Continuously study the relations between the demands of society and the prevailing needs of children as both affect the school program.

18. Search for constructive ways in which parents and laymen can participate in the formulation of the goals of the school.

19. Attempt to become skilled in group processes and in such matters as leading group discussions.

20. Study school problems and issues sufficiently to make thoughtful proposals for action which members of the group may approve, reject, or modify into useful form.

21. Seek to improve the quality of communication between all elements of the school community.

22. Tend to use the term "we" rather than "I" in discussing the school and its activities.

23. Maintain and demonstrate a genuine faith in education as an instrument of human progress.

24. Try to maintain a professional imagination that kindles the creative tendencies of staff members.

25. Be a student of the school community.

26. Spearhead a continuous inventory of resources and attempt to help people bring available resources into use in the program of the school.

27. Continuously seek for the effective merger of sound theory and good practice.

28. Have a working knowledge of developments and research findings in the field of elementary education.

29. Strive to develop processes within the school which will encourage leadership on the part of teachers, parents, and children.

30. Actively participate in community and civic affairs.

31. Seek to provide opportunities for members of the staff to discuss school matters informally under pleasant conditions.

32. Attempt to discover and apply the relationships between the democratic way of life and the processes of the school.

33. Attempt to discover resources for improving the quality of his leadership.

34. Participate in the activities of professional associations in the area of administrative and supervisory leadership.

35. Sense the real significance of his opportunity for leadership.

36. Evaluate his own activities in the light of the goals of the school.

37. Be motivated and guided in day-to-day activities by high personal and professional ethics.

SELECTED REFERENCES FOR EXTENDED READING

ADAMS, HAROLD P., and DICKEY, FRANK G. *Basic Principles of Supervision.* New York: American Book Co., 1953, chap. 3.

CAMPBELL, CLYDE M. (ed.). *Practical Applications of Democratic Administration.* New York: Harper & Bros., 1952.

HAGMAN, HARLAN L. *The Administration of American Public Schools.* New York: McGraw-Hill Book Co., Inc., 1951.

MILLER, VAN, and SPALDING, WILLARD B. *The Public Administration of American Schools.* Yonkers, N. Y.: World Book Co., 1952.

PITTENGER, BENJAMIN F. *Local Public School Administration.* New York: McGraw-Hill Book Co., Inc., 1951.

REAVIS, WILLIAM C., PIERCE, PAUL R., STULLKEN, EDWARD H., and SMITH, BERTRAND. *Administering the Elementary School.* New York: Prentice-Hall, Inc., 1953, chaps. 11 and 12.

SEARS, JESSE B. *The Nature of the Administrative Process with Special Reference to Public School Administration.* New York: McGraw-Hill Book Co., Inc., 1950.

SHANE, HAROLD G., and McSWAIN, E. T. *Evaluation and the Elementary Curriculum.* New York: Henry Holt & Co., 1951, chap. 13.

SHANE, HAROLD G., and YOUCH, WILBUR A. *Creative School Administration.* New York: Henry Holt & Co., 1954, chaps. 1-3.

WILES, KIMBALL. *Supervision for Better Schools.* New York: Prentice-Hall, Inc., 1950, chap. 2.

Chapter 2

CHARACTERISTICS OF EFFECTIVE
ADMINISTRATIVE LEADERS

*'Tis the flight and not the cry of the wild goose that determines
the way the flock flies—Old Proverb*

Leadership cannot exist except in its relation to members of a group. Therefore, evidence regarding the quality of leadership is not necessarily obtained from the administrator himself, but is more likely to be found in the activities and accomplishments of the group. This observation is not intended to diminish the importance of the administrative leader but rather to emphasize his significance in the modern concept of educational leadership. It suggests that the real value of the administrator lies not so much in what he is able to do as in what he is able to stimulate and help others to do.

This chapter is directed toward the exploration of the attributes essential to the elementary school principal if he is to assume his role as leader in a competent manner. As administrative leader, the principal is faced with both opportunity and responsibility. The vision to see the opportunities and the courage and competence to meet the responsibilities of the job are important. The kind of person the principal is and the pattern of behavior he demonstrates bear directly upon any valid appraisal of his work. Simply stated, much of the evaluation of the principal's competence will be derived from *what he is* and *what he does*. Observation and analysis of the work of successful principals lead to the conclusion that certain types of personal attributes and professional resources are possessed almost uniformly by those who experience greatest success as leaders.

Underlying Principles Regarding the Role of Administrative Leader

It seems difficult, if not impossible, to characterize the success of the administrative leader in the elementary school except in relation to the job to be done. As implied earlier, his role is catalytic and must be judged by the extent to which the activities and behavior of others are influenced in a positive manner. Justification for administration in education lies in the assumption that it facilitates learning as well as the efforts of all persons who contribute to the process of learning. In large measure, then, the effective administrator is one who possesses the personal and professional qualities necessary for meeting his responsibilities to others in educative endeavor. It therefore seems appropriate and desirable at this point to analyze briefly the nature of some of the responsibilities facing the elementary school principal.

1. *The effective administrative leader recognizes his responsibility to those who appoint him.* This implies a loyalty to the general purposes and welfare of the school system as a whole. It demands execution of policy and respect for authority in the development and implementation of policy. The principal should realize that in his hands is placed the responsibility for the successful operation of an important segment of the total educational enterprise; he must further realize that he should demonstrate a professional fidelity commensurate with the size of his task.

There is a difference, however, between *loyalty* and *conformity.* Loyalty is a matter of spirit or attitude; conformity is a matter of form or structure. The obligation of professional loyalty on the part of the principal does not demand that he become a "rubber stamp." It does require that professional disagreement be dealt with impersonally, in a friendly but forthright manner, and through the proper channels. The effective principal is both honest and cooperative in his relations with those who select him.

2. *The effective administrative leader recognizes his responsibility to his immediate professional associates.* Genuine educational leadership is both inspiring and enduring to those affected by it. Certainly the principal owes it to his fellow workers to encourage their efforts in every legitimate way. At the same time, his leadership must lend stability to the situation, serve as an integrating force for unifying ideas and activities of members of the staff, and help provide the necessary thread of continuity in planning and executing the school program. The principal has the obligation to listen sympathetically to the proposals of the individual staff members even though, in the interest of the total program, he cannot support the ideas. If the efforts of his professional associates are to be stimulated to an optimum degree, the principal must encourage the freedom on their part to make proposals of debatable merit and must allow them the privilege of making occasional errors in judgment without being unduly penalized for such mistakes.

3. *The effective administrative leader recognizes his responsibility*

THE ADMINISTRATIVE LEADER

DISCHARGES HIS
RESPONSIBILITY ――――――――――▶ THROUGH HIS ROLE
TO   AS:
        │   │
        ▼   ▼

THE PROFESSION   EXECUTIVE OFFICER

SOCIETY   COORDINATOR

THE COMMUNITY   MOTIVATOR

PARENTS   ADVISOR

EMPLOYER   MEDIATOR

NON-PROFESSIONAL   INTERPRETER
STAFF

PROFESSIONAL   SUPERVISOR
STAFF

THE CHILD   EVALUATOR

                               DEMOCRATIC
                               EXAMPLE

                               EDUCATIONAL
                               PROPHET

Figure 2

The Nature of the Leader

to nonprofessional members of the staff. The effectiveness of the school program depends to a very large degree on the quality of service rendered by the technical but nonteaching staff of the school. This group is composed of secretarial and clerical assistants, members of the custodial staff, the school nurse, bus drivers, and cafeteria workers. In a great many instances, particularly in large school systems, the work of these various staff members is administered and supervised by someone other than the school principal. For example, school custodians are often administratively responsible to a superintendent of buildings and grounds. However, this does not relieve the principal from his responsibilities to such workers.

It is the direct responsibility of the school principal to provide means whereby the efforts of technical workers are suitably related to the educational purposes of the school and are effectively merged into the best possible total organization for achieving these purposes. This necessitates a genial working relationship between the principal and each staff member, with regular provision made for all such staff members to participate in appropriate ways in developing policies regarding or affecting their duties. It also suggests that these services should not be taken for granted by the administrator but should receive commendation commensurate with their value to the school program.

4. *The effective administrative leader recognizes his responsibility to the chief educational consumer of the school: the child.* Although it seems trite in modern educational circles to make such a statement, it is advisable for educators to keep reminding themselves that schools exist for children, rather than the converse. One of the basic obligations of the school, then, is to provide for maximum adjustment to the child's needs and development and for the fullest possible utilization of the child's interests and resources in the process. This prime obligation of the school obviously is one of the strongest challenges to the ingenuity and leadership of the administrator. How well he performs this particular professional feat indicates to a very strong degree the extent of his total effectiveness.

The principal should bring all available resources to the task of providing leadership in the development of a school program which promotes the happiness, comfort, and success of each child. Indeed, the tone of the school will be set largely by the attitude of the administrator toward children and by what he conceives to be the school's responsibility to them. The effective principal invariably knows children, loves them, and recognizes clearly his responsibility to them as leader of the school.

5. *The effective administrative leader recognizes his responsibility to*

parents and citizens of the community. The establishment and phenomenal growth of public schools in this country have demonstrated a strong, persisting faith in education as a desirable instrument for constructively influencing the lives of individuals with a resulting salutary effect on society as a whole. When a mother, proud but often tearful, takes her five- or six-year-old by the hand and leads him to school for the first time, she is concretely attesting to that faith. She expects that her child will profit from his days and years at school. She anticipates that the same kind of tender, sympathetic interest she feels in his problems and his progress will be demonstrated by those to whom she entrusts his educational fortunes. The faithful and competent administrator will sense the faith thus imposed in the school and will exert every professional effort to help provide educational experiences that fully justify such faith.

The school has a responsibility to the community which goes beyond its obligations to individual parents and families. Through adult education programs, as well as through its espousal of various cultural activities of the community, the school can be a vital force for community improvement. One of the marks of distinction of the effective principal is his sensitivity to the social structure of the community and to possible means whereby the school and community may mutually complement each other in providing activities for improving and enriching the lives of its citizens.

6. *The effective administrative leader recognizes his responsibility to society as a whole.* In this era in which we are living, there are few limits to the contributions individual citizens may make to the country or to the world. Whereas once there was a strong likelihood that a person would spend much of his life in the community of his birth, modern communication and transportation have brought an increasing mobility of families throughout the various regions of the nation and world.

The child who attends an elementary school is being educated not only for community citizenship but for world citizenship as well. The quality of the education he experiences affects his own individual development and, in addition, has an impact in many direct and indirect ways on society as a whole. The educator cannot escape awareness of the obligation this places upon him. Furthermore, he will encourage his associates in their attempts to develop and provide educational experiences consistent with this broader responsibility.

The principal, as an administrative leader with broad perspective and professional specialization, is often in a position to make individual contributions to the welfare of society by serving in various civic roles.

While this should not be considered the primary role of the principal, his effectiveness may be enhanced considerably through such contributions.

7. *The effective administrative leader recognizes his responsibility to the educational profession.* A very popular work of fiction[1] portrayed with dramatic and forceful impact the interrelationships between the fortunes and misfortunes of individual members belonging to a group with common purposes. The essence of its theme is that any misfortune which befalls one member of a group must in effect be felt by all other members dedicated to the common purpose.

The principal of a school is an important member of a great profession. Membership in such a profession carries with it the obligation to perform one's responsibilities in such a manner as to reflect credit upon the profession as a whole. It further requires an active regard for established codes of professional conduct. This respect will be equally demonstrated in the performance of duty and in the principal's relations with his fellows.

Another way in which the principal may contribute to his profession is through the active support of professional organizations. Service to and through these organizations usually helps the profession as a whole and contributes to the growth of the participating principal. At the same time, participation in such activities by the administrator himself demonstrates to those working with him his recognition of the value of professionalization of the educational enterprise. The judicious participation of the principal in professional activities will bring benefits to himself and to his associates, and recognition to the school in which he works.

8. *The effective administrative leader recognizes certain responsibilities to himself.* Certain attitudes of the principal toward himself and his work have considerable bearing on his total professional efficiency. It is important that he respect himself and his own ideas without becoming dogmatic or intolerant of the ideas of others. It is equally essential to good administration that he possess a sense of proportion regarding his responsibilities and that he be able to view matters in terms of their relative importance. Otherwise, there will be a strong temptation to succumb to the persisting pressures of routines and deadlines without giving the desirable attention to broader and more significant problems and policies. When the principal thus becomes entangled in the maze of administrative detail, he often loses much of the challenge inherent in his position of leadership.

The personal life of the principal is often another factor in his total

[1] Ernest Hemingway, *For Whom the Bell Tolls* (New York: Chas. Scribner's Sons, 1941).

effectiveness as a leader. The responsibilities of administration are so numerous and so broad that they constitute a severe drain on the energy of the principal. Long hours must be given to meeting the demands of the job. For his own sake, and indeed for the sake of the school program, the principal should attempt to lead a life as normal and as rich as possible. He can thus bring to his position each day his very best efforts. The principal who limits his interests and energy entirely to the confines of his office is ignoring one of the strongest resources of the leader—a rich and well-rounded personal life which brings vigor, interest, and perspective to the situation.

9. *The effective administrative leader is one who shares both responsibility and recognition.* The principal's awareness of the importance of the responsibilities listed in preceding paragraphs does not suggest that he alone should be concerned with them. By sharing many of the duties related to the operation of the school program, the principal thus relieves himself of the impossible task of attending to all the details involved. At the same time, delegation of duties encourages active participation of members of the staff with the corresponding opportunity for improved perspective of the over-all structure of the school program. It should be remembered, however, that in the final analysis it is impossible for an administrator to delegate his responsibility for providing a good educational program. Even though he shares certain duties, he still retains administrative responsibility for seeing that they are fulfilled in an effective manner.

The principal should share credit and recognition as readily as he shares responsibilities. One of the distinguishing marks of the democratic leader is his eagerness to reward honest effort and unusual achievement with the recognition they deserve. Giving credit for work well done will go far toward increasing the willingness of members of the school staff to participate actively in the development of the educational program.

10. *The effective administrative leader seeks to develop in himself the qualities necessary for successfully meeting his responsibilities.* The successful principal is one who, regardless of years of experience, still possesses the capacity to grow and to learn. Thoughtful reaction to experience, along with the use of all available opportunities for extended study, provides the fertile ground for the development of the attributes needed for productive leadership. By taking a wholesomely critical attitude toward himself, the principal may identify his relative weaknesses and do much to eliminate them and their possible interference with his complete effectiveness as the leader of the school. Certainly, many of the personal traits that make the principal an appealing person

will also contribute to his success as a leader. Some of these characteristics which seem particularly essential to the administrative leader will
be discussed in detail in a later portion of this chapter.

The fact that the administrative leader possesses many splendid
personal qualities will not, in itself, guarantee success in meeting the
obligations of his position; maximum professional understanding and
competence are also helpful to his effectiveness. Some of this competence
can be obtained through advanced professional study and through keeping up with educational research and the contents of pertinent educational literature. Contacts with other educational leaders, individually
and through the work of professional associations, may also contribute
to this type of growth. It seems sufficient to say that the principal should
avail himself of all opportunities for becoming a better person and an
improved professional practitioner.

Varying Roles of the Principal

The demands of the job of being a successful administrator in the
elementary school are so varied that versatility is one of the primary requisites for proficiency on the part of the principal. It is not enough
to be strongly equipped in one or two aspects. The job of administering
the modern elementary school is such that the principal must be able to
assume several different roles with equal ease and competence. It seems
appropriate here to comment briefly on the nature of some of these roles.

The Principal as Executive Officer of the School.—Although
school policy is often developed by the superintendent and board of
education, the responsibility for its interpretation and implementation
rests with the principal. In the interest of good administration, it is
necessary for him to study the policies of the school thoroughly, explain
them clearly and accurately to members of the staff, make provisions for
action to be taken, and ultimately to appraise their effect on the school
program. The privilege of leadership carries with it the obligation of
directing the implementation of school policy both democratically and
efficiently.

The Principal as Coordinator.—As has been implied earlier in this
volume, the science of administrative leadership is composed very
largely of the inclination and the ability to coordinate, in an optimum
manner, all the environmental and human resources available in order
to insure the greatest benefits to all persons involved in the process.
The effective fitting together of all pieces of the educational effort is

the very strongest justification possible for the existence of the administrator.

The Principal as Motivator.—Another essential quality of the successful administrative leader is his power to stimulate people in the attainment of their goals. This is valuable in the principal's relationships with other members of the staff, with parents and citizens of the community, and with the pupils of the school themselves. One of his most challenging jobs is that of helping people do better the things they need to be doing. Nowhere is the principal more appreciated than in his sincere attempts to furnish the inspirational spark to help motivate the efforts and activities of his fellows and followers.

The Principal as Expert.—It is a compliment to the principal that teachers, parents, and pupils often look to him for expert opinion regarding their problems. It is obligatory on the part of such a leader to attempt to develop the necessary understanding to deal with these opportunities for service in a sympathetic, helpful manner. The earnest desire to keep abreast of educational developments, coupled with the effort to be a serious student of education and of people, will do much to insure a reasonable degree of such understanding.

The Principal as Adviser.—This role is closely related to that of serving as an educational expert in the school. However, it is possible for the principal to possess the technical competence and information necessary for expertness without being able to serve as an effective adviser to persons bringing problems to him. As adviser he must possess not only professional understanding of the problem involved, but also a spirit and manner which invite the discussion of the problem.

The Principal as Mediator.—Even in the most favorable circumstances, situations occasionally arise which require that the principal act as professional mediator. Although the role of adjudication is seldom an enviable one, it can be performed in such a manner that complete respect can be maintained for all concerned. Such situations sometimes involve conflicts between teacher and teacher, teacher and parent, or teacher and pupil. In any instance, the principal should attempt to help the participants to clarify the conflicting issues, to identify and to evaluate points of difference and possible areas of agreement, and to offer possible solutions for easing conflict. In a few cases, the principal may find it necessary to arbitrate the matter by suggesting the action to be taken. At such times, his best and most reliable weapons are objectivity and a complete sense of fairness.

The Principal as Interpreter.—The principal is in the center of the educational process, and thus in a position to interpret to the superintendent the activities and needs of the school. At the same time, policies developed by the superintendent and board of education are transmitted to the staff and local community through the principal. Furthermore, the principal is in a position to capitalize on his contacts with parents and citizens of the immediate school community by interpreting to them the purposes and activities of the school. In each case, faithful and accurate interpretation are essential to the operation of the modern school program.

The Principal as Supervisor.—In a considerable number of schools the only supervision available is that furnished by the principal. In such instances, a heavy responsibility for the improvement of instruction rests on his shoulders. It becomes necessary for him to assist teachers in the study, evaluation, and improvement of the teaching-learning situation. Other ways in which he can be helpful involve the location and use of new instructional materials and guidance in adapting and experimenting with new or modified instructional methods in the classroom. Even in schools where general and/or special supervisors and consultants are available, the principal still retains much responsibility for the over-all supervision of the school and for directing efforts for its improvement.

The Principal as Evaluator.—The manner in which the principal assumes his role as evaluator is an extremely accurate indication of his concept of leadership. Mention of the importance of this aspect of administrative leadership does not imply any sympathy whatever with the practice of the administrator who goes about, pencil, notebook, and rating sheet in hand, eager to rate any and all with whom he comes in contact. On the contrary, the suggestion here is that he use all available means—and employ all the staff in the process—to appraise the outcomes of the school program in terms of the values and purposes held by the school. To perform this function well, he needs to be clear on the purposes of the school and well informed regarding the various instruments suitable for educational evaluation.

The Principal as a Democratic Example and Advocate.—A chief goal of American education is the development of the attitudes and skills necessary for democratic living. This aim involves a guarantee of the rights of individuals as well as a corresponding obligation of self-direction and self-determination of the individual. It further demands respect for minority voices, although either consensus or majority usually is the basic determiner of regulation and policy. Such a goal emphatically demands that all members of a group have a voice in making the rules by which they are required to live.

The principal's own behavior is the best single instrument he possesses for promoting the democratic attitudes of members of his staff and others with whom he works. There is no more sincere way of subscribing to the democratic way of life than by practicing it. The principal who believes and practices the basic democratic tenets in his relations with teachers in the school finds it much easier to stimulate similar practices and attitudes on the part of teachers in the classroom. On the other hand, the autocratic administrator will be conscious of many deaf ears when he extols the virtues of democratic action to members of his staff.

Administrative leaders occasionally find it necessary, in order to protect the rights of individuals or groups, to uphold principles which may not be generally popular in the community. Although he will exercise the greatest tact in such situations, the leader of stature will not shrink from the role of advocate of a just cause.

The Principal as Educational Prophet.—Without proclaiming the necessity for supernatural vision on the part of the administrative leader, it must be said that his job requires a considerable amount of projective judgment. Operation of the school from year to year demands the systematic and scientific analysis of population trends, birth rates, turnover in teaching staff, and depreciation of equipment and facilities. The effective administrator is not only interested in the present but tries to determine the needs of the future, and to make an intelligent and continuing inventory of resources in terms of anticipated needs. It is well also for the principal to sense the directions in which educational organization and practice seem to be moving in terms of their relationship to such things as building construction and the use of facilities.

PERSONAL ATTRIBUTES OF THE ADMINISTRATIVE LEADER

There is an old adage that expresses well an aspect of the effective administrative leader. It is stated as follows: "What you are speaks so loudly that I cannot hear what you say." Basically, the principal of an elementary school will be known for the kind of person he is; likewise, his professional effectiveness will be determined largely by the nature of his personality.

A considerable number of studies have been made of the attributes which teachers most appreciate in their principals and supervisory leaders. Analysis of these studies reveals rather unanimous agreement regarding the characteristics which teachers consider virtues in the principals with whom they work.

In the first place, they want him to be *kind* and *sympathetic* in his relationships with staff members and with children in the school. Such a principal places the most favorable interpretation on all the actions of others, and is understanding of the guilty; he is easily approachable and arouses in his fellows a feeling of complete confidence. Ridicule and sarcasm are avoided by him. He is the professional exemplar of the Golden Rule in all that he says or does. He is a gentleman in the finest sense of the word.

Teachers want their principals to be *human*. Nothing delights them more than the presence and demonstration of a sense of humor by the principal in the face of apparently insurmountable problems. A positive boost to the morale of teachers is often the knowledge that their administrative leader can make mistakes, will admit them, and can forgive others for making similar ones. Administrators who operate with the efficiency and impersonality of a machine are not likely to be either effective or appreciated. It takes the warmth of human personality to evoke the professional gratitude and loyalty such a leader might desire. In the performance of his duties and in creating a favorable impression upon his followers, the principal will find no satisfactory substitute for human graciousness.

A third trait which teachers desire in their administrators is *dependability*. They want to be able to respect him and to be bolstered by the support of his judgment. They like to feel that they can depend upon him to bring both feeling and reason to bear on the solutions to their problems, and to have the assurance that his decisions and actions are based on sound knowledge of educational theory and practice, with due consideration for all persons involved in the teaching-learning process.

Closely related to dependability is *consistency*. The principal who greets staff members, pupils, and parents on one day with backslapping hilarity and extreme cordiality, and on subsequent days is obviously despondent and moody, cannot expect to command maximum appreciation from those whom he meets and with whom he works. Unnecessary problems are created by unpredictable and contradictory decisions. The principal who operates in a framework of consistency and reliability lends a substantial degree of stability to the school and earns the extended efforts it stimulates on the part of professional associates.

Although it is a matter of organization as well as attitude, it seems appropriate to mention here the high value teachers place on the *accessibility* of the administrative leader in the school. Obviously, this problem varies according to the size of the school, but it appears to be a safe assertion that the professional morale of teachers suffers from the necessity of making appointments long in advance to confer with the principal, or from other applications of a strong closed-door policy in the operation of his office. Of course it is important for the principal to protect himself from a continual round of insignificant, trivial chit-chat and from the tendency of some to make his office a lounge. However, he must be reasonably accessible to visitors if he is to do his job well and is to be appreciated by his staff.

Aside from the attributes discussed above, upon which teachers seem to agree rather generally, there are other personal characteristics of the effective educational leader which seem to merit attention. One extremely valuable asset of the administrator is a good *memory*. The ability to remember faces and names is a superlatively useful factor in establishing and maintaining good human relations. It is desirable also for the principal to remember his experiences as a classroom teacher, or even as a child, in order that he may more effectively sense the feelings of teachers and children as he works with them.

Professional *imagination* in exploring the frontiers and experimental possibilities of educational practice can be of great benefit to the administrator in his role of professional leader. In addition, he should attempt to develop a kind of social imagination whereby he may see himself in the place of those with whom he comes in contact. This can be an asset in dealing with the problems of teachers, children, and parents since it helps to establish a basis for mutual understanding and communication.

Certainly the principal should be *physically* and *mentally healthy*. Physical and emotional vigor and stability give a feeling of confidence to him and to those around him, in addition to strength to meet his responsibilities capably. Further importance is attached to the physical and mental health of the principal in that it also affects his disposition and temperament, with a direct bearing on his social relationships. *Personal grooming* and *neatness* also are essential to the development of this feeling of confidence and to the creation of a favorable impression of him as a professional leader in the community.

AREAS OF PROFESSIONAL COMPETENCE

It is difficult to distinguish personal traits from professional competencies in viewing and analyzing the effectiveness of the principal. Obviously, they are not mutually exclusive as expressed in the behavior of a person. For discussion, however, it seems profitable to give attention to some aspects of competence not necessarily inherent in the principal.

In this group are included those resources and strengths over which he himself exercises almost complete control through his own initiative and application.

The principal builds his professional strength largely through (1) preservice preparation, (2) experience, and (3) utilization of all types of current opportunities for personal and professional growth. All are essential to one who chooses administration as a career; but the stature of professional competence can be developed only in a person possessing intelligence and, to a reasonable degree, the personal characteristics mentioned earlier in this chapter.

Preservice Preparation.—The preservice study by the elementary school principal should be of two types. One aspect of his education is that designed to give him a broad cultural background and a rich fund of knowledge of the various fields of human interest and endeavor. Study in any area which contributes to making the potential principal a better informed and more interesting person can be a step toward making him a more effective principal.

A substantial portion of the prospective principal's preservice study should be concerned with the development of professional and technical competencies. Certainly, a person with administrative aspirations should gain an understanding of the philosophical, psychological, and sociological foundations of education. He should have specialized knowledge of accepted theories of the nature of learning and of the basic aspects of child growth and development. In addition, the organized study of curriculum and curriculum development, supervision, organization and administration of schools, and the use and interpretation of common forms of research in education are all indispensable to the well-rounded preparation of the principal. Competency in educational guidance and personnel techniques is also necessary for educational administration in the elementary school.

The two predominant aspects of the principal's preparation—cultural and professional—should be supplemented by work in areas designed to meet certain specialized needs. Competency in public speaking and knowledge of legal and financial structure of units of government are desirable components of the administrator's professional equipment. An honest self-inventory by the potential principal usually will reveal the areas of this nature that should receive attention in his preservice preparation.

Background of Experience.—The person who assumes, or expects to assume, the responsibilities of the elementary school principalship can derive major benefits from experience as a student, classroom teacher, or assistant administrator of some type. This experience is often one of the most productive resources on which the principal can draw. It is particularly helpful to him in his efforts to incorporate the teachers' point of view into the structure and development of the school program.

The real benefits to be derived from experience, however, usually accrue from one's reaction to it and critical examination of it. It is possible, therefore, for a principal to have twenty years of experience or to have one year of experience twenty times. The administrative leader should reflect intelligently upon his years of experience in the hope of sifting from them the most successful approaches to educational problems.

While there may be virtue and convenience in remaining in the same teaching position for many years, there is much reason to believe that a reasonable tenure in several different positions offers a richer background of experience for the prospective elementary school principal. Of course, this will vary with persons and situations. At any rate, a varied experience can be invaluable as a foundation for the leadership role in education.

Many modern programs of preparation for elementary school principals include some type of internship experience under the supervision of a mature, successful principal on the job. While the pattern for such experience differs from place to place, the internship usually involves a cooperative arrangement between an educational institution of higher learning and one or more public schools. The experience ordinarily is integrated with professional study courses and activities and is carried on under the general supervision of college or university personnel.

In-Service Growth.—There are numerous channels, aside from continued study and experience, through which the principal may direct his efforts to improve himself professionally. It is important for him to survey these possibilities continually and carefully as the means for improving his effectiveness. A few such sources for improvement warrant particular attention.

One of the first steps a principal can take in his desire for self-improvement is to establish a professional library for himself. He may wish to start with only a few books and build his collection as his interests demand and his financial status permits. In selecting books to own he should seek volumes representative of various fields of education rather than those whose contents are all confined to one aspect of education. Recency and authenticity are probably more important criteria than the number of volumes in appraising the value the professional library holds for the principal. In addition to books in such professional areas as psychology and child development, administration, supervision, curriculum, personnel management, and teaching methods, the professional library should contain some volumes of inspirational materials, often useful to the principal. From the list of professional journals, the principal should read regularly those which best represent his basic interests and responsibilities and which will best keep him in touch with educational developments at the local, state, national, and international levels.

The administrator may contribute further to his in-service development through affiliation with, and participation in, appropriate professional associations. In addition to national and state associations for teachers, there exist particular organizations for elementary principals at the national, state, and local levels providing opportunity for increased stimulation and improved professional status. Comparable organizations exist in supervision and curriculum development, and offer similar opportunity for self-improvement.

Many benefits can come to the elementary school principal through his participation in community and civic affairs. His contribution to religious and civic organizations not only helps the organizations but also serves the administrator as a resource for self-improvement. Public speaking, community surveys, forum discussions, and group work of all types may enhance the professional competence of the principal. He certainly should avail himself of all the opportunities for cultural growth offered by the local community, and often can further broaden his cultural perspective through travel within the country and abroad, both to vitalize himself and to extend his store of knowledge.

Another way in which the administrator may grow is by maintaining professional contact with institutions of higher learning in his state or region. Particularly, he can profit from maintaining a working relationship with the personnel of the institution from which he gained his professional training. Such colleges and universities frequently offer specialized services to public schools and sponsor valuable educational conferences and professional clinics.

GOALS OF THE ADMINISTRATIVE LEADER

The professional study, experience, and activities of the principal, both at the preservice and in-service levels, are presumed to equip him in areas of competence necessary for his work as administrator and educational leader. While there are numerous secondary benefits to be derived from his education and experience, the principal's main concern should be the acquisition of certain basic components of professional understanding and competence. Some of these are:

1. An emerging *philosophy of education* based on the best that is

known regarding the learner, the nature of the learning process, the comparative effectiveness of various teaching methods, and on a sound set of ethical values.

2. A clear *concept of the purposes of education* in a democracy as they relate to all phases of human development and to the social and historical orientation of the school as an instrument of society for improving the lot of mankind.

3. An *understanding of the basic principles of school organization* and the necessary techniques for adapting and applying these principles to a particular school situation.

4. A developing *competence in human relations* and personnel leadership based on social sensitivity and on the technical and human aspects of group processes.

5. An *informed and critical interest* in community, state, national, and world affairs and events and the relationship of education to social, economic, and political developments at all these levels.

6. A growing *interest and proficiency* in performing, encouraging, and interpreting *educational research* and experimentation with the corresponding ability to apply, and help others to apply, the findings of research to the daily operation of the school program.

7. An expanding *faith in education* as both the support and chief motivating factor of advancing civilization.

ACTION SUGGESTIONS FOR THE PRINCIPAL

1. Study the attributes and actions of persons who have achieved outstanding success as educational leaders.

2. Keep in mind the importance of *school success* rather than personal success.

3. Be loyal to the school system and the welfare of the people it serves. A principal should not continue to serve a community to which he feels no sense of loyalty.

4. Listen sympathetically to proposals of staff members or citizens and utilize the best elements of such proposals.

5. Try to maintain relations with the staff that will allow professional disagreements without personal conflicts.

6. Encourage teachers to use as much initiative as they can.

7. Permit staff members an occasional error of judgment and treat such errors in a casual and friendly manner.

8. Encourage nonteaching personnel to participate in the development of all-school policies.

9. Keep in mind that the chief criterion of school operation is the welfare of the children.

10. By example set a friendly "tone" for the school and recognize others who contribute to the creation of such an atmosphere.

11. In dealing with parents try to sense and appreciate the feelings they hold for their children.

12. Participate in professional groups with programs designed to improve leadership.

13. Support appropriate professional organizations in their work to improve education.

14. Reserve some time for personal and family recreation.

15. Develop a planned program for personal improvement to include extended reading, travel, hobbies, or special interests, and participation in community life.

16. Give associates credit for carrying out responsibilities assigned to them.

17. Keep the superintendent informed regarding ideas, proposals, and significant actions of the local school staff.

18. Keep the staff informed of policies and actions of the superintendent and board of education.

19. Be honest but try to eliminate the element of cruelty from relationships with staff, children, and parents.

20. Merit the reputation of being fair in all instances requiring mediation.

21. Try to keep the interpretation of school activities and problems on a constructive plane, and encourage others to do so.

22. Demonstrate a concept of supervision which is dedicated to helping others do their very best.

23. Demonstrate democracy in action.

24. Try to envision community and school conditions and needs well in advance.

25. Maintain a sense of humor.

26. Be consistent in manner and performance.

27. Remain accessible to staff members, children, parents, and other citizens; avoid the "closed door" policy.

28. Try to remember occasionally how it feels to be a child of elementary school age.

29. Set an example of good health and good grooming.

30. Build on past experiences; keep a file of constructive ideas.

31. Keep abreast of educational literature pertaining to administration and leadership.

32. Keep faith in education as a major hope of the world.

SELECTED REFERENCES FOR EXTENDED READING

ADAMS, HAROLD P., and DICKEY, FRANK G. *Basic Principles of Supervision*. New York: American Book Co., Inc., 1951, chap. 3.

AYER, FRED C. *Fundamentals of Instructional Supervision*. New York: Harper & Bros., 1954, chaps. 3 and 4.

CAMPBELL, CLYDE M. (ed.). *Practical Applications of Democratic Administration.* New York: Harper & Bros., 1952, chap. 12.

DEPARTMENT OF ELEMENTARY SCHOOL PRINCIPALS. *Bases for Effective Learning: Thirty-First Yearbook.* Washington, D. C.: National Education Association, 1952, chap. 2.

ELSBREE, WILLARD S., and MCNALLY, HAROLD J. *Elementary School Administration and Supervision.* New York: American Book Co., 1951, chaps. 1, 2, and 29.

HAGMAN, HARLAN L. *The Administration of American Public Schools.* New York: McGraw-Hill Book Co., Inc., 1951.

MILLER, VAN, and SPALDING, WILLARD B. *The Public Administration of American Schools.* Yonkers, N. Y.: World Book Co., 1952.

OTTO, HENRY J. *Elementary School Organization and Administration.* New York: Appleton-Century-Crofts, Inc., 1954, chap. 16.

REAVIS, WILLIAM C., PIERCE, PAUL R., STULLKEN, EDWARD H., and SMITH, BERTRAND L. *Administering the Elementary School.* New York: Prentice-Hall, Inc., 1953, chaps. 11 and 12.

SHANE, HAROLD G., and MCSWAIN, E. T. *Evaluation and the Elementary Curriculum.* New York: Henry Holt & Co., 1951, chap. 13.

SHANE, HAROLD G., and YAUCH, WILBUR A. *Creative School Administration.* New York: Henry Holt & Co., 1954, chap. 2.

SPEARS, HAROLD. *Improving the Supervision of Instruction.* New York: Prentice-Hall, Inc., 1953, chap. 10.

WILES, KIMBALL. *Supervision for Better Schools.* New York: Prentice-Hall, Inc., 1950, chaps. 2, 3, and 4.

YEAGER, WILLIAM A. *Administration and the Teacher.* New York: Harper & Bros., 1954, chap. 24.

PART II

PURPOSES AND FUNCTIONS OF THE SCHOOL

Chapter 3

THE EDUCATIONAL SETTING OF THE
ELEMENTARY SCHOOL

The influences of the past, the activities of the present, and the hopes of the future all meet in the public school

Education is as old as man's yearning for comfort and as persistent as his dreams of a better world for his children. It is true, of course, that primitive man had no systematic structure to guide the education of his children. Thus it was largely a family enterprise conducted in connection with the problems of living. Even physical survival depended largely on the family's ability to pass along to its younger members the knowledge and skills necessary for protecting themselves from the rigors of their environment and for procuring from that environment the basic necessities of food, clothing, and shelter.

The earliest groups were probably formed for two reasons: (1) to improve their security from the forces of a hostile environment, and (2) to share their common resources and efforts for mutual progress. Throughout the years this tendency toward the formation of ever broadening social and political units among men has been accompanied by an awareness that, if they are to live long and well, they must recognize the common needs of men—among them, a basic educational program.

While its evolution has sometimes been marked by an obvious concern for certain purposes or groups, the elementary school of the modern era probably is the best single expression of this recognition of the need for a common educational program for all members of our society. The passage of compulsory attendance laws in this country has attested to a belief in the universal benefits to be derived from the basic educational program in our schools. Today the elementary school is concerned with the development of individuals who possess the knowledge, the degree of understanding, the skills, and the kinds of habits and attitudes necessary for living fruitfully and happily among one's fellows. It has become truly the laboratory for developing proficiency in citizenship for current and future generations.

Any valid perspective of the modern elementary school requires a consideration of both the historical and sociological factors underlying its development. Its present structure represents a refinement of elements from many stages of its evolution. At different stages of its development, varying emphases have dominated its purposes and program; it has been through successive periods in American history an instrument for religious training, for literacy in communication and basic general knowledge, for social improvement, for character development, and for general competency as a basis for citizenship. The modern elementary school represents, in many ways, a composite of the characteristics of the school program in effect during these various stages.

Certainly the elementary school principal, as administrative leader, must have a clear and complete understanding of the forces which have shaped the structure and function of the elementary school if he is to assume his obligations in an adequate manner. It is hoped that this chapter will contribute to such an understanding of the elementary school through a discussion of (1) certain basic considerations underlying its structure; (2) some of the more significant contributing factors in its historical development; (3) some of the more important relationships existing between it and other social, political, and professional agencies; (4) its scope and characteristics; and (5) some trends and promising frontiers in elementary school organization and structure.

PRINCIPLES AND CONSIDERATIONS AFFECTING THE DEVELOPMENT OF THE ELEMENTARY SCHOOL

Justification for the elementary school, as for any other organized unit of education, lies in its relation to human well-being and civilization. The school represents a conscious effort of society to accomplish commonly accepted ends; it is an integral part of the functional structure of a community, state, or nation for developing an informed and competent citizenry, and certain basic considerations underlie any comprehensive analysis of the development of the elementary school as we know it today.

1. *Increasingly, the elementary school has become a concern of all the people.* In its earlier forms, even in this country, the elementary school served certain limited purposes. As a result, the opportunity for even a rudimentary program of education was not extended to all. However, with the development of a form of government in America which demanded participation by all and, in turn, emphasized the importance of individual rights, increasing importance was attached to the improvement of the personal and civic competence of citizens through education.

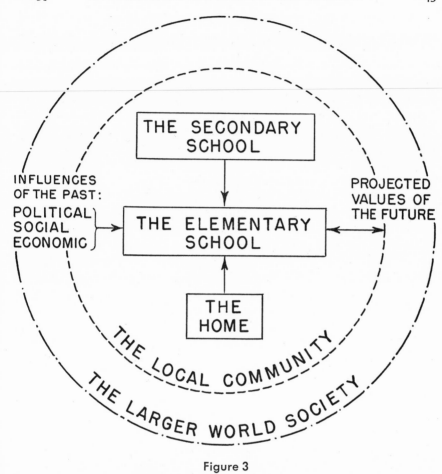

Figure 3

The Setting of the Elementary School

This relationship between education and the responsibilities of citizenship has been recognized increasingly until the present day, in which it appears obvious to most thoughtful citizens. This relationship has been felt in two ways. In the first place, the elementary school has gradually become a school "for all the children of all the people." In the second place, schools are enjoying greater active participation from parents and laymen in assuming responsibility for providing facilities for education and in the development of broad educational policies for schools.

2. *The usefulness and importance of education have endured and been extended because the forms of education have changed in accordance with changing man and changing conditions.* As mentioned earlier

in this chapter, education was recognized and practiced in its more casual forms before it became a public responsibility. Evolving generations have associated learning with improved status. Therefore, as men have extended their knowledge, broadened their understanding, and become aware of new needs, they have established new purposes for themselves. These unfolding purposes, in turn, have become the directing guideposts for the developing educational structure. The most constructive purposes of education during any age have been those that have been related to helping man adjust to his environment, operate effectively within it, and contribute to its improvement. Schools thus have found it necessary to remain sensitive not only to the changing nature and purposes of people but to changing world conditions as well.

The fact that changes in educational practice sometimes come slowly is not wholly unfortunate. The imagination of professional educators can project technical advancements in education beyond the point where proper interaction with society can be maintained by the schools. On the other hand, schools which remain static in a changing world will soon lose their usefulness entirely. An essential of good education is the ability to foresee, then to make intelligent changes.

3. *The purposes of the elementary school change in relation to the desires and needs of the people served by the school.* Schools always exist within a framework of time and location, and invariably have reflected the period and place in which they have operated. For instance, during colonial times in this country, the schools were limited largely to moral and religious concerns. During succeeding generations the aims of the elementary school have shown the influence of successive social, economic, and political developments. The schools of a generation reflect in their goals the things which the citizens of that generation consider important.

The purposes of the elementary school also are affected by the nature of the region or community in which the school is located. They bear a genuine relation to the persisting culture patterns of the group inhabiting the community. They tend to be structured according to dominant occupational groups and by the things which are held to be important by such groups. The tradition of local control in American education has permitted great diversity in the nature and quality of the schools from one community to another. Although this condition has some unfortunate results, it does tend to allow the people of a community to provide the kind of school which they desire for their children, at least up to the existing level of financial resources.

4. *As the purposes and basic philosophy of the elementary school have been modified, they have been accompanied by corresponding*

changes in method. The destination one sets for a trip determines to a large degree the manner in which he expects to travel and the road he will follow. In similar manner, the existing purposes of the elementary school during a particular period, or in a particular region, have tended to shape the nature of the educational methods employed in the school.

While there is still great disparity among elementary schools throughout the nation with respect to the value and quality of instruction, there has been a gradual, yet constant, acceptance of democratic citizenship as one of the predominant purposes of education. As a result, a corresponding diminution of regimentation as an instructional and administrative device has been noted. There also has been an increase in the utilization of actual experience and activity in the school program. These changes in organization and method are based on the premise that learning to participate effectively as a member of a group can be best learned through some experience in participating.

5. *As the purposes, basic philosophy, and methods of the elementary school change, a corresponding change in the nature of facilities is required.* It is no accident that the school plant which housed the elementary school of a few decades ago resembled a factory building in the same community. The operation of the school of that era demanded little more than four walls and a few simple furnishings. A premium was placed on silence and inactivity. Lack of room was not a major problem, since the purposes and methods of the educational program demanded little or no movement, exploration, or investigation.

In the modern elementary school, with its concern for active citizenship, an entirely different kind of educational setting is needed. Room for activity, group work, and for the storage and use of varied instructional materials is essential. The search for resources of all types requires interaction within the school and between school and community.

6. *The structure of the elementary school program of today is the result of the same kinds of influences which have brought advances in other aspects of human endeavor.* It is true that the nature of the modern elementary school has been shaped largely in terms of the expanding purposes of education in our democracy. However, certain other factors have produced very notable modifications in the organization and instructional procedures employed in the elementary school.

Just as in the other professions, or in industry, research has played a major role in the determination of the most effective educational processes and facilities. In the main, the changes most obvious in the development of the modern elementary school may be directly attributed to the results of educational research. Such research has revealed rather complete knowledge of how children develop, how learning takes place most efficiently, as well as information regarding the comparable effectiveness of various devices and materials of learning. In turn, these findings have affected, at least indirectly, the administration of the school program.

7. *The basic function of the modern elementary school is to promote maximum self-development of each child and to provide experiences that will equip him to understand and interact with his physical and social environment in a constructive manner and to an ever-expanding degree.* In organizing the elementary school, one must remember that the educated citizen's effectiveness is based on his individual skills, habits, understanding, and attitudes and on the facility with which he can use these personal attributes in his relations with others and with his environment. This calls for a school program which includes experiences and opportunities for individuals to gain proficiency along both lines.

Historical Background of the American Elementary School

History may not repeat itself, but historical events are felt beyond the period of their occurrence. The component factors of civilization are largely cumulative, and education is no exception. The elementary school of today is what it is because of many things. Numerous personalities out of the past have helped to mold the contemporary structure of elementary education. Countless events of other ages have indelibly marked the educational processes of this generation. To understand the evolution of the elementary school, it is necessary to consider some of the forces which have contributed historically to its development.

European Influences.—Although the educational patterns developed by the Greeks and Romans, and, during the Renaissance, by other Europeans, represented significant rungs on the ladder of systematic approaches to education, the real forerunner of modern education was Comenius. Although he spent a great part of his relatively long life in exile, largely as a result of the religious struggle of the time, he managed to make some very significant contributions to educational thought and practice. Among his major contributions was his idea regarding the proper organization of the school system. He suggested that the educational program be divided into four units. The first was to be the *school for infants* for children from birth to six years, administered in the home by the mothers themselves. The second unit of education was the *vernacular school* for children between the ages of six and twelve. This corresponded roughly to our elementary school of today. The third phase of the educational program was the *gymnasium* for children from twelve to eighteen years of age. This was followed by six years given to a *university* education. Comenius felt that such an organization followed logically the periods of growth of children.

Comenius was a forerunner of democratic education in that he persisted in his advocacy of a single-track plan of education for all children. He frowned upon the idea of separate educational programs for children of the poor and those of the wealthy. He believed that a common elementary school program for the children of all would result in mutual social benefits to all. In fact, many modern ideas of education may be found in one of his greatest publications, the *Great Didactic*.

Roughly a century after Comenius, the influence of Rousseau began to be felt in religious, political and educational circles. The publication of his book *Emile* revealed many of his ideas regarding education. He placed strong emphasis on the child himself rather than on subject matter as such. He called for consideration of natural interests of children in formulating learning materials and experiences. He placed considerable emphasis on physical activity. In many of his ideas set forth in describing the education of the young boy in *Emile,* many similarities to modern educational theories and practices may be noted.

Pestalozzi was another European who exerted a great deal of influence on the ultimate pattern of educational organization in America. He was a native of Switzerland and early came under the influence of the philosophy of Rousseau. He may be said to be the father of the activity program in school. On one occasion, he established a school on the farm and combined experiences in farm activities with the study of regular school subjects. Later he established and operated an institute at Yverdon, where he developed and demonstrated his methods of teaching. Pestalozzi insisted on humane treatment of the child and attempted to fit educational experiences to the child's nature and needs. His methods of teaching were observed and studied not only by other prominent Europeans but by visitors from America as well.

Among the students of Pestalozzi was Friedrich Froebel, who later was destined to influence educational organization almost as much as Pestalozzi himself. Froebel had a rather unhappy childhood, and little success as a student in the university at Jena in Germany. After his contact with Pestalozzi at Yverdon he developed a strong passion for the idea of building a lifelike program of education for young children. This ultimately led him to establish the first kindergarten in Blankenburg. Aside from devoting most of the remaining years of his life to the operation of his kindergarten, he also started a training school for kindergarten teachers. Subsequently, the idea of the kindergarten based on activity and social participation spread throughout the world.

Another contemporary of Pestalozzi who was to exercise a marked influence on educational organization and methodology was Johann Friedrich Herbart. He was a German scholar and university professor who worked mainly in the fields of methodology and psychology. Many think of Herbart as the father of the organismic concept of psychology, since he believed that the mind operates as a unitary force and is not divided into compartmentalized "faculties." Needless to say, the years since his time have seen many refinements of Herbart's theories into more usable patterns, but he must be given credit for his pioneering efforts in the field of psychology of learning.

Herbart's greatest contribution to educational practice probably was made in the area of teaching methodology. He attempted to reduce teaching to a completely scientific process. Later he was responsible for the development of the five formal steps in teaching: (1) preparation, (2) presentation, (3) comparison, (4) conclusion, and (5) application. Although it seems obvious to educators now that it is impossible to apply such formal steps uniformly to the teaching-learning process, it can readily be understood that such a structured teaching methodology would exert a very concrete influence on teaching and planning for years following their proposal. This is exactly what happened, and even today some of the traces of Herbart's thinking can be identified in school organization and practice.

Early American Influences.—An understanding of the emerging structure of the elementary school in this country must take into account the fact that elementary education took three entirely different forms in the colonial period. The southern colonies, with their great plantations, were populated chiefly by members of an aristocratic society, Negro slaves, and a white poor class with little property of value. The plantation owners hired tutors for the education of their children; the children of the servants and slaves received no education. It was not until the middle part of the nineteenth century that Virginia, for instance, advanced beyond a modified private tutorial practice in the establishment of a school system as such.

On the other hand, in New England men had settled for entirely different reasons. They had come to this country to find religious freedom and freedom from autocratic rule. These motives, not surprisingly, were reflected in the forms of education which emerged in New England. Even though the schools were patterned after those in England, these pioneers wished to make education available to all and in turn developed public support for the schools. Even though the motivating factor in education was a religious one, the New England schools were, to a great degree, community-centered and oriented.

A third type of education came into being in the Middle colonies. A major concern of the people of these colonies was also religion and their educational programs were motivated by the desire to equip their children to read the Bible. However, their schools were controlled and supported by the churches rather than by the communities.

Obviously, it is not the purpose of this volume to treat in detail the history of public education in this country. However, any comprehensive and thoughtful review of how the structure of the present school came into being must include some mention of a few of the persons, among many, who have made outstanding contributions to the molding of our educational system in America.[1] Of the numerous persons who have thus contributed, at least two seem to deserve special consideration for the impetus they gave to public education during the crucial early stages of its establishment and development in the nation.

Thomas Jefferson, throughout his years of distinguished public service, recognized the strong relationship between the quality of education of the common man and the effectiveness of a democratic form of government. He was a believer in the rights of the common man and in the premise that the power of men to govern themselves could be increased through education. These basic beliefs were carried into action by Jefferson in several concrete ways. During his term as a member of the Virginia state legislature he introduced a bill for the establishment of free public education. His proposal for such a system, though made in 1779, contained many of the features of our present organizational and administrative structure of schools. It provided for three years of education at public expense to be extended, if desired, at parents' expense. Sentiment in the southern colonies at that time did not favor such a development, and Jefferson failed to get approval for his plan. However, it did exert considerable influence on the nature of subsequent developments in education. It may be said that Jefferson, though not a professional educator, did much to emphasize the importance of education and undoubtedly influenced the growth and patterns of emerging American schools.

Another man who cast a profound influence on public education in America was Horace Mann. As a member of the Massachusetts state legislature and later as secretary of the first Massachusetts state board of education, which had been created on his proposal, he waged a very successful fight for free public education. He dedicated himself to the tasks of getting financial support for schools, of improving their methods and facilities, and of educating teachers specially qualified to guide the

[1] See George Willard Frasier, *An Introduction to the Study of Education* (New York: Harper & Bros., 1951), pp. 25-66.

learning of children. Largely through his efforts and interest, the first normal school was founded in Lexington, Massachusetts, in 1839. In fact, Mann may well be considered the father of teacher education in America. As a further major contribution to education, Horace Mann, acting as secretary of the state board of education, made twelve annual reports in which he discussed many aspects of educational aims and conditions in Massachusetts. These reports reflect very clearly his belief in the extreme importance of free public education of a nonsectarian nature. He later became the founder and president of Antioch College in Ohio, which he served during the remainder of his years.

Still a third man who should not be overlooked in viewing the development of schools in this country was Henry Barnard. He, too, like Mann, was a lawyer, and he too served in a state legislature, in Connecticut. Later he deserted the legal profession and devoted most of his remaining life to the cause of education. Again, like Mann, he became secretary of a state board of education (Connecticut) and, with a corresponding passion for free public education, worked unceasingly to improve educational conditions. Later he carried his ideas and efforts into Rhode Island, where he became the first commissioner of education for that state. Still later he served as president of the University of Wisconsin and terminated his career of public and professional service by serving, with distinction, as the first United States Commissioner of Education. During his professional career, Barnard became interested in the kindergarten movement and exerted considerable influence on teaching methodology as it applied to young children.

As the frontiers were being extended westward, each state in turn faced the problems of providing adequate educational systems for their people. Aside from the pioneering vision and efforts of the three men previously mentioned, the contributions of such men as Thaddeus Stevens in Pennsylvania, Calvin Wiley in North Carolina, Caleb Mills in Indiana, and John D. Pierce in Michigan should not be overlooked. Each in his own way hastened the establishment of a system of free public schools throughout the nation.

Later American Influences.—As Jefferson's conviction that an enlightened citizenry constitutes a basic prerequisite to effective democratic government began to find expression in the universal establishment of free public schools, many varied influences continued to shape the ultimate structure of these schools. As a result of this slow evolutionary process, schools of today are different in many respects from those which existed during the earlier periods of our history. There have been at least five major educational developments which have left indelible impressions on the elementary school as it has emerged in its modern form.

1. *The gradual change in the nature of the school population to be served by the schools.* Much of this change has been quantitative in nature. For example, in 1880, approximately 10 million children were attending elementary schools in the United States; in 1950 this number had doubled and conservative official estimates now indicate an enrollment of more than 25 million in 1955, with approximately 30 million expected by 1960. This increase in numbers, along with the concentration of population due to industrial expansion, has influenced the number, size, and structure of elementary schools immeasurably.

Not only has the size of the school population increased but its nature has changed as well. An increasing interest and faith in public education gradually has made the elementary school an institution for all the people. Compulsory attendance laws have legalized this concept, resulting in a school population composed of the wealthy and the poor, the interested and the disinterested, the gifted, the average, and the handicapped. This is an entirely different situation from that of an earlier day when the school population beyond the primary grades was comprised largely of the more capable children of interested parents. In the earlier school the rigors of a highly standardized textbook curriculum usually served as a very effective instrument of selection, and generally only the able and persistent survived the entire graded program of the elementary school.

2. *The gradually broadening functions of the elementary school.* The program of the modern elementary school is complex as compared with that of schools in the early American colonies. Schools of that period were devoted mainly to morality and simple literacy. As the general population of the country has become more enlightened in many respects, there have been increasing demands for adding various subjects to the program of the elementary school. This trend has continued until the present day; now the educational program embraces a multitude of activities and responsibilities which previously would have seemed ridiculous. Obviously, this extension of responsibility has necessitated corresponding changes in the organization and structure of the schools.

3. *Gradually changing professional concepts of education itself.* One reason for a rather continuous change in the structure of the elementary school during its development in this country is the change that has occurred in our notions of what constitutes good education. Both philosophic and psychological bases of education have undergone revision as the system of American public schools has evolved. Roughly, the history of education since the colonial period reveals three successive concepts of education. In the earliest period of our history, education was considered to be *training for specific or limited tasks and activities.*

This training was characterized by narrowness of purpose and by intensive drill.

As we moved into the mid-period of our national history, people gradually began to accept *education as preparation for life as a whole*. As a result the curriculum gradually was broadened to include an increasing number of aspects of living. Teaching methodology and elementary school organization necessarily were influenced by this evolution in educational thought.

The third concept of education can be attributed, to a great degree, to the influence of John Dewey on the modern elementary school. His insistence that *education is living* rather than preparation for living has done much to extend the frontiers of the classroom and to bring many elements of the environment into a natural relationship with the school curriculum. His plea for capitalizing on interest as a factor in the educational process has done much to vitalize the elementary school program and to carry it beyond the realm of abstractness and artificiality which characterized traditional curricula.

To a great extent, patterns of teaching methodology and school organization have paralleled changing concepts of educational psychology. For example, when "faculty psychology" dominated educational practice, it was quite natural that drill and memorization should be utilized as basic approaches to learning. As educators began to conceive of learning as a unified and integrative process, there has been a corresponding trend toward organizing school efforts around "units of work" or "centers of interest."

4. *The standardized testing movement in education.* The whole development of education as a science and the scientific approach to education had an important effect on educational practice in the schools. The standardized testing movement, which got its great initial emphasis about the time of the First World War, had some very direct effects on the organization of the elementary school. Mental tests soon became administrative instruments for classifying learners, since such tests furnished the first scientific basis for categorizing children of different abilities. Achievement tests gained a similarly favorable response in schools and have continued to influence methods and policies of evaluation and pupil progress up to the present time. Likewise, the creation of diagnostic tests directly contributed to a clamor for remedial work in the various areas of the curriculum. All of these, and many other outcomes of the standardized testing movement, have helped determine the present structure of the elementary school.

5. *The centralization movement in education.* Since 1869 when the state of Massachusetts enacted legislation which permitted the consoli-

dation of school districts, the tendency toward the creation of larger school units through centralization has been almost continuous. Many factors have contributed to this development. Part of it is certainly due to the natural desire of parents in isolated rural areas for their children to have educational services and opportunities equal to those offered their city cousins. Purely economic considerations have played their part in the elimination of small one-room schools with few children in attendance. The improvement of roads and highways has made it possible to transport children greater distances in a shorter time with a minimum of hazard. Whatever reasons are involved, the fact remains that administrative school units have grown increasingly larger in size. This has had an obvious effect on the organization of the school. While the general effects of such consolidation have been educationally wholesome, many problems have at the same time been created. For example, the problem of providing adequately for the individual differences of children appears to become increasingly difficult as the children are regimented into very large educational units. However, it should be said that, even though the larger schools are not without problems which attend their size, the advantages of such schools far outweigh their disadvantages as compared with the smaller schools to be found throughout the country.

This regrouping of school children into larger school units has necessitated serious thought on the part of administrative leaders with regard to such matters as home-school relations, classification, grouping, and pupil progress, in addition to such school service problems as transportation and the school lunch program. All in all, the centralization movement has been a principal factor in shaping the pattern of the typical elementary school of today.

Contemporary Setting of the Elementary School

Over and beyond the historical factors which have helped to mold the elementary school into its present form, modern society also provides numerous elements which condition the nature of the school. Many social elements and agencies are so related to the function of education that it is difficult to consider one without a corresponding consideration of the others. Several of these relationships merit the serious study of the administrative leader as he seeks to define, develop, and appraise the basic educational structure of schools today. For that reason, a limited discussion of a few of them is included here.

The Relationship of the Elementary School to Other Educational Units Within the Profession.—Although the elementary school has evolved from specific purposes rather uniquely related to the basic tenets of an expanding American democracy, its history cannot be adequately considered apart from other organized aspects of American education. In fact, one of the most persistent problems confronting public education in this country has been the effective articulation of the efforts of the various educational units into a unified pattern of learning throughout the educational system.

One of the mutually important relationships is that existing between the elementary school and the secondary school. It will be remembered that the origin of the secondary school was quite different from that of the common, or elementary, school. In fact, the first high schools bore no relationship at all to existing elementary schools, having been developed along completely independent lines for entirely different purposes.[2]

Admission to high school was based on entrance examinations, and rigid selection of students was the rule. Later these examinations were increasingly based on the curriculum of the elementary school, and ultimately the completion of the work of the grammar school, as it was called, served as a satisfactory credential for entering the secondary school. Gradually, and somewhat logically, the elementary school came to be considered a preparatory institution for high school.

It has been pointed out that the two educational units, elementary and secondary, originated and developed for different purposes and along different lines. As a result it has been a difficult task to implement the wholesome, yet slow, trend toward the unification and integration of the programs of the two school units into an effective pattern of education consistent with modern knowledge of human growth and the role of education for American citizenship. At any rate, the superimposing of the secondary school on the common school program in this country undoubtedly has affected the structure and program of the elementary school of the twentieth century. In recent years, there appear to be rather promising indications that increased compatibility is being developed between the programs of the elementary and secondary schools.

Two other and interrelated extensions of the school program are leaving their marks on the elementary school. One of these is the extension of the elementary school downward through providing programs for five-year-olds, four-year-olds, or for children even younger. Modern knowledge and understanding of child development have given a marked impetus to the establishment of kindergartens and nursery schools as integral parts of the public school system. Although such programs are relatively few compared with the total number of elementary schools in

[2] Hollis A. Caswell and A. Wellesley Foshay, *Education in the Elementary School* (New York: American Book Co., 1950), p. 24.

the country, the recognition of their value is being demonstrated by a gradual increase in their number each year. It must be recognized also that the great increase in the number of working mothers during the recent years of war and military expansion has stimulated the enrollment in, and demands for, nursery schools and kindergartens. The growing acceptance of the idea of extending the organized educational program downward through the early years of the child's life is a concrete step in the direction of active demonstration of the fact that education is actually a lifelong process extending from "the cradle to the grave."

The extension of the organized educational program downward into the earlier years of children's lives has been accompanied by an increased interest of parents in child development. This naturally has brought about a closer articulation of home and school in providing more consistent approaches to the task of helping children grow and learn. Many communities have seen the organization and development of parent study groups and adult classes covering various aspects of knowledge and understanding of the nature of children and how they learn. Undoubtedly these developments have influenced greatly the effectiveness of the elementary school program in many communities, and it seems likely that the trend toward the integration of the educational efforts of home and school will continue.

The upgrading and refinement of public education in the United States has been due in large part to a corresponding growth in provisions for teacher education throughout the country. From the time of the establishment of the first normal school in Lexington, Massachusetts, in 1839, as mentioned earlier, the preparation of teachers has become the principal link in the whole educational system. As the nature and purposes of the public schools themselves have changed through the years, the somewhat limited pattern of the earlier normal schools has given way to the broader and more scientifically conceived programs of the teachers colleges and schools of education connected with universities. In the modern era of education, teachers are licensed to teach after a systematic program of teacher education rather than on the basis of an examination over a few factual fields of subject matter.

Recent years have brought about an increasing tendency to develop programs of teacher education on the basis of critical analyses of the competencies required for successful teaching, in so far as they can be determined. Some such studies have been undertaken locally by teacher-educating institutions, while others have been conducted on a state or national basis. Some statements of specific competencies are given in Chapter 8 as they are related to the improvement of teachers in service.

Public schools, as well as institutions of higher learning, have a genuine stake in the supply of well-qualified teachers. The quality of instruction in the elementary schools of any community, or in the country as a whole, for that matter, is largely dependent upon the adequacy of the professional preparation given to persons planning to teach. Since there is now a trend toward the use of public schools for laboratory and teaching experiences as a part of the professional training sequence in many regions, the personnel of these schools are presented with a genuine opportunity to influence constructively the nature and quality of the future generation of teachers. The interest and sympathetic guidance given to student teachers in such schools by the administrative leader and the staff will help determine the benefits to be derived from the experience. Principals, supervising teachers, and other staff members might well ponder the ways in which they can make a maximum contribution to the upgrading of public education through efforts directed toward providing a rich professional experience for student teachers located in their schools.

The Relationship of the Elementary School to Family and Community Factors and Change.—Many economic and technological developments in this country have been accompanied by changes in the attitudes and living habits of its people. Population shifts have reflected the change from an agrarian society to an urban one. The self-contained and compact family unit has become much more elastic through the varied interactions of its members with the other forces and components of the community and world society. The family has shifted its role from that of producer of materials for its own needs to that of consumer of products which are the results of the labors of many people, far removed and generally unknown. The activities of members of the typical family are taking them more frequently beyond the limits of the home, and more and more of the world is being brought across the threshold to affect the lives of those residing within the home. All these factors have affected the total education of children from generation to generation and have continued to influence indirectly the role, the objectives, and the program of the school in recent years.

The nature of family life has a bearing on the function and organization of the elementary school in numerous and varied ways. In the first place, the family is the educational agency for the child from the time of his birth until he enters school. For most children this covers an important five-year span. It is a time when they learn the important skills of elemental language and the processes of movement and walking. But these are not all. The child also learns the values and attitudes that are to influence his subsequent life in school and through later years. Because the family guides so completely the impressionable and formative years of the child's life during the preschool period, many of his patterns of personality and performance are rather clearly indicated by the time he enters into the organized program of the elementary school. What the children bring with them when they enter school—needs, experiences, attitudes, resources, limitations—have a great effect in shaping the nature of what the school can offer in return. One of the greatest challenges facing educational leadership is the obligation for providing experiences for children in school that will, on the one hand, supplement all previous desirable learning and, on the other, alleviate the effects of the deprivation experienced by some children during the preschool years.

In this modern age there has been brought into the typical home much educative information which formerly the family could have procured only through reading. Radio and television programs have rearranged family schedules and have provided a continuous diet of information, drama, music, and miscellaneous offerings, many of which have been directed toward youthful auditors and viewers. As a result, in many instances, children are coming to school with broader backgrounds of information than previously. However, at the same time, when the emotional pull of such media is not present in school activities, some problems of motivation are almost inevitable. Currently, one of the problems confronting both parents and educators is that of reconciling effectively and consistently the educational opportunities which children have in home and school.

Ease of communication and ease of transportation also have affected family life as well as opportunities for learning. More and more children enjoy the privilege of travel with their families, usually during the earlier years of their lives. Such experiences of children not only enrich their own lives but provide material to be shared through the organized activities of the classroom.

In addition to the many direct changes that have occurred in the pattern of living in the typical American family in recent years, several economic and cultural aspects of community life have affected, indirectly at least, the complexions of both home and school. One of these is the fact that less and less of the energies of family members are devoted to the actual production of the goods and services utilized by them. On the one hand, this has created a situation in which members of a family or community are dependent upon many persons both within and outside the boundaries of the community in which they live. At the same time, these increasingly specialized vocational endeavors have resulted in more and more time for leisure. Naturally, both of these developments affect in many ways the lives of children as they mature.

Modern community life is much more impersonal than formerly. The family is not so closely knit as previously and is no longer the sole source of recreation for its members. Intercommunication and visiting among neighbors have diminished in favor of various interest groups, social and civic, which have developed in most communities and consume much of the spare energies of family members. In a similar way, community agencies such as the Boy Scouts, Girl Scouts, and other youth groups have enjoyed a phenomenal growth in this country and have supplanted, in a way, some of the functions previously assumed to be the domain of the family. Although these agencies represent independent programs, their effectiveness depends rather heavily upon a constructive working relationship with the home and school.

Another condition which has affected both community living and the effectiveness of educational provisions for children has been the increased mobility of the population of this country in recent years. Although a certain proportion of our people has always been affected by the nomadic tendency to move from one supposedly green pasture to another, the extent of this problem has been accentuated considerably by some of the conditions of recent years. During the war years and since, the lure of relatively high-paying jobs in areas with rapidly expanding construction has attracted many such families. Seasonal harvests seem also to encourage a migration of workers and their families from one place to another, depending on the agricultural activity in each community. Members of this transient population, motivated by such conditions as those suggested above, usually do not become integral and stable elements of the communities in which they live. Children from such families find it difficult to profit from any sustained program of education, since they suffer from frequent interruptions in their schooling. Obviously, the schools must take into account the fact that a sizable part of their enrollments is highly mobile and must attempt to make adjustments, wherever possible, to meet this problem.

A great many of the children of elementary school age now have come through prolonged periods in which their fathers have been absent from the home for military service. This condition has influenced very materially the nature of the school population and has limited the possibilities of family living for these children. Such situations have tended to focus attention of school personnel more sympathetically on the emotional stresses and problems of children as a whole.

The Relationship of the Public Elementary School to Various Units of Government.—The principle of local control has been an important one in the development of the American public school. However, the elementary school cannot accurately be considered an autonomous educational unit because of its relationship to and dependence upon local, state, and federal agencies of government. The regulation and contributions of these agencies have affected both the resources and the nature of the program of the elementary school.

The elementary school must look to the local district for its primary support. Local districts are governed by boards of education composed of from three to fifteen members. These boards have the power to levy taxes for the support of local schools and to employ personnel and provide facilities for operating an educational program in the community. As a rule, these boards are considered policy-making bodies and are expected to delegate the responsibility for professional administration to a superintendent or to other administrative officials of their own selection. In some states and communities, board members are appointed; in others they are elected directly by the vote of the people. Some local school districts are fiscally independent, while others must have their budgets submitted to city officials for approval and action. In recent years there appears to be a trend toward fiscal independence for school districts.

Although state legislatures have delegated most of the control of education to local communities, there are many ways in which the state controls and influences the nature and quality of the educational program at the local level. Part of this control is exercised directly by legislatures through laws and through appropriations to the various districts. Although such statutory provisions vary from state to state, legislation even regarding various aspects of the curriculum has been passed by state legislatures. Usually, however, state legislatures have set up state agencies and commissions whose regulations, though not law, often have the force of law. The most common state agency of this kind is the department of public instruction headed by a state superintendent or commissioner of schools.

State agencies play a large part in determining the nature of the school program through certification and licensing of teachers, creation of textbook commissions, administration of general and special appropriations, supervision of school transportation, and through curriculum control and development. State departments of education also have assumed supervisory functions over the schools of the states. In recent years this function has become increasingly a service activity of the state rather than being primarily inspectorial in nature. State agencies further aid local districts in some cases by operating testing and research services as well as consultant services for general and vocational programs in the schools.

Although public education traditionally has been a state and local responsibility, it has profited from certain contributions from the federal government. One of the ways in which education is influenced at the national level is through the activities of the United States Office of Education. This department of government was created in 1867; and, although its name has changed three times, it has functioned continuously from that date, when Henry Barnard served as the first Commissioner of Education. In 1953 the Office of Education became a part of the newly created Department of Health, Education and Welfare whose administrator was given cabinet status in the executive branch of the government. Much of the work of the Office of Education has been concerned with the collection, organization, interpretation, and distribution of data regarding education and the schools.

Another manner in which the contribution of the national government has been felt in the operation of local schools has been through provision of funds for school lunch programs. State funds have been supplemented for this use and commodities frequently have been supplied by the federal government for use in the schools.

ACTION SUGGESTIONS FOR THE PRINCIPAL

1. Formulate a clear and workable definition of the role of education in our modern society.

2. Realize that the elementary school is a school for "all the children of all the people."

3. Welcome constructive change.

4. Always view the purposes of the school in terms of the people it serves.

5. Help the staff study its efforts to determine whether they are consistent with the school's purposes.

6. Strive to provide facilities that are consistent with modern methods of learning.

7. Study the history of the local school to sense its achievements, note its directions, and determine its persisting needs.

8. Study the socioeconomic patterns of the community served by the school.

9. Become acquainted with the great educational leaders of this and other eras and their contributions to the evolving elementary school.

10. Make careful enrollment studies to determine current and future obligations of the school.

11. Furnish leadership in establishing concrete approaches to the articulation of elementary and secondary school programs such as creating a joint committee for studying means for making easier the transition from one unit to the other.

12. Cooperate fully with secondary school officials in any constructive efforts to achieve articulation.

13. Seek to establish some means of developing close school ties with parents of preschool children so that early growth of the children may be affected in a positive way.

14. Cooperate closely with teacher-educating institutions in any appropriate preservice or in-service efforts to provide better teachers.

15. Provide opportunities for parents and teachers to discuss jointly the problems of mutual concern regarding the home, school, and community experiences of children.

16. Be completely informed regarding the contributions of the state and federal governments to the resources or program of the local school.

SELECTED REFERENCES FOR EXTENDED READING

ADAMS, FAY. *Educating America's Children: Elementary School Curriculum and Methods* (rev. ed.). New York: The Ronald Press Co., 1954.

BRAMELD, THEODORE. *Ends and Means in Education.* New York: Harper & Bros., 1950.

BRUBACHER, JOHN S., (ed.). *Eclectic Philosophy of Education.* New York: Prentice-Hall, Inc., 1951.

CASWELL, HOLLIS L., and FOSHAY, A. WELLESLEY. *Education in the Elementary School.* New York: American Book Co., 1942.

COLE, LUELLA. *A History of Education.* New York: Rinehart & Co., 1950.

DEPARTMENT OF ELEMENTARY SCHOOL PRINCIPALS. *Human Values in the Elementary School.* Washington, D. C.: N.E.A., 1952.

EDUCATIONAL POLICIES COMMISSION. *Education for All American Children.* Washington, D. C.: National Education Association and American Association of School Administrators, 1948.

FRASIER, GEORGE WILLARD. *An Introduction to the Study of Education.* New York: Harper & Bros., 1951.

HART, JOSEPH K. *Education in the Humane Community.* New York: Harper & Bros., 1951.

JOHN DEWEY SOCIETY. *The American Elementary School.* Yearbook, New York: Harper & Bros., 1953.

OTTO, HENRY J. *Elementary-School Organization and Administration.* New York: Appleton-Century-Crofts, Inc., 1954, chaps. 1 and 2.

RAGAN, WILLIAM B. *Modern Elementary Curriculum.* New York: The Dryden Press, Inc., 1953, chaps. 1, 2, and 3.

REAVIS, WILLIAM C., PIERCE, PAUL R., STULLKEN, EDWARD H., and SMITH, BERTRAND L. *Administering the Elementary School.* New York: Prentice-Hall, Inc., 1953, chaps. 1 and 2.

SAYERS, E. V. *A First Course in Philosophy of Education.* New York: Henry Holt & Co., 1953.

SHANE, HAROLD G., and MCSWAIN, E. T. *Evaluation and the Elementary Curriculum.* New York: Henry Holt & Co., chaps. 2 and 4.

STANLEY, WILLIAM O. *Education and Social Integration.* New York: Teachers College, Columbia University, 1953.

Chapter 4

THE EDUCATIONAL CONSUMER: THE CHILD

A small child is the clearest symbol of humanity's hope

The justification for the energies devoted to education resides in learners—individually and collectively. The virtues of an educational program are revealed in the development of the children; at the same time, the deficiencies which may be attributed to education usually result from inadequate regard for the learner. Complete knowledge of and consideration for the child are basic to the establishment and operation of an effective school program.

Since schools are fashioned, supported, operated, and evaluated chiefly by adults, it is easy to lapse into the subconscious tendency toward shaping the learning experiences of children to conform to adult standards. One of the most difficult, if not impossible, tasks facing parents and professional educators is that of remembering, or trying to determine, what it is like to be a child. In view of these observations, it is essential that a conscious effort be made to select and organize learning experiences for children in proper keeping with the basic characteristics of childhood and in terms of the ways in which children grow and develop.

If leaders in education understand the nature of the learner and can share such understanding with their associates, they thus can progress toward the formulation of a program of learning experiences consistent with the needs, capacities, and maturity levels of those for whom the school exists—the children. This chapter sets forth a few basic considerations regarding the relationships between the school and the child, along with some aspects of the nature of children which merit the attention of all who assume leadership roles in the elementary school.

PRINCIPLES AND CONSIDERATIONS AFFECTING RELATIONSHIPS BETWEEN THE SCHOOL AND THE CHILD

The school is an instrument of society, dedicated to the welfare of the individuals who attend it. All who have a part in educational effort must always remain aware of the necessity for balance between the purposes and needs of society and those of the individual. However, in a democratic way of life such as prevails in our country, concern for the individual must permeate and guide our educational enterprise as well as other forms of human endeavor. In view of this, certain considerations are worth noting.

1. *Schools were created to serve, not to be served.* Schools came into being as expressions of man's faith in the future and of his aspirations for an informed and effective citizenry. Their justification is based on the assumption that organized public education can do certain things for people which they would not be likely to do if left to their own individual initiative and devices. The outcomes of the school, then, must be viewed in relation to the extent to which they serve the current and future needs of individuals affected. If these things be true, and the author sincerely believes they are, then every proposal and development of the school should be considered in the light of this basic function of education—service.

2. *The elementary school is operated by adults but exists for children.* Even though much progress has been made in recent years in discovering means whereby learners may participate in the planning of their own learning experiences, schools and classrooms still are predominantly managed by adults. This probably is necessary and not an undesirable situation in itself. The dangers of it lie in the extent to which adult standards of behavior are imposed on children, and the extent to which adult convenience and comfort supersede the educational needs of children as the bases for educational activity. While administrative expediency must often be considered in any realistic situation, the prime factor in determining what is done in our schools must always be the welfare of the children served by them.

3. *The program of the elementary school should be designed so as to operate with the grain of human development rather than against it.* Common sense, as well as educational considerations, suggests the wisdom of capitalizing on the natural phases and attributes of human development in the formulation of the sequence of learning experiences which comprise the program of the elementary school. In many phases of education, as in navigation, progress is faster when we operate with the current rather than against it. Most educators recognize that it is extremely wasteful of human energy to attempt to teach things for which learners have neither the maturity nor readiness for learning. It has been suggested that many distressing problems of education, including behavior problems, could be solved if efforts to teach children things they cannot learn were terminated. Certainly a first thought of all who par-

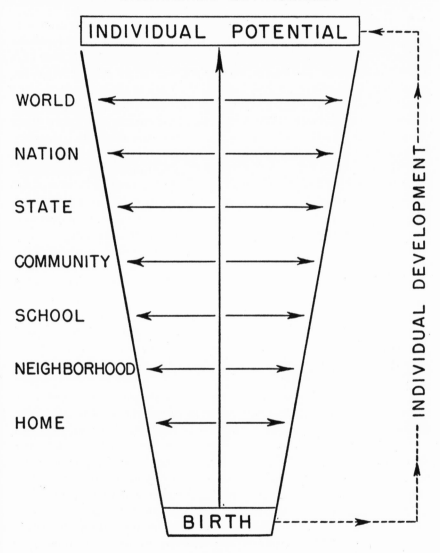

Figure 4

Individual and Social Growth of the Child

ticipate in the development and organization of the elementary school program should be a consideration of the characteristics of learners at various levels of growth.

4. *Certain characteristics of children of elementary school age have a direct bearing on the organization of the school.* If the school is to be organized in terms of the way children develop, administrators and teachers must continuously attempt to provide an educational setting which evidences due regard for the nature of children. It must be recognized that children have certain common characteristics that can serve as guides in the formulation of common patterns of knowledge and learning; at the same time, the individual differences in the growth and learning rates of children demand provisions for flexibility in the program of the school if the needs of all children are to be met.

While the attributes and attitudes of children change somewhat with each year in school, certain general characteristics of children are sufficiently related to the total organization of the school as to warrant special attention. In the following section of this chapter, therefore, some of these prevailing attributes are discussed in more detail.

SOME CHARACTERISTICS OF ELEMENTARY SCHOOL CHILDREN

Each child is the product of his own hereditary background and is molded by his own experience. This means, of course, that each child is different from all others in numerous respects. Yet in spite of this, children tend to have certain characteristics in common. At least some of these more common attributes have a direct bearing on the manner in which school experiences should be organized in order to be effective. Certainly they represent factors that should guide teachers and administrators in their efforts to provide optimum conditions for fruitful living and learning in school.

Children Are Human.—As human beings, children are complex organisms. They think, react, and feel in terms of situational stimuli. Their behavior is not always predictable nor is it necessarily consistent in terms of logic. They usually experience many of the emotional impulses and responses found in adults without having developed the social restraints to govern them. Reason is often overpowered momentarily by strong emotional feelings. Even more than adults, children are alternately enthusiastic and reluctant. Similarly, this human quality carries with it the susceptibility to motivation or, for that matter, to discouragement.

The fact that children are human should be a basic consideration for all who seek to provide good situations for learning. The activities of children cannot be organized in the same manner as the inanimate elements of the school environment. Provision must be made for sensible flexibility, and the child must be respected as a *reacting, responsive,* and *human individual.*

Children Are Uniquely "Childlike."—One of the most delightful creatures in the world is a child. The simple trust, the unceasing curiosity, and the relative lack of artificial inhibitions combine with numerous other intriguing characteristics to produce the appeal of the child. Children definitely are not miniature adults, although the recognition of this fact represents something of a departure from ideas which prevailed in previous eras of educational history. In spite of this changed attitude of many teachers and parents, the purposes and standards for child behavior and activity, both in home and school, still appear to be set up largely in terms of desirable adult behavior and characteristics rather than being oriented to the basic, typical nature of children.

Children Are Individualistic.—Children of elementary school age, like members of the human race in general, have many things in common. Yet each is an individual different from all others. This is one of the marvels of humanity as well as one of its greatest virtues, and, perhaps, also one of its most challenging problems. The regulation of human affairs certainly would be relatively simple, though perhaps uninteresting, if all men were alike in their abilities, interests, and standards of conduct. Much time and effort might be saved if all twelve-year-old boys automatically found twelve-year-old suits to fit perfectly. However, in view of existing reality, such conjecture becomes ridiculous, for it is obvious that such common traits do not exist. It is similarly obvious that much of the value of an individual in our society stems from his distinctive characteristics rather than from the fact that he is like others. One of the greatest privileges of democracy is the right to be different without being penalized for it. This should also represent one of the concerns of the modern elementary school for each of the children it serves.

Certainly some social conformity is desirable in a good group learning situation. There are many aspects of learning that can and should be applied to all pupils. It does, however, seem desirable to guard continuously against the tendency toward unjustified uniformity and regimentation of learning experiences to the extent that simple conformity is commended while individualism is condemned. In later sections of this book dealing with the instructional program of the elementary school, certain specific suggestions are made concerning appropriate provisions for children as individuals.

Children Are Active.—The nature of the child is such that growth comes through activity. Since the child is normally in the elementary school during a period of considerable physical growth, much of his activity needs to be of a physical nature. It is obvious to students of child psychology that a school program which demands long hours of continuous inactivity is not being operated in terms of the characteristics of children. One of the great challenges faced by the school is whether or not it can guide the natural activity of children into constructive educational channels. Although many schools of an earlier day appeared to be dedicated to keeping children quiet and moored to a desk throughout the day, most educators now recognize that a good learning situation, though requiring much planning and organization, demands a reasonable degree of flexibility and activity of various kinds on the part of the learners.

Children Are Responsive.—Because they have not yet learned to moderate judgments and feelings in the manner to be expected of persons possessing more maturity and experience, children of elementary school age usually react to persons and situations in terms of strong likes and dislikes. Many of their emotional reactions are likely to be somewhat extreme in nature. They often find incidents very funny and frequently see elements of humor in situations which evoke no such responses from their elders. At the same time, children of this age are sensitive to the misfortunes of others, particularly if they involve pain or injury to their friends, their pets, or members of their family. This characteristic of responsiveness in children obviously has many connotations for the organizing, and more particularly for the motivating, of learning experiences in the elementary school.

Children Are Curious.—An even greater factor in the motivation of children toward desired goals of learning is the fact that they are characteristically curious about the world around them. Anyone who has had the experience of accompanying a child of six years on a walk through the woods, for instance, will attest to the eager enthusiasm he displays toward the trees, the birds, the animals, or the rocks he encounters on the excursion. He wants to learn. He wants to know the answers to numerous questions. He wants to expand his horizons and extend his experience. All these are vital conditions and elements in a good learning situation, whether in a classroom or out under the blue sky. Those who organize and operate schools and classrooms should consider well how this typical intellectual curiosity and enthusiasm can be captured and maintained throughout all the years spent in the school program and beyond.

Children Are Basically Social.—It is true that children begin their lives with rather highly egocentric purposes and attitudes and that they must learn consideration for others. It is equally true, as pointed out in an earlier part of this discussion, that each child is individualistic in many respects. Notwithstanding these observations, it must be realized that children are typically and basically social. At the same time that they seek independence for themselves, they abhor isolation. Although the extent of social sensitivity gradually increases through the years of the elementary school, most children of this age want to identify themselves with some sort of social group even though the nature of the group changes.

Some Differences in Children Related to Stages of Development

The preceding section of this chapter has been concerned with some of the typical and common characteristics of elementary school children. It is essential to consider these because a great part of the school program must be planned on a common experience basis. However, the effective school must recognize the differences in children as well as their similarities. The intelligent planning and organization of the program of the school, therefore, must be based on an awareness and understanding of the various types of differences found in pupils.

The elementary school is directly concerned with the growth of the child from the time he enters the kindergarten, or before, until the early adolescent period of his development. During these years the child passes through several stages of physical, social, and psychological development. Particular differences may be noted in the child during his preschool years, his primary years, and his intermediate years in school.

During the preschool years, prior to his entrance into school, the child is engaged in the refinement of muscle activity. At the time he enters kindergarten, he usually has rather complete big-muscle control but he does not yet have the skills necessary for smaller muscle manipulation. The child of six years is growing at a relatively slower rate than he was during his earlier years. He is going through a stage of marked physical activity. This particular characteristic points up the need for considerable space for the activities of children of this age. As the child proceeds through the primary grades to the age of eight or nine, his growth becomes relatively steady and his motor control much more refined. The comparative advancement in maturity of girls over boys (which appears to be present from rather early ages) becomes much more noticeable from the ages of nine or ten upward through adolescence.

Although the earmarks of each stage are not as concrete and obvious as in physical growth, children also grow through rather distinctive social and emotional levels of development. At the time of his entrance into the elementary school, the child is somewhat egocentric in his desires and usually requires assistance and encouragement in learning to consider others, as in situations which demand joint use of play facilities or the sharing of them. He is dependent on others for his feeling of security and yet he is continually seeking to establish himself as an individual in his own right. As children approach the age of nine or ten, they become more conscious of the approval of their peers and are likely to show a tendency to organize themselves into new social groups or "gangs" of their own devising. Such groups at this age are usually confined to members of one sex, largely on the basis of mutual interest, rather than on any marked heterosexual consciousness. During the very late years in the elementary school, however, children often begin to become conscious of the opposite sex as well as to begin efforts to free themselves from the domination and protectiveness of parents.

It is important that school administrators and teachers understand the general characteristics of children at the different levels of development and accept them as normal. It is equally important that the organization of learning experiences at the various levels be structured as much as possible in terms of the nature and needs of children of each particular age.

INDIVIDUAL DIFFERENCES IN CHILDREN

If educational opportunities and experiences are to be adapted to individual differences in children, the nature of some of these differences must be considered. Certainly it is a mistake to believe or suggest that all kinds of deviations can be provided for in the same manner. A few of the basic ways in which children at any given age level differ are given here because of their usefulness in the adaptation of the program of the elementary school.

Basically, *hereditary* and *environmental* influences make each child what he is. While the comparative weights of these two factors in the life of the child have been debated for many years, it is sufficient here to state that each is significant in determining the status and potentialities of the learner. Simply stated, it may be said that a person's hereditary strength tends to set the limits of his achievements, while the quality of his environment is a chief factor in determining how near his potential level he performs. The value of this distinction seems obvious for those who help determine the nature of the elementary school. While the school cannot retroactively assist a child in the selection of his grandparents, it does have control over the process of providing a program that will allow and encourage each child to achieve as nearly as possible to the limit of his powers.

The democratic concept does not limit education to any particular group of people; rather it suggests that each person shall have the opportunity for education. One of the obligations and challenges of educational leaders is to assist in the development of educational programs that will properly benefit persons who appear all along the scale of human ability and potentiality.

The task of providing effective educational experiences for any given child at any stage of the elementary school program presumes a knowledge of (1) his cultural and experiential background, (2) his present status in terms of behavior and achievement, and (3) his educational potentialities as far as they can be determined. Since children differ widely in all three respects, the intelligent adaptation of instructional materials and procedures must be based on thoughtful attention and scientific study of these differences along with their connotations for the school. For that reason, a brief discussion of these factors is included here as a prerequisite to the actual formulation of the school's purposes and organization.

Differences in Background.—Aside from the wide variation in ancestral endowment which occurs from child to child, there are also marked differences in the environments into which children are born and in which they develop. Thorpe, in his splendid discussion of the relationship between the fundamental needs of the child and the basic influences of family life on the child, has suggested four areas in which these influences are especially significant. They are:

1. Influences relating to the physical well-being.
2. Influences pertaining to self or ego security.
3. Influences relating to social growth.
4. Influences touching the development of social values.[1]

It has been generally accepted by educational psychologists that many of the essential needs of children in the process of optimum all-round development are related to such things as the physical contacts and care which the child enjoys, the social status and recognition allowed him, and the opportunities for self-expression provided for him. It is usually

[1] Louis P. Thorpe, *Child Psychology and Development* (New York, The Ronald Press Co., 1946), p. 217.

conceded that, even though the purely physical needs may be met to a greater degree through institutional care of a child, there is an element of psychological security in the natural family unit that is difficult, if not impossible, to duplicate elsewhere outside the home. This is not to say, of course, that there are not instances in which an excellent institutional environment is to be preferred to inadequate family life, but rather to emphasize the importance of the home in determining the nature and quality of the child's personality and development.

Differences in physical vigor of children may be based on variations in their family and community backgrounds. There appears to be some correlation, at least, between the socioeconomic background of a child and the nutritional adequacy of the diet provided for him during his early years. There is great variation from home to home and in various communities regarding the attention given to the dental and medical problems of children. Even such matters as the heating and lighting of the home have some bearing on the physical well-being of children. As these things differ, children undoubtedly differ also. As will be pointed out in detail in a later part of this book, this suggests careful study by school personnel in order that these deficiencies may be alleviated as far as possible through the program of the school.

Many of the emotional problems encountered by children in later life appear to be rooted in early childhood experiences. Either rejection or overprotection of children by their parents has been found to contribute to lack of stability and mental health in children as they develop. Conflicts between members of the family leave deep-seated scars on children. Fears and frustrations, as well as overt aggressiveness, often may be traced to the quality of the family relationship experienced by a child. The extent to which children learn to share and to have respect for the rights and property of others is dependent to a large degree on the social relationships of the families of which they are a part. Social and moral values as well seem to have their nature and quality influenced notably by the standards of conduct and the attitudes evidenced within the family pattern of interaction. Even the parents' attitude toward school and education may go far toward determining the child's interest in school.

Opportunities for the child to express himself in an independent manner, while enjoying the security of a good social environment, are vitally important to the development of a feeling of confidence. This is equally true in terms of physical activity and verbal expression. The urge to create and to turn one's ideas into some form of concrete expression is a natural one which should be encouraged. Actually much of the recognition a child needs for persistent motivation may be related to his efforts at self-expression. Unfortunately, great variance may be noted in the extent to which this basic need is met in family life. In fact, it may be observed that in some families even the slightest efforts of the child toward independent self-expression are frowned upon and actively discouraged. When children enter school from all types of home backgrounds, the situation presents a real challenge to the school to try to adapt its program accordingly in terms of individual experiences.

Proper language development is another aspect of growth that depends heavily on early childhood experiences for its optimum realization. In the first place, the manner in which the child is accepted as a member of the family group has a marked influence on his initial efforts at speech. Obviously, a child must have both occasion and opportunity to express himself orally if he is to be expected to become facile in his language skills. An environment based on the notion that "children should be seen but not heard" is not conducive to such facility.

A second way in which the home influences the speech patterns of children is through the standards and example set by parents and older brothers and sisters. Early patterns of speech acquired by the child are so largely imitative that the child's language reflects rather accurately the level of language proficiency demonstrated in the home and neighborhood environment.

The richness of the experiences enjoyed by the child is another contributing factor in his language development. Since a child must have rich and varied experiences for the development of an expanding vocabulary, limited experience is a very real deterrent to vocabulary development. This is true with regard to the growing conversational ability of the child and will become noticeable in connection with his readiness for reading after he enters school.

Bilingualism in the home and community is often felt to be still another very important factor which may complicate the early growth of the child. Although studies differ somewhat in their conclusions about the extent to which bilingualism in the home affects the educational background of the child adversely, it still remains a factor to be taken into account when the individual differences of children are being considered.

There are still many other ways in which the backgrounds of children differ and most of these environmental variations bear some relation to subsequent school experiences and achievement. Some children have the opportunity to travel widely, both in the United States and abroad; others hardly venture from their immediate neighborhoods during the preschool period of their lives. Some children live in homes where they are surrounded with books and periodicals and enjoy radio and television; others are confined by virtually bare walls which house few, if any, such cultural stimuli. In some homes children engage in family conversation concerning events of the day, while in others no time is given to such activities. All these things, and many others, help to make children different, at least in the background they bring to school with them when they enter.

Differences in Status.—The behavior or the achievement of any six-year-old or nine-year-old in the elementary school is different in some respect from that of all other six-year-olds or nine-year-olds, respectively, within that school. The nature and extent of these differences vary according to the hereditary and environmental backgrounds of each. It is just too much to expect, and wholly unrealistic to assume, that each six-year-old child should evidence the same readiness for reading as all others do, or that each ten-year-old boy should weigh exactly the same as all other ten-year-olds. We have been generally willing to accept physical differences but much slower to accept, and provide for, the intellectual differences found in children of the same chronological age.

Some of the aspects of child status which bear a very direct relationship to the formulation of the instructional program of the elementary school are:

1. *Personal well-being.* Only a child normally healthy, physically, mentally, and emotionally, can derive maximum benefits from school. It becomes the responsibility of the school to identify and alleviate, in so far as possible, any deficiencies along these lines.

2. *Educational achievement.* Certainly it is vital to know to what extent a child is achieving his goals and the relation between his achievement and his educational potential. The intelligent formulation or revision of the school program must involve appropriate consideration for the differences displayed by children in the achievement of essential skills, knowledge, and understanding of the physical and social environment, and in the development of constructive attitudes toward themselves and others.

3. *Educational ability.* Mental ages of children differ widely. Therefore, it is not only essential to consider how children vary in terms of achievement but also how their inherent abilities differ at any given time. Numerous tests are available that are useful in determining the general ability to do school tasks. It is imperative that intelligent use be made of all instruments available to determine the range of ability represented in various classrooms of the school, and that the structure of the school program reflect a recognition of these differences.

4. *Interests.* Since interest is a prime requisite for motivation, the differences in the interests found in children take on considerable educa-

tional significance. These differences have very direct implications for the organization of the school, for variations in teaching methodology, and for the selection of instructional materials.

  5. *Strengths and deficiencies.* Any consideration of the variations in the status of children certainly should include some appraisal of the specialized abilities as well as the special problems of children. It is a part of the educational obligation of the school to identify these abilities, analyze existing weaknesses, and provide appropriate opportunities in terms of each condition.

  Potentialities.—It is extremely important to understand the differences in background of children if schools are to be organized for children. It is likewise important, as has been suggested, to be wholly aware of the wide variations in status represented by a group of children of any particular chronological age. However, valuable as such understandings are, they do not form the complete basis for considering individual differences in children of elementary school age. Beyond studying and knowing the past history of a child or evaluating his current cumulative behavior, it is also essential to consider the differences in the potentialities of children. It is comforting to assume that each child has an equal chance to succeed in life, but such an assumption is valid only if we are willing to adapt the definition of success to the limiting potential of each child. It is completely unrealistic for the school to assume, or appear to assume, that all children are headed toward the same educational goals.

  While there is no completely accurate instrument for predicting future educational performance of the learner, considerable use can be made of standardized prognostic and mental ability tests for this purpose. Of the individual tests of mental ability the *Stanford Revision of the Binet Scale* is the most widely used. Numerous group tests such as the *Pintner-Cunningham Mental Test* and the *California Tests of Mental Maturity* are available. In tests such as the latter, both language and nonlanguage scores are given, along with a general total score which can be translated into mental age. In turn, the intelligence quotient (I.Q.) is derived from the ratio of the mental age to the chronological age.

  The value of the I.Q. as a predictive device depends rather largely on the degree to which it remains constant throughout the growth period of the learner. Numerous studies have been directed to this problem in recent years, resulting in varying conclusions. It seems safe to assume that the intellectual stature represented by the I.Q. remains more constant than does the ability to measure it. It seems fair to admit that so many variable factors enter into this type of testing that some fluctuation must be expected. At the same time, this does not deny, on the basis of what is now known, that intelligence may be affected by environmental conditions and motivating circumstances, at least to a degree. Until better and more scientific devices are produced, however, the intelligence quotient can be used to advantage in determining roughly what the school justifiably may expect from each child in terms of his indicated capacities for learning things of the type involved in school tasks.

SOME TECHNIQUES USED FOR STUDYING CHILDREN

Although many of the individual characteristics of children are so obvious that they lend themselves readily to casual observation, there are many other traits of children which require thoughtful and skillful study. Even the most modern and refined approaches to the problem of child study do not produce wholly satisfying results, although they do provide extremely beneficial data. Some of the more acceptable techniques of child study are discussed briefly here on the assumption that as complete knowledge of children as possible is required as a basis for developing a school program dedicated to the maximum growth of children.[2]

Use of Tests.—The findings from various types of tests may be very useful in determining the nature of a school population, individually and collectively. Individual and group tests of intelligence, or academic aptitude, offer valuable information regarding what may reasonably be expected from a child or group of children. Achievement tests based on established norms reveal considerable information about the comparative status of children with regard to school achievement and are also helpful in determining the extent of growth experienced by a particular child from one testing period to the next. In addition, certain diagnostic tests are available which can be used to help isolate particular learning difficulties of individual children. Of course, all these types of standardized instruments are susceptible to abuse through overemphasis on their accuracy in any particular moment or case. However, if they are assumed to be indicative rather than completely conclusive, and if their results are interpreted wisely and in the light of all other known factors, they can be quite useful as devices for learning about children.

Teacher-made tests also can be used to advantage if they are objective and are carefully constructed. They appear to play a more useful role in determining and evaluating academic achievement than in other areas of child development.

Various scales and inventories constitute another group of testing

[2] See Ruth Strang, *An Introduction to Child Study* (New York: The Macmillan Co., 1951) ; Theodore L. Torgerson, *Studying Children* (New York: The Dryden Press, Inc., 1947).

devices which occasionally can be utilized to advantage in professional child study. Of these, interest inventories appear to be especially helpful in identifying the particular interests of boys and girls in the elementary school. They have been used readily in terms of general interests, play interests, and radio and television preferences of children of this age.

Use of Observations.—The effectiveness of the study of children through observational techniques is determined chiefly by the extent to which *natural* behavior is observed and the skill with which the behavior is interpreted and translated into conclusions. The former problem has been largely resolved by one-way vision screens; these have been used successfully in clinics and are gradually finding their way into other school situations. The second difficulty can be met only by the analyst's increasing professional skill and understanding.

Observational techniques often reveal personality traits and emotional problems not uncovered through more highly controlled devices such as tests. They have a similar value in detecting personal mannerisms which in turn may indicate problems of a more serious nature.

Use of Anecdotal Records.—Closely related to the observation of children's behavior is the use of the anecdotal record. Briefly stated, anecdotal records are written, descriptive notations of behavioral incidents. Such records appear to be valuable in the process of gaining a longitudinal and cumulative pattern of a child's performance and attitudes. They also sharpen the sensitivity of teachers to the behavior of children and its significance. Of course, the value of such records, in the final analysis, is directly proportional to the understanding and objectivity of those who employ them as a means for child study. Certainly, they should not be considered solely and independently reliable on all occasions, but should justifiably be included in the battery of instruments utilized by educators in their efforts to discover and analyze the traits of children which affect the educational benefits they derive from the school.

Use of Clinical Case Studies.—This approach to child study is usually employed with children whose educational problems tend to be acute, but it has merit for other situations as well. It involves the exhaustive analysis of numerous factors which appear to affect the personal, social, emotional or educational adjustment of the learner. Case studies usually make use of such things as the personal and family history, the educational history, the social acceptance and sensitivity of the subject, as well as his habits and motivating interests. This method of child study has the limitations which ordinarily accompany subjective processes but can be valuable if the data are sufficiently complete and varied to present a comprehensive picture of the child's prior life. It should also be noted that the rather technical knowledge of the specialist is usually needed to achieve the fullest benefits from the use of this technique.

Use of Experimental Studies.—Much can be learned about children and the way they learn best through experimental techniques. Though controlled experimentation is rather difficult in the typical classroom, more and more teachers and administrators are becoming experiment-minded and are exploring the possibilities of this approach in finding out more about children. The experimental method depends, for its effectiveness, upon the control of as many variable factors as possible, the precision of its methods and measurements, and its susceptibility to scientific verification. It is frequently utilized in situations where the learners are divided into two groups matched on the basis of common attributes— one a control group and the other an experimental group—which are subjected to identical experiences except for the experimental factor which operates within the latter group. Even though it is extremely difficult to control all the variables in growing children of elementary school age, the method still has much to offer as a device for investigating psychological and instructional phenomena.

Use of Projective Techniques.—Recent years have seen the development of the projective technique as an instrument for child study. It is so called because extended meanings are attributed to the activities or imaginative expressions of persons being studied. Through the analysis of children's wishes, their imaginative play activities, or the stories they create, considerable insight can often be gained into their attitudes and problems. One of the most standardized and widely used devices of this sort is the Rorschach test, which involves the application of the child's imagination to a series of ink blots. In these tests, the blots serve as stimuli to evoke interpretative responses from the child which reveal his feelings without the necessity for him to express them directly. While such techniques have not yet been uniformly accepted as valid and scientific instruments, they do give promise of being beneficial as one further approach to the problem of child study.

Use of Sociometric Devices.—Another method of child study of rather recent origin is sociometry, or the study of the social interrelationships existing among children of a group. A great deal of insight into how children feel about their associates may be gained through the use of sociometric techniques. This method usually involves having each child choose from among his fellows those he wishes to be closely associated with him in terms of some existing problem, such as the seating arrangement of the group, or the formulation of committees for class work or projects. These choices are then charted in a systematic manner which reveals varying degrees of popularity or isolation existing among members of the group. Since it has been shown in some studies[3] that there is little correlation between the actual social acceptance enjoyed by children and that attributed to them by teachers, these techniques appear to have notable value in sensitizing teachers to the actual social relationships of the children they teach.

ACTION SUGGESTIONS FOR THE PRINCIPAL

1. Remember that the school exists to serve children.
2. Keep informed about research and literature in child development.
3. Encourage teachers to make case studies of children.
4. Develop a knowledge of leaders in the field of child study and of major centers where continued study is being carried on.
5. Work with the staff on the analysis of the school testing program.
6. Develop school records that actually reveal pertinent information about children.
7. Use parent conferences to help evaluate and analyze pupil behavior.
8. Encourage the occasional use of interest inventories.
9. Develop a complete school history of each child.
10. Develop means for identifying special talents and aptitudes of children.
11. Develop means for identifying special problems of individual children.
12. Encourage the use of "clinical sessions" at which staff members pool information about individual problem cases.
13. Keep a file of clinical resources which might be used to get assistance for particular children or parents.
14. Try to capitalize on the natural interests of children wherever feasible in the school program.
15. Help the staff develop an understanding of the characteristics of children at various age levels.
16. Refrain from evaluating child performance solely by adult standards.
17. Within reason, allow children to be individuals.
18. Try to provide wholesome outlets for the natural activity of children.
19. Maintain a school program that feeds and encourages the curiosity of children along positive lines.
20. Take a positive approach to the fact that each child is different from all others; do not insist on conformity for conformity's sake.
21. Study the home and community backgrounds of children as a means of analyzing behavior.
22. Provide bulletins and other professional materials for the use of parents in improving the experiences of children outside school.

[3] For example, see Marion Vere DeVault, *Relationship of Sociometric Status to Selected Factors in Grades One Through Twelve* (Indiana University, unpublished doctoral study, 1953).

23. Encourage teachers to make intelligent use of anecdotal records of children's behavior.

24. Help teachers make appropriate use of projective and sociometric techniques in studying children.

25. Try to send children home each day happy with the satisfaction that comes from a full but interesting day.

Selected References for Extended Reading

ADAMS, FAY. *Educating America's Children: Elementary School Curriculum and Methods* (rev. ed.). New York: The Ronald Press Co., 1954.

BAXTER, BERNICE, LEWIS, GERTRUDE M., and CROSS, GERTRUDE M. *Elementary Education*. Boston: D. C. Heath & Co., 1952.

BURTON, WILLIAM H. *The Guidance of Learning Activities*. New York: Appleton-Century-Crofts, Inc., 1944, chap. 5.

GANS, ROMA, STENDLER, CELIA B., and ALMY, MILLIE. *Teaching Young Children*. Yonkers, N. Y.: World Book Co., 1952.

LEE, J. MURRAY, and LEE, DORRIS MAY. *The Child and His Curriculum*. New York: Appleton-Century-Crofts, Inc., 1950, chaps. 2, 3, 4, and 5.

MEHL, MARIE A., MILLS, HUBERT H., and DOUGLASS, HARL R. *Teaching in the Elementary School*. New York: The Ronald Press Co., 1950.

MILLARD, CECIL V. *Child Growth and Development in the Elementary School*. Boston: D. C. Heath & Co., 1951.

SHANE, HAROLD G. (ed.). *The American Elementary School: Thirteenth Yearbook of The John Dewey Society*. New York: Harper & Bros., 1953.

STRANG, RUTH. *An Introduction to Child Study*. New York: The Macmillan Co., 1951.

TORGERSON, THEODORE L. *Studying Children*. New York: The Dryden Press, Inc., 1947, chap. 3.

YEAGER, WILLIAM A. *Administration and the Pupil*. New York: Harper & Bros., 1949, chap. 1.

Chapter 5

THE EDUCATIONAL PROCESS IN THE ELEMENTARY SCHOOL

Living to learn is one of the best guarantees of learning to live

The primary business of the school is to help children learn. A school, then, may be considered successful to the degree that it stimulates and promotes learning. This suggests that those who assume the responsibilities of leadership in the formulation of the program of the elementary school must possess a thorough understanding of both *the learner* and *the learning process*. An attempt was made in the preceding chapter to give a brief survey of the characteristics of children of elementary school age, the ways in which these children differ, and some of the acceptable means whereby the attributes and resources of children can be studied. The present chapter points out briefly some of the basic aspects of the learning process and how that process may be facilitated through the control and adjustment of the conditions which make up the learning situation.

MODERN CONCEPTS OF LEARNING

The history of education in America reflects the influence of various schools of thought with respect to the nature and process of learning. While individual theories of learning have been numerous, modern study and research in educational psychology have evolved largely around three systems of thought: behaviorism or conditioned response psychology; Gestalt or organismic psychology; and connectionism or stimulus response psychology.[1] Though some of the earlier ideas of the more prominent proponents of each of these theories have since been either revised or discredited through further study and research, they have left their marks on school organization and practice and have contributed materially to the emergence of the modern functional concept of learning. In fact, the organismic field theory of learning, with its emphasis on in-

[1] Arthur Gates, Arthur Jersild, T. R. McConnell, and Robert Challman, *Educational Psychology* (New York: The Macmillan Co., 1948), p. 9.

sight and understanding, has much support among educators and possesses many features in common with modern concepts of learning through experience directed toward recognized goals of the learners.[2]

Late in the seventeenth century John Locke formulated one of the real bases of modern education when he proposed his *tabula rasa* theory, which for the first time related learning to the experience and activity of the learner.[3] This was opposed to earlier concepts of learning which portrayed the process as a passive, receptive phenomenon. From that time, with increasing emphasis, learning has been associated with the activity and reactions of the learner. It is easy to see how this has affected the whole concept of teaching.

Another great influence on modern concepts of learning and teaching has been exerted by Thorndike throughout many years of experimental research in various aspects of learning. He is associated with connectionist theories of learning although he did not emphasize the mechanistic ideas proposed by the conditioned reactionists, or behaviorists. Chief among the contributions of Thorndike have been his laws of learning which, in their earliest forms, were the Law of Use, the Law of Disuse, and the Law of Effect. As might be surmised from an analysis of these laws of learning, much of his effort was directed toward research concerning such things as drill and motivation in learning.

From the sources indicated in the preceding paragraphs, and many others, have come our modern ideas about how children learn. The increasing quantity of research with children themselves in recent years[4] has done much to improve professional insight into the growth of children and the factors which deter or accelerate that growth.

Learning is now considered to be interaction with the environment in such a way that behavior is modified. It involves experience, or more technically, reaction to experience, as it also necessitates continuous reorganization, reconstruction, and integration of experience. It is based on the assumption that the learner reacts as a whole to environmental stimuli. Such learning is obviously susceptible to the influences of inner motivations or extrinsic conditions and can thus have its rate and effectiveness improved or hampered through the manipulation of the conditions surrounding the learning situation or through changes in the learner himself. It is purposeful, meaningful, and reality-centered,

---

[2] See J. Murray Lee and Dorris May Lee, *The Child and His Curriculum* (New York: Appleton-Century-Crofts, Inc., 1950), p. 164; and National Society for the Study of Education, *Psychology of Learning: Forty-First Yearbook* (Bloomington, Ill.: Public School Publishing Company, 1942).

[3] *Ibid.,* p. 163.

[4] Such as the research of Willard Olson at the University of Michigan and Arnold Gesell at Yale University.

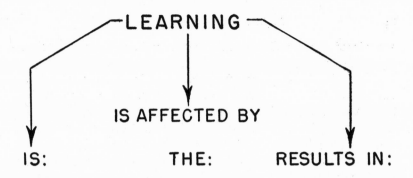

LEARNING

IS AFFECTED BY

IS:	THE:	RESULTS IN:
INDIVIDUAL	CONDITION	CHANGED BEHAVIOR
EXPERIENTIAL	ABILITY	
INTEGRATIVE	PURPOSE	
MODIFIABLE	INTEREST	
	ATTITUDE	
	EXPERIENCE	
	METHOD	
	SUCCESS OF THE LEARNER	

Figure 5

Some Basic Factors in the Learning Process

as pointed out by Cantor in a recent volume on the teaching-learning process.[5]

Most of the changes that have occurred in educational practice in the elementary school in recent years have been direct outgrowths of two basic aspects of modern learning: (1) the emphasis on activity and experience in learning as expressed in the belief that *we learn by doing* and (2) the role of integration in learning which leads to the conclusion that *we learn all over* in a simultaneous and unified manner. The author is reminded that, during his early childhood, he was often assured by his father that "experience is the best teacher," which is a kind of popular and common-sense expression of the more scientifically derived functional theories of learning which are implemented in good modern schools of the current era. Obviously, this experience-based concept has gained much more universal acceptance in some learning tasks than in others. Educators and laymen alike have little difficulty in subscribing to the principle that the quickest and best way to learn to ride a bicycle is through a gradually refined trial-and-error process which very actively involves *riding the bicycle*. They can easily see that a person could read and even memorize all available manuals *about* bicycle riding without gaining skill in the process. Similar illustrations could be pointed out in situations involving other types of motor skill, such as swimming or typing.

In all such cases, the role of activity is accepted as apparent. However, no such uniform understanding exists among laymen or educators when they think of learning in terms of reading, thinking critically, solving problems, or making wise decisions. Educators know, of course, that learning to read depends very heavily upon the breadth and richness of the experience brought by a child to the printed page. In fact, it is wholly impossible to read without some background of experience on the part of the learner. While it must be admitted that there are some very real distinctions between motor learning and that involving a greater degree of abstraction and symbolism, enough common elements exist to dramatize clearly the essential role of experience in education.

The integration concept has influenced the organization of learning experiences in the school for some years and has found expression in the project method, correlation, fusion, the unit method, and the core curriculum. It is based on the idea that aspects of the whole—facts, skills, habits, understanding, and attitudes—are learned in relation to each other and in terms of the extent to which they become a part of the total makeup of the learner through the integrative process of unification.

[5] Nathaniel Cantor, *The Teaching-Learning Process* (New York, The Dryden Press, Inc., 1953), chap. 5.

The learner does the integrating through his interpretation of his interaction with his environment. The best that can be done by the school is to assist the learner in the selection and organization of learning experiences so that they are psychologically profitable and digestible. From the standpoint of the elementary school curriculum this means providing learning experiences that are (1) related as naturally as possible to each other, and (2) related to the on-going activities of life. As will be seen from more detailed discussion of the program of instruction in later sections of this book, this concept is implicit in the program of the modern elementary school.

Learning may be conceived of as both a process and a product. As a process, it is essentially activity on the part of the learner interacting with a stimulating environment; as a product it is a set of unified, and unifying, responses that increases the effectiveness of the learner in coping with the problems he meets in living. The real challenge of education is to make the process psychologically efficient and the product desirable from the standpoint of both the individual and society.

Some Basic Principles of Learning in the Elementary School

It is impossible to reduce the complexities of learning to neatly contrived, discrete laws or principles. However, out of the abundance of research in educational psychology and child development, certain clear-cut characteristics of learning have emerged. Since some of them bear a direct relationship to the organization of the school, their consideration is an important element in the formulation of the policies and procedures of the modern elementary school.

1. *The most important element in learning is the learner.* The major control of the learning process resides in the learner himself. There is an element of truth in the old adage, "You can lead a horse to water but you can't make him drink," when it is applied to human beings and learning. The physical condition, the intellectual capacity, the maturity, the emotional attitudes, the background of experience, and many other factors all are agents which control the effectiveness and rate of learning. Since the learner must learn through his own reactions, learning cannot be done for him nor imposed upon him.

A child may be exposed to a splendid school plant, well-trained teachers, and rich instructional materials, desirable as they are, and still not learn. Learning begins to occur when he starts to react to the environment, to utilize the materials, or to be stimulated by the teacher. It is *his own experience* that brings meaning to a word he encounters in reading, or that sets his standards of behavior as he enters school. It is likewise through his own extended experience that he will grow through the years of the elementary school. This is not to minimize the importance of teaching. It is rather to emphasize the importance of *good* teaching— a process of planning, selecting, and guiding learning experiences which provides for each child a fertile field for wise, purposeful, and productive activity.

2. *Learning involves goals.* The fruitful activities of mankind are directed toward the accomplishment of purposes. Purpose generates enthusiasm, which in turn fans the flame of human effort. Life itself becomes vitalized through the anticipation of realizing pre-established aims. In the life of the young child the prospect of a visit to grandmother's, a trip to the zoo, the arrival of the circus, or the impending approach of a holiday all provide interest and zest. As he grows older such things as dates, marriage, graduation, or his first regular job become motivating factors. In a similar fashion learning, to be effective, must be directed toward goals or purposes. Such goals must not only be present but must be recognized by the learner as his goals. It is also well to remember that, in terms of the psychological principles involved, if goals are to be effective as motivation they must be rather immediate for the young child even though they can be extended in remoteness with additional maturity of the learner.

3. *Learning involves the medium of content.* Learning cannot occur in a vacuum, for there are no automatic connections between the past experiences of a learner and the purposes which he hopes to accomplish. Occasionally modern education is accused of no longer recognizing the importance of subject matter, or content. Such comments appear to be wholly unjustified in terms of the basic tenets of modern education endorsed by responsible educators. One of these basic tenets certainly is to the effect that when we learn, we learn *something*. Furthermore, it is held to be true that content, in the truest sense, can take many forms and that much respectable "subject matter" can be found outside the covers of books. In other words, content should be varied enough to serve as a useful agent in the development of all facets of learning, not just in the acquisition of textbook material alone. The selection of the content of the elementary school curriculum is another of the controls of the nature and quality of the learning that takes place.

4. *Learning requires continuous evaluation.* The continuous analysis and reappraisal of the learner's progress are important for two reasons: (1) knowledge of success is one of the prime motivators of human behavior and (2) because learning involves trial-and-error activity on the part of the learner, it is necessary to make provision for refining and revis-

ing the learning process as it develops toward established purposes. Such evaluation also points up specialized needs, such as the lack of essential learning skills or unwholesome emotional attitudes toward educational tasks. In addition, continuous examination of the teaching-learning process is one of the paramount guideposts to the teacher in formulating and developing his own activities.

5. *Learning is influenced by environmental factors.* The importance of the status, attitudes, and activity of the learner have been deliberately emphasized in the foregoing paragraphs. Important as they are, however, they represent only a part of the story of effective learning. In fact, these facets exist within, and are influenced by, some sort of environment. The nature of these environmental conditions affects the physical and psychological condition of the learner, his attitudes toward learning, and the interest he displays in pursuing educational experience. As Seagers says: ". . . the physical environment sets the stage for social, emotional, and intellectual growth [and] constitutes an important base upon which we build an effective school program."[6]

The quality of his relations with his associates—child and adult alike —is another factor which determines what and how well a child learns. The personality of the teacher, the teaching methods he utilizes, and his own ideas about the proper outcomes of education all contribute to the efficiency of the child's learning.

The nature, abundance, variety, and availability of instructional materials constitute still another integral element of the learning situation. Learning is facilitated by the accessibility of varied materials which offer opportunities for experiences of both manual and abstract types. Rich and varied sources of information and understanding are necessary to a good learning situation.

6. *Learning can be facilitated but it cannot be forced.* It is as much a mistake to assume that a learner will learn because he is commanded to do so as it is to believe his attention can be guaranteed by demanding it. Both stem from erroneous concepts of learning. The purpose and readiness of the learner are so essential to effective learning that it is unwise and wasteful to attempt to force learning when they are not present to the degree necessary to assure reasonable facility. We can help clarify purposes of learning activities, assist in locating sources of information, guide children's judgments, help in establishing associative connections with things already known, recognize and develop motivating interests, and assist in cooperative forms of continuous evaluation that will give

[6] Paul W. Seagers, "Providing an Environment for Effective Learning," *Bases for Effective Learning, Thirty-First Yearbook of the Department of Elementary Principals* (Washington, D. C.: 1952), p. 254.

children knowledge of their own successful achievements and will point out aspects of the learning situation which need further attention. The proper role of the teacher must be defined in terms of these activities rather than of pure direction, which has too often been assumed to result automatically in learning. Children do not learn because someone tells them to, or threatens them if they do not. They learn when they want to learn. It is the job of the school to guide them in such ways that they want to learn, that they see opportunities through which they can learn, and that they see relationships among these desires, opportunities, and constructive ends, or outcomes.

By way of illustration, it is interesting to note the behavior of the child just learning to talk. His parents, eager to display his newly acquired skills to friends and relatives, insist that he "say something for the folks." If this fails to produce results, they then may even invoke mild threats or offer simple bribes, often to no avail. Such activity may proceed until the parents become angry, the guests disturbed, and the child provoked to tears. However, after the episode is forgotten and the child suddenly realizes he wants a cookie from the kitchen, he bursts into expressions of his desire without hesitation.

7. *Learning results in changed behavior.* Presumably, schools exist to help produce certain kinds of people because it is an accepted premise that some kinds of behavior are more desirable for the individual and for society than are other kinds. Through learning a child expands his fund of knowledge, improves his understanding, and develops fundamental skills for rich living and further learning; but the real test of learning lies in the extent to which these things are reflected in his behavior. The genuine measurement and evaluation of educational achievement, then, must be related to *what the learner does* as well as to *what he knows.* As will be discussed in Chapter 19 of this book, the development of more scientific means for the evaluation of behavioral change is one of the greatest challenges modern educators face.

SOME CONDITIONS UNDER WHICH LEARNING PROCEEDS BEST

The foregoing section has been devoted to a discussion of the general aspects of learning as they apply to the elementary school. It has been pointed out that the effectiveness of the learning process is determined by the condition and activities of the learner, the methods and materials used, and the quality of the surrounding environment. Since all these factors are variable, it is obvious that improvement in any or all of them should result in a corresponding effect on the rate and quality of learning. For that reason, it seems appropriate to indicate some specific considerations relating directly to facilitating the learning process. Many fine compilations and statements of principles of learning are available in educational literature. Two such statements with which the author has been closely acquainted are included here:

Some Principles of Desirable Teaching and Learning[7]

1. A child learns best when his own purposeful goals, needs, and desires guide him.

It is not enough for the teacher to understand the purpose of an experience and to set up the learning goals. Unless the child also works with a purpose and his purpose is in harmony with that of the teacher, the goals set by the teacher cannot be attained satisfactorily. If the teacher sets up as her purpose certain achievements and learning and the child purposes merely to do what the teacher asks him to do but has no learning purpose of his own, little of lasting value can come from the experience.

2. A child is capable of purposing only when the learning situation has grown out of and is close to his experience and interests and within the range of his ability to comprehend.

Unless the child understands the learning situation with which he is working and its potentialities it is impossible for him to have a purpose of his own. As interest and experience expand he will learn to purpose more and more wisely. Growth in purposing is as important as growth in achievement of purposes; the child needs wise guidance to set up better and better purposes as well as better and better methods of attaining his goals.

3. A child learns best when he is free to participate in the creation of his own organization of materials as he satisfies his purposeful goals.

There is no one method of arriving at learning goals, nor is there any single organization or set of materials which is indispensable. Children and teacher must work together on the selection of materials and sources and on the organization of them.

4. A child learns best when he can share in the management of the learning experience with the other children in the group, guided but not controlled by adults.

Skills such as working together, locating and organizing materials, reaching conclusions, and evaluating results are just as necessary to child development as are the more commonly recognized skills of the three R's. Experience in planning and participation in managing lead to better and better planning and managing. Child planning does not do away with the need for teacher planning. It has been wisely said, "The teacher *must* plan so that the children *may* plan." Life in the adult world at the present time calls for better planning than has ever been done before and better managing of the affairs of men and nations than the world has ever witnessed. Only through experience in planning and managing can children

---

[7] *A Good Start in School,* Curriculum Bulletin No. 158 (Indianapolis: State of Indiana, Department of Public Instruction, 1944), pp. 28-33.

develop the insight and skill which they will need as adults to do their share in the task of straightening out the snarl into which human relationships in the world have fallen.

5. A child learns best under the guidance of sympathetic adults who understand him as a growing personality.

Respect for the personality of each individual is the foundation upon which democracy is built. The needs of a democratic society demand that each citizen contribute to the common good whatever of ability and talent he possesses. Abilities and talents can reach their highest development only in a climate of respect for the personality and ability of each individual child, regardless of his mental capacity and his physical skill. Self-respect and a wholesome sense of one's own worth are absolutely necessary to mental health and without mental health no child can achieve up to the level of his capacity. The challenge to teachers here is especially great.

6. A child learns the meaning and interpretation of cooperative, democratic living best when he experiences it day by day.

Children cannot spend twelve or more years of their lives in authoritarian schoolrooms and go out prepared to participate in democratic processes and contribute to life in a democracy. Only through day-by-day living in a child-size democratic society in the classroom, sharing its responsibilities, making its decisions, and solving its problems, can children be prepared for the assumption of the privileges and responsibilities of free men in a democracy later on. The need for such preparation has never been greater than at the present time.

7. Other things being equal, a child's learning is increased as he increases his sensory experiences within the learning situation.

A tremendous amount of verbalism has been incorporated with public school method in the United States. The reason is easily understood when one realizes that the pioneer schools of the country were set up to teach only a few fundamental skills. All the rest of the child's education took place in the home and community, where his learning included firsthand experiences in great abundance. With the decrease of intimate contact in the home with the sources and processes by which man's needs are met, the school gradually took over the responsibility for such basic knowledge but attempted in many instances to teach it verbally and through books only, without recourse to actual experience and its supporting battery of sense impressions. Bringing real experiences into the classroom and going outside for experiences is now considered essential to good teaching.

8. The greater the number of avenues of impression and the broader the avenues of expression the more complete the learning.

Impression and expression are interwoven in the learning process. Impressions are clarified through expression and enriched by it. Expression is of many types and utilizes many media; it may be original creation, reproduction, or the mere living through of vital, firsthand experience.

9. Meaningful experience is the basis of comprehensive learning and is the stuff out of which ability to deal in generalizations and abstractions grows.

Children's minds move more readily from experience . . . to generalization and abstraction than . . . from verbalism alone. Many children learn arithmetical thinking only on the verbal and manipulation level and never achieve genuine understanding. Real learning and understanding come only through meaningful experience.

10. Any specific learning is part of a total pattern of learning and the effect on the child is the result of the interaction of all factors within the pattern.

A spelling situation may call upon a child to learn the letter sequences required in spelling certain words correctly, but the spelling itself is only a part of the learning. The motivation behind the learning—whether it stems from need for spelling which the child himself recognizes or merely from arbitrary assignment or teacher compulsion—the method used in the learning, the opportunities to utilize the learning in meaningful situations, the child's previously developed attitude toward spelling—these and other elements are part of the learning pattern. Whether the child builds spelling skill, concern for correct spelling, or actual dislike of spelling is determined by the way in which the elements in the total pattern interact.

11. Learning is enhanced when opportunities are provided for seeing relationships and when these relationships are drawn out and made clear.

It is often true in teaching, whether in kindergarten or college, that teachers assume that learners see in a situation the relationships and interactions which their own mature minds take for granted. The teacher of young children has a special obligation to draw out and call attention to relationships and to help the children see and understand them.

12. Opportunities to appraise such materials, organize and reorganize data and information, arrive at solutions to problems, and evaluate results are important factors in learning.

These abilities develop only as a result of many opportunities for guided experience. All of them are abilities essential to a democracy and should be developed in each individual citizen to the highest level of which he is capable.

13. A child learns best when he is conscious of his progress toward his own goals and those which society has set for him, and can evaluate his own achievement.

Few avenues of satisfaction afford the child keener enjoyment that the realization that he is growing in power and in knowledge. Confidence has been defined as "Memory of past successes." Observing and evaluating his own growth builds confidence in his potentialities and confidence, together with self-understanding, carry him on to ever higher levels of growth.

SOME GUIDING PRINCIPLES OF LEARNING[8]

A. *Readiness is a prerequisite to learning.*
1. A child learns best when the experiences are related to or grow out of his environment.
2. A child learns best when he feels comfortable and secure in a situation.
3. A child learns best when he is in a happy frame of mind.

[8] Adapted from a statement compiled by members of a workshop in Elementary Education held at Indiana University during the summer of 1953.

4. A child learns best when he feels he is needed in the group.
5. A child learns best when he feels the need to add more ideas to his store of information.
6. A child learns best when the experiences and material are at his level.

B. *Motivation is a prerequisite to learning.*
1. A child learns best when he experiences feelings of success.
2. A child learns best when goals are intrinsic rather than extrinsic.
3. A child learns best when his creative interests are aroused.
4. A child learns best when the purposes for learning are apparent to him.
5. A child learns best when the activities of the learning situation have meaning to him.
6. A child learns best when a happy rapport exists among him, the group, and the teacher.

C. *Participation is a prerequisite to learning.*
1. The child learns best when he carries out group tasks as well as individual tasks.
2. The child learns best when he engages in solving problems that are significant.
3. The child learns best when he sees the relation between materials and purposes to achieve.
4. The child learns best when he develops a concern for the success of the group.
5. The child learns best when he learns to solve problems by critical thinking.

D. *Individual differences affect learning.*
1. The intelligence test does not accurately test learning ability; it reflects to a large extent the child's experience background.
2. A child's physical condition greatly affects his learning ability.
3. A child's emotional problems at home and school greatly affect his learning.
4. A child acquires multiple learning (academic and social) along with presentation of subject matter.
5. Children start at different levels and learn at different rates because they have different social and economic backgrounds, different intellectual backgrounds, and different experience backgrounds.

E. *Effective human relations improve learning.*
1. Children can be encouraged to know and to practice the Golden Rule.
2. Learning to get along with people is highly important.
3. The child learns best the spiritual values exemplified by the teacher.
4. Children learn best when we expect them to do their best.
5. Children reflect the emotional attitudes of the teacher.
6. Honest and immediate praise, with few exceptions, will do more in fostering learning than will punishment.
7. Emotional atmosphere of the classroom greatly affects learning, for we do not teach children; we create an atmosphere in which learning can take place.

F. *Evaluation of the child's learnings are essential to him as they provide:*
1. A satisfying summary of his achievements.

2. A starting place or a background from which to begin again.
3. A means to recognize how happy he is with his group.
4. A goal toward which he grows in ability to meet life's situations.

From the considerations enumerated on the preceding pages, it is clear that both the quality and extent of learning can be substantially affected by the school conditions which prevail. Because the administrator has such direct and broad responsibility for creating, maintaining, and improving the quality of the school environment, it is essential that his efforts toward this end be soundly conceived and courageously executed.

ACTION SUGGESTIONS FOR THE PRINCIPAL

1. Develop a sound and clearly conceived understanding of the learning process based on the best information available. Reduce this concept to terms and illustrations which can be used in interpreting the school program to laymen.
2. Help teachers and pupils organize work in naturally related blocks of experience.
3. Keep opportunities for learning varied.
4. Build on the experiences of children.
5. Strive to create a school environment rich in resources for learning.
6. Encourage teachers and learners to establish goals toward which their efforts may be directed.
7. Develop means for continuous evaluation of content required of pupils.
8. Encourage the staff to use all legitimate means for motivating learners. Keep motivation on a positive plane.
9. Utilize changed behavior as one of the chief elements in the evaluation of learning.
10. Strive to keep learning experiences within the extended reach of children.
11. Encourage teachers to utilize pupil planning as far as feasible in the classroom.
12. Provide opportunities for children to learn to share in the responsibility for the management of the school.
13. Use faculty meetings or teacher study groups to discuss new and/or significant ideas with respect to how children learn and develop.
14. Devote occasional clinical sessions to the exploration of improved approaches to teaching children who have learning difficulties.
15. Help children learn democratic procedures through appropriate participation in the day-to-day processes and decisions made in the school.
16. Provide audio-visual facilities which extend learning opportunities. Simplify the use of such facilities as much as possible.
17. Encourage learning through firsthand experience in the community but develop means for systematizing and evaluating such experiences.
18. Encourage learning through the creative urges and efforts of children.

19. Try to maintain a school dedicated to the task of making successes of people.

20. Remember that children learn to be like the persons with whom they live, work, and associate.

SELECTED REFERENCES FOR EXTENDED READING

BRECKENRIDGE, MARIAN E., and VINCENT, E. LEE. *Child Development.* Philadelphia: Saunders Publishing Co., 1943.

BURTON, WILLIAM H. *The Guidance of Learning Activities.* New York: Appleton-Century-Crofts, Inc., 1944, chaps. 2, 3, and 4.

GARRISON, KARL C. *Growth and Development.* New York: Longmans, Green & Co., 1952, chaps. 1 and 4.

GESELL, ARNOLD, and ILG, FRANCES. *The Child from Five to Ten.* New York: Harper & Bros., 1946.

JENKINS, GLADYS G., SHACTER, HELEN and BAUER, W. W. *These Are Your Children.* Chicago: Scott, Foresman & Co., 1949.

JERSILD, ARTHUR T. *Child Psychology.* New York: Prentice-Hall, Inc., 1947.

LEE, J. MURRAY, and LEE, DORRIS MAY. *The Child and His Curriculum.* New York: Appleton-Century-Crofts, Inc., 1950, chap. 5.

MEHL, MARIE A., MILLS, HUBERT H., and DOUGLASS, HARL R. *Teaching in Elementary School.* New York: The Ronald Press Co., 1950, chap. 4.

MILLARD, CECIL V. *Child Growth and Development in the Elementary School Years.* Boston: D. C. Heath & Co., 1951.

OLSON, WILLARD C. *Child Development.* Boston: D. C. Heath & Co., 1949, chaps. 1 and 5.

SHANE, HAROLD G. (ed.). *The American Elementary School, Thirteenth Yearbook of The John Dewey Society.* New York: Harper & Bros., 1953.

SPEARS, HAROLD. *Principles of Teaching.* New York: Prentice-Hall, Inc., 1951, chap. 5.

Chapter 6

FORMULATING THE PROGRAM OF THE SCHOOL

*If we know not what harbor we are making for, no wind is the
right wind—Seneca*

Education represents one of society's greatest hopes and efforts for
its own improvement. This is particularly true in America where great
faith has been placed in public education as a means of perpetuating and
refining the concept of self-government by a people. Obviously, under
such a concept of government, the common destiny cannot easily rise
above the level of the aspirations and competencies of the individuals
who compose the masses of our population. This being true, it follows
that the role of education in determining the future of the democratic way
of life cannot be easily overestimated. Furthermore, as a vital agency in
the lives of the people, education must be intelligently conceived, and
based on wise analyses of experience viewed in the light of new demands
and discoveries. It cannot be a haphazard process subject to the unjustified whims of individuals or groups. It must represent a *program* which
rests on a solid foundation of the best that is known, up to the present,
about educational processes.

As stated in earlier chapters, the functions of the elementary school
are derived from two sources: (1) the demands and desires of society,
and (2) the nature and needs of the individual. Important as it is, the
self-development of the individual child is only one of the determinants of
the school program; the other involves his varied relationships with his
environment, human and physical. From the time a very young child in
his crib begins to realize that his needs and desires can be met only
through contact with the world outside that crib, the process of social
interaction continuously expands as a part of his learning pattern.

The program of an elementary school may be defined as its conscious
efforts to carry out its responsibilities—to educate individuals to operate
with maximum effectiveness in the environment in which they will live
and work. Such a program may be thought of as a continuum of designed opportunities for growth. Although the education of children
extends far beyond the walls of the school, the responsibility for studying

and planning the school program is not thereby diminished. In fact, the ultimate success of the school is determined very largely by the inclination, wisdom, and clarity with which school personnel utilize and organize the resources which can be welded into a program of educational activities.

PRINCIPLES UNDERLYING THE FORMULATION OF THE SCHOOL PROGRAM

Human behavior is admittedly a complex phenomenon. It follows, therefore, that the motivation and guidance of human behavior are difficult to reduce to simple rules or predetermined structures. So many variable factors operate in the educational growth of a child that it is impossible to assume that certain outcomes will result from any given program of instruction. However, the results are likely to be even less predictable if the educational experiences of children are left solely to chance. The presence of a program, which represents the studied attempt to develop a situation in which each child can do his best, does not necessarily involve rigidity. It merely serves as a meeting ground for security and flexibility. Because of these considerations, it seems advisable to suggest a few basic principles underlying the development of a program in the elementary school.

1. *A school program is based on a philosophy of education.* It is often mistakenly felt in some quarters that philosophy exists only in an abstract realm of its own, far removed from the practical world. Actually nothing could be a more inaccurate interpretation of the role of philosophy in human affairs, since most of the planned activities of people are based on some set of beliefs or assumptions. To a very marked extent what we believe, as individuals, determines what we do. The same observation seems to be equally true, on a composite basis, of communities, nations, or of the human race as a whole.

Professional educators and laymen alike, whether it is recognized or not, hold to certain values as significant bases for effective living. These we wish to perpetuate and refine through the process of education. Such a process, then, must be designed in terms of these particular values. We cannot, for example, expect to foster or teach honesty in situations which place a major premium on dishonesty. We do not expect to teach respect for the individual, one of the basic tenets of democracy, in a completely regimented program which seeks to compress all individuals into a common mold of conformity. If we believe that schools exist for children, not children for the schools, we will seek to guarantee an element of flexibility in the formulation of the school program.

The school program is the expression of the beliefs and values of all the people who are responsible for it. This is especially true of the profes-

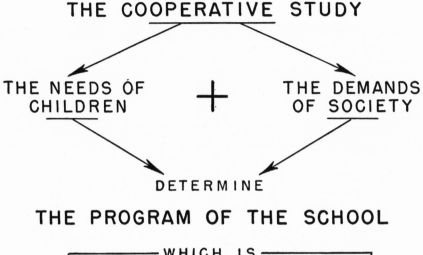

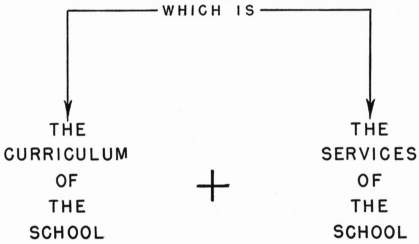

Figure 6

The Program of the School

sional staff of the school. If we expect to have schools which reflect and promote the democratic way of life, it seems essential that we staff them with leaders who know, appreciate, and practice the basic tenets of democratic processes.

2. *A school program should be directed toward known purposes.* Out of a philosophy of life one formulates his purposes; out of a philosophy of education the goals of the school emerge. If it is felt that effec-

tive communication between people is a vital aspect of our culture and civilization, we normally make an effort to devise a school program with considerable emphasis on the development of the skills of communication. By the same reasoning, when it is felt that the progress, if not the salvation, of the world depends on people learning to live and work together toward common goals, then some conscious effort should be made to organize a school program devoted to the acquisition of such competencies. This same relationship between values and purposes, or goals, can be illustrated in many other areas of living and learning. It seems sufficient to suggest here that, in the final analysis, the nature and success of the school program must be determined in the light of what it sets out to do—its purposes. We may assume further that the program is effective to the extent that the purposes are known and understood by all who are expected to contribute to their realization. This offers one of the great challenges to leadership at a vital level of the educational process.

3. *The school program depends upon appropriate and fruitful methods for achieving its purposes.* Purposes remain sterile until they are activated by some method or activity for achieving them. Such methods, whether administrative or instructional, must not only be directed toward the accomplishment of identified goals but must also be consistent with the philosophy underlying the whole process. In education, it is a fallacy to assume that the nobility of the ends justifies any means for their realization; in education, both the product and the process are important and must be consistently interrelated.

The method of the school program may be considered the total machinery through which the learning experiences of boys and girls are guided and stimulated. It involves classification and grouping, guidance, instruction, motivation, and many other phases of the educational process. Obviously, in all these and other areas, some techniques bring more favorable results than others. Bringing into operation genuinely skillful methods in the school program is one of the more significant contributions to be made by effective leaders.

4. *The ultimate effectiveness of the school program depends heavily upon the quality of the personnel responsible for its operation.* The program of a school can be little, if any, better than the wisdom and understanding of the professional staff of the school. For optimum effectiveness, those who formulate and carry out the program of the school should know and accept its purposes and be skilled in its methods. It is conceivable that a barber can be skillful at his trade without his interest extending beyond the price he is to receive for a haircut, but he probably will be a better barber if he is conscious of the role a good appearance

plays in the success of his customers and takes a corresponding pride in his own work as a result of this recognition. It is conceivable that a salesman may experience considerable success selling a product in which he has little faith and no interest, but it is usually conceded that one of the basic factors in sales success is the enthusiasm of the salesman for his product. It is almost inconceivable that one engaged in the profession of education will experience any degree of success without a strong belief in the purposes to which education is dedicated.

5. *A school program, to be successful, must have the faith and support of those outside the educational profession.* High level and intelligent interaction between school and community is one of the typical earmarks of a good school. A school program, no matter how scientifically and wisely conceived by educators, cannot long endure in isolation with respect to those whom it serves. Consequently, parents and laymen in the community play a very significant role in the formulation of the school program. Their contributions should be made mainly in the realm of *what* the school is to do rather than in the area of *how* it is to be done, which is more appropriately considered a professional function. The real obligation of leadership in this regard is to develop conditions for optimum and balanced contributions from all persons and agencies, professional and lay, who have a genuine stake in the work of the school.

6. *The school program must be realistically related to the basic functions of education in American democracy.* Theoretically, it would be quite possible for many individuals to develop themselves to a rather high level of personal knowledge and proficiency without the benefit of public education or, for that matter, without the type of group processes or contacts usually found within the classrooms of America. Though such an approach to education might be possible, not many would wish to recommend it. This is true largely because most people recognize that the learning acquired by an individual usually becomes useful at the point of his interaction with the things and people around him. Arithmetic would seem to be a relatively unimportant study if one were the only human being on earth with no possible chance for any kind of transactions with others. The same would be equally true of many areas of learning if education were conceived wholly in terms of the individual without regard for his orientation to his surroundings. This observation should not be construed as viewing unfavorably the increasing tendency to consider each pupil as an individual and to help him as much as possible to achieve his potential level of accomplishment. It is merely to emphasize the opinion that good education goes a bit further and considers the individual in relation to the environment in which he lives and may expect to live. If one accepts this premise, those who formulate the

program of an elementary school will be concerned with at least three effects that program should have on children who attend the school.

A basic obligation of the school is to help children *adjust increasingly to an expanding environment*. Regardless of age, most of us are surrounded continuously by two types of environment: the physical world and the social world. One involves things; the other people. It is difficult to say just how much of the actual energy of an individual is consumed in merely adjusting to the physical conditions which surround him. It is generally felt that conditions which demand eyestrain or make hearing difficult leave us exhausted after a relatively short period of time. Extreme temperatures or uncomfortable seats in a classroom appear to have a direct effect on the amount of energy one has left for productive endeavors. Such conditions merely illustrate that there is a genuine relationship between adjustment and productivity as far as the physical world is concerned. The social adjustments of an individual probably are even more vital to his well-being and his ability to lead a happy, successful life among his fellows.

Optimum adjustment to one's environment involves getting satisfactions from, and seeing the best in, the people and things about one. It is based on extending knowledge, increasing understanding, and expanding interests. It often requires the imagination to put one's self in another's place and occasionally demands the inclination and ability to endure an unpleasant fact or incident without becoming too emotional about it.

Certainly one of the prime jobs of the school is to offer opportunities for children to learn about the environment, both physical and social, and to understand relationships existing among its various elements.

A second important task facing the elementary school is that of *developing individuals who can operate effectively within their physical and social environments* to an ever increasing degree. To do so children must develop positive attitudes toward others and toward life itself. In addition, they must develop the skills necessary to communicate with their fellows and to meet the day-to-day demands of successful living. They must learn efficient work habits and develop a respect for quality and beauty. They must learn to know, within the limits of their capacities, the features of the American heritage and the historical and sociological orientation of our culture. They must learn to be self-reliant and yet, at the same time, develop the ability to pool resources with others effectively when it is for the common good—the ability to live, work, and play with others. They must learn the necessity for assuming responsibility and develop the persistence to see essential tasks through to their culmination.

Many factors obviously affect the fulfillment of the functions cited above. Both the content of the curriculum and the manner in which learning experiences are organized undoubtedly have a direct bearing on the development of the ability to operate effectively as a member of society and of its component groups. It seems futile to expect that the assumption of responsibility will be acquired suddenly by a child at a particular stage in his educational growth. Certainly this trait must be gradually developed through a succession of opportunities for putting it into practice. The same holds true for the basic skills of learning, for the understanding of the scientific world about us, and for the development of moral and ethical attitudes. All these need to be considered when the program of the school is planned.

Some individuals may feel that the purposes of their existence have been fulfilled when they have adjusted to the physical and human world around them sufficiently well to lead a normally happy life. Others may suggest that certainly successful living does not go beyond the ability to gain individual recognition and satisfactions while operating happily among one's fellows. It is the opinion of the writer that the person truly successful in the art of living strives not only to adjust, or to sustain himself, but also to *improve* the environment in which he lives. A third function of education may well be that of helping individuals to *develop the desire and the competence to improve their surroundings.* This again requires attention to all aspects of learning—knowledge, understanding, appreciation, attitudes, habits, and skills. It means that the program of a school should be designed to give children an understanding of their world, near and remote, the skills to get along in it with maximum success, and, in addition, a zest for better things.

Simply stated, before we can have a school program we must seek the answers to the following questions as they relate to any particular elementary school:

1. What is important to the people who operate and support this school?
2. For the achievement of what goals does this school work?
3. By what processes does this school expect to achieve each of its goals?
4. To what extent do members of the staff understand the goals and to what extent are they skilled in sound methods for achieving them?
5. To what extent does the school enjoy and utilize resources and support from outside the professional ranks?

Other Considerations.—The *sociological structure* of the school community must be considered in determining the nature of the school program. The primary justification for a high degree of local administrative control in public education is to provide maximum assurance that each community shall have a major voice in determining the quality of its provisions for educating its children. It is felt that such local control makes it more nearly possible to tailor local educational offerings to the conditions and needs of each particular community.

Most modern educators would agree generally with the necessity for a careful consideration of community structure as a prerequisite to the wise formulation of school objectives. The economic character of the community, the nature and mobility of the population, and the existence and activity of other cultural agencies in the community all are factors to be analyzed in shaping the educational program.

The determination of the nature of the school program also is influenced, to a substantial degree, by the *concepts of learning* which prevail in any given situation. Certain principles relating to the learning process were discussed in Chapter 5. The effective implementation of these principles is one of the major tasks of the school, and the program provided must reflect a recognition and understanding of them.

If the learner is the integrating unit of primary concern in the total teaching-learning situation, then it follows that the program of the school must be conceived and developed with the learner as the foremost consideration. Thus from this primary concern for the learner objectives are derived and get their greatest meaning. In a similar way, this consideration of the child should guide the effort to develop a program of activities and to provide services which facilitate these activities.

Another principle of learning which should serve as a guide in the formulation of the school program is one which suggests that learning is facilitated rather than forced. If this principle is accepted, it is readily seen that stimulation must replace coercion as the chief agent for the acceleration of learning. This point of view should lead to efforts to bring into the school program a richness and variety of educational activity that will serve to motivate learners in a maximum way.

Similarly, other principles of learning should be studied carefully by educational leaders in order that the school program may be psychologically adequate as well as society-centered.

ELEMENTS OF THE ELEMENTARY SCHOOL PROGRAM

The school program is really the means by which a school attempts to accomplish its tasks; it includes the steps through which it goes in order to transform its objectives into actual outcomes; it is the organized effort we expend to gain the things we want for our children. If such a program is to be wisely conceived, many factors must be considered. Three of these basic factors are: (1) a consciousness of the purposes for which we attempt to formulate a program, (2) the development of the best possible means for achieving these objectives, and (3) the presence and use of some effective methods for evaluating the results of the program. Each of these will be treated in some detail in following sections of this chapter as well as in later chapters which are concerned with curriculum development and evaluation.

STEP ONE: THE FORMULATION OF PURPOSES

Intention usually precedes constructive action. What we do seems very directly related to what we hope to do. This is as true in connection with the development of a good educational program as elsewhere. Our first task, then, in the formulation of the school program is to decide on what we wish to accomplish through the activities of the school. This responsibility involves certain prerequisite considerations before it can be successfully met.

Necessity for Wide Participation.—It is important that wide participation be encouraged in the formulation of the purposes to which a school dedicates its efforts. Such participation should be sought from teachers, staff members, pupils, parents, and all others who have a legitimate stake in the school and its activities. This not only broadens the base of resources from which school purposes can be drawn, but it also assures a higher quality of understanding of these purposes at the point of their implementation into action. The administrator who assumes sole responsibility for formulating the aims of a school is probably demonstrating an educational omnipotence which is unjustified; and, at the same time, he is missing the opportunity for creating understanding among members of the staff through participation. Parents and other laymen also are in much better position to react positively to a school program if they have been active in its development. In fact, it is at the stage of delineation of purpose that the involvement of laymen is most urgent. In a system of education such as ours, which is chartered by society in the hope of achieving beneficial goals, it is imperative that members of the profession remain alert to opportunities for utilizing lay resources for determining these goals. At the technical, or professional, level, however, it seems best to rely on professional personnel for decisions regarding the methods and techniques which are best for achieving the goals which have been cooperatively devised. Simply stated, this merely means that many different people should help determine what our schools should accomplish but that the methods of accomplishment should rest in the hands of professional personnel especially trained in educational processes. This places the responsibility where it belongs; it does not, of course, negate nor minimize the desirability of professional personnel seeking and using the contributions of parents and laymen in all possible constructive ways to strengthen the school program.

Recognition of Wide Range of Purposes.—A second essential ingredient in the determination of purposes is the recognition that several different levels of objectives are necessary for a well-rounded program. It is usually agreed that certain broad educational objectives may be applied rather universally to all elementary schools throughout the country. For instance, few would doubt that the development of the skills of critical thinking is a worthy objective for any elementary school. The same can be said for the development of effective communication skills. These and other commonly accepted purposes may be regarded as *general objectives*. They are highly important for a number of reasons. In the first place, since all American schools serve to perpetuate and improve the American way of life, it is essential that all of them be dedicated to certain basic tenets. These will be reflected in corresponding common purposes. In the second place, there is a high degree of mobility of school children through the United States, and it is desirable that schools retain enough of a common structure so that children moving from one region or school to another will not be hopelessly lost. A third valid assumption is that the purposes of education generally are derived from exhaustive study and deliberation by some of the most competent groups of people in the country and should represent a sound base around which to build local programs of education.

In addition to the general purposes of education in American democracy, certain *community-based objectives* frequently become integral determinants of the nature of the school program. If the educational program is to be a functional enterprise, it must be responsive to the community which it serves most directly. From its community, it will draw many resources which will breathe into the program the practicality and vigor of reality. Schools devoted to the task of educating for effective living certainly cannot remain aloof from the scene in which current living is occurring to the greatest degree—the local community.

Even within a school system itself, each school should consider the necessity for *local school objectives*. The school population of a particular building within a city school system often differs from that of other buildings in the common and dominant needs of its children. When an analysis of the enrollment of a school reveals unique characteristics of its population, the purposes which guide its program demand corresponding adjustment.

In the final analysis the scale of educational purposes applicable to the elementary school includes objectives that are even more specific. Since general objectives, community-based objectives, and school objectives gain fruition mainly at the classroom level, it is obvious that adaptations must be made in terms of specific *group* and *individual* needs and purposes. In the formulation of the purposes, therefore, which chart the course of a school program, it is essential that all types of objectives, broad and specific, be given due consideration.

Provision for Common Understanding of Purposes.—In addition to wide participation in the development of a school's purposes, which include those that are both broad and specific, it is also necessary that all who are to contribute to the successful achievement of these purposes must have a *common understanding* of them. It is important that each teacher in an elementary school have a very clear notion of the philosophy and major objectives of the school. It is further essential that all staff members see clearly the direct relationship of their own assignments and activities to what is to be accomplished through the program of the school. Such understanding results both in improved efficiency and professional satisfaction of the personnel charged with the responsibility of carrying the objectives of the school into action.

Common understanding can be developed only through sufficient involvement of all members of a school staff to guarantee the emergence of common denominators of communication and concepts. This can be done through rotating responsibilities, shifting opportunities for leadership, and encouraging and seeking group deliberations and decisions regarding broad policies of the school. Detailed attention is given to effective use of group processes in a later chapter.

Statements of Purposes.—Changes in conditions in this country have been reflected in the statements of educational objectives that have emerged from time to time. During the period of strong emphasis on a developing nationalism in America, the objectives of education were largely political, with considerable influence being exerted by religion. Schools served as instruments for developing a citizenry with sufficient intelligence to carry out successfully a system of self-government. This emphasis did much to shape the nature of the elementary school program and the purposes around which it developed.

During the period of rapid expansion from the latter part of the nineteenth century to the period following World War I, the necessity for re-examination of educational objectives became more and more apparent. School populations expanded immensely during this period, creating a very natural situation for the mass production concept of industry to be carried over into the schools. Even the mechanistic stimulus-response psychology with its great emphasis on repetition as a factor in learning fitted rather well into the school pattern of that particular period, the basic features of which had earlier been brought from Europe. This period of expansion, however, saw the beginnings of many educational reforms which were to be refined in later years. Greater emphasis on teacher education, with its corresponding improvement, became increasingly apparent toward the latter years of that period. With the development of standardized measuring instruments came greater recognition of individual differences in learners; this encouraged examination of traditional practices in evaluating learners and their progress. Although the curriculum was still almost completely compartmentalized into specific subject areas, these subjects had become more numerous and the curriculum as a whole was much more comprehensive than previously.

Beginning at about the time of the great economic depression in this country in 1929, a new emphasis began to be felt in education. Economic problems and insecurity led to general unrest, which in turn focused considerable attention on the remoteness of education from the actual problems and processes of living. As a result of these and numerous other influences, the schools began to undergo rather thorough reorganization. They became increasingly sensitive to the philosophical, social, and psychological concepts receiving wider acceptance among members of the profession and laymen as well. Efforts were promoted to inject functionalism and realism into the program of the school by relating the learning experiences of boys and girls to the actual problems of living in the home and community. Emphasis was placed on the child as the principal focus of education rather than on subject matter as such. Attempts were made to differentiate instruction according to the abilities and growth rates of individual children.

As in most reform movements, extremists undoubtedly carried the newer concepts of education far beyond the point indicated by either scientific evidence or common sense, with the result that unwarranted suspicion of the concepts themselves may have been encouraged. However, as a whole, much educational progress has been realized during the past two or three decades, particularly in individualization of instruction, enrichment of the curriculum through extended use of resources beyond the textbook, and in creating a more natural and flexible learning environment for children.

New and more complex demands upon education in the modern era have been reflected in the statements of educational objectives which have been formulated and accepted by the profession. A tendency to express such objectives in specific behavior has been evident. It may also be noted that modern objectives of education involve much broader sets of skills and competencies than has been true in former years.

The major trends of objectives for the modern elementary school are well demonstrated by the following set of purposes which have been widely accepted since their formulation in 1938:

I. THE OBJECTIVES OF SELF-REALIZATION

The Inquiring Mind. The educated person has an appetite for learning.

Speech. The educated person can speak the mother tongue clearly.

Reading. The educated person reads the mother tongue efficiently.

Writing. The educated person writes the mother tongue effectively.

Number. The educated person solves his problems of counting and calculating.

Sight and Hearing. The educated person is skilled in listening and observing.

Health Knowledge. The educated person understands the basic facts concerning health and disease.

Health Habits. The educated person protects his own health and that of his dependents.

Public Health. The educated person works to improve the health of the community.

Recreation. The educated person is participant and spectator in many sports and other pastimes.

Intellectual Interests. The educated person has mental resources for the use of leisure.

Aesthetic Interests. The educated person appreciates beauty.

Character. The educated person gives responsible direction to his own life.

II. THE OBJECTIVES OF HUMAN RELATIONSHIP

Respect for Humanity. The educated person puts human relationships first.

Friendships. The educated person enjoys a rich, sincere, and varied social life.

Cooperation. The educated person can work and play with others.

Courtesy. The educated person observes the amenities of social behavior.

Appreciation of the Home. The educated person appreciates the family as a social institution.

Conservation of the Home. The educated person conserves family ideals.

Homemaking. The educated person is skilled in homemaking.

Democracy in the Home. The educated person maintains democratic family relationships.

III. THE OBJECTIVES OF ECONOMIC EFFICIENCY

Work. The educated producer knows the satisfaction of good workmanship.

Occupational Information. The educated producer understands the requirements and opportunities for various jobs.

Occupational Choice. The educated producer has selected his occupation.

Occupational Efficiency. The educated producer succeeds in his chosen vocation.

Occupational Adjustment. The educated producer maintains and improves his efficiency.

Occupational Appreciation. The educated producer appreciates the social value of his work.

Personal Economics. The educated consumer plans the economics of his own life.

Consumer Judgment. The educated consumer develops standards for guiding his expenditures.

Efficiency in Buying. The educated consumer is an informed and skillful buyer.

Consumer Protection. The educated consumer takes appropriate measures to safeguard his interests.

IV. THE OBJECTIVES OF CIVIC RESPONSIBILITY

Social Justice. The educated citizen is sensitive to the disparities of human circumstance.

Social Activity. The educated citizen acts to correct unsatisfactory conditions.

Social Understanding. The educated citizen seeks to understand social structures and social processes.

Critical Judgment. The educated citizen has defenses against propaganda.

Tolerance. The educated citizen respects honest differences of opinion.

Conservation. The educated citizen has a regard for the nation's resources.

Social Applications of Science. The educated citizen measures scientific advance by its contribution to the general welfare.

World Citizenship. The educated citizen is a cooperating member of the world community.

Law Observance. The educated citizen respects the law.

Economic Literacy. The educated citizen is economically literate.

Political Citizenship. The educated citizen accepts his civic duties.

Devotion to Democracy. The educated citizen acts upon an unswerving loyalty to democratic ideals.[1]

Statements of purposes based on modern concepts of the responsibilities of education, such as these above, almost invariably are related to the kind of person we wish to emerge from our schools rather than to the mastery or completion of certain academic tasks. In other words, they are based on a recognition of the importance of both the *human process* and the *human product.* As pointed out in a bulletin of the State Department of Public Instruction of Indiana, when parents or teachers are asked the question, "What kind of person do you want this child to be when he finishes school?" their answers will not be formulated in terms of textbooks, grades, or test scores but rather will be stated in terms of such personal attributes as:

[1] *The Purposes of Education in American Democracy,* The Educational Policies Commission of the National Educational Association (Washington, D. C.: The National Education Association, 1938), pp. 50, 72, 90, and 108.

A healthy, well-developed body and habits and knowledge that will enable him to keep it so.

A clean wholesome mind.

Strength and integrity of character.

Ability to get along happily with others, knowing the courtesies and rules of the game, how to cooperate, how to lead, and how to follow.

Initiative to get a job and the ability to hold it.

An appreciation of his personal and civic responsibilities and the will to live up to them.

Resources within himself to care for work and leisure time.

Interest in the world about him with knowledge to understand and appreciate it.

Skill to do the work he needs to do—command of the tools of communication.

Understanding of what it means to be free and to live in a democracy.[2]

Another trend that may be noted in recent formulations of educational purposes is the effort to relate such purposes to democratic values. A striking example of this approach is found in the statement of "The General and Continuing Points of Emphasis" developed by the faculty for the University School of Ohio State University. The major goals are suggested by the topical divisions of the statement which follows:

A. Continuous Curriculum Experiences Directly Related to Democratic Values
    1. Developing social sensitivity
    2. Developing cooperativeness
    3. Developing the ability and zeal to utilize the method of intelligence in solving all problems of human concern
    4. Developing creativeness
    5. Developing skills in democratic living
    6. Interpreting democracy
    7. Developing self-direction

B. Continuous Curriculum Experiences Implied by Democratic Values
    1. Developing communication skills and appreciations
    2. Developing skills in measurement and the use of quantitative symbols
    3. Developing skills in utilizing goods and services
    4. Promoting social adjustments
    5. Promoting health and safety
    6. Developing vocational adjustments and standards
    7. Developing adequate recreational outlets
    8. Developing standards of personal appearance and grooming[3]

Adaptation of General Purposes in the Elementary School.— Thoughtful study of statements of purposes such as the ones which have been used here may be very helpful to a school staff in its efforts to get a

[2] *A Good Start in School* (Indianapolis: State of Indiana, Department of Public Instruction, Bulletin No. 158, 1944), p. 15.

[3] *The Philosophy and Purposes of the University School* (Columbus, Ohio: The Ohio State University, 1948), pp. 9-11.

comprehensive and clear view of the job confronting it. However, it must be understood that such purposes usually require adaptation before they become meaningful in a local school situation in a particular classroom. These adaptations take two forms: (1) interpretation of each goal in terms of the stage of development of the children involved, and (2) revision and/or emphasis of goals in terms of local conditions and specialized needs. For instance, communication skills purposes would demand different approaches and activities for six-year-olds, twelve-year-olds, or in a community where bilingualism created a special communication problem among children.

Supplementation of General Purposes.—A statement of general purposes is usually a splendid springboard from which the staff of a school can launch a study of its objectives, but such a general statement should never be construed as a terminal point of concern. Actually, it is essential that each school community, each school unit within the community, and even each classroom group have its activities guided by clearly understood purposes. General purposes may be thought of as a kind of educational platform, but they need the specificity and reality of locally devised objectives to bring genuine meaning to them in their relation to the school program.

Preparing Statements of Purposes.—While it is readily recognized that written statements of purposes do not in themselves carry the assurance that they will be translated into action, it is felt that the process of creating such statements usually has a very salutary effect on the personnel involved. In addition, written objectives tend to clarify and crystallize the tasks confronting teachers as they attempt to provide learning opportunities for children under their guidance. In the preparation of objectives, certain characteristics are worth noting:

1. Objectives ordinarily should be basically related to expected outcomes of *learners* rather than to those of *teachers*.
2. Objectives should be in terms of desired behavior.
3. Objectives should be consistent, one with another.
4. Objectives should include all aspects of growth.
5. Objectives should be based on both individual and group needs.
6. Objectives should be clearly stated and thoroughly understood by those who are expected to use them.
7. Objectives should be such that evaluation of progress toward their achievement is possible.

STEP TWO: THE DEVELOPMENT OF A PROGRAM

It is not enough to indicate what is to be done; it is equally important to decide how it is to be done. This is especially true with regard to the relationship of the purposes and program of the elementary school. *The school program is the designed plan for achieving the purposes of the school.* It is composed chiefly of the curriculum of the school, the services for which the school assumes responsibility, and the policies which govern both. Each of these will be considered in its relation to the total program here and will be discussed in detail in later chapters.

In order to appreciate fully the relation of the various components to the total school structure, it seems worth while to note a recent statement with respect to the indispensable elements of good living in the elementary school:

The characteristics, then, of an elementary school which provides the "good life" may be defined specifically as follows:

1. A school program with clearly stated purposes, defined cooperatively by teachers, parents, and children, and subject to change as conditions and needs may indicate.

2. A school staff with the ability to plan, execute, and evaluate educational activities in terms of purposes; individuals who believe in the coordinated intelligence of the group, and who understand and use the method of intelligence in the solution of problems.

3. A school principal who can lead classroom teachers, pupils, and parents to exercise their best efforts toward the achievement of agreed-upon goals; one who is a leader by virtue of ability rather than by position.

4. A community whose citizens participate actively in the school program; whose participation is sought and utilized by school personnel in all phases of school life.

5. A student body that has respect and understanding of teachers; where the worth of each individual child is appreciated, and where each individual is provided opportunities for growth.

6. A physical plant which allows for a changing program of activities; where facilities are provided to assist teachers and children in the learning-growing process.

7. A program of activities for children developed in relation to the achievement of the purposes of the school; activities that reflect teacher understanding of student needs, abilities, and interests; activities which, in their scope and sequence, indicate a knowledge of and sensitiveness to the total development of the whole child.[4]

Relation of the Curriculum to the School Program.—The curriculum of the elementary school is the heart of its program, for it consists of the learning experiences, planned and unplanned, which the school utilizes to achieve its desired ends. The curriculum takes on life at the

[4] *Bases for Effective Learning,* Thirty-First Yearbook of the Department of Elementary School Principals (Washington, D. C.: National Education Association, 1952), p. 22.

point of contact with learners. It is not a course of study although, admittedly, a course of study may set forth the intentions and resources which enter into the curriculum and its implementation. It is probably safe to assume that no school program is much better than the concept of the curriculum held by members of the professional staff of the school.

If it is to be effective, the curriculum of the school must be consistent with the purposes set up for a school. For example, if one of the purposes of a school is to develop the ability on the part of children to plan a course of action on a cooperative basis, then it would seem to be an obvious kind of folly to insist on a rigid, completely preplanned curriculum for children at all times. Such a purpose appears rather to call for the use of resource units for learning that will provide a general framework for learning but will permit, within that framework, the free operation of creativity and thoughtful planning together.

Since it is such a vital part of a unified school program, it is essential that the curriculum be consistently conceived throughout all levels of the school. This is not to suggest conformity or restriction, for it is imperative that each teacher be free to exercise initiative in guiding the learning experiences of her pupils. It does mean, however, that children should not be subjected to a series of learning experiences, some of which tend to counteract the constructive effect of the others. In order to get the necessary thread of consistency into the program, curriculum development and revision require the participation of the full resources of the professional staff, individually and collectively. In this way, common understandings can be established around which each teacher may develop her own classroom program of activities.

The Relation of Services to the School Program.—School services have come to be considered as an integral part of the modern school program. Health, library, and pupil personnel services, and other similar supplements to the instructional program are found in most good elementary schools today. More and more schools are operating school lunch services. While each of these services makes its own unique contribution to the administration and instructional program, all of them can and should be justified in terms of their assistance in increasing the effectiveness of learning and living in the school.

In the first place, the services of the school contribute to the all around development and growth of children. If the program is to be based, as it obviously should be, on the idea of the unified growth and development of the whole child, it is necessary to give appropriate attention to his health, his nutrition, and his resources for working and learning independently.

School services also provide a functional setting for employing habits and information learned by the child. The school lunch room is an excellent place to put into practice the things that have been learned about proper nutrition or dining etiquette. The library provides an equally lifelike opportunity to apply the skills of research and independent study.

A third function performed by school services is the removal of obstacles to effective learning on the part of some children. Through the school health program, certain health deficiencies of children may be discovered and proper corrective treatment prescribed and provided. Visual and hearing impairments are often screened out through the school health services at a time when correction is usually possible. The attendance and personnel services of the school often identify children with guidance problems so that proper attention can be given to their needs.

The Relation of Policy to the School Program.—Policies may be considered broad, sustaining agreements which guide specific day-to-day decisions. We might think of them as the operating "ground rules" of the school. Some policies, of course, are handed down from the administrative offices of the school system, having emanated from that office or from the board of education. In addition to all such policies, however, there is need for each school to set up for itself a framework of principles and policies to guide the actions of members of its staff. These policies provide for better coordination of effort and lend a greater degree of security to members of the staff as they discharge their respective responsibilities.

As a simple example, one might consider the problem of the action to be taken by a teacher in case of an injury to a child on the playground during the lunch hour while the teacher is the assigned supervisor of the playground. Obviously, the problem might be met in many ways. One way, though undoubtedly a ridiculous and wasteful approach, would be to have a meeting of the staff called each time such an accident occurred in order that the resources and thinking of all members might be utilized in arriving at the best possible decision. Another approach would be to assume that the principal was to be called each time for his decision regarding the best course of action for the teacher. Still another possibility would be to allow the teacher to do as she thought best at the time of the accident without regard for consistency of action from time to time or from person to person. In the face of such accidents, there is a need for some previously agreed-upon policy or practice, as to who should be notified and what actions might reasonably be expected from the teacher under such circumstances.

Matters such as pupil progress and classification, the joint utilization of facilities and services, the requisition, allocation, and distribution of supplies, and some aspects of pupil accounting are illustrative of other areas of mutual concern that often require corporate consideration that will lead to the development of guiding policies.

All schools operate within the framework of policy although they may not be conscious of doing so. The policies which guide the program of instruction and services in a particular school may be issued from an authoritarian source or they may be democratically developed through the participation of members of the school staff and community. It is felt by some that the participation of the many which is necessary for democratic development of policy is highly wasteful of energy and time in relation to the benefits derived from the method. However, others feel that the democratic approach to problem solving and policy development actually saves time when the over-all cycle of policy development and implementation is considered. For example, when an administrator suddenly announces a new policy to his staff and demands immediate implementation, little time is taken for policy formulation but much time will be necessary for interpretation, common understanding, and proper activation of the policy. Possibly the action stimulated by such a policy will be varied from person to person and, in some instances at least, will be reluctantly initiated. On the other hand, while there is a greater length of time taken for a group to come to a decision as to the nature of a policy to be used, much less time will be necessary for carrying policies thus developed into intelligent action, since such action will be based on common understanding to a much greater extent than in the former case.

ACTION SUGGESTIONS FOR THE PRINCIPAL

1. Emphasize the importance of specific purposes or goals for the school.
2. Find constructive ways to involve teachers, children, parents, and other citizens in the selection and formulation of school purposes.
3. Work continuously on the development of a school program that will achieve the purposes the school holds.
4. Help all persons involved to formulate, in clear and simple terms, the philosophy of the school.
5. Seek and examine the stated philosophies of other schools for comparison, discussion, and stimulation.
6. Encourage teachers to become increasingly skilled classroom practitioners; provide opportunities for in-service inspiration and growth.
7. Select personnel who are professionally openminded.
8. Strive to make the school a genuine instrument of democracy.

9. Develop a school atmosphere that promotes the adjustment of children to it.

10. Continuously examine the processes through which school personnel expect to achieve school objectives.

11. Utilize community resources in developing school policies and practices.

12. Utilize available professional resources such as consultant services.

13. Work for wide participation in developing school policies.

14. Survey community needs and resources as a basis for program development.

15. Develop, for distribution to interested citizens, bulletins and handbooks setting forth the major features of the school program.

16. In planning the building or remodeling of the school plant, consider first the aims and functions of the school.

17. Plan occasional workshops or in-service seminars on school improvement. Invite both professional staff and laymen to participate.

18. Develop a plan for the continuous evaluation and revision of the curriculum.

19. Develop needed pupil services as an integral part of the total program of the school.

20. In performing the responsibilities of leadership distinguish clearly between the *development* of policy, which is a cooperative activity, and the *administration* of policy, which is largely the responsibility of the principal.

SELECTED REFERENCES FOR EXTENDED READING

ASSOCIATION FOR SUPERVISION AND CURRICULUM DEVELOPMENT. *Organizing the Elementary School for Living and Learning, 1947 Yearbook.* Washington, D. C.: National Education Association, 1947.

AYER, FRED C. *Fundamentals of Instructional Supervision.* New York: Harper & Bros., 1954.

CAMPBELL, CLYDE M. (ed.). *Practical Applications of Democratic Administration.* New York: Harper & Bros., 1952, chap. 5.

CASWELL, HOLLIS L., and FOSHAY, A. WELLESLEY. *Education in the Elementary School.* New York: American Book Co., 1950, chaps. 3 and 4.

DOUGHERTY, JAMES H., GORMAN, FRANK H., and PHILLIPS, CLAUDE A. *Elementary School Organization and Management (revised).* New York: The Macmillan Co., 1950, chap. 3.

ELSBREE, WILLARD S., and McNALLY, HAROLD J. *Elementary School Administration and Supervision.* New York: American Book Co., 1951, chap. 6.

KYTE, GEORGE C. *The Principal at Work.* Boston: Ginn & Co., 1952, chap. 7.

MEHL, MARIE A., MILLS, HUBERT H., and DOUGLASS, HARL R. *Teaching in Elementary School.* New York: The Ronald Press Co., 1950, chaps. 3 and 4.

OTTO, HENRY J. *Elementary School Organization and Administration.* New York: Appleton-Century-Crofts, Inc., 1954, chaps. 2, 4, and 7.

RAGAN, WILLIAM B. *Modern Elementary Curriculum.* New York: The Dryden Press, Inc., 1953, chaps. 5-7.

REAVIS, WILLIAM C., and OTHERS. *Administering the Elementary School.* New York: Prentice-Hall, Inc., 1953, chaps. 1, 4, and 5.

SHANE, HAROLD G., and YAUCH, WILBUR A. *Creative School Administration.* New York: Henry Holt & Co., 1954, chaps. 7, 8, and 9.

PART III

IMPROVING THE ORGANIZATION AND MANAGEMENT OF THE SCHOOL

Chapter 7

IMPROVING THE MANAGEMENT OF SCHOOL PLANT AND FACILITIES

The educational plant may be merely a schoolhouse—or it may be a schoolhome

The organization of an elementary school is the total coordinative process used to regulate and promote its activities. It is organization which most often determines the extent to which the varied elements of the school program become working parts of a unified, integrated effort. The organization and management functions of school personnel are not ends in themselves; they can be justified only in that they are means for providing optimum conditions under which effective learning takes place.

While there are many facets of management, its major purposes usually have three foci: to provide for (1) the best possible use of educational facilities, (2) the maximum utilization of staff energies, and (3) optimum classification and grouping of children for effective learning. Each of these aspects of organization is discussed in subsequent chapters. In this chapter we shall consider the management and utilization of the physical facilities of the educational environment.

Principles Underlying Effective Use of Plant and Facilities

Educational facilities are rather concrete and specific in nature and may be used constructively, ignored, or actually misused according to the understanding and motives of their users. For this reason, it seems desirable to suggest a few basic concepts, or principles, which profitably might guide one's thinking with regard to important features of the physical plant of the school.

1. *The school plant should be accessible and harmonious with its surroundings.* The site for the elementary school should be selected with consideration of its surroundings and the character of the community. This means that selection cannot always be made wisely on the basis of population density alone, although the distribution of children

in the community is always a factor to be considered. The distance of the school site from its current and potential customers is important. In addition, the relation of the site to railroads, busy highways, or dangerous intersections or crossings cannot be overlooked.

It is usually desirable to think of the school plant in relation to the nature of its surroundings in order to insure a reasonable element of coherence. This may involve the type of building materials used as well as the architectural design and orientation of the building in relation to its environment. The site should be selected also with regard to its possible use for community activities, such as the use of the playground for recreation. In communities made up of several rather distinct cultural groups, it is important to try to plan for a site and building that give equal consideration to all elements of the community.

2. *The school plant should reflect a recognition of the nature of the groups to be served by it.* An elementary school should be designed for elementary school children. Such a statement seems utterly trite until one takes a critical look at many elementary school buildings in use today. In too many instances, factors of architectural logic and aesthetic considerations, rather than educational function, appear to have determined the general features of school plants with the result that they might with a few internal adjustments serve just as well as hospitals or factories. It is well known that young children need space and yet many plants do not reflect the awareness of this fact. Such minor things as the number and kinds of steps leading into a building, the height of drinking fountains and bulletin boards, and the types of flooring used are important.

3. *The school plant should reflect a recognition of the type of curriculum around which school life is organized.* The nature of the plant and physical environment may impose numerous restrictions on the operation of a modern school program. Many school plants do not encourage the degree of activity and social grouping and interaction that have come to be accepted as important parts of the total educational process. The community-school concept almost demands some adjustment in the planning of the typical school plant in order to facilitate the types of functional learning which so largely comprise the activities of the genuine community school.

As the curriculum of the school is increasingly extended beyond the covers of the textbooks, provisions must be made for storage, distribution, and easy accessibility and use of varied kinds of instructional materials. This requires careful thought by those who plan school plants and by all who are responsible for working out plans for making optimum use of such facilities.

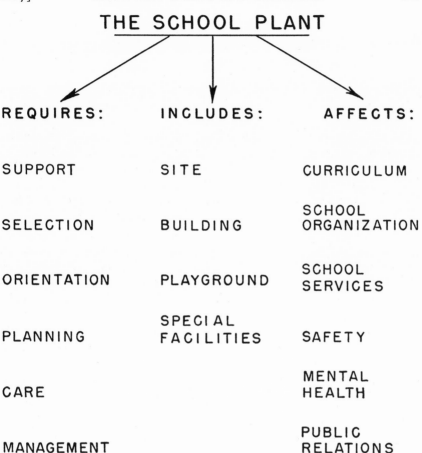

Figure 7

The Elementary School Plant

4. *The school plant should reflect a recognition of modern methods of teaching and sound concepts of learning.* This is a corollary to the immediately preceding principle. In a good school, provision must be made for individualized activity, small group activity, and for activities that involve sharing with large groups in an audience situation. In addition, attention should be paid to facilities for making maximum use of audio-visual materials of instruction and for creative kinds of activity on the part of learners. The size and arrangement of classrooms and buildings were not so important when teaching was defined mainly as question and answer recitations. Now that teaching-learning very wisely involves so many varied approaches, it is imperative that corresponding adjust-

ments be made in the educational facilities of the school in order to provide the most productive setting possible for learning.

5. *The school plant should reflect and facilitate the close relationship that exists between the instructional program of the school and its specialized services.* The location and nature of the quarters provided for special services of the school have much to do with establishing their relationship to the instructional activities of the school. If they are located and operated in comparative isolation from other aspects of the life of the school, no real integration is likely to occur between these two important aspects of the school program. This is especially true of health services, school lunch services, and library services. Much more than the mere specialized functioning of these services is involved if they are to make their maximum educational contribution to good living for children. To create conditions wherein these desirable relationships can exist in a natural manner is a definite challenge to thoughtful planning.

6. *The school plant should be adaptable to community needs and use.* It is true, as mentioned above, that the basic consideration in the construction, maintenance, and utilization of a school plant should be the educational welfare of the children served by the school. However, with the increasing recognition of the importance of school-home-community interaction in effective education, the utilization of the school plant by the community cannot wisely be ignored. Provisions should be made for the direct use by parents and other adults of such facilities of the school as the library services. The recreational facilities may also be utilized by laymen along with such other facilities as the school auditorium or dining room. Parent and adult study groups are becoming common in many school communities and usually meet at school. All such groups profit from these activities and, in addition, contribute to a growing mutual understanding between school personnel and citizens of the community.

7. *The school plant should reflect an emphasis on flexibility rather than permanence.* Two trends in school plant planning appear to be entirely wholesome from a professional point of view. The first is the trend away from standardization of school building design. In fact, many communities and states are making deliberate efforts to encourage functional imagination and individuality in the planning of elementary school buildings. They feel that if a school is to reflect the unique needs of a community, it should be planned accordingly rather than on the basis of standard architectural design.

Another noteworthy trend in school plant planning is the increased emphasis on flexibility and expandibility. With the mobility of population now being experienced in many communities, it seems unwise to plan for permanent buildings for the future. Rather it seems advisable to provide for a plant that can easily be modified in terms of future community needs, or even be replaced at moderate cost.

8. *The school plant should reflect the desire for a good living environment for the children of a community.* Children spend a large proportion of their waking hours at school. The environment provided by the school has a strong day-by-day effect on the attitudes of these children. Unfortunately, many parents who want only the best of living conditions for their children at home appear to show very little concern about the quality of the physical environment at school. Dilapidated buildings, crowded classrooms, and inadequate special rooms and equipment all appear to affect attitudes toward other children and adults and toward property and equipment. Healthful and functionally planned plants, on the contrary, tend to develop a sense of pride and loyalty on the part of children who are privileged to enjoy them.

Some Criteria for Evaluating the School Plant

The foregoing principles naturally lead us to a consideration of the specific characteristics of a school plant which must be met if these principles are to be observed. A good statement of such criteria appears in a recent yearbook of the American Association of School Administrators. The statement sets forth the following criteria for educationally effective buildings:

Curriculum adequacy—Do they provide the space and facilities for the educational program that your community needs for its children, youth, and adults?

Safety and well-being—Do they not only protect against danger but also provide a positive influence for improving the health and physical welfare of pupils?

Interfunctional coordination—Are they so planned that the activity in each part of the building may be coordinated harmoniously with related activities and may be carried on effectively without disturbing other activities?

Efficiency and utility—Are they so planned that the handling of materials and the comings and goings of pupils, school staff, and the public are accomplished with a minimum of interference and a maximum of ease and satisfaction to all concerned?

Beauty—Are they pleasing in appearance, with simplicity, usefulness, and balance as ideals, rather than ornamentation and symmetry?

Adaptability—Are they so planned that they can be enlarged or rearranged internally to meet new educational demands with a minimum of additional cost?

Economy—Are they so planned that in original outlay and in future operation the utmost in educational utility can be secured for every dollar spent?[1]

[1] American Association of School Administrators, *American School Buildings,* Twenty-Seventh Yearbook (Washington, D. C.: American Association of School Administrators, 1949), p. 8.

Essential Elements of the School Plant

The school plant includes all the permanent physical facilities of the school, both within and outside the school building itself. The total design and resources of the modern elementary school are intended to provide wholesome quarters for group living and learning and, in addition, to serve the specialized needs of children as they participate in a well-rounded program of elementary education. To serve these purposes well, the school plant must be functionally planned and constructed.

Initially, of course, the plant must be visualized in terms of the size of the school population to be served by it. Although local geographic and economic factors naturally are basic considerations in determining the size of a prospective school unit, the question of what constitutes optimum size for an elementary school certainly should get serious consideration in planning it. Actually, there is limited evidence to indicate the exact size at which a school is both effective and economical to operate. However, much thought on the part of many serious students of the situation has bestowed favor on the moderate-sized school. It is felt that an extremely large school requires a regimentation and impersonal operation that limits its effectiveness. At the same time, schools that are too small cannot provide many of the essential services of education on an economical basis. An illustration of the growing feeling that the size of the school unit is important is the resolution passed at a recent meeting of the Department of Elementary School Principals which recommended that schools have an enrollment no larger than five hundred.[2]

Each component part of the school plant should be considered in relation to its educational functions and the persons it is expected to serve. Both quantitative and qualitative features require careful study if maximum results are to be obtained from the facilities of the school. A few of these elements of the school plant appear to merit discussion at this point.

Classrooms.—The greater part of the educational activity of an elementary school occurs in classrooms. Teachers organize their work there. Children spend most of their day in their respective classrooms. To a group of elementary school children, their classroom is their "schoolhome." The classroom is the place where educational plans are made and carried out; it serves as a common ground for sharing; it is the proving ground for growth in group living and learning.

In recent years the emphasis on the whole child has influenced the

[2] Meeting of the Department of Elementary School Principals at Atlantic City, New Jersey, on February 11-13, 1954.

nature of classrooms to a tremendous degree. The recognition of the role of experience and activity in learning has resulted in a corresponding awareness of the need for space adequate for multiple activities in the classroom. The increased concern for children as individuals has prompted many attempts to differentiate instruction through methods utilizing a wide range of materials. This condition has necessitated the emergence of a more flexible classroom with provisions for diversified arrangement and activities in terms of needs to be met. The attempts to unify learning experiences through the unit approach and other integrative devices have required classrooms which could house varied types of instructional materials. This emphasis on relatedness in learning also has resulted in an increasing respect and demand for self-contained classrooms as opposed to departmentalized forms of instruction at the elementary school levels.

Elementary school classrooms should be sufficiently large to permit freedom of movement and to promote the effective use of multiple learning activities. This is particularly true of rooms which house very young children, since they require space for big-muscle development even in their indoor activities. School building specialists now usually recommend that regular elementary school classrooms have at least one thousand square feet of floor space with nursery school and kindergarten space substantially larger.

Recent study of and research in the psychological effects of factors of the physical environment, such as lighting and color, have led to some rather drastic departures from the conventional types of classroom decoration. Many modern schools now are being decorated in different colors from room to room, in accordance with the kind of effect desired. Multiple colors are frequently used even within a single classroom in order to produce a bright and interesting environment. Certainly, in planning or modernizing school buildings, sufficient study should be given to the matter of color to insure cheerful and livable surroundings for the children who are to occupy the quarters.

The amount and quality of light necessary for effective vision throughout the room are other matters for careful consideration. Since scientific instruments that are simple to use and relatively inexpensive are now available for measuring intensity of light at different points in the classroom, it is possible for any school to get rather reliable information regarding lighting conditions in its various classrooms. The effective use of color, as mentioned above, and the utilization of newer types of indirect lighting also serve frequently to improve the quality of the lighting within a room.

It is important that classrooms in the elementary school have facilities within the room itself to sustain the educational activities which occur within its walls. This means that each classroom should be equipped with running water and the work space necessary for carrying on art and construction activities and for caring for materials. Such facilities should include a sink, a work counter, and storage shelves and cabinets suitable for the materials of various sizes in use. Ample bulletin boards and suitable chalkboards are also essential features of a good classroom, as well as appropriate space for such centers of interest as a science corner and library corner.

The School Office.—Fortunately, the concept of the principal's office as a center for penal operations is a fading notion. As the principal has become a professional leader, his role as school disciplinarian has been considerably modified. It can easily be seen that under the former concept of the principal's police function, it was completely consistent to have him occupy an office designed, furnished, and operated along rather severe lines. With the gradual advent of the belief that the principal can best serve the school in the role of sympathetic adviser and participant, the function of the school office has been viewed in a different light. Obviously, it should be a place which seeks to attract rather than awe people, a place from which comes help rather than punishment.

It is highly desirable that the school office be located in a convenient and readily accessible part of the building, since most school visits are initiated at this point. It should be warm and inviting with proper staff and facilities for making callers comfortable and for giving reasonably prompt attention to their particular missions or problems. A pleasant, though not necessarily large, reception room is desirable for the school office. If it is impossible to employ a clerk or secretary for the office, or if the principal is not regularly available to greet visitors, it is often valuable to allow children to serve as school hosts or hostesses. At any rate, someone should be in the office at all times to receive visitors and telephone calls. Nothing is so distressing to a busy parent, or to any other hurried visitor, as the necessity for waiting for long periods of time in the school office for someone to appear. The particular method for receiving guests, of course, must be worked out by each school in terms of its size, office quarters, and other contributing factors.

In addition to the outer office usually occupied by the school secretary, there should be a private office for the use of the principal for conferences and other situations demanding privacy. The outer office ordinarily is equipped with accessible mail boxes for teachers and other staff members, and often with a teachers' bulletin board for the exchange of messages. If it is used as a reception room, as it usually is, it is helpful to provide current magazines or interesting school materials for visitors to read while they wait to confer with principal or teachers. Somewhere within the office structure there should be available adequate files and storage for records. It is also desirable to provide a safe for money and for materials which could not be replaced.

The Work Center.—Every school needs a room equipped with clerical and duplicating facilities, as well as other supplies, for planning and carrying out room and school projects. Such a room should have a regular typewriter and one with primary type. It also should house duplicating equipment, materials for making charts, and paper cutters for all sizes of paper used within the school. This type of work center probably should be located near or adjoining the office of the school, although in large schools it is helpful to have two such work rooms, particularly if the school building is a two-story structure. It has been suggested by some persons that one such work center should be provided for primary teachers with an additional room provided for intermediate and upper-grade teachers. The main thing is that appropriate opportunity and facilities be provided for teachers to get their clerical work done expeditiously and for them to prepare teacher-made instructional materials when they are needed. Such centers are also invaluable as quarters for preparation of school bulletins, news sheets, and notices that are to be sent to parents and laymen throughout the community.

The Health Unit.—A vital part of the equipment of the modern school is the health service unit. Such a unit usually serves as headquarters for the school nurse. As such it should include facilities for both the clerical and technical work of the health personnel who perform their duties in the building. The unit customarily comprises at least three rooms. One is used for the health office, the second for an examination room, and the third as a rest room for children who become ill or who, for any reason, need to lie down during the day. The size of each room will be determined, of course, by the size of the school and the number of children to be served. The same will be true, to some extent, regarding the equipment and facilities needed for the health quarters. In a large school, for instance, it would be necessary to provide more rest facilities than would be the case in a small school.

Certain basic health equipment is essential in all schools which provide adequate health services for children. Such equipment includes modern facilities for administering screening tests to detect possible difficulties in vision and hearing. Devices such as the telebinocular and the audiometer, though more expensive than some of the simpler screening instruments in common use, appear to be much more effective and comprehensive in identifying possible difficulties in sight and hearing which children may have. It is also essential that facilities be provided for periodic checks on heights and weights of children. Some schools are also providing a dental chair and equipment needed by the dental hygienist if regular dental examinations are a part of the health service program of the school. As the years pass, more and more schools are adding this service, sometimes within the school itself and, in other cases, through a joint arrangement between two or more schools.

The School Library.—The gradual implementation of the concept that the child learns and grows as a whole has placed increasing emphasis on the self-contained classroom as opposed to the departmentalization of instruction in the elementary school. This development also has influenced the ideas of teachers regarding what constitutes the best means for enduring availability and use of supplementary and independent reading materials. Some have held that each classroom should have its own library as a vital part of its own unitary facilities and activities and without regard for what others may have. Others have felt that sole dependence on classroom libraries is unrealistic and uneconomical and often leads to wasteful and ineffective duplication in the purchase and use of materials. Actually, the study and experience of the writer have led him to believe that a good modern school must have both a school library and rich room collections if it is hoped to get maximum utilization of the reading materials provided for children.

The school library should be planned in accordance with the purposes and people it hopes to serve. It is important that it be light, airy, and pleasant in as many respects as possible. Since it will be used chiefly by children, shelves and furniture should be selected and arranged in such a way that children can use them efficiently and as independently as possible. A small work room off the main part of the library is an essential part of the unit. In such a room worn books can be repaired and materials for picture files can be clipped and sorted.

Some schools are also providing space within the library of the school for both a teachers' professional library and a parents' library. These can well become integral parts of the library service of the school.

The School Dining Room.—An integral part of the modern school plant is the school lunch unit. As in the case of the school library, it is essential that the quarters used for this purpose have the necessary physical characteristics to make them attractive and healthful. The room should be well lighted and ventilated in such a manner that strong or unpleasant food odors and other fumes can be removed effectively. The tables and chairs should be sturdy and capable of being easily cleaned.

There is also some advantage, particularly in smaller schools, in providing furniture in the school lunch room that is sufficiently portable that it can be moved without difficulty, thus providing the possibility of using the space for other purposes at times when meals are not being served.

Experience has shown that much care should be exercised in planning the kitchen facilities to be used in the preparation of school lunches. The arrangement of the kitchen has a great influence on economy of time and effort in food preparation. Therefore, it should be arranged in such a way as to save unnecessary steps and activity and, at the same time, contribute to ease in serving the meals. Aside from regular cooking and sterilizing facilities and equipment, it is desirable to provide sufficient storage space for such foods as meats and frozen foods. In this way, foods can be purchased in quantities that will effect considerable savings for the school. This is particularly important in situations in which it is possible to acquire surplus foods at little or no cost that can be used over a period of time.

The lunch room is a center of social and educational activity as well as a place for the distribution of food. Furnishings and facilities should be such that an atmosphere is provided in which children acquire proper habits of eating together courteously and pleasantly. To do this is to fulfill one of the social purposes of the school.

The Playground and Play Rooms.—It has been pointed out earlier that one of the basic needs of children of elementary school age is for the development of their muscular systems through extended physical activities appropriate to their maturity. This suggests that one of the jobs of the school is to provide proper facilities for such activity. It further suggests that one of the integral elements of a good modern school is the playground.

The first requirement for a good playground is that it be of adequate size to accommodate the number of pupils enrolled in the school. Although some studies have been made in an attempt to determine the amount of space necessary for each pupil enrolled, it is educationally dangerous to assume that the solution of the playground problem is that simple. So many factors are involved in determining the educational adequacy of playground facilities that any well-founded conclusions can be made only after careful study of the local situation. At any rate, the amount of available space should be considered in such matters as the purchase of playground equipment. If space is limited, it is probably wise to acquire the types of equipment that lend themselves to multiple and mass use without requiring an unusual amount of space. The individual and team games, which children at the upper-grade levels begin to engage in, usually demand much more room if they are to be carried on with complete safety. A good playground provides sufficient space for free play and activity, for use of playground equipment, and for the organized games of older children.

The surface and topography of the playground are other aspects that demand consideration. Even though it is expensive, and probably not entirely desirable, to provide an all-weather surface for the entire playground if it is large, it is almost necessary to have at least a part of the playground surfaced in such a way that activities can be carried on at times when inclement weather has left the ground muddy. This is a factor in building maintenance as well as in getting maximum use of the grounds.

Even maximum playground facilities do not completely preclude the necessity for some indoor space that can be used for physical activities and games during inclement weather. Many people feel that indoor activity rooms for elementary schools should be designed more in terms of the typical activities of elementary school children than in the pattern of the customary gymnasium. Certainly such rooms should be of sufficient size to accommodate ordinary classroom groups as they engage in organized and informal group activities.

Provisions for storage space for physical educational equipment and materials and adequate toilet and shower facilities are other aspects of the school plant that deserve consideration if it is to serve all phases of the educational program according to modern standards.

The Teachers' Room.—One of the important factors contributing to teacher morale is the provision of one or more rooms for the use of teachers. Wherever possible, separate teachers' lounges should be provided for men and women. These usually serve as places where teachers may rest during lunch periods or other free periods. They should have ample rest and toilet facilities as well as comfortable and relaxing furnishings. It is considered desirable also to provide periodical and professional reading materials for the use of teachers, as well as facilities for writing.

The Community Room.—The modern elementary school is becoming increasingly a community school; as such, it draws upon educational resources of the community and shares its facilities with other community agencies engaged in educational pursuits in the interest of boys and girls. However, over and above this general school-community interaction, it is desirable, whenever possible, to provide special quarters for community use. Such a room, or rooms, should be large enough and sufficiently flexible to serve as the setting for scout and club meetings of both boys and girls and for meetings of parents and adult study groups. Facilities should be provided for the storage of work materials. It is also desirable to have the minimum kitchen facilities for the preparation and serving of refreshments and simple meals.

The Auditorium.—If a school is to perform a genuine community function, a suitable school auditorium seems almost essential. Its size will be determined by the school population and by existing and prospective community use. Aside from merely being a place where a large number of people may be seated, it should also have appropriate facilities for dramatic and musical activities and performances as well as projection equipment for use in showing films and other audio-visual materials. The auditorium, if possible, should be equipped with a public address system for use at large group meetings.

The Audio-Visual Center.—Although it is desirable that many audio-visual materials will be used in the setting of the classroom itself, there seems to be considerable justification for including in the school plant a room that can be used for carrying on audio-visual activities. Such a room customarily houses equipment for projection of slides, film strips, and films, for recording, and for listening to records and transcriptions of various sorts. It can also serve as the logical center for using television and radio receivers if these facilities are not provided in regular classrooms. The audio-visual center also may well serve as a place where teachers and older pupils may construct simpler forms of audio-visual materials, such as slides and other graphic media.

Management of the School Plant and Facilities

School facilities are educationally useful to the extent to which they are maintained in suitable condition for use. In the first place, it is a matter of false economy to fail to provide for proper maintenance of a plant and facilities which represent the kind of investment that is required for a modern elementary school. In the second place, the condition of a school plant and facilities has a corresponding and direct effect on the physical well-being of the school's inhabitants and on the development of habits and attitudes that are felt to be desirable. For these and many other reasons, much attention should be given to ways and means of guaranteeing maximum effectiveness in the maintenance and operation of school facilities.

At least three aspects of school maintenance and management bear such close relationship to the purposes of the school that they deserve detailed attention. They are (1) the custodial care and maintenance of the school plant and equipment, (2) the acquisition of supplies and equipment for the school, and (3) the distribution and utilization of school supplies and equipment. Each will be discussed at some length in the following sections.

Custodial Care and Maintenance of the School Plant.—The most important step that can be taken to assure good school maintenance is the *selection of competent custodial personnel.* While the actual selection and appointment of members of the custodial force often does not lie within the jurisdiction of the school principal, in any case he should use whatever influence he has to insure that competent people are hired to care for the school plant. A school custodian should be a person who can work congenially with adults and children, who is sensitive and sympathetic to the operating philosophy of the school, and who sees in his daily tasks a challenge to his inherent pride in well-kept surroundings. It is true that such a person cannot be secured for the salaries typically paid for custodial work, but it is the feeling of the writer that improved salaries for such competent people would be a small additional investment in terms of the great dividends the school could reap from his services. If schools are of sufficient size to warrant more than one custodian, it is usually advantageous to have a woman as a member of the custodial staff to be responsible for some of the lighter cleaning chores.

The *standards of care and cleanliness* maintained by the custodial staff go a long way in setting the general tone of the school. A clean, attractive school building is a matter of pride to teachers and pupils alike and creates an atmosphere for living and learning that is conducive to the development of positive attitudes concerning the rights and property of others. Children who are inclined to apply their artistic and literary talents to corridor and washroom walls are much less likely to do so if the walls are kept clean and free from mutilation.

The cleaning schedules of the custodial staff should be arranged in such a way that minimum interference with the regular activities of the school results. Many schools are finding it advantageous to have the building and rooms cleaned at night after the activities of the day are over. At any rate, the possibility of children coming to school in the morning to an uncleaned room should be rigidly avoided.

Perhaps it should be pointed out that, important as it is, a clean building is not an end in itself. Therefore, it should always be remembered that custodial services are employed to expedite and improve the quality of the educational environment and program and are good to the extent that they achieve this purpose. At no time should the educational activities of the school be subordinated to the desire for a spotlessly clean and completely orderly building. Such an attitude defeats the very justification for having the building in the first place.

It appears to be a sound educational practice for children to assume some responsibilities for housekeeping in relation to their own room activities. This is an outgrowth of the emphasis on personal and group responsibility that is evidenced in most modern school programs. Children are usually willing to assume the obligation of cleaning up after engaging in activities that tend to disarrange the functional livability of the room. They can be responsible for putting away art and construction materials and for cleaning tools and paint brushes after use. The assumption of such responsibilities tends to develop good work habits and to create a positive sensitivity to the values of order and cleanliness. Children or teachers should not be asked to do regular custodial chores for which others have been hired just because these chores may not otherwise be done. Such work seems to have little educational value for children and may result in a kind of destructive resentment toward the school.

Another important function of the custodial staff is the *maintenance of service facilities* of the school. Part of this responsibility is related to the professional staff with such chores as moving room furniture, hanging maps and pictures, or making minor repairs and adjustments of furnishings and equipment. Another aspect of this responsibility involves the vigilant attention that insures that soap dispensers contain soap and are in a usable condition, that washrooms are always equipped with the necessary supply of toilet paper and towels, and that washbowls, toilets, and urinals are clean at all times and free from obnoxious odors. Proper and continuing attention to the service needs of the school is one of the most significant contributions of the custodial force.

Closely related to the maintenance of the service facilities of the school is the necessity for prompt and efficient provisions for *making minor repairs* of the equipment and school plant. Early attention to broken window shades, desks, or plumbing insures continuous use and, at the same time, forestalls more expensive repairs that become necessary when the difficulty is allowed to continue until it becomes acute.

One of the ways in which an administrative leader can be beneficial to a school is to assist the professional and custodial staff in working out practical and efficient means for cooperating so that the best possible service will result. Especially in larger schools, it usually has been found to be necessary to decide upon some systematic manner in which teachers request custodial service. This is often done through the school office or in some other manner which is found to be feasible and effective. It is important also that the school custodian understands completely the manner in which requests for major repairs and custodial supplies are to be made.

Definite arrangements should be made and understood by all persons concerned regarding the services of custodial personnel in connection with community meetings held in the school at irregular hours. Unpleasant situations often arise as a result of lack of understanding regarding policies governing such situations. On the other hand, good custodial service on such occasions is an important factor in the establishment and maintenance of pleasant and workable school-community relations.

The Requisition of Equipment and Supplies.—Maintaining proper equipment and a continuous supply of instructional materials in a large elementary school is a comprehensive enterprise. It is a matter of great importance because the on-going activities of the school depend upon a continuous availability of educational materials and also because the lack of such supplies has an immediate and devastating effect on morale within the school. Since the acquisition and management of these materials exert so great an influence on the quality of the school program, it seems appropriate to suggest a few considerations with respect to this problem.

School equipment and supplies always should be selected in terms of the program and needs of the school. There is little, if any, virtue in the possession of elaborate equipment for which there is small use in the activities of the school and for which there appears to be limited prospective use. It is often necessary, in the face of typical budgetary limitations, to set up priorities of need and urgency when purchases of equipment are anticipated. Certainly some pieces of equipment are more necessary than others and the only way to exercise wisdom in the matter of selection is to study the situation carefully enough to arrive at sound criteria upon which conclusions may be made regarding pending requisitions.

If school equipment and supplies are to be truly functional, *the people who are to use them must be taken into the process of their selection.* This suggests the undesirability of one or two persons assuming full responsibility for the selection and purchase of such materials. If equipment is to be used by the entire school on a shared basis, it is often desirable to select a committee of teachers, teachers and pupils, or teachers, pupils, and parents, to deliberate about the matter and to submit their composite judgment. If supplies are to be used solely or largely by one teacher or in one classroom, certainly that teacher's judgment regarding the types of materials desired should be given considerable weight.

Budgets for supplementary books and supplies are often divided equally among the teachers of a school in order to provide some assurance of fairness in the distribution of resources. This type of practice undoubtedly tends to simplify the rationing of limited funds and does insure some degree of justice in the allocation of instructional materials. However, such a procedure has its limitations. It is based on the assumption that the needs of all classrooms are the same regardless of grade level, methods of instruction, or particular problems inherent in each group. Generally speaking, there seems to be a need for the establishment of criteria to determine the worthiness of items requested as well as the degree and nature of the need to be met through the acquisition of the supplies. In any case, teachers should be aware of the bases for honoring requisitions and should be informed of the disposition made of their requests as well as the reason for the action taken.

Teachers and staff members should be kept wholly informed regarding the steps necessary for requisitioning supplies, the dates, if any particular ones, when orders are submitted, and any changes that occur in the methods customarily used to secure additional instructional resources and materials. Much can be said also in favor of simplifying as much as possible the forms used for inventory and requisition. In the busy day, a teacher has no time to waste on seeking and recording information that is not essential. It is unfortunate, though too often true, that much of the time of the teacher is taken for the clerical preparation of reports and information that are never used. Such unjustified efforts make no real contribution to the organization and operation of the school and often result in a decline in the morale of faculty members involved.

The selection of textbooks presents a particular problem in many schools, although the legal provisions governing their purchase differ among the various states. Even though there appears to be no genuinely sound educational reason for doing so, many states and school systems place some sort of restrictions on textbook selection by local schools or by individual teachers. This is done frequently through the action of a textbook commission or committee which selects a list of approved books from which local schools are permitted to choose. These ultimate choices at the local level are best made when there is a high degree of participation among staff members and when a systematic study of school needs and book characteristics is conducted in an analytical and deliberate manner.

Several considerations are fundamental in the selection of textbooks for a school. In the first place, the trend toward the supplanting of a single textbook with many books of different authors and types requires careful study regarding the contributions which are expected from each of several books selected. In some fields, however, such as reading, it is desirable to provide for the sequential development of the many facets of reading skill. This appears to be best done through the use of some particular basic reading materials which have been developed in systematic fashion for such use. In such cases, it is advisable to have other supplementary reading materials available to lend scope and variety to the program.

Two dimensions must be recognized when books are being provided for any particular classroom in the modern elementary school. First, there must be variety in terms of *interest* and *scope*. It is usually better to provide a few copies of several different books in science or social studies than to place a copy of the same book at the disposal of each child in the group. In the second place, there must be a variety in terms of *difficulty*. It is a good practice to attempt to provide reading materials at as many different levels as are represented by the reading abilities of the individual children in the group.

The Distribution and Utilization of Supplies.—The purchase of varied and generous instructional materials for a school is in itself no guarantee that they will be utilized effectively. Proper provisions have to be made for storage, distribution, and use. In making such provisions due consideration should be given to simplicity of administration and easy accessibility. It is standard practice to provide a central supply room, often as a part of the office suite. This simplifies accounting for and continuous checking of available supplies. It also eliminates the necessity for utilizing valuable classroom space for storing future stocks of supplies for the group. If such a plan is to work well, however, the process of obtaining materials from the supply room must be direct and simple and free of unnecessary red tape. For the sake of maintaining a continuing inventory and of estimating needs, it is customary in such situations for a teacher to indicate on a simple form the nature and amount of supplies taken from the central stock. This form is then filed in some designated place.

The sharing of equipment and facilities can work well only if the staff plans and agrees upon effective means for equitable distribution. This often applies to audio-visual equipment and other facilities not in continuous use in any one classroom. It is sometimes necessary to share certain supplementary and reference materials such as maps, globes, and books. The chief objective in working out means for joint use of facilities should be to get maximum use of them without jeopardizing the quality of the learning experiences planned and carried out in each classroom.

Simple administrative provisions should be made for the easy transfer of supplementary book collections from the school library to a particular classroom where they are to be used in connection with the development of special projects or units of study. Such a scheme enriches the resources of individual classrooms and, at the same time, precludes the necessity for undue duplication of materials.

ACTION SUGGESTIONS FOR THE PRINCIPAL

1. Think of the school plant as a *school home*.

2. Keep a continuing census of children of preschool age so that future plant needs can be anticipated clearly and accurately.

3. Read regular issues of professional journals in school administration to help keep abreast of modern developments in buildings and equipment; plan staff discussions of stimulating articles.

4. When planning educational quarters, begin with the functions they are to serve and then seek to design them according to need.

5. Work with the staff toward a common understanding of the relationship between teaching methods and the nature and amount of building space.

6. Seek ways to make children, staff, and parents proud of the school plant.

7. Seek to employ, or recommend for employment, the best possible custodial force; avoid the false economy of limited or inefficient custodians.

8. Help develop a sense of pride and responsibility on the part of custodians by giving them opportunities to understand and contribute to school policies, particularly with respect to building care and use.

9. Both in planning and in use, try to adapt the building and classrooms to the activities of children.

10. If possible, set aside a room where parents may assemble to study or work.

11. Involve all members of the staff in planning building or remodeling projects.

12. Work as far as possible toward making each classroom a self-contained unit with facilities for all types of curricular activities.

13. Try to promote the community school concept which envisions the school as a community center but develop simple but systematic policies for plant use.

14. Make flexibility of use a keynote for school building design and construction.

15. Plan the school plant in such a way that functional expansion can be achieved economically.

16. Try to incorporate the same features for good living in the school as are found in a good home.

17. Be sure that frequent checks are made to insure as complete safety as possible in the school and on the playground.

18. Encourage teachers and children to exercise initiative in planning, arranging, and using facilities of their own classrooms.

19. Develop a positive and pleasant atmosphere in the school office.

20. Keep the school office easily accessible to visitors and to school personnel.

21. Work for wide use of school facilities and supplies but attempt to develop a sense of intelligent thrift on the part of those who use them.

22. In the educational utilization of the school plant and facilities place human values above the concern for material things.

23. Work for "livability" in the school but encourage staff and children to exercise reasonable standards of good housekeeping.

24. When equipment and supplies are selected, involve persons who use them in the selection process.

25. Furnish simple and clear instructions regarding the requisition and distribution of supplies—especially for the benefit of teachers new to the school.

SELECTED REFERENCES FOR EXTENDED READING

ADAMS, HAROLD P., and DICKEY, FRANK G. *Basic Principles of Supervision.* New York: American Book Co., 1953, chap. 10.

AMERICAN ASSOCIATION OF SCHOOL ADMINISTRATORS. *American School Buildings: Twenty-Seventh Yearbook.* Washington, D. C.: The Association, 1949.

CHAMBERLAIN, LEO M., and KINDRED, LESLIE W. *The Teacher and School Organization.* New York: Prentice-Hall, Inc., 1949, chap. 16.

DEPARTMENT OF ELEMENTARY SCHOOL PRINCIPALS. *Bases for Effective Learning: Thirty-First Yearbook.* Washington, D. C.: National Education Association, 1952, chap. 8.

ELSBREE, WILLARD S., and MCNALLY, HAROLD J. *Elementary School Administration and Supervision.* New York: American Book Co., 1951, chaps. 21, 22, and 23.

ENGELHART, N. L., ENGELHART, N. L., JR., and LEGGETT, STANTON. *Planning Elementary School Buildings.* New York: Dodge & Co., 1953.

JACOBSON, PAUL B., REAVIS, WILLIAM C., and LOGSDON, JAMES D. *Duties of School Principals.* New York: Prentice-Hall, Inc., 1950, chap. 21.

MCNERNEY, CHESTER T. *Educational Supervision.* New York: McGraw-Hill Book Co., Inc., 1951, chap. 11.

NATIONAL SOCIETY FOR THE STUDY OF EDUCATION. *The Community School: Fifty-Second Yearbook,* Part II. Chicago: University of Chicago Press, 1952, chap. 9.

OTTO, HENRY J. *Elementary School Organization and Administration.* New York: Appleton-Century-Crofts, Inc., 1954, chap. 15.

REAVIS, WILLIAM C., PIERCE, PAUL R., STULLKEN, EDWARD H., and SMITH, BERTRAND L. *Administering the Elementary School.* New York: Prentice-Hall, Inc., 1953, chaps. 15, 16.

SHANE, HAROLD G., and YAUCH, WILBUR A. *Creative School Administration.* New York: Henry Holt & Co., 1954, chap. 15.

TAYLOR, JAMES L., and HERRINGTON, JACK D. *Designing Elementary Classrooms.* Publication No. 1, Department of Health, Education, and Welfare. Washington, D. C.: U. S. Office of Education, 1953.

WILSON, G. T. "School Buildings and Equipment to Serve Modern Educational Needs," *American School Board Journal.* CXV (August, 1947), 40-41.

Chapter 8

IMPROVING THE EFFECTIVENESS
OF THE SCHOOL STAFF

Every true teacher is a merchant of success

The most vital element of a good school program is a competent staff. The quality of the learning experiences which the school provides cannot rise above the individual and corporate competencies of members of the professional team of the school. Although physical facilities exert a very important influence on the level of quality at which a school operates, the lifeblood of the program is derived from the character, imagination, technical competence, and efforts of the teachers who daily conduct the instructional affairs of the school.

Teachers in the elementary schools of today are generally much more competent than in previous periods of our history. With the gradual professionalization of teachers, the position has acquired increasing prestige and has moved toward salary standards comparable with those of other vocational groups. As a result, the teaching profession increasingly is attracting competent and interested young people. The development of teacher education programs in colleges and universities based on the thorough study of the psychology of learning, child development, and modern methodology of teaching has been a very significant factor in the improvement of teachers. This professional work is usually merged with a comprehensive program of general education to provide a well-rounded higher education for prospective teachers during their years in college.

Many different factors determine the competency of a teacher in his position. His own personality and interests have a strong bearing on the outcomes of his teaching. The nature and quality of his preservice professional preparation are vital to his success, as are also the opportunities that are provided for continuing his personal and professional growth in service. In addition, the appropriateness of his particular assignment may go far in determining his success on the job.

This chapter explores some of the pertinent aspects of the problem of developing an effective corps of teachers and other staff members in order that the greatest possible benefits may be derived from the school program. It is evident that an intelligent approach to this problem involves the discovery and recognition of basic principles governing the improvement of teaching effectiveness, the identification and selection of potentially competent staff members, and the wise utilization of instruments and channels through which improvement may be expected. These aspects of the problem, along with some of their ramifications, are discussed in the following pages of the chapter.

Some Basic Principles Underlying Staff Improvement

The serious study of teaching competencies almost invariably points to certain basic considerations that must be recognized and understood if one is to attack the problem of professional improvement. Some of these premises, at least by implication, also suggest points of departure that may be expected to lead to positive results in the effort to improve one's efficiency or to assist others in improvement. A few of these considerations are included here in some detail.

1. *The professional effectiveness of a teacher is related directly to his own personal character and resources.* There is little, if any, scientific support for the old saying that "teachers are born rather than made." Yet it must be readily admitted that all persons cannot and should not attempt to become teachers. One of the historical deterrents to good education for children has been the prevalence among laymen of the idea that all that is necessary for teaching is "to know more than the kids." Unusually discouraging has been the marked persistence of this notion with reference to kindergarten and primary teachers. Many unenlightened people have insisted that such teaching assignments require little professional preparation. This is, of course, a wholly fallacious opinion, and it is fortunate that our citizenry are growing in their recognition of, respect for, and insistence on professionally qualified teachers to guide the lives of their children.

It is difficult to overestimate the importance of the professional preparation of teachers. Yet, unless a person has the personal qualities and potentiality necessary for teaching, a thorough program of teacher preparation alone will not guarantee success for him. Basically, then, the first factor to consider in analyzing the reasons for success, or lack of it, is the nature and personality of the person himself.

Successful teaching usually requires more than average general ability. While exceptions can always be cited, genuinely competent teachers are usually persons of high average or superior intelligence.

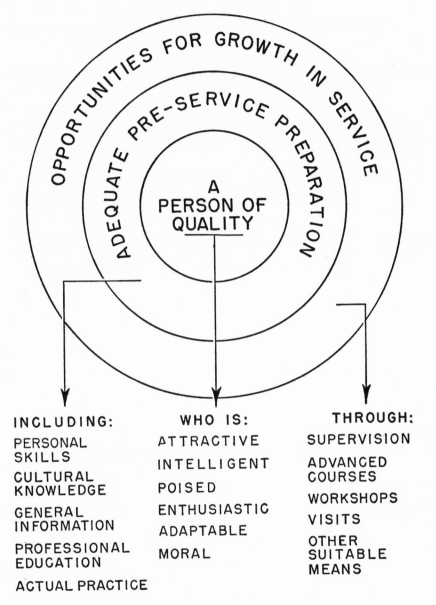

Figure 8

Some Basic Factors in Teaching Competence

A relatively high level of intellectual ability and social sensitivity is an essential resource of the competent teacher in the job of educating children. In this connection, it must be remembered that a teacher's effectiveness is dependent, to a considerable degree, on his cooperation and interaction with other adult members of the school community. This demands that he be able to earn the respect of other professional, business, and community leaders. A teacher with less than adequate intellectual strength cannot be expected to assume a comfortable and productive role in community relations.

The personal attractiveness and poise of a teacher are vital attributes related to his success. This is not intended to imply that only potential beauty contest winners can expect to be or become competent teachers. It is intended to suggest that, since teaching is a social process involving the interacting effects of one person on another, the person who is equipped through appearance and mode of behavior to affect others in a pleasing manner possesses one of the primary characteristics for successful teaching.

A rich personal life, full of the varied interests and pursuits that our modern age affords, is an excellent resource for those who wish to enrich the lives of others whom they teach. The breadth of a teacher's interest, his sensitivity to life around him, and his knowledge of the contemporary interests of children and youth all make a contribution to the degree of teaching success he can expect to enjoy. It is the teacher who has achieved the art of successful living who can best inspire others in their pursuit of the good life.

The teacher's voice is one of the most useful tools at his command. Its quality and the manner in which it is used go a long way in creating a good social climate for living and learning in the classroom. With the opportunities for speech development now offered in many institutions which prepare teachers, voice quality and effectiveness can be improved immeasurably in teachers and prospective teachers.

Many other components go to make up the galaxy of personal resources necessary for good teaching. One's interest in, and enthusiasm for, other people is a paramount virtue in assuming his role as teacher. His physical and mental vigor and his emotional stability are prime requisites for being the kind of person who achieves success in teaching. All these things can be summed up by suggesting that the first prerequisite for being a splendid teacher is being a *splendid person*.

2. *The professional effectiveness of a teacher is related directly to the nature and quality of his professional preparation for teaching.* All of us have wonderful friends whom we would not trust nor expect to pilot an airplane in which we expected to ride, to extract a tooth for

us, or to repair the television receiver. They may be excellent people who possess in full degree the personal attributes desirable in all these vocations. Our reluctance to allow them to perform such services for us is based solely on the fact that they do not possess the necessary training in these fields to become successful practitioners. The same relationship exists between the personal attributes of a person and his success as a teacher. To succeed he must possess an appropriate background of professional preparation suitable for developing the skills essential to good teaching.

The preparation of a competent teacher for the modern elementary school is made up of several different types of components. It must include the opportunity for a broad understanding of the cultural heritage and environment, the development of the basic educational skills of literacy and critical thinking, the acquisition of sound knowledge of human development and the learning process, and the development of proficiency in the methods of teaching through study and actual laboratory experiences with children in the classroom. The characteristics of some of the more effective programs for preservice education of teachers will be treated in more detail in subsequent sections of this chapter.

It is a mistake to assume that all the necessary competencies for successful teaching can be developed through an exemplary program of teacher education at the preservice level. It is increasingly evident that some of the techniques and understandings can be learned best through experience in the classroom. Even such in-service growth, however, can most effectively be built on a sound background of preservice preparation.

3. *The professional effectiveness of a teacher is related directly to existing opportunities for continuing growth on the job.* As stated above, not all aspects of teaching competence can be completely acquired through a program of preservice preparation for teaching. Both initial and ultimate levels of success enjoyed by a teacher are dependent on the opportunities provided within the teaching situation for continued personal and professional growth. Thoughtfully conceived and graciously executed plans for helping teachers grow on the job are evidences of leadership that pay in educational outcomes as well as in human satisfactions.

Opportunities for in-service growth of teachers may be provided through many different means. The professional library of the school is one way to provide such an opportunity. The encouragement of professional study through summer work, extension courses, and local and regional workshops often leads to constructive results. Travel refreshes the teacher and broadens his information simultaneously. Participation in community activities and enterprises often results in an improved knowledge and appreciation of the social and economic setting in which the school must operate.

In-service growth of teachers is a process that can be stimulated and guided but cannot be forced. In fact, there is some doubt that the best approach to teacher improvement can be made through carefully organized and announced "programs" of in-service training, since it often has a bit too much indoctrination in its process. It is usually better to provide rich opportunities for extending personal and professional interests and resources, encourage staff members to explore them fully, and then give proper recognition to any benefits noticeably derived from the in-service activities. True in-service growth appears to be fully as much a matter of spirit as of structured program.

4. *The professional effectiveness of a teacher is related directly to working conditions and environment.* Inspiring surroundings invariably have a salutary effect on a professional worker. Conversely, it is difficult to develop a sense of challenge toward one's work in a situation that lacks all the elements of stimulation and satisfaction. Morale of teachers is based on feelings of belonging, opportunity for success, and a sense of being appreciated. The effectiveness of a teacher is influenced by the quality and tone of the physical atmosphere surrounding the teaching-learning situation. Restful wall decorations, clean floors, and acoustically treated ceilings all contribute to the quality of teaching and learning that occurs in a classroom or throughout a school building. The freedom a teacher feels in adapting existing facilities to the needs of any particular day or moment is an important factor contributing to his professional morale.

Freedom from unnecessary administrative regulations is another element of teacher improvement on the job. The right to exercise professional initiative and to carry on professional experimentation is fundamental for improvement. While the competent teacher will not expect to operate in isolation from the rest of the school, he should possess considerable freedom and independence in planning and carrying out the activities for his own classroom group. One of the ways a teacher may sense opportunities for improvement is through "trying his wings" on new approaches to the task of organizing learning experiences for the children of his group.

If a teacher is to perform in a competent manner, he must be furnished with the necessary materials for getting his job done well. A teacher should evidence an abundance of ingenuity; but it is too much to expect that he should be able to overcome through sheer adroitness the limitations created by lack of supplies, inadequate books, and unreasonably crowded classrooms. Even the very best teacher cannot demonstrate unusual competence under such conditions.

5. *Positive professional growth is not attained through negative means.* The first step toward increased proficiency is the desire to improve. Such a constructive attitude toward one's own improvement cannot be brought about through negative approaches and techniques. Improvement is not a condition that is to be had through demanding it, or even through financial incentives; it is rather a product of self-motivation operating in a field fertile with opportunities for growth. Criticism directed toward teachers by administrators and supervisors is not likely to bring improvement unless it is offered constructively and in a setting replete with optimum conditions for good human relations and understanding.

Expanding responsibility is more likely to produce improved teaching behavior than is direct help. When a member of the staff is given a responsibility that stretches his professional imagination a bit, it is likely to result in two benefits. In the first place, his selection for the assignment may contribute to his self-respect and self-confidence. In addition, such a responsibility may require exploratory study and systematic thought that will in itself produce numerous secondary benefits as a result of the additional effort.

If growth in teaching effectiveness is to be continuous, it must have the stimulation of periodic evaluation and corresponding recognition for goals achieved or difficulties eliminated. Such credit does not need to be given in any formal way, but in the many casual opportunities that present themselves from day to day as the work of the school is accomplished. Self-evaluation is an essential element of the improvement process. A sense of accomplishment resulting from a critical appraisal of one's activities is a great stimulus to attempts to gain even further proficiency.

The Identification and Selection of Competent Teachers

It is trite to suggest that all teachers are not equally competent. This is true even when they have similar backgrounds of experience and preparation. As a result it is virtually impossible to build a staff all of whose members are individuals of outstanding competence. This difficulty, however, does not negate the desirability of developing an efficient staff who can work together with maximum effectiveness. Some aspects of teacher selection and some accepted criteria for judging teaching competence are presented here.

Three categories of strength should be examined carefully in attempts to identify promising prospective teachers. They are:

1. Personal qualities and resources of the person
2. Nature and amount of general education and professional preparation for teaching
3. Potential for personal and professional growth through experience

These were treated briefly in the preceding pages of this chapter but merit fuller consideration for those who participate in the continuous quest for competent teachers.

Personal Qualities.—The kind of person one is determines to a large degree his fitness for teaching. A teacher needs a wholesome personality, an interest in people and in his surroundings, and the emotional stability essential to good adjustment. The personal attributes of a teacher also sometimes help to determine the age level of the children with whom he might best work. The qualities for guiding very young children in an effective manner may not be identical with those necessary for work with older children or adults.

The whole teaching-learning process is dependent on adequate communication, which lends importance to the quality of speech attained and practiced by the teacher—voice quality, pitch, volume, and modulation. Equally important is clear, correct pronunciation, free from unusual or distracting accents. The teacher should develop a speech consciousness that will prevent his developing mannerisms which affect adversely the effectiveness of his speech. It is essential that the speech of a teacher be pleasant to hear, clear in transmitting its message, and adaptable enough to be adjusted to formal or conversational use with equal effectiveness.

The *personal appearance* of a teacher is important to his success. While some studies[1] suggest that the behavior of a teacher is more important to students than his appearance, their findings do not refute the generally accepted impression that neatness and good grooming are valuable assets to the teacher. The keys to acceptability in appearance are good taste, neatness, and appropriateness. Certainly the appearance and dress of a teacher should reflect the same awareness of refinement and culture that one might expect from any respected professional person in the community.

Another indispensable asset for teaching is *physical vigor*. The task of teaching is strenuous. The intensity of the activities of the elementary school teacher, the continuous nature of these activities, and

---

[1] Robert W. Richey and William Fox, *A Study of Some Opinions of High School Students with Regard to Teachers and Teaching.* Bloomington: Bulletin of the School of Education, Indiana University, XXVII, No. 4, (July, 1951).

the length of the day all combine to demand an unusual amount of physical stamina. A physically weak teacher finds it very difficult to maintain the necessary enthusiasm for children and teaching in the face of the persistent drain on his physical resources.

There is a second reason for the importance of a teacher's physical health. Since one of the avowed purposes of the elementary school is to develop good health habits in children, it is important that the teacher represent, in so far as possible, a pattern of good health.

Closely related to good physical health are *emotional stability and mental health*. The teacher should possess a sense of proportion and value that allows him to discriminate between triviality and importance. He should have developed a degree of adaptability that equips him to adjust to unexpected situations without undue alarm. His day-to-day performance should reflect a mode of operation not given either to unusual aggressiveness or to extreme shyness. He should manage to be self-reflective and self-critical without suffering the pangs of the frustrated perfectionist. He should demonstrate an active alertness to surrounding conditions without developing undue suspicion regarding them or the motives of those responsible for them. The emotionally stable teacher is one who is positively responsive to the demands of living and of teaching.

Other attributes of the competent teacher are *flexibility and resourcefulness*. The day in the life of an elementary school teacher can never be completely anticipated. Unexpected situations always arise. It will be necessary many times to make momentary adjustments in the procedures and activities being carried on. To do this wisely requires a knowledge of alternative plans of action, and ability to develop new plans on the spur of the moment, as well as freedom from rigid and structured methods and patterns of teaching behavior. A sensitivity to the uses that may be made of various school and community resources in teaching stems from a strong personal resourcefulness on the part of the teacher. Such a teacher foresees multiple approaches to a difficulty, should it arise, and judges soundly the best course of action. Teachers possessing this professional and personal maturity are invaluable to a school in its functioning.

The teamwork necessary in the successful operation of a modern elementary school requires an unusual amount of *social sensitivity and competence*. The ability to live and work with others, while desirable for all, is essential to the success of teachers. A teacher cannot teach alone. The learning activities he plans and guides are built upon the efforts of other teachers and, in turn, will be built upon by those to follow. He is daily associated with children, with professional associates, with service employees, with parents, and with casual visitors to the school. In addition, the teacher's contacts in the community often serve as the chief bases for the opinions which detached laymen form regarding the school and its program. All these considerations point up the necessity for the teacher to cultivate wholesome attitudes and techniques in establishing effective working relations with others. The inclination and ability to imagine one's self in the place of another is very useful to the teacher. It helps him adapt himself not only to the ideas of children, but also to the point of view of adults from whom he seeks understanding and support. The kind of cooperation essential to effective school organization is based on social sensitivity and competence in human relations.

The attitude of a teacher toward *responsibility* is another important element of competence. The eagerness with which a teacher assumes his share of routine tasks, the willingness with which he accepts the role of leadership in his special areas of competence, and the extent to which he contributes to group endeavors are all indications of professional responsibility. The truly competent teacher needs little regulation, since he always considers his own activities in the light of the total school concern. To be thoroughly responsible is one of the marks of the successful teacher.

It is impractical to attempt to include here all the personal traits that contribute to teaching success. Aside from the particular attributes discussed above, some of the characteristics which usually have been mentioned in studies of the personal traits of successful teachers are self-control, enthusiasm, honesty, impartiality, forcefulness, and punctuality. From any study of available analyses, it is obvious that there is a relationship between the personality of the teacher and the level of success that is likely to be attained by him.

Nature and Extent of Professional Preparation.—Young people with excellent personal traits and resources do not automatically become competent teachers. They must be trained for the job. Because the task of teaching is so complex and comprehensive, the preparation of a teacher must at once be both broad and specialized. It must be broad in furnishing understanding of the cultural, economic, and political forces which have shaped history and which play upon mankind's current fortunes. At the same time, the teacher, through preparation, must become a specialist in child behavior and in the methods of skillful teaching. The professional preparation of a teacher should include attention to those activities designed to make him a stronger person and, at the same time, provide experiences that will develop his skills as a practitioner in the classroom.

During the relatively short period of its history, teacher education has expanded greatly in its offerings and has involved an increasingly greater number of teachers. The influences of research in psychology and education and the broadening functions of the public school have correspondingly affected the nature of teacher education and have focused attention on its importance.

Considerable variation is found among the states and teacher-educating institutions in the components of the teacher-education program. Investigation in educational institutions and in the public schools indicates certain directions in which teacher-education has been extended and refined. As a result some agreement as to the nature of a good program of teacher education for elementary school teachers appears to be emerging.

Both the certification patterns for elementary school teachers in many states and the programs of institutions ascribe importance to the following aspects of teacher education:

1. General education designed to broaden the prospective teacher's understanding of the historical, sociological, scientific, and aesthetic features of our culture
2. Basic professional courses in philosophy and psychology of education and in human development
3. Professional methods designed to develop proficiency in teaching techniques appropriate to various curricular areas and various age levels
4. Professional laboratory experiences with children in the classroom through observation, participation, and student teaching
5. Elective pursuits through which dominant interests may be developed, weaknesses corrected, or skills improved

Most institutions engaged in preparing teachers for elementary schools give some attention to each of the above areas. They differ somewhat in the proportionate part of the total program devoted to each. There is some division of opinion, for example, as to the relative importance of general education and professional education in the teacher's preparation for his work. Persons working in the liberal arts and humanities are sometimes critical of the importance which they think professional educators attach to courses in the methods of teaching; on the other hand, some professional educators appear to belittle knowledge of subject matter as a requisite for good teaching. Probably extreme positions on either end of this scale are likely to be held by persons not well informed in both general and professional education. Those who have a constructive attitude toward teacher education and who possess knowledge of the contributions that should be made by both subject matter specialists and professional educators are likely to see virtue in both.

General Education.—The elementary school teacher, as an interpreter of our culture, should be well grounded in the major areas of human knowledge and experience. Education has new meaning when it is related to the historical and sociological background of contemporary civilization. A general knowledge of the sciences and literature adds breadth and depth to the resources a teacher brings to the job, aside from the personal enrichment it affords. Similarly, the arts are important to the teacher in developing in children a sensitivity to beauty. These and other academic fields have much to offer to the well-rounded development of a competent teacher. It does not seem necessary, or even desirable, for most teachers to have highly specialized knowledge in particular fields mentioned above; rather a more useful goal is a well-balanced general understanding in several areas. This is particularly true of the elementary school teacher.

General Professional Courses.—The teacher must operate in terms of his understanding of the role of the teacher and the teaching profession, the learning and growth processes, and the characteristic features of the major philosophies of education. Although the patterns through which institutions attempt to meet these needs vary somewhat from one to another, there is considerable similarity in their programs. For instance, a course in the introduction to teaching is common among institutions preparing teachers. Such courses, or activities, are usually devoted to developing in the prospective teacher an understanding of the role of the teacher as it is related to the school, to the community, and to the profession as a whole. One of the functions of such a course is to present a complete overview of teaching suitable for the person taking the initial steps in his preparation to become a teacher.

Required study in the areas of educational psychology and human growth and development is also common among the institutions preparing teachers. These equip the prospective teacher with an understanding of the various stages of growth and what may reasonably be expected from children at the various stages. They also give the teacher technical knowledge of the learning process and how it may be suitably motivated.

Some institutions emphasize heavily the study of the philosophies of education in the pattern of teacher education; others place less stress on it. In either case it should be recognized that it is desirable for a prospective teacher to have sufficient knowledge of the theories of education to serve as a background for his own philosophy of the subject.

It is important for a teacher to have convictions about education along with reasons for having them.

Professional Methodology.—Knowledge and understanding do not completely equip an elementary school teacher for his duties. These must be supplemented and activated by professional skills and techniques. Courses designed to educate teachers in sound methods of teaching are usually referred to as methods courses. Again, institutions do not follow the same pattern in providing courses of this type. Some provide courses that correspond mainly to the major curricular areas of the elementary school program, such as language arts, number experiences, social studies, sciences, and fine arts; others combine the specific areas into broader "method blocks" of a more general nature. At any rate, attention is customarily given to the development of teaching skills in the various fields of the curriculum, to the organization of learning experiences into units of work, and to appropriate means for evaluating pupil achievement.

Professional Laboratory Experiences.—Most modern educators subscribe to the concept of "learning by doing." It is not surprising, then, to find among teacher educators the widespread belief that actual experience with children is a part of a person's preparation for teaching. Problems of classroom management and pupil behavior cannot be understood fully nor studied effectively outside the classroom. For this reason, a considerable emphasis has been placed on "laboratory experiences" in good teacher education programs. Such experiences usually include graduated and differentiated visiting and observation in the classroom, participation in the routines of the classroom, and actual student teaching in which the prospective teacher is given individual responsibility for planning and carrying through learning experiences for children. There has been a trend in recent years toward longer periods of student teaching on a full-time basis. These experiences are arranged in such a manner that the student teacher spends the whole day in an elementary school for several weeks, and in some cases, for a whole semester or more.

Guided Electives.— In many institutions those responsible for teacher education feel that the prospective teacher should be allowed to elect a considerable portion of his program. This seems sensible in the light of the differences existing among students preparing to become teachers. Complete conformity to required patterns of professional preparation seems to be unjustified for many reasons. Many institutions attempt to guide students in planning their programs so that they may use elective work to greatest advantage. They thus may select courses that will help to alleviate specific weaknesses in speech, art, or music, or, on the other hand, use these courses to extend their skills. First aid or camping education is often useful to the prospective teacher. In still other cases, a student may pursue in elective courses a particular interest such as folklore, public affairs, writing, crafts, or sociology. Elective courses, under proper guidance, may fill a genuine need in the preparation of the competent teacher for the modern elementary school.

As in the nature of specific offerings, institutions and states differ also in the proportionate emphasis given each of the above facets of preparation in the various programs and patterns for certification. Typically, in four-year programs of teacher preparation, from one fourth to one third of the total program is given to professional courses and frequently much less is devoted to such courses. The remainder is devoted to courses in general education and liberal arts and to electives chosen by the prospective teacher.

Potentiality as a Factor of Competence.—It has been suggested earlier that the identification of teaching competence involves the personal qualities of the teacher, the nature and extent of professional preparation, and the teacher's potentiality for growth. The last of these does not always seem to get the attention it merits from persons charged with the responsibility for the selection of teachers for the elementary school. It is often recognized that a professional worker cannot remain static in his efficiency. Either he grows through experience or he regresses through boredom, indifference, or frustration. In selecting teachers of promise, then, it is desirable to learn what the prospective teacher thinks about the future. The degree of motivation he possesses, the level of professional aspiration, and the ability to sense his strengths and weaknesses all are symptomatic of the potential professional growth of a young teacher.

The factors which have contributed to the current status of a teacher may also serve as clues to his capacity for growth. The persistence displayed in getting a college education, the reasons for his selection of teaching as a vocation, unusual evidences of independent effort to broaden his educational horizons, and the general tendency to pursue various interests all suggest certain things about the future attitudes and actions of a teacher. Experience is itself a great teacher. If a person has the inclination and the sensitivity to make use of it, he may grow immeasurably during the years devoted to teaching. The really successful teacher is one who is still willing and able to learn.

SOME STATEMENTS OF TEACHING COMPETENCE

As implied throughout the previous discussion, the components of teaching competence are difficult to isolate and measure because of their interrelationships. Genuine competence involves an intermingling of knowledge, attitudes, personal attributes and habits, understandings, and skills into an integrated pattern of behavior.

Several statements have been issued in recent years that attempt to set forth some of the major attitudes and attributes essential to competence in teaching. As an illustration of the competencies felt to be significant in teaching success, there appears below a statement prepared by a group of representatives from teacher-educating institutions and public schools of the State of Indiana :[2]

The competent teacher :

1. Is guided in all his thinking and doing by democratic concepts based upon a profound respect for the dignity of the individual.

2. Maintains himself in a state of maximum efficiency and promotes the health of others.

3. Appreciates fully the relationship to good living of the creative and aesthetic; and comprehends fully the import of the scientific method, and is objective and realistic in his approach to social problems.

4. Has developed his personality for harmonious living with himself and with others.

5. Is conscious of the values in his own and others' cultures, continually re-examines and interprets them in the light of new conditions and experiences; is able to work understandingly with those of other cultural groups.

6. Participates effectively in school and community affairs.

7. Has intellectual vigor; has an inquiring mind; is well informed, and continues to keep abreast of social and economic information; sees the relevancy of knowledge and applies his knowledge to specific situations.

8. Has a continuing mastery of subject matter in a subject area and insight into its basic assumptions; has facility in interpreting content to students in terms of their experiences.

9. Has adequate facility in communications.

10. Has a thorough knowledge of all relevant aspects of human growth and development and uses his knowledge to create and foster appropriate learning situations.

11. Uses the school as one of several agencies for progressive improvement of man.

Another more detailed statement of teaching competencies was issued by the California Council on Teacher Education. While the statement was prepared in an attempt to reduce the functions of student

[2] From Workshop on Teacher Education held at McCormick's Creek State Park, Indiana, November 15-18, 1949.

teaching to behavioral dimensions, it applies equally well to teaching in general. It follows :[3]

THE CALIFORNIA STATEMENT OF TEACHING COMPETENCE

The competent teacher :

1. Provides for the learning of students.
  a) Uses psychological principles of learning.
    (1) Uses effective and continuing motivation.
      (a) Recognizes and makes use of the interest, abilities, and needs of students.
      (b) Uses the experiences of students and draws upon life situations and the interests inherent in subject matter.
    (2) Provides varied learning experiences.
    (3) Uses a variety of teaching procedures, such as discussion, review, etc., effectively.
    (4) Plans cooperatively with students.
  b) Uses principles of child growth and development in learning situations.
    (1) Provides for differentiated activities and assignments to meet the needs and abilities of students.
    (2) Knows the health (mental and physical) status of his students and adapts activities to their needs.
  c) Maintains an atmosphere in the classroom that is conducive to learning and is marked by a sense of balance between freedom and security.
    (1) Maintains an effective working situation.
    (2) Helps students increasingly to assume leadership and responsibility.
    (3) Provides opportunities for students to cooperate and to exercise leadership in the activities of large and small groups.
    (4) Provides opportunity for expression of independent critical thought with emphasis on freedom of expression and open-mindedness.
  d) Plans effectively.
    (1) Aids the students to define worth-while objectives for large units, daily class work, and special class activities.
    (2) Organizes his teaching well by choosing wisely learning experiences, subject matter content, and materials of instruction.
    (3) Selects and uses a wide variety of materials of instruction (e.g., books, pamphlets, films, bulletin boards, flat pictures, radios, recordings, etc.).
    (4) Uses resources of the school library and the community.
  e) Uses varied teaching procedures.
    (1) Uses teaching procedures (such as group reporting, discussion, planning with pupils) designed to achieve desired purposes in teaching.
    (2) Builds effectively upon the students' participation in class activities.
    (3) Develops study skills of students.

[3] *The Evaluation of Student Teaching*, Twenty-Eighth Annual Yearbook (Lock Haven, Pa.: The Association for Student Teaching, State Teachers College, 1949) pp. 7-11.

(4) Stimulates creative activities of students.

(5) Aids the students to evaluate their own achievements.

f) Uses diagnostic and remedial procedures effectively.

(1) Is familiar with common diagnostic tests in his own and related fields.

(2) Constructs, administers, and interprets diagnostic tests.

(3) Uses other appropriate diagnostic procedures.

(4) Plans and uses remedial procedures.

g) Uses adequate procedures for evaluating the achievement of students.

(1) Uses informal evaluation procedures (anecdotal record, interview, questionnaire) for collecting and interpreting needed information.

(2) Uses standard achievement tests.

(a) Is familiar with the more common ones in his field.

(b) Selects, administers, and interprets the results of tests and uses them in planning.

(3) Uses teacher-made tests.

(a) Constructs appropriate tests skillfully.

(b) Interprets the results and uses them in planning.

(4) Keeps accurate and adequate records, e.g., case studies, cumulative records.

(5) Makes effective reports to students and parents concerning the progress of students in their growth.

h) Manages the class effectively.

(1) Plans satisfactory routine for the handling of materials, equipment, and supplies.

(2) Uses own and pupils' time effectively.

(3) Is attentive to the physical well-being of students in such matters as hearing, lighting, ventilation, and seating.

2. Counsels and guides students wisely.

a) Uses sound psychological principles concerning the growth and development of children in guiding individuals and groups.

(1) Maintains objectivity when dealing with behavior that is aggressive and abnormal.

(2) Is sympatheic with and sensitive to students' personal and social problems as well as their academic needs.

(3) Makes adjustments in the curriculum and other requirements in the light of pupils' needs.

(4) Secures sufficient rapport with students so that they come voluntarily for counsel.

b) Maintains effective relationships with parents.

(1) Explains the needs, abilities, interests, and problems of the students to their parents.

(2) Obtains cooperation from parents in helping students with their problems.

c) Collects and uses significant counseling data.

(1) Administers aptitude and intelligence tests.

(2) Interprets the results of such tests.

(3) Uses results collected in counseling with students.

(4) Keeps research suitable for guidance.

d) Uses suitable counseling procedures.

e) Maintains appropriate relations with guidance specialists, recognizing their role, and the limitations of his own skill and ability.

3. Aids students to understand and appreciate our cultural heritage.

a) Organizes the classroom for effective democratic living.

b) Directs individuals and groups to significant life applications of classroom learnings.

(1) Uses subject fields to develop understanding of social, economic, and political problems.

(2) Develops an understanding of the wide significance of various fields of subject matter.

c) Draws on his own background of experience to elicit the cultural growth of individuals and groups.

d) Helps students to know and to apply in their daily lives the democratic principles which are rooted deep in our historical development.

4. Participates effectively in the activities of the school.

a) Plans cooperatively the means of achieving educational objectives.

(1) Shares effectively in curricular revision and is able to evaluate progress toward attaining education objectives.

(a) Defines objectives clearly.

(b) Collects data efficiently and draws appropriate conclusions from them.

(c) Employs appropriate remedial procedures.

(2) Shows flexibility in modifying his plans and procedures to fit with those of the entire school.

b) Assumes his share of the responsibility for school activities.

(1) Carries out effectively the administrative responsibilities delegated to him.

(2) Participates in planning and administering extracurricular activities.

c) Maintains harmonious personal relations with his colleagues.

5. Assists in maintaining good relations between the school and the rest of the community.

a) Acquaints himself with available community resources and uses them in classroom activities.

b) Obtains the cooperation of parents in school activities.

c) Aids in defining and solving community problems.

(1) Helps in defining community problems and in developing awareness of them in students and parents.

(2) Draws on available and appropriate resources within the school in attacking community problems.

d) Takes part in community affairs and projects.

e) Observes professional ethics in discussing school problems particularly with lay persons.

6. Works on a professional level.
   a) Gives evidence of the social importance of the profession to parents, students, and other members of the professions.
   b) Adheres to a professional code of ethics.
   c) Contributes to the profession by membership in professional organizations and participation in their activities.
   d) Assumes responsibility for his own professional growth by planning an appropriate program for professional betterment.
      (1) Continues professional study through courses, lectures, institutes, professional reading, and other activities.
   e) Aids in supervising student teachers and in the orientation and induction of beginning teachers.

Providing Opportunities for Growth in Service

Most educators now recognize that the development of teaching proficiency is a process that extends beyond the preservice period and into the years of actual employment as a teacher. Such a process begins with the orientation of the new teacher on the job and continues throughout the years of his service. It involves conscious planning and numerous individual and group techniques. A genuinely valuable in-service program involves the voluntary participation of teachers, supervisors, administrators, and representatives from the community.

Teachers should not only bring a commendable attitude and a strong background of preservice to the teaching job but should continue to grow in many aspects of competence. A list of some of these might be expected to include growth in such things as:

Understanding of the learning process
Ability to measure and evaluate growth in children
Utilization of an ever widening field of resources for teaching
Individualizing of the learning experiences of children
Grouping of children for effective instruction
Enlisting and using community resources and agencies
Classroom management and organization
Guidance of children in grouping processes
Establishing good human relations within and without the school
Interpretation of the educational program
Sensing needs and opportunities for further growth

The conscious efforts exerted within a school to provide the setting, encouragement, and means for teachers to grow on the job are usually considered to be the in-service education program of the school. Some of the approaches through which this program may operate will be discussed in some detail in the following sections.

Characteristics of Effective In-Service Education Programs.—
Certain observations can be made regarding the features which make
in-service education programs produce positive results. These features
of the program in general apply equally well to the various activities
included in the total program. First, it is essential that such a program
be carried into operation on the basis of the needs of the participants.
Some of these needs may be recognized while others may not. Relatively greater motivation is experienced if participants in the program
see that their own felt needs are being considered in the formulation of
in-service opportunities and activities.

In the second place, it is important that in-service education include
many types of opportunities for professional experience and growth.
This means that some attention should be given to organized group
activity at the same time that many opportunities exist for individuals
to work on their own problems and according to their own interests.
It is as foolish to assume that all teachers should experience growth
through the same means as to insist that all children in a classroom
should have identical learning experiences and should be expected to
profit equally from them.

A third consideration in providing in-service growth opportunities
is that much of the planning should be cooperatively done and cooperatively evaluated on as continuous a basis as feasible. Neither the initiation nor the subsequent planning of in-service activities should be considered the sole responsibility of the principal or of any one person on
the staff. The program will be productive to the extent that the involvement of many persons is achieved at the levels of planning, operation, and evaluation. This, of course, does not diminish the responsibility of leadership by those who should be exercising it, as in any
other phase of the school program.

Finally, it should be recognized that an in-service program loses
its effectiveness when participation in it is gained only through coercion. Genuine motivation for an effective in-service education program
comes from the members of the group involved. It cannot be imposed
successfully or even generated from outside the group, without a proper
consideration of the needs of the members of the group.

Orientation of New Teachers.—A useful function of the in-service
program is that designed to orient new members of the staff to the
physical and social environment of the school in which they are to work.
Two types of new teachers are concerned, the inexperienced and the
teacher with experience who is new to the particular school or school
system. The same general considerations apply in each case except that

perhaps the orientation should be somewhat more inclusive in the case of the wholly inexperienced teacher.

There are at least three general ways in which beginning teachers may be helped to succeed on the job: (1) by furnishing them necessary *information* for carrying out their daily responsibilities from the beginning of the school year, (2) by assisting them in their social and professional *integration* into the staff as a full-fledged member with a sense of comfort and belongingness, and (3) by contributing to the *motivation* of new members through early and regular recognition of their efforts and successes. Nothing is as frustrating to a new teacher as being ignored and left uninformed regarding the extent to which he is being accepted or is succeeding as a member of the staff. Many administrative leaders feel that the staff and school as a whole may be stimulated through encouraging, maintaining, and utilizing the enthusiasm of the new teacher as he approaches his job.

Numerous studies have been made which reveal particular ways in which teachers feel they may be assisted in their orientation to the school. Some of these areas of help on which there is rather common agreement are:

1. Knowledge of personnel policies of the school regarding such things as sick leave, arrangement for substitutes, and contractual policies.
2. Understanding the school's philosophy.
3. Interpretation of community conditions and mores.
4. Information regarding routines of the school—attendance, health referrals, reports, supervision schedules, and lunch provisions.
5. Policies governing marking and evaluation in the school.
6. Acquaintance with facilities and the means for securing and utilizing instructional resources.
7. Knowledge of accepted school standards of discipline and the sources of help with pupil problems.
8. Orientation to the staff and to the community.

In discussing the characteristics of effective orientation programs Weber[4] has suggested nine essential features which should govern such a program:

1. The orientation program should be based upon purposes which are developed in advance and which are understood by all those concerned with carrying out the plans.
2. The orientation program should be timely; that is, it should give new teachers help at the time it is needed, not three weeks late or three weeks too early.

4 Clarence A. Weber, *Personnel Problems of School Administrators* (New York: McGraw-Hill Book Co., Inc., 1954), p. 61. By permission of the publisher.

3. The orientation program should be authoritative and accurate. Information presented should be accurate information.

4. The orientation program should be sufficiently comprehensive to ensure that the new teacher has seen the basic structure of the school and the community, the basic philosophy of the school in the community, and the essential elements of the administrative machinery.

5. The orientation program should be carried out by all large segments of the people concerned with the welfare of the new teacher.

6. There should be periodic evaluations of the orientation program to discover weaknesses and strengths.

7. The professional personnel of the schools should take the initiative in developing an orientation program.

8. The orientation program should have the full support of the board of education.

9. The orientation program should be the product of cooperative thinking and planning of the entire professional staff.

Consideration of Teachers' Problems.—Both experienced and inexperienced teachers have problems to face in the day-to-day discharge of their responsibilities. The manner in which these problems are looked upon by the principal is a factor in the morale of teachers. Even more important is the manner in which the teacher is assisted in meeting his problems.

A five-point program is suggested in a recent article by Stottler[5] for the establishment of a good human relations program in dealing with the problems of teachers. His suggestions are: (1) Let each teacher know what is expected of him; (2) give the teacher credit where credit is due; (3) tell teachers in advance about changes which affect them; (4) make the best of each teacher's ability; (5) treat teachers as individuals.

Sometimes very minor occurrences or adjustments create problem situations among members of the staff. Rumors regarding staff changes, rotation of assignments, or adjustments in the school calendar are good examples of conditions which create unrest among teachers. Apparent inequality in teaching load or lack of teacher representation on decision-making groups is often responsible for morale problems. As in the case of most of life's problems, a bit of prevention is much more valuable than a lot of cure. The creation of a working atmosphere and working relations that are friendly, yet straightforward, does much toward eliminating the conditions for conflict and misunderstanding which sometimes occur. A group in which each member has status and in which each member can trust his fellows is relatively free from the

[5] Richard H. Stottler, "Human Relations in School Administration," *School and College Management*, XX, No. 8 (March, 1951), 19.

kind of situation which breeds problems in human relations. It is a good policy to grant each member of a staff the luxury of an occasional mistake without the accompanying feeling that he must fear being penalized for making it.

Development and Practice of Good Human Relations.—Professional relations and their development will be treated in detail in a later chapter of this book. However, it seems appropriate to mention here that genuine growth on the part of teachers can be fostered only in an atmosphere of pleasant human relations. Real professional growth is so dependent on cooperative group action and participation that it is difficult to see how it can be expected to abound in a situation dominated by rugged and ruthless individualism, devoid of common courtesy and mutual consideration among staff members. A congenial atmosphere is one of the greatest guarantees of effective working relations.

The tone and quality of human relations existing in any school are set by the attitudes of the administrative leader. If he is dictatorial, suspicious of his fellows, eager to grab credit for all commendable activities of the school, or generally disagreeable in his contacts with associates, he cannot expect the level of interaction among staff members to rise above his example. On the other hand, if he is genial, though businesslike, with a genuine liking for and interest in people, he very likely will set a standard of human relations that will be widely adopted among teachers and even among the children who attend the school.

Effective human relations demand a positive attitude in all the activities of the school. If teachers and principal are positive in their approach to parents they are much more likely to enlist a deserved degree of cooperation and support. Even progress reports which emphasize the growth and strengths of pupils tend to promote good relations between school and home to a far greater extent than reports which are consistently negative in tone. The same is true of principal-teacher relationships in the school. If each can make it habitual to look for the best in the other, an atmosphere will be established that will permit real growth of all concerned.

Continuous Opportunities for In-Service Growth.—The in-service growth of teachers is not a thing which flourishes for a time, then dies. The ideal in-service program is a set of related and continuous opportunities. As stated before, some must be individual while others are related to the group activities of the staff. Some may be initiated at the administrative level while others originate with members of the staff themselves.

The *faculty meeting* may meet a real in-service need if it is a *faculty* meeting rather than the *principal's* meeting. If meetings of the staff are to be used solely for administrative announcements or directives, there is little justification for meeting together. There are briefer means for the transmission of one-way messages. If, however, interaction and exchange of ideas are encouraged and needed, it seems necessary and desirable to meet together as a group. Many administrators are finding that teachers are much more highly motivated toward faculty meetings if they participate freely in them and have frequent opportunities for bringing ideas to the attention of the group. Productive faculty meetings are more likely to occur when they are used for group discussion of mutual problems and their possible solutions. Teachers often have the opportunity to grow through participation in stimulating faculty meetings for which they must assume some responsibility.

POINTERS FOR FACULTY MEETINGS

Some pointers for faculty meetings are :[6]

1. All the persons affected by a decision should have some part in that decision.

2. Decisions and policy based upon group action are superior to the decisions of one or two individuals.

3. Leadership defined by function and service rendered is more realistic and useful than the concept that leadership resides only in status.

4. Decisions made by a group are more frequently put into action than decisions made without the support and commitment within the group.

5. The group serves as a standard-setter. A consciously interactive and participative group possesses great strength in the matter of standard-setting.

6. It is generally accepted that some basic changes in curriculum and school organization are necessary to meet the demands of the present world. An understanding of the basis for change and the re-statement of goals necessary to change may be accomplished best through group action.

7. The participative group supports its members in their changed ways of thinking and doing.

8. A cohesive group has a superior chance to meet frustration and adversity with decreased damage to itself.

When the implications of group life are understood, the traditional faculty meeting is as outmoded as the maintenance of thousands of blacksmith shops. The need is for a working group with a problem-solving, policy-making function, a group that recognizes the cooperative nature of the teaching job. It is encouraging that it is possible for any group to learn the skills and acquire the attitudes necessary to becoming a truly productive group. The rewards for membership in such a group are very great.

[6] From contribution of Marie M. Hughes to "Pointers for Faculty Meetings," *National Elementary Principal*, XXXIII, No. 4 (February, 1954), 18-20.

Study groups within the staff often contribute to harmonious efforts and to the sharpening of professional insights of individual teachers. Often primary teachers get together regularly to compare notes and to exchange ideas. In a similar way, teachers of older children may wish to pool their resources and ideas in discussing their common problems. Such specific study groups have great possibilities for contributing to the teacher's growth on the job.

Some schools have found that teachers' *workshops* are beneficial in fostering increased understanding among teachers. Both the process and the products of such workshops have a salutary effect on the professional efficiency of teachers. Teachers gain much from working together on common problems and from the give-and-take of the group processes involved. In addition, greater insight into the problems studied can result from the intensive attention given to them by the members participating in the workshop. Curriculum improvement is now being approached in many schools through local workshops in which teachers, usually with the help of one or more outside consultants, work on their own curriculum and instruction problems. The workshop is being used extensively also during the pre-opening activities of the school year.

Most colleges and universities offer *extension courses, summer workshops and courses,* and *in-service seminars* designed primarily for the teacher in service. Full utilization of these opportunities is another way in which teachers may work on the continuous upgrading of professional understanding and proficiency.

Travel and *independent study* often make a real contribution to the personal and professional well-being of the teacher. The intellectual effect of such activities is reflected in the performance and attitudes of the teacher. Many school systems encourage this activity for their teachers, and institutions of higher learning frequently allow a nominal amount of credit for well planned experiences of this sort.

Another way teachers may improve professionally is through *classroom experimentation,* either of the controlled or action-research types. Creative approaches to teaching carried into action often benefit both the teacher and the children for whom he is responsible. The teacher always in search of better ways of teaching is very likely to be a growing teacher. The administrator can favor both the teacher and the school by encouraging the spirit of experimentation in the school.

Teacher Participation in Policy Development.—Teachers grow in their understanding of the school through opportunities to study its problems and determine its policies. Through such participation in developing policies to govern the activities of the school, teachers come to know and appreciate the relationship which exists between their own individual responsibilities and the total operation and well-being of the school as a whole. They also become much more familiar with the various elements of the school program through the increased perspective which such participation gives them. As a further result of teacher participation in policy development, certain previously undiscovered strengths of individual teachers may reveal themselves. It is often surprising to discover the composite wisdom and strength of a group when their experiences are pooled effectively for their mutual welfare and that of the school.

Growth Through Administrative Adjustments.—Sometimes growth can be gained through administrative adjustments in the assignments of teachers. A teacher may profit from the opportunity to be relieved from his regular duties to carry out a special project for the school. Likewise, a teacher who has taught at the same age level for many years, and indeed other teachers, may gain a great deal from working with a group of another age, or by assuming responsibility for the same group through a two- or three-year cycle. For such approaches to be productive, they must be free from coercion and administered in such a way that the teacher involved is not given a sense of failure in the process.

ACTION SUGGESTIONS FOR THE PRINCIPAL

1. Treat teachers as professional associates rather than subordinates.
2. Keep alert to opportunities for building the morale of teachers.
3. Include teachers in cooperative policy decisions.
4. Avoid encroaching on the personal lives of teachers.
5. Encourage teachers to develop broad and wholesome interests outside of school.
6. Ask teachers to share suggestions or information about good books they read.
7. Help teachers locate sources of varied instructional materials.
8. Rotate responsibilities for planning and conducting faculty meetings.
9. Show some interest in the activities, achievements, and problems of individual teachers.
10. Keep before teachers the evidence which shows the value of increased professional education.
11. Offer incentives for improvement and give credit for it.
12. Start in-service study programs with problems of interest to teachers.
13. Avoid forced attendance at in-service meetings of the staff.
14. Consider it one of the basic responsibilities of the principal to help each teacher become successful.

15. Provide working conditions that foster good mental health.

16. Recognize that teachers, as well as children, have the right to be different one from another.

17. Try to capitalize on the special interests and talents of teachers in the operation of the school program.

18. Demonstrate a genuine faith in members of the staff.

19. Encourage teachers to cooperate with teacher-educating institutions by working with student teachers.

20. Encourage teachers to do experimental teaching.

21. Plan occasional, informal "sharing sessions" at which teachers present particular devices or methods which have contributed to successful teaching.

22. Confer with teachers well in advance of any anticipated change in their teaching assignments.

23. Comment occasionally on the attractiveness and good taste of teachers.

24. Plan a professional library with and for teachers.

25. Encourage teachers to visit other teachers and other schools periodically.

26. Induct new teachers gradually into the operational activities of the school and be sure such teachers have definite instructions regarding the schedule and nature of their responsibilities.

27. Make faculty meetings pleasant affairs.

28. Always let teachers know in advance why they are called together for a meeting or group conference.

29. Keep informed as to existing opportunities for teacher improvement through study at neighboring colleges or universities.

30. Keep teachers informed about possible sources of help with particular problems.

31. Never let teachers forget the importance of their work; help them become true "salesmen of success."

SELECTED REFERENCES FOR EXTENDED READING

ADAMS, HAROLD P., and DICKEY, FRANK G. *Basic Principles of Supervision.* New York: American Book Co., 1953.

ASSOCIATION FOR SUPERVISION AND CURRICULUM DEVELOPMENT. *Group Processes in Education.* Washington, D. C.: National Education Association, 1945.

AYER, FRED C. *Fundamentals of Instructional Supervision.* New York: Harper & Bros., 1954.

BROWNELL, SAMUEL M. "Importance of Prepared Teachers for the Schools of America," *Educational Outlook,* XXVIII (May, 1954), 149-53.

DEPARTMENT OF ELEMENTARY SCHOOL PRINCIPALS. *Bases for Effective Learning. Thirty-First Yearbook.* Washington, D. C.: National Education Association, 1952, chap. 5.

ELSBREE, WILLARD S., and McNALLY, HAROLD J. *Elementary School Administration and Supervision.* New York: American Book Co., 1951, chaps. 26 and 27.

ELSBREE, WILLARD S., and REUTTER, E. EDMUND, JR. *Staff Personnel in the Public Schools.* New York: Prentice-Hall, Inc., 1954, chap. 9.

GOODLAD, JOHN I. "Some Frontier Issues in Educating Elementary School Teachers," *Elementary School Journal,* LIV (November, 1953), 139-44.

McNerney, Chester T. *Educational Supervision*. New York: McGraw-Hill Book Co., Inc., 1951, chaps. 12 and 13.

Mehl, Marie A., Mills, Hubert H., and Douglass, Harl R. *Teaching in Elementary School*. New York: The Ronald Press Co., 1950, chaps. 23 and 24.

Prall, Charles E., and Cushman, Leslie C. *Teacher Education in Service*. Washington, D. C.: Commission on Teacher Education of the American Council on Education, 1944.

Reavis, William C., Pierce, Paul R., Stullken, Edward H., and Smith, Bertrand L. *Administering the Elementary School*. New York: Prentice-Hall, Inc., 1953, chap. 27.

Reeder, Edwin H. *Supervision in the Elementary School*. Boston: Houghton-Mifflin Co., 1953.

Shane, Harold G., and McSwain, E. T. *Evaluation and the Elementary Curriculum*. New York: Henry Holt & Co., 1951, chaps. 13 and 14.

Shane, Harold G., and Yauch, Wilbur A. *Creative School Administration*. New York: Henry Holt & Co., 1954, chap. 4.

Spears, Harold. *Improving the Supervision of Instruction*. New York: Prentice-Hall, Inc., 1953, chaps. 17 and 18.

Weber, Clarence A. *Personnel Problems of School Administrators*. New York: McGraw-Hill Book Co., Inc., 1954, chaps. 4 and 5.

Wiles, Kimball. *Supervision for Better Schools*. New York: Prentice-Hall, Inc., 1950.

Witty, Paul. "In-Service Growth of Teachers Through Cooperative Programs," *Forty-Eighth Yearbook of the National Society for the Study of Education*, Part II, *Reading in the Elementary School*. Chicago: University of Chicago Press, 1949.

Yauch, Wilbur. *Improving Human Relations in School Administration*. New York: Harper & Bros., 1949.

Yeager, William A. *Administration and the Teacher*. New York: Harper & Bros., 1954, chaps. 12, 13, and 14.

Chapter 9

GROUPING CHILDREN FOR EFFECTIVE
LIVING AND LEARNING

*In an ideal group everyone gains without the necessity for
anyone losing*

Grouping of children in the elementary school is both an administrative expedient and an educational process. The enrollment of approximately 25 million children in the elementary schools of the United States completely precludes the possibility of providing instruction on a strictly individual basis, even if such an arrangement were desirable. Throughout the history of schools in this country, as school populations have expanded, it has become increasingly necessary to explore possibilities for the grouping of learners. In the earlier periods of our history, the grouping was done largely on a school basis, some children attending one type of school and others attending an entirely different kind of school, largely in terms of anticipated vocational pursuits. The graded system, on a vertical basis, was another manner of grouping children for instruction that has been a persistent feature of schools for many years and still is commonly characteristic of elementary schools. The very fact that the number of school children in this country is so much greater than the number of teachers almost assures that children will continue to have their learning experiences organized on a group basis for some time to come.

The interest of modern educators in grouping, however, goes far beyond the administrative necessities of the situation. Developments in the field of sociology, as well as in psychology, have focused attention on the educational implications of group dynamics as a factor contributing to the social development of children and as a means of sharing experience. The child's first entrance into school at the kindergarten level is marked by concern for the success with which he adjusts to the group of which he is a part. While it is true that much emphasis has been placed on the individual in the learning process in recent years, the development of the individual is only a part of the obligation of education. A desirable program for learners gives appropriate attention to a learner's reactions and contributions to groups of which he is a member, as well as to the effects of such groups on him as an individual. Serious study of the psychological and sociological implications of grouping should be the natural forerunner of the formulation or adoption of any particular plan or plans for organizing children into teaching units.

Two types of grouping occur in the typical elementary school: (1) grouping children into classroom groups which are conducive to good living and to wise economy of effort, and (2) instructional grouping within the classroom for the purpose of facilitating learning. Before discussing these in greater detail, it may be best to examine some of the principles which should guide the organization of educational grouping.

SOME BASIC PRINCIPLES OF EDUCATIONAL GROUPING

Grouping, like most aspects of organization, is not an end in itself. Rather, it is a means whereby progress toward desirable ends may be facilitated. It is reasonable, then, to assume that grouping should always be considered in its relation to other components of the total educational program. It is on the basis of this assumption that certain guiding principles are suggested.

1. *Grouping should be related to purpose.* The writer recalls a visit to a school in which he had the opportunity to observe the work of a teacher at the junior high school level. On that particular occasion, the teacher "taught" for the entire period but there was virtually no activity, and apparently little interest, on the part of the pupils. Yet in a subsequent conversation the teacher complained rather bitterly because her classroom group was relatively large. One got the impression that, unless modification were made in the teaching methods employed, it would have made little difference in the quality of learning if the size of the group had been doubled.

If the purpose to be achieved through grouping is that of providing the best possible situation for the use of effective instructional methods, then groups should be created with such criteria in mind. If, on the other hand, the motivating purpose is to simplify administrative routines, the criteria for the formation of groups may be entirely different. If the social competence of pupils is the dominating goal in a particular situation, then still different considerations may guide the manner in which groups are formed. The first consideration always should be the determination of what is to be expected from dividing children into groups. If no purpose is present, perhaps there is no good reason for the grouping.

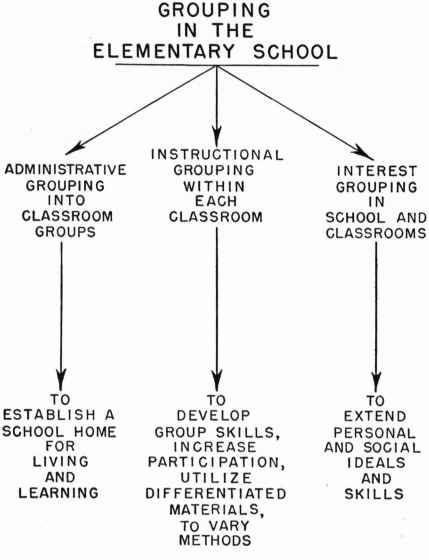

Figure 9

Some Major Aspects of Grouping

2. *Grouping should contribute to improved learning.* The primary justification of any educational device rests on its effect upon learning; this is true in the grouping of children. The assumption underlying the division of large groups into smaller units is that, through such means,

learning improves. Grouping often simplifies the adaptation of methods and materials, facilitates use of instructional resources, increases the participation of pupils, and aids in attempts to individualize and differentiate instruction. Through such grouping, varied approaches to learning may be utilized to greater effect. Grouping also bears a direct relationship to the development of independence and individual work habits of children.

3. *Grouping should be reasonably flexible.* Strict rigidity in grouping can be as unwholesome as general regimentation. To avoid such unrelenting structure in the elementary school, care should be taken to permit and encourage flexibility of groups. Even in the home room grouping of children, there is little reason to assume that a child must remain in the same group throughout a year or semester if there is some evidence that his learning might proceed more effectively in a different situation. This is even more important for instructional groups within the classroom. Educational purposes seem to be served best in situations where there are provisions for easy transfer from one group to another and for continuous formation of groups in terms of particular educational tasks to be accomplished.

4. *Grouping should be based on multiple factors of growth.* Aside from the predominant purpose for a group's structure, it is necessary also to consider all elements of growth in the formation of learning groups. At the primary levels, for instance, one of the legitimate bases for grouping may be the degree of readiness for reading, but this does not preclude the necessity for considering other factors in grouping. A particularly shy child may need the security that comes from being initially assigned to a group in which he has friends. Throughout various levels of the elementary school, the developing interests and competencies of children become increasingly important factors to be considered in assigning them to groups. The mental health and emotional stability of children are essential elements of growth which cannot be overlooked in setting organization patterns for the classroom and the school. In fact, all possible facets of well-being should be included in setting up the conditions governing the social and intellectual interactions of learners.

5. *Grouping should facilitate effective use and adaptation of facilities and materials in terms of the differing learning rates of children.* A problem of education is provision of means for differentiation of instruction to comply with individual growth rates within the structure of a school organization designed for mass education. One partial solution to the problem is the judicious use of instructional grouping of children. Such an approach permits the adaptive use of instructional

materials in a manner consistent with the needs, interests, and maturity levels of individual pupils. Variety of instructional materials can thus be made available without the necessity for providing all types of materials for all pupils.

6. *Grouping should be natural and realistic.* The groups in which children participate at school should be as life-like and functional as possible and as free from artificiality as it is possible to make them. Children should be urged and encouraged to assume group responsibility in all manners consistent with their levels of maturity. In the main, common interest should be a strong motivating factor in the activities of school groups. This suggests both heterogeneity and flexibility as essential characteristics of effective groups, since most community groups in which people ordinarily participate are neither static nor homogeneous except on the possible basis of mutual interest.

Another aspect of realism in the formation of school groups is the extent to which learners' choices are utilized, or even considered. In adult society, membership in a group ordinarily involves some degree of volition of the participating member, except, perhaps, in the case of the family group. One's eagerness to affiliate with groups in the community is determined by interest, identification with a valued cause, anticipated benefits, and prospects of participation in the affairs of the group. If school groups are to be wholly functional, they must minimize, wherever possible, the extent to which groups are formed in a manner totally arbitrary and which ignores the attitudes and interests of learners.

7. *Grouping should be free from negative effects and stigmas.* As discussed in an earlier chapter of this book, it is not to the discredit of children that each of them is different from all others. It is to the discredit of a school program that penalizes a child because he is different from others racially, culturally, physically, intellectually, or in any other way. It is important, therefore, that the machinery for implementing the instruction of children should not itself contribute to feelings of inferiority and resentment or, on the other hand, to delusions of superiority. One of the justifiable criticisms of homogeneous grouping, or ability grouping as it is sometimes called, is that it categorizes children in a manner that can easily result in an academic caste system. Such results, and the conditions which create them, are not consistent with our dedication to the democratic principle of respecting the feelings and worth of individuals. The manner in which the teacher refers to groups, what they are called, provisions for a flexible and rotating membership, and the extent to which differentiated standards are applied to

the work of groups, all have a direct influence on the eagerness or reluctance with which a child accepts membership in his group.

SOME BASES FOR GROUPING IN SCHOOL

Grouping may be done in terms of several different bases. As indicated above, the reason for grouping may be either administrative or instructional. In any case, children are grouped for some reason or on the basis of some criterion. The main reason for grouping, of course, is to provide a physical, social, and intellectual setting that will be conducive to good learning. Some of the attempts to add to the effectiveness of teaching and learning through grouping procedures have stood the test of time fairly well; others have not proved to be effective in the light of all educational factors involved. A few of the common bases for grouping are discussed in the following paragraphs.

Environmental Bases.—One of the most simple and obvious reasons for grouping is to establish a good learning environment. If ninety children enter the first grade of an elementary school at the beginning of the school year, it is evident that, without further division, such a group is far too unwieldy to constitute a reasonable classroom group. Large groups reduce the opportunity for participation and demand a regimentation in their management that is not in accordance with the kind of self-direction and self-discipline that we hope to develop in children.

Little objective evidence exists regarding the optimum size of classroom groups. Most educators who have studied the matter tend to believe that approximately twenty-five children constitute an effective and workable group. Undoubtedly, the size should vary some with the age level of the children involved, the activities to be emphasized, and the degree to which members of a group are able to do independent work under guidance.

Maturity Bases.—For some purposes it has seemed feasible and desirable to group children for instructional activities on the basis of certain aspects of maturity. At the six-year-old level, for instance, it is obvious that all children who report to school are not equally equipped, intellectually and through experience, to enter into formalized reading activities. It may be desirable, therefore, to group them in terms of intellectual or social maturity. This makes it easier for each group to proceed from the approximate point of development of its members. This is customarily done in the skills areas such as reading, since growth in those areas of the curriculum is sequential in character and it is essential that instruction be organized in such a way that the development rate and status of each child are taken into full account.

Social Bases.—A condition for effective membership in a group is the feeling of social comfort or belongingness. The social relations of members of a group, their reactions to each other, and the mutual bonds of interest and trust they possess, are all invaluable to the effectiveness of the group for educational purposes. Considerable progress has been made in recent years in gathering data regarding the social acceptance of children by other members of their peer groups.

One of the more helpful techniques developed for observing and recording the social appeal children have for each other is *sociometry*. Much of the pioneer work in this field was done by J. L. Moreno, who published a significant book on the subject in 1934.[1] Recent studies have further refined the uses and techniques of sociometry, so that currently it is an educational science contributing a great deal to the understanding of children by teachers who apply it to the problems of grouping in the classroom. One of the rather surprising facts revealed by a recent exhaustive sociometric study is that teachers' estimates of the social acceptance of various children by their peers are notably unreliable.[2] Children just do not respond to each other in the manner expected by teachers.

Sociometry, simply stated, is a technique through which children's choices and preferences regarding their relationships with their associates are sought in connection with some particular situation. (See Chapter 4.) They then are tabulated and transferred to a chart which pictorially depicts these relationships. For example, children may be asked to choose persons with whom they would like to work on a research committee in social studies. These choices are usually limited to three in number. In turn, these choices are tabulated and charted. If such sociometric responses are sought regularly and in terms of various activities, there soon begins to emerge a rather definite picture of the social preferment which children enjoy or lack in the opinion of their fellow pupils.

Interest Bases.—Common interest is the cohesive ingredient that lends unity to a group action. To some extent, it is also the motivating element of a group situation. Both children and adults tend to persist in activities that follow the lines of their major interests. At the same time, they develop continuing and expanding interests in these activities

[1] J. L. Moreno, *Who Shall Survive?* (New York: Beacon House, 1934).
[2] Marion Vere DeVault, *Relationship of Sociometric Status to Selected Factors in Grades One Through Twelve* (Bloomington: Unpublished Doctoral Study, Indiana University, 1953).

as they gain proficiency in them and derive satisfactions from them. These tendencies have a very obvious and direct effect on group opportunities for interaction. The good elementary school will incorporate into its organization the recognition of these facts in two ways: (1) the interests of children will be used, to the extent of reason and effectiveness, in motivating all learning activities of the children at any developmental level of the school program, and (2) there will be occasional opportunities for children to group themselves solely on the basis of common interests and purposes in order to develop group skills while working on constructive activities.

Many of the on-going activities of the school offer opportunities for group work. Committees are often utilized for planning special occasions, such as programs, field days, or an open house for parents. Even in developing broad units in social studies, for instance, there is no reason why children should not be allowed to work on research committees of their own choosing in terms of interest. The organization and operation of the school provide a fertile field for pupil participation. Interested children may assist with traffic and safety through the school patrol. Others may serve on student government groups. Still others may wish to belong to clubs organized around special interests of boys and girls. In fact, there are numerous ways in which pupils may enjoy the opportunity to pursue matters of particular interest and, at the same time, develop wholesome group attitudes and skills. Some of the more common activity groups are discussed in a later part of this chapter.

Age Bases.—Many persons feel that the best way to take maturity into account is to group children on the basis of age. Some insist that mental age, derived from so-called mental ability tests, can best serve as the criterion for dividing children into realistic educational groups; others are equally convinced that chronological age is the most natural and, in terms of all considerations, the most effective basis for such grouping. It seems probable that neither factor alone is a sufficient consideration in the formation and organization of school groups, even though, in many modern elementary schools, considerable emphasis is placed on the desirability of keeping children of the same chronological age together.

Composite Bases.—Since children are complex creatures whose development has many facets, it is unrealistic and psychologically unsound to assume that any single factor can serve effectively as a sole basis for grouping children in such a manner that they live happily and learn well. Therefore, two considerations are important in this aspect of organizing the school program: (1) groups should be formed in terms of the purposes to be served by them, and (2) many factors—physical, social, intellectual, and emotional—should be utilized in the formation of educational groups.

HOMOGENEOUS VS. HETEROGENEOUS GROUPING

Homogeneous grouping attempts to reduce the wide range of differences in children by bringing together, for instructional purposes, children who are somewhat alike in age, in ability, or in background of achievement and experience. Numerous attempts to establish varying degrees of homogeneity have characterized American education for many years.[3] In fact, the graded system adopted by elementary schools is, in essence, an attempt to reduce the diversity of physical and scholastic attributes of the members of school groups. The concept of homogeneity, though incapable of complete implementation in practice, can be useful in meeting some of the instructional purposes to be served in the typical elementary school. For example, at the primary levels of the elementary school, it is common practice to form groups somewhat homogeneous in reading maturity. Similarly, in the later grades, social studies research groups may be selected on the basis of homogeneity of interest. Other groups may be composed of pupils who have similar status in other ways. One can find little objection to such groupings if they remain temporary and flexible in nature.

Unfortunately, homogeneous grouping is often considered synonymous with ability grouping. In reality, these two concepts are quite different. Homogeneous grouping does not preclude the possibility of incorporating the consideration of many factors in the formulation of groups; ability grouping is usually based on a single criterion such as I.Q. or mental age. The narrowness of this criterion causes skepticism of the usefulness and appropriateness of ability grouping as an administrative device, although the research directed toward determining the educational value of ability grouping, as compared with other means, is generally inconclusive.

In general, when the school population is being divided into workable, livable classroom groups, it seems desirable to allow for considerable heterogeneity. Social factors, age, and achievement all seem to be factors to be considered but not to a restrictive degree. On the other hand, when specific purposes are to be achieved within each classroom group, various types of homogeneous grouping undoubtedly have merit.

[3] See Henry J. Otto, *Elementary-School Organization and Administration* (New York: Appleton-Century-Crofts, Inc., 1954), pp. 199-200.

Self-contained Classroom Plan vs. Departmentalization

The school is faced continuously with the problem of trying to provide, on a group basis, for educational growth that is largely individual in character. The fact that children differ so notably in rate of growth, interests, and experiential backgrounds makes it extremely difficult to organize them into administratively convenient groups without violating their individual rights. The situation is further complicated by the fact that bases other than the educational adjustment of children must be considered in dividing a school population into classroom groups. Three prime considerations underlie administrative grouping in a school:

1. How can children be grouped in order to provide for the best possible learning environment for each during his hours spent at school?
2. How can the maximum contributions of teachers be encouraged through the organization of school groups?
3. How can the facilities and resources be best utilized through the manner in which the school is organized?

Recognition of this three-fold problem is one of the factors which have led to various innovations in classification and grouping of pupils in the elementary school. Homogeneous grouping, as mentioned earlier, has been justified on the ground that it makes teaching more effective through reducing the disparity existing among children in the ability to achieve. In this way, it was hoped to improve instruction through this particular type of grouping. Experience and a considerable body of research have created much doubt among educators as to the value of this type of administrative grouping, although, as stated earlier in another connection, certain types of homogeneity are often utilized in temporary groupings within the classroom.

Departmentalization.—One form of organization that has been used typically in the secondary schools and frequently in elementary schools is departmentalization according to subject areas. The defense of this plan has been based largely on the argument that it provides for much greater utilization of a teacher's special strengths, interests, and training. Through such a plan, children are shifted from one teacher to another, throughout the school day, in accordance with curriculum requirements. Although this approach to grouping has never been universal in elementary schools of the country, research has indicated that about half of the schools of the United States have practiced some form of departmentalization during the last decade. One factor which earlier caused schools to move toward departmentalization was the inclusion in the curriculum of so-called special subjects such as music, art, and physical education. Though there is a current trend away from departmentalized forms of organization, many schools still operate a program that is at least partially departmentalized. There are relatively few instances of departmentalized programs at the primary levels of the elementary school and the incidence of such programs increases as the age level of pupils rises.

One of the particular forms of departmentalization that met with considerable favor is the *platoon system*. It was originated as an administrative device for coping with the problem of large numbers of pupils in schools with limited classroom space. It enjoyed its greatest popularity after the First World War and has been gradually disappearing during recent years. According to the platoon plan, children are divided into groups. The children of each group pursue regular subjects of the curriculum with the home-room teachers during one half day, and during the other half day engage in special activities that necessitate special kinds of equipment or unusual space. Usually one teacher taught two general groups. Through this plan the children come in contact with several different teachers each day, often having as a consequence a compartmentalized and disunified kind of program.

Special Organization for Individualization.—A few schools have developed special types of organization to aid in the individualization of instruction. Notable among these are the plans developed at Winnetka, Illinois, and Dalton, Massachusetts. In each case, instruction in the basic subjects is developed in terms of *individual contracts* based on each child's rate of achievement. Other aspects of the school program are organized on a group basis in order to assure that some attention is given to the social aspects of learning. Such plans have the advantage of being geared to the individual capacities of children but they also have certain disadvantages. Among these limitations are the unusual demands such a plan places on teachers in keeping individual records, assisting with individual contracts and planning, and in evaluating progress. Some educators feel that an undue amount of importance is attached to certain tool subjects under such an arrangement. While the contract approach to organization has flourished in a few school systems, its advocates apparently are becoming fewer all the time.

Ungraded classes have been organized in many schools as an attempt to provide a setting conducive to individualization of instruction for children who are exceptional in their deviations from average. Most such classes are provided for children who are slow learners, for children with orthopedic handicaps, or who deviate in various other respects.

Occasionally, speech correction classes are maintained for children with speech difficulties. The main advantage of the ungraded class is that it is usually small, permitting almost completely individualized instruction, particularly if it is staffed by a teacher with appropriate training and experience. Such a class also makes it easier to maintain and use special facilities which cannot be so successfully utilized in the typical classroom. The chief disadvantage of such an arrangement is that children assigned to special classes often are deprived of normal social contacts with other children. More will be said about provisions for exceptional children in a later chapter devoted to that problem.

The Self-contained Classroom.—Much can be said in favor of each of the various attempts that have been made to organize children for more effective learning in the elementary school. Each plan that has been proposed to date appears to have some particular advantage to recommend its adoption. However, when one considers the problem of providing the best possible atmosphere for the all-round growth of children, there is no evidence that any arrangement is superior to the self-contained classroom in which children of about the same chronological age are placed under the guidance of one teacher for most, if not all, of the day's activities. It is further recommended that such groups be determined on a generally heterogeneous basis with ample provision for easy transfer from one group to another if there occurs any valid reason for doing so. There is little evidence to indicate that the problem of individual differences among children can be met more effectively through plans of organization other than the self-contained classroom if the teacher has the inclination and qualifications necessary for dealing with them.

The self-contained classroom is the administrative expression of the modern concern for the "whole child." It makes it possible and feasible to unify his efforts and activities, to identify his individual difficulties, and to maintain a balance between self-development and social development. It provides for the meaningful and continuous use of learning materials and establishes a functional relationship between living and learning in that the child pursues his academic tasks in an environment that is partially of his own planning and making. The fact that the same teacher remains with the group throughout the day lends security to the children and permits the teacher to gain the maximum amount of knowledge and understanding of pupils. The real success of the plan depends upon the well-rounded professional preparation of the teacher and his unlimited devotion to the task of providing the best possible place for children to live and learn.

GROUP PROCESSES AND OUTCOMES

Grouping is more than an administrative device for dividing children into groups commensurate with the supply of teachers and the dimensions of classrooms. Of course, the school should be organized in such a manner that groups are not unwieldy in size and teachers are not overloaded. Other considerations, however, should not be overlooked.

An important part of the educational process is group interaction. Children learn from each other and from their experiences in reacting to each other. This process takes many forms, a few of which are:

1. *Group discussion*—which may be either organized or informal, depending upon the setting and purpose. It may occur when a classroom or school problem faces the group, or it may be directed toward the initiation or development of a unit of work or some part of it. Group discussion should involve all members of the group and elicit as many ideas as possible from the members. Its success as an educational process depends upon freedom of the individual to express himself and his consideration for other members of the group. Group discussion and sharing can be invaluable as means for developing social skills.

2. *Group planning*—which is the means whereby ideas become the bases for subsequent action. If the most is to be gained from group planning, all members must be encouraged to contribute, opinions must be respected by members of the group, and sufficient time must be allowed for the effective pooling of suggestions and for weighing all suggestions carefully and deliberately. The more closely a problem is related to the felt interests and needs of children, the more effectively and enthusiastically they engage in the group planning process. It is not a device that succeeds in the consideration of problems that are artificial or remote.

3. *Group activity*—which is directed toward the achievement of plans. Such action may be carried out by groups delegated to deliver a message, make a simple survey, or carry on research in a problem selected for study. There are many occasions throughout the school day when group activity is an essential part of the day's work. The effectiveness with which it is done depends upon the group experience of the children, the quality of planning, and the degree of motivation possessed by the children. Just as it is important that each child develop his own individual skills, it is also essential that he learn to work well with others through the opportunity for group work.

4. *Group evaluation*—which encourages children to view outcomes in terms of purposes and original plans, is an important activity, de-

veloping the ability to be objective and self-critical. Though the teacher is responsible for the evaluation of group work, it is valuable for pupils to share in the evaluation process. This is particularly true when the results of group planning and group work are being appraised.

From the types of group interaction mentioned above, and from others, children gain maturity and competence in working out problems on a cooperative basis. In addition, their learning experiences are enriched through the process of sharing with members of the group and their judgments are sharpened as they approve, accept, modify, or reject ideas that are projected into group discussions.

The Effect of Group Dynamics on Behavior.—Some of the problems of behavior in individuals can be alleviated to a considerable degree through the power of group dynamics. At all levels of the elementary school the effect of a group on individuals may be noted, though it may differ in terms of the ages of the children involved. Often the attitudes and reactions of a group may be invaluable in assisting individuals to overcome personal behavior problems. Some striking examples of how desired effects may be produced through group dynamics have been reported by members of the staff of the University Elementary School of the University of Michigan.[4] Some of them follow:

TECHNIC: DIRECT DISCUSSION OF PROBLEM BY THE GROUP RESULTING IN GROUP
ACTION

Example A : How can a child whose clowning becomes obnoxious be helped?

Jerry, an eight-year-old, is very fond of telling humorous stories, but each story-telling situation becomes a moment of superfluous clowning. The children were greatly amused during its early stages but as the clowning progressed, the children became disgusted. In time the group refused to hear his stories. As a result, Jerry continually interrupted other children's stories with his obnoxious clowning. Jerry has a keen sense of humor. How can the group help him?

The children discussed funny stories they had heard. How did the person tell that particular story? The group decided that a humorous story is funnier to the listeners if:

1. The story teller told it without exaggerated expression or gesture.

2. The story teller stopped as soon as the punch-line was delivered. Jerry was given other opportunities to tell humorous stories. He tried again and again. When his story delivery improved slightly, the group commented favorably. Then, one day, Jerry's story ended with a terrific punch-line. The laughter was spontaneous and the applause tremendous. One little boy shouted, "Don't you

---

[4] Virginia Copeland, Jessie Dypka, Trude Kinnel, William Mills, and Robert Fox, "Group Dynamics and Individual Behavior," *Bases for Effective Learning,* Thirty-First Yearbook of the Department of Elementary Principals, XXXII, No. 1. (Washington, D. C.: National Education Association, 1952), 210-13.

like the way Jerry tells a funny story!" Jerry rarely resorts to clowning to get group attention any more.

Example B: How can a child who is easily angered be helped?

Tommy, an eight-year-old boy, became easily angered when situations did not meet with his approval. At first he broke into tears, ran out of the room, and refused to return. The group was very fond of him when he was agreeable. How could the group help him?

The group discussed, "What makes a person angry?" Then the children discussed how the total group could assist an individual in controlling his anger:

1. A person has the right to show that he is displeased.

2. They would comment favorably when displeasure was demonstrated without anger or tears. This week a situation angered Tommy. He flushed slightly and clenched his fists. With a forced smile he remarked, "I don't care to do this. I'm going to sit and watch for a while." Emily spoke up, "That's all right with us. You did that very well. You became angry but you didn't let your feelings show. We'll try not to do what we did, to keep you from feeling unpleasant again." The other children smiled and nodded in agreement. Several other comments of approval were made. Tommy beamed with pride. The day was saved for him.

Example C: How can a child who disregards the safety of others be helped to realize his responsibilities?

Robin had a highly developed ethical sense (for others) but could not hold himself to acceptable behavior. Private conferences and isolation had no effect on preventing acts of cruelty to other children.

One day Robin was discovered poking a broken piece of metal coat hanger up through the boards of the slide.

The teacher guided group discussion of the problem with the idea that the group should help, not blame, Robin. The children suggested all the things that could have resulted if a child had slid over this sharp object. They then asked Robin what he felt would make him remember. He chose isolation, but they felt that could be too enjoyable because he liked to read alone in the classroom. It was finally suggested that Robin be an observer during play period, that he tell the class all the careful or safe ways of playing he saw, and that he rejoin the group when he felt he was ready to accept responsibility for his actions.

That was two months ago. No incidents of Robin hurting others have been reported since.

Comments regarding use of discussion technic:

1. Direct discussion of the problem by the group may not only be an effective way of influencing individual behavior, but also be an essential element in the democratic process.

2. The use of this technic is dependent upon the maturity level of the group and upon its level of operation as a group. A less mature group will need careful guidance and direction in setting up standards for individual behavior. A group exhibiting a high degree of interaction and cohesion is more able to assist its indi-

vidual members to alter their patterns of behavior in such a way as to be the least damaging to themselves and to the group.

3. Direct group discussion may focus too much on a problem that may be peculiar to one individual.

4. Care needs to be taken that the group does not set standards too high.

5. Discussion in itself will not alter the individual's behavior. The group needs to provide situations in which the more desirable behavior may operate.

6. There may be a tendency for the individual to perform in such a manner as to win group approval without a complete understanding of the actions taken.

TECHNIC: PROVIDING THE INDIVIDUAL WITH MEANS OF SECURING GROUP APPROVAL

Example A : How can a child who lacks finesse in sharing his own talents be helped?

Richard was musically inclined and talented. However, he had become so engrossed in and conceited over his ability to play the piano that the group was finding it difficult to accept his comments: "Don't applaud so long. I'm not quite Vladimir Horowitz yet." Or "I'm not sure I can do this piece perfectly; I've practiced it for only six weeks."

In order to channel this type of behavior into something useful, the teacher enlisted Richard's aid in playing bass clef notes only as she played the melody of popular and folk tunes. Later other children offered to pick out the tune and have him contribute the bass and rhythm. Soon both boys and girls were taking turns playing with Richard for the class. He discovered it was fun to play folk and popular songs, and to compose songs with others; that trivial mistakes were not of great consequence; and that others could learn notes, rhythms, and enjoy music with his help. He ceased being so engrossed in classical music as his only bid for success and became respected for the excellent assistance he could give to the whole class during music period.

Example B : Can a child who is low in reading and language skills be encouraged to improve?

Martha Jane was a child with low reading skills, high problem tendencies, and general lack of verbal ability. The class suggested a time during its unit in which all children could bring and explain items relating to the unit study. Martha Jane's family had many items relating to pioneer study—a venison roasting grill, old flat irons, and bellows. These Martha Jane brought and achieved recognition in telling about them. She became more interested in each unit by looking for things to share (a rock collection, bird pictures, magazine pictures). Her verbal power increased and she was also instrumental in interesting other children in starting collections. She began reading about specific items and drawing pictures to explain her ideas. She became so busy in these activities she was welcomed as a contributing member of the group.

Comments regarding use of group approval technic:

1. Excellent rapport with the group and with the individual child is necessary

before any technic for providing group approval can be undertaken. The children must have an experience basis for faith in the teacher's fairness, consistency, and helpfulness before they can place their confidence in her action for any or all of them.

2. In the case of Richard, had the teacher used the discussion technic with the group regarding the necessity for rechanneling Richard's conceit, such frankness would have placed him in a defensive position. Had the teacher forbidden their natural reaction to his overbearing manner and demanded appreciation of his talent, the result would have been mere lip service to adult power and an invitation for them to project their resentment on him. Had she removed all opportunities for his playing in a school situation, he could easily have withdrawn more deeply into his feeling of superiority or turned to other less desirable means of attaining group recognition.

3. By unobtrusively placing herself in a learner's role, the teacher directed attention from the individual to herself. Rediversion to other children as soon as possible placed the situation on a participating and contributing basis involving the individual child and the whole group in more constructive roles.

TECHNIC: ROLE PLAYING

Example A: How can skill and confidence in meeting new social responsibilities be gained?

A group of fourth-grade children had planned a choral speaking program, an arts and crafts display, and a party for their parents at Hallowe'en. Many of the children and their parents were new to the school and this was the first opportunity of meeting as a group.

In planning the organization of the party and seating arrangements for serving, the children asked each other, "How will we know whose parents are whose?" The need for knowing how to introduce strangers to each other was discussed. Rules for introductions were explained and listed on the board. The teacher suggested the formation of "pretend" families among class members for practice. A movie roll was made of cut-out magazine pictures explaining the introduction of a gentleman to one's mother with the words to say beside it, of a younger man to an older man, of a father to the teacher, etc. Then each group of four children elected various members to be fathers, mothers, aunts, sisters, or grandfathers. Other children were elected as the principal, the teacher, a doctor, a very important person, and an old man. As each "family group" came into the room, they were introduced by "their" child to others in the room.

On the day of the program the real visitors were ushered into the room by their own children and introduced graciously to the other visitors present. The children, by previous role playing, had oriented themselves in both what to do and how to do it long before the actual necessity arose.

Comments regarding use of role-playing technic: It is clear that role playing must be carefully selected and structured so that no individual is hurt and everyone participates. There must be an understanding of how and why something is being done. Much learning and pleasure, however, can come from a well-prepared and carefully selected role-playing experience.

SPECIAL INTEREST GROUPS WITHIN THE SCHOOL

The broadening of the purposes of the elementary school in recent years has led inevitably to a greater variety of approaches to the achievement of desired goals. One of the ways this recognition has found expression is through the organization of special interest groups related to some aspect of the school's operation or program. Such groups are useful in two respects:

1. They provide a functional setting for the application of attitudes of responsibility.

2. They utilize special interests of children as a motivation for further learning. The possibilities for the formation of groups of this kind are almost infinite in number and form. A few of the more common types are included for illustration.

School Clubs.—Children of upper elementary school age are going through what is commonly called "the gang age." They tend to organize themselves into clubs of various sorts. Many of these are developed on a neighborhood basis and frequently adopt rather rigid rules and regulations administered by a group of duly elected officers.

This rather natural urge can serve as bases for some very constructive club work in the elementary school. Science clubs, art clubs, hobby clubs, outdoor clubs, aviation clubs, and many others can be organized around a nucleus of pupil interest. Interest, of course, will vary somewhat between boys and girls and in terms of the local community situation and the timeliness with which a club is organized. Club work should make as much use as possible of pupil initiative and leadership with, of course, sufficient guidance from the teacher to insure constructive activities in a wholesome direction.

A detailed listing of some of the kinds of activities that can be carried on effectively through club work is suggested by Lindahl in a recent yearbook of the Department of Elementary School Principals.[5]

Dramatic Club

Group and individual pantomiming of imagined situations.

Group pantomiming of scenes from familiar stories.

Individual pantomiming of the action of characters from well-known books or stories.

Group evaluation of the interpretation of characters.

Group dramatizations of favorite stories.

Group creation of additions to various scenes in stories.

[5] Hannah M. Lindahl, "Club Activities in the Intermediate Grades," *Creative Schools,* Twenty-Third Yearbook of Department of Elementary School Principals, (Washington, D. C.: National Education Association, 1944), 117-20.

Group planning and presentation of plays adapted from books of plays.
Group creation and presentation of original plays.

Science Club

Collecting specimens and identifying them.
Reading to secure information about specimens.
Giving reports of reference reading.
Making booklets containing specimens or drawings of specimens.
Taking hikes for purposes of firsthand observation.
Assisting in making a science collection for the school.
Using the microscope and discussing observations.
Making science scrapbooks containing pictures and articles about birds, trees,
    wild flowers, gardening, or some other subject of special interest.
Keeping class diaries on "Birds We Know."
Doing wood construction, such as making birdhouses and feeding tables.
Writing letters for information and material.
Collecting science news and posting it on the bulletin board.
Making bibliographies of science references.
Playing science quiz games.

Choral Club

Preparing programs for assemblies, meetings of the parent-teacher association,
    or meetings of some civic organization.
Singing on the radio.
Making records of individual and group singing.
Going caroling during the holiday season.
Composing music for verses written by the club members.
Creating folk dances to illustrate certain European folk music.
Reading about well-known composers and reporting interesting information to
    the group.

Junior Red Cross Club

Making stuffed toys for gifts to children.
Making table decorations and tray covers for use in hospitals.
Knitting afghans, articles for soldiers, and articles for children in war areas.
Making Christmas cards for hospitalized servicemen.
Making cartoon and puzzle scrapbooks for servicemen in hospitals.
Packing Christmas gift boxes to be sent to war areas.
Collecting games for hospitalized servicemen.

Art Club

Making gifts of paper, cloth, clay, leather, and other materials.
Making a frieze to hang in the hall at school.
Making posters for school campaigns.
Doing freehand drawing and painting.
Designing simple costumes for the members of the dramatic club.
Making puppets and giving puppet shows.

Sewing Club

Sewing aprons, luncheon cloths, towels, and other useful articles.
Learning to knit.
Mending tears in garments; sewing on buttons; darning hose.
Embroidering dresser scarfs and pillow tops.
Making simple costumes for members of the dramatic club.
Making simple chair covers for the rest room at school.

Stamp Club

Collecting and mounting stamps; exchanging stamps.
Locating and discussing countries represented in stamp collections.
Giving reports on noted people who collect stamps as a hobby.

Reading Club

Engaging in recreational reading.
Discussing and sharing reactions to books read.
Writing riddles or poems about book characters.
Impersonating book characters in a guessing contest.
Illustrating scenes from favorite books.
Making a classroom frieze of well-known book characters.
Making book posters to advertise interesting books.
Reading children's magazines and participating in group discussions of the leading features of the various ones.
Advertising books through brief reports that do not divulge the way the stories end.
Discussing authors and collecting news items about favorite authors of today's books.

First-Aid Club

Discussing what to do in case of accident or illness.
Observing proper bandaging; practicing proper bandaging.
Discussing school accidents with emphasis upon preventive measures.
Describing accident victims and discussing appropriate first-aid measures.
Making safety posters.
Writing safety slogans and jingles.

Current Events Club

Discussing current events.
Making scrapbooks containing news in word and picture.
Giving individual reports of today's leaders in national and international affairs.
Listening to news broadcasts.

Choric Speech Club

Participating in poetry appreciation.
Discussing favorite poems.
Group learning of poems through choral reading.
Presenting poems in choric-speech assembly programs.

Gardening Club

Discussing essential steps in gardening.

Writing invitations to members of the community's adult garden club, inviting them to attend meetings of the school's own garden club.

Writing for seed catalogs; buying and selling seeds.

Planning a home garden.

Reading to secure needed information for home gardening.

Sponsoring a flower and vegetable show at school.

The Student Council.—The student council has become an integral part of the secondary school but the elementary school has made less use of such a group largely because of the immaturity of the children involved. However, an increasing number of student councils are being included in the organization of modern elementary schools. They are usually composed of one or more representatives from each grade or age level along with one or more sponsoring teachers. Sometimes they take the form of an advisory council to the principal. Some of the functions such a group can perform are: (1) To present the child's point of view regarding changes or needed changes in operational routines; (2) to assume responsibility for assisting in planning school activities; (3) to serve as a clearing house for pupil surveys, etc.; (4) to assume leadership in special projects of the school; (5) to exercise leadership in school citizenship.

The School Patrol.—Another group which makes a tremendous contribution to the program of the school is the school patrol. Besides performing a direct service to the safety program, the school, and the community, this organization provides opportunity for children to exercise leadership in a constructive way, and to learn the importance of assuming obligations in a responsible manner.

School patrols are usually established in cooperation with local civic or traffic agencies particularly interested in safety. However done, the principal should make sure that proper equipment and facilities exist to reduce hazards to an absolute minimum. In addition, he should know the legal implications involved in terms of the laws of his particular city or state. Generally speaking, the patrol has performed a real service to communities and schools and, at the same time, its members have had some valuable citizenship training not available through less concrete means.

Scout Programs.—Not all elementary schools will have in attendance children whose ages permit membership in the Boy Scouts of America and Girl Scouts of America. Virtually all elementary schools, however, will have some sort of connection, directly or indirectly, with Cub Scout and Brownie programs for younger boys and girls. Many of these units are sponsored by school or school-affiliated organizations such as the P.T.A., Fathers' Club, or Mothers' Club. They often meet in the school in quarters provided for them and frequently include school personnel as sponsors and leaders. Such activities are not without their problems, but the relationship between the school and other such educational agencies is valuable and should be encouraged and protected in every constructive way.

It is necessary that all persons involved agree on the responsibilities of each as well as on the arrangements for utilization of school facilities and the conditions under which they are used. Clarity of understanding prevents later conflicts and insures better working relationships in general.

ACTION SUGGESTIONS FOR THE PRINCIPAL

1. Remember that children learn best when they are socially comfortable.

2. Try to help the teaching staff and parents understand fully the educational reasons for grouping.

3. Group children in terms of purposes to be achieved.

4. Keep classroom groups socially functional.

5. Encourage teachers to use varied types of instructional grouping within the classroom groups in order to achieve different educational purposes.

6. Help provide instructional materials of varying nature and difficulty for use with instructional groups at different levels of achievement.

7. Never consider *any* grouping arrangement either sacred or permanent.

8. Develop administrative machinery for the easy transfer of a child from one classroom group to another.

9. Avoid the establishment or perpetuation of groups to which social or scholastic stigmas are attached.

10. Create a situation in which children have some choices in their assignment to groups.

11. Help teachers understand the uses of sociometry in the grouping of children.

12. Encourage the use of committee work and group research by children.

13. Organize school clubs on the sole basis of interest.

14. Encourage children to participate in school government through group discussion.

15. Encourage group evaluation.

16. Promote occasional parent-teacher forums on the social development of children.

17. Become reasonably well informed in the field of group dynamics.

18. Encourage children to develop group pride.

19. Wherever possible, minimize the discreteness of grade groups.

20. Have unusually competent teachers demonstrate or share with other teachers successful experiences with instructional grouping.

21. Develop specific and natural means for integrating new pupils into their classroom groups.

22. Give children opportunities to participate in large group activities both as performers and as courteous members of an audience.

SELECTED REFERENCES FOR EXTENDED READING

ASSOCIATION FOR SUPERVISION AND CURRICULUM. *Organizing the Elementary School for Living and Learning: 1947 Yearbook.* Washington, D. C.: National Education Association, 1947.

BAXTER, BERNICE, LEWIS, GERTRUDE M., and CROSS, GERTRUDE M. *Elementary Education.* Boston: D. C. Heath & Co., 1952.

CASWELL, HOLLIS L., and FOSHAY, A. WELLESLEY. *Education in the Elementary School.* New York: American Book Co., 1950.

CUNNINGHAM, RUTH and OTHERS. *Understanding Group Behavior of Boys and Girls.* New York: Teachers College, Columbia University, 1951.

DEPARTMENT OF ELEMENTARY SCHOOL PRINCIPALS. *Bases for Effective Learning: Thirty-First Yearbook.* Washington, D. C.: National Education Association, 1952, chaps. 6 and 7.

DOUGHERTY, JAMES H., GORMAN, FRANK H., and PHILLIPS, CLAUDE A. *Elementary School Organization and Management* (rev. ed.). New York: The Macmillan Co., 1950, chap. 6.

ELSBREE, WILLARD S. *Pupil Progress in the Elementary School.* New York: Bureau of Publications, Teachers College, Columbia University, 1943.

LEE, J. MURRAY, and LEE, DORRIS MAY. *The Child and His Curriculum.* New York: Appleton-Century-Crofts, Inc., 1950.

NATIONAL SOCIETY FOR THE STUDY OF EDUCATION. *The Grouping of Pupils: Thirty-Fifth Yearbook,* Part I. Chicago: University of Chicago Press, 1936.

OTTO, HENRY J. *Elementary School Organization and Administration.* New York: Appleton-Century-Crofts, Inc., 1954, chap. 5.

RAGAN, WILLIAM B. *Modern Elementary Curriculum.* New York: The Dryden Press, Inc., 1953, chaps. 5 and 6.

Chapter 10

MEETING PROBLEMS OF PUPIL PROGRESS
CONSTRUCTIVELY

Without going one can get nowhere—*Chinese Proverb*

Administrative provisions for pupil progress through the school program have always been a necessity. Pupil progress and promotion did not present a serious problem, however, during the earlier periods of our educational history when the program of the school was rigidly prescribed on a strictly graded basis with the same standards set for all children of a particular grade. Pupils either learned enough of the factual subject-matter to "pass" or they repeated a study of the same material during the succeeding year or years until such time as their examination scores were above the line which arbitrarily separated success from failure. Whatever may be said of such practice otherwise, it must be admitted that it simplified the decisions that had to be made regarding promotion and nonpromotion.

Pupil progress and promotion based on uniform grade standards are consistent with the philosophy of the early graded school. As schools have become more concerned with the individual and his own rate of growth, they have found it necessary to face the growing problem of how to provide for continuous growth of children as they progress through a program that is designed largely on a graded subject-matter basis. As a result, much thought and many studies have been directed toward attempts to alleviate the problem, although the difficulty of reconciling individual growth and mass instruction has of course been recognized.

Rebellion against the inflexible forms of pupil progress which have persisted for so long has led to various kinds of attempts to develop promotional policies more in keeping with the current understanding of children and the ways in which their growth is stimulated. Before discussing some of these attempts in detail, perhaps it is advisable to suggest some basic considerations related to pupil progress and promotion.

SOME BASIC PRINCIPLES RELATED TO PUPIL PROGRESS

Someone has said that if he knew a principal's philosophy with respect to pupil progress and promotion, he could then describe the kind of elementary school the principal might be expected to administer. While this may be a slight exaggeration, it does suggest an awareness of the fact that policies and practices of promotion influence materially all the other aspects of the school program. Before studying or recommending particular plans, then, one should consider all facets of educational growth as well as the organizational arrangements through which such growth is fostered.

1. *Pupil progress should be as continuous as possible.* Unfortunately for administrative purposes, the human growth curve does not correspond to school years, semesters, or other units of time spent in academic pursuits. Learning is not an additive, mechanistic process but is rather a cumulative, integrating process which requires continuous reaction to and reconstruction of experience. If pupil progress is to be continuous, attention must be directed toward (1) elimination of the concept of repeating a grade as a means of improving learning, and (2) reduction of the learning gaps that often occur between grades or between administrative units of the school system. No plan for promotion can be wholly infallible, but the better approaches to this problem are those which take into account the necessity and desirability of continuity in the learning process.

2. *Pupil progress should be determined on the basis of multiple factors.* One of the most questionable features of earlier promotional practices was the disproportionate amount of emphasis placed on academic achievement, with little or no consideration being given to other aspects of educational growth. Wherever the criterion of "subject-matter mastery" has been the sole criterion for promotion, an unusual amount of overageness has been the inevitable result. In turn, such overageness has led to problems of social and emotional adjustment which have far overshadowed any possible advantages of nonpromotion in most cases.

Human behavior and adjustment are far too complicated to lend themselves to evaluation by index numbers and percentages. Although grade records, test scores, and intelligence quotients are valuable components of appraisal, decisions which involve the adjustment of a child for a year or more should not be based on these factors alone. Physical size, social adjustment, personality factors, and home conditions and

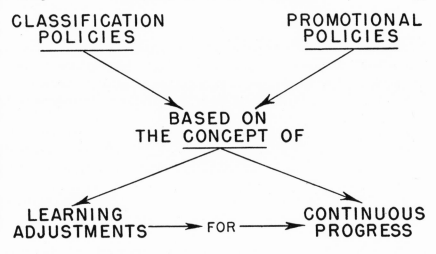

CLASSIFICATION   PROMOTIONAL
POLICIES   POLICIES

BASED ON
THE CONCEPT OF

LEARNING   CONTINUOUS
ADJUSTMENTS ──► FOR ──► PROGRESS

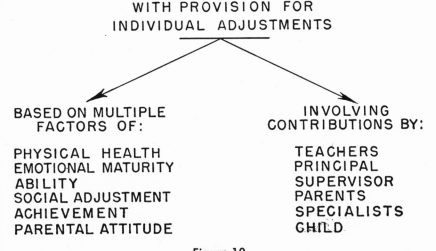

WITH PROVISION FOR
INDIVIDUAL ADJUSTMENTS

BASED ON MULTIPLE   INVOLVING
FACTORS OF: CONTRIBUTIONS BY:

PHYSICAL HEALTH   TEACHERS
EMOTIONAL MATURITY   PRINCIPAL
ABILITY   SUPERVISOR
SOCIAL ADJUSTMENT   PARENTS
ACHIEVEMENT   SPECIALISTS
PARENTAL ATTITUDE   CHILD

Figure 10

Some Important Aspects of Pupil Progress

attitudes all should be considered in the process of pupil progress through school. A report of a school in New York[1] as to its policies on promotion refers to the use of two sets of criteria, one general and the

[1] Lawrence O. Lobdell, "Results of a Nonpromotion Policy in One School District," *Elementary School Journal*, LIV, No. 6 (February, 1954), 333-37.

other specific, to be applied when decisions as to the classification of individuals must be made. They are as follows:

General Criteria

1. Which of the alternatives—promotion or nonpromotion—promises to serve best the *long-range* welfare of the child?
2. No one child shall, except in the most unusual circumstances, repeat more than one grade in his progress through the six grades.
3. No child shall repeat Grade VI if such repetition can possibly be avoided.
4. No child shall repeat a grade with the same teacher with whom he failed.

Specific Criteria

Seven specific criteria are taken into account when deciding whether or not to retain a particular pupil:

1. The pupil's marks for the present year. This is the teacher's assessment of the quality of the pupil's work.
2. The pupil's scores on the standardized achievement tests given to all pupils in May of each year.
3. The pupil's score on a test of mental ability.
4. The social, emotional, and personality characteristics of the pupil.
5. The pupil's chronological age.
6. The pupil's physical size.
7. The attitude of the pupil's parents toward their child's progress in school, and particularly toward the choice which must be made now.

3. *Promotion and pupil classification are means rather than ends.* Historically, promotion has been associated with success. As a result there has developed a strong tendency to consider promotion and school success as synonymous concepts. Inevitably, this has led to an emphasis on promotion rather than learning, with parents and teachers frequently holding the threat of nonpromotion over the head of the reluctant learner. This degree of emphasis seems wholly unjustified. Promotion should be considered only in the light of what it is—an administrative device for moving groups of children, as well as individuals, through the school program in a manner consistent with their development. If a promotional policy facilitates the educational development of the children involved, it is undoubtedly a good policy; if it hinders such development, it certainly is open to question and should be studied carefully with a view to improvement or elimination.

The difficulty of controlling or manipulating human behavior in terms of mechanical processes has been mentioned. The problem of promotion is a concrete illustration of this difficulty. The administration of promotion is a definite example of a point in the educational process at which educational principles and practices come into conflict.[2] The con-

[2] See William A. Yeager, *Administration and the Pupil* (Harper & Bros., New York, 1949), p. 147.

cern for the individual growth rate of the child must be reconciled with the necessary regard for administrative problems to be met when many children are involved in the school program. There is no perfect answer to the problem at present; it is unlikely that there will be developed a perfect solution to this dilemma. However, the problem is one to be studied and met by schools through (1) considering the child first, then the administrative machinery, and (2) by keeping in mind that promotion is a means rather than an end.

4. *Promotion policies should be socially and emotionally humane.* The basic consideration in administering a promotion policy is what it does to each individual. Feelings of success or failure directly affect the status and security of an individual child and, therefore, exert an influence upon the efforts of the child in many directions. His relationship to his peers is one of the most important elements of his life. Therefore, consideration for the feelings, status, and reactions of a child are necessary to effective machinery for administering pupil progress.

Several aspects of considerateness merit attention. Often it may be painful to a child, and harmful to his social adjustment and personality development, to be retained at any grade level for a second year when all his classmates are promoted to the next grade level and enjoy all the attendant blessings of success. Such a situation is agonizing to the retained pupil because he is described in the terminology of failure, because his fellows may pity him, ridicule him, or "look down upon him," or because his retention may invoke upon him the wrath of unsympathetic parents. Such conditions do not necessarily have to accompany nonpromotion, but they appear to do so in far too many cases.

Whatever administrative schemes may be devised for promoting and classifying children should be built upon a prerequisite respect for the feelings and attitudes of children as human beings. Anything less is to contribute to the loss of self-respect in the individual and, in all probability, to influence negatively his motivation toward educational goals. The best plans for classifying pupils for instruction are those which provide for the best possible adjustment of children and are free from unnecessary humiliation or embarrassment.

5. *Promotion policies should be flexible and adaptable to particular cases.* There is definite danger in categorizing children on a rigid and permanent basis. Much damage is often done to a child because he is persistently classified on a long-term basis in terms of the results of a single test score or other limited data. Probably no grouping in the elementary school should ever be considered other than tentative. There should be provisions within classification procedures for the reconstruction of groupings as needs and status of children demand.

No single type of promotion procedure or standards should be applied to all cases. Policies concerning promotion should include the possibility and means for dealing with individual cases in terms of the extenuating factors involved. By the same token, no policy or regulation should become so sacred that human considerations and educational circumstances cannot bring about its modification when it is desirable to alter it. Such modifications do not indicate a disrespect for school policy; rather, they reflect a reasonableness in the interpretation of policy which should permeate all aspects of administering a program for elementary school children.

Policies are developed in order to encourage consistency of action; they should not be construed as regulations which demand absolute conformity. It is wise for the staff of an elementary school, therefore, to establish policies to guide its administrative decisions and procedures. At the same time, such policies must permit sufficient flexibility to make them both useful and susceptible to the fluctuating characteristics of human behavior.

6. *Promotion policies should be based on a knowledge of research concerning pupil progress.* The promotion practices of many schools are based on false assumptions which ignore the findings of research into the effects of promotion and nonpromotion on the learning of children. Many of these assumptions appear reasonable on the surface and, as a result, have been accepted by teachers and administrators as bases for administrative procedures for regulating pupil progress throughout the elementary school. Some of these assumptions are: (*a*) that nonpromotion is necessary to maintain high standards of achievement; (*b*) that nonpromotion spurs a child on to greater efforts through firsthand experience with failure; (*c*) that nonpromotion contributes to homogeneity of groups and thus, indirectly, to good social and emotional adjustment of pupils; (*d*) that nonpromotion is effective conditioning for children who will, it is assumed, ultimately have to face the successes and failures of adult life.

In the case of each of these assumptions, there is sufficient evidence to question if not indeed to refute its validity.[3] Furthermore, the simple application of psychological principles and common sense to practices based on these assumptions raises many questions regarding them.

SOME ORGANIZED PLANS FOR ADMINISTERING PUPIL PROGRESS

The procedures designed to bring the children into contact with the school program constitute the administrative expression of the

[3] For an excellent general discussion see Willard S. Elsbree, *Pupil Progress in the Elementary School* (New York: Bureau of Publications, Teachers College, Columbia University, 1943).

kind of philosophy which motivates the procedures. Some practices in classifying and promoting pupils appear to assume that children should be adjusted to the school program; others seem to indicate the belief that a program should be devised to fit the needs of the children involved. As some of the historical and revised plans for administering pupil progress are considered, it will be seen readily that each is rooted in some underlying assumption of the child's relation to the program of the school.

Promotion in Terms of Grade Standards.—The graded school has been the tradition in American public education and it is still the typical plan of organization in most elementary schools of this country. In fact, elementary schools are usually called "graded" or "grade" schools. As indicated in the previous chapter, the graded school was developed as an organizational device for dividing the school population into instructional groups somewhat homogeneous in achievement.[4] The school curriculum was divided into vertical segments corresponding to what was considered appropriate work for children at each grade level. Correspondingly, standards were set for each grade in terms of the degree to which the subject matter for each grade was mastered. A pupil who did not meet the standards for entering the work of the next grade was retained and required to repeat the work of the grade just completed. This practice dominated the regulation of pupil progress in elementary schools until well into the twentieth century, and, even yet, has not been eliminated from the operational structure of schools.

During the first quarter of the twentieth century a gradual rebellion against such rigid interpretation and application of grade standards began to develop among educators. Two major developments contributed to the growing skepticism with respect to the grade-standard theory of pupil progress. The first was the advent of *standardized tests* and the so-called scientific movement in education. With the introduction and use of intelligence tests came the strong and growing realization that children may be created with equal rights but that they are not created with equal resources for learning. Educators began to call attention to the great differences in maturity existing in children at school entrance age, and to the fact that these differences become even more apparent as children advance in age. These developments, along with experimental research, began to focus attention on the unfairness involved in a scheme which set the same standards of educational success for all pupils regardless of ability or circumstances.

[4] Hollis L. Caswell and A. Wellesley Foshay, *Education in the Elementary School* (New York: American Book Co., 1950), pp. 333-34.

Another factor which led to the de-emphasis of grade standards as the sole bases for promotion was the growing insistence on *equal educational opportunity* for all children. The implementation of this concept in school practice has demanded that children have an opportunity to progress continuously through school at their own particular rates of growth. This, in turn, required that standards be established in terms of individuals rather than in terms of the total group. The impact of this growing concept on the existing school structure has led to many attempts to revise administrative practices in such a way that grade standards would remain important and, at the same time, proper consideration could be given to differentiation according to the needs and resources of individuals. Some of the organizational attempts to alleviate the questionable effects of the grade-standard theory of pupil progress will be discussed in some detail in the following pages.

1. *Shortening the period on which promotion is based.* One of the major attempts to reduce the unwholesome effects of nonpromotion has involved the adjustment of the promotion period. This usually has meant a reduction in the length of the academic period on which the child is evaluated and a corresponding increase in the frequency of promotion periods. Instead of the customary practice of promoting children each year, semiannual promotion came into being and, in a few instances, children have been promoted at the end of periods even shorter than half a year. Although this practice has tended to eliminate the repetition of a whole year's work at any one time, it has not been materially beneficial in adjusting the school program to the differences in learning rates of the children who attend school. Recent years have brought a gradual, but definite, trend away from semiannual promotion. Many educators have felt that such a plan merely increases the administrative routines involved without resulting in corresponding improvements over regular annual promotion plans.

2. *Ability grouping.* This device was hopefully expected to contribute to the wholesome adjustment of pupils and to increased effectiveness of teaching. It came into being on the assumption that children will profit both educationally and emotionally from being placed with other children who have similar abilities and needs. As has been pointed out earlier in connection with the grouping of pupils, there are times when the grouping of children in terms of particular status or need is legitimate. However, available evidence has not supported the superior value of ability grouping on a school-wide basis as a means of improving pupil adjustment and reducing the existing evils of other promotion plans and practices. Opinion, as well as practice, is divided as to merits of ability grouping but it is now felt by many educators that such a plan offers

little toward insuring the continuous progress of children through school.

3. *Conditional promotions.* Another plan tried as a means of alleviating the rigidity of promotions based on grade standards is that of conditional, or trial, promotions. Through the opportunity for a trial promotion, a child whose status is doubtful is given a chance to proceed with the work of the next grade along with others of his classroom group. Presumably, such children remain on educational probation until they demonstrate whether or not they can continue with the prescribed work of the grade, or until the end of some definite, predetermined period. In actual practice, however, very few children once promoted ever are demoted to their previous classification status. As a result, trial promotions have had little effect of any kind on existing patterns of promotional policy and practice, except whatever possible harm may be attributed to the practice of demanding that a child spend a period of several weeks or months in a state of uncertainty with regard to his status as a member of a group.

4. *"Social" promotions.* A fourth approach to the alleviation of the more acute difficulties arising from conventional promotion practices has been referred to as "social adjustment" promotion. Many teachers and administrators who lean heavily on grade standards as the chief criterion for promoting children from grade to grade do recognize the extreme problems which such a plan creates. They see the fallacy in suggesting that a large, overage child remain in the same grade for years while the gap between him and his classroom associates gradually widens. They, therefore, send such a child along to the next grade but with the stipulation that it is being done only as a "social promotion." This limited concession to human individuality is commendable as far as it goes, but it is not likely to exert much influence in establishing any generally workable plan for pupil progress.

Promotion on the Basis of Chronological Age.—From the foregoing observations, it can be seen that many problems have arisen from attempts to reconcile the individual and continuous growth of the child with the administrative machinery of the elementary school. It has become increasingly apparent that not all children grow in a manner consistent with the vertical segments of the graded school. As a result, children have been penalized in many cases, parents have been made unhappy, and teachers have faced the end of the year with the frustration which comes from trying to mix human sympathy with the objective ruthlessness of achievement standards. It is little wonder that such conditions have led to the search for more realistic bases for determining the rate of a child's progress through the various stages of the school program.

Reaction against undesirable ideas for practices often is expressed by moving to an opposite position. As doubts have grown of the soundness of the grade standard theory of pupil progress, even when modified, many teachers have come to feel that nonpromotion, or retardation of any kind, should be entirely eliminated. They reason that, if nonpromotion has ill effects out of proportion with its advantages, the simplest way to cure the situation is to promote all children automatically at the end of each school year. This has come to be known by various terms, such as "automatic promotion," "100 per cent promotion," or "promotion by chronological age." In the main, available evidence seems to show that this plan is as feasible as any yet proposed as a general means of regulating pupil progress.

Many educators feel, however, that universal promotion is open to many abuses unless the philosophy of those who operate it is consistent with the purposes of the plan. It obviously will present many problems when it is applied administratively by teachers who have rigid conceptions of the curriculum at any particular grade level. However, when chronological age is used as the chief criterion for promotion, along with suitable provisions for making decisions occasionally on an individual basis, it does much to reduce failure among children and to eliminate a disproportionate amount of overageness in the school. In turn, these effects tend to alleviate some of the social and emotional problems which might otherwise be encountered.

In order for a plan of promotion based on chronological age to be consistent with provisions for continuous progress, certain considerations are necessary:

1. *There must be both opportunity and means for dealing with the cases of individual children whose adjustment cannot best be served through regular promotions with the group.* Such children may be those with particular physical, social, intellectual, or emotional problems, or those whose educational experiences have been interrupted unduly for various reasons. When decisions are necessary with respect to a given individual's classification, three principles should be followed: (*a*) The welfare of the individual should be the prime factor of consideration; (*b*) all elements of educational growth—physical, social, academic, and emotional—should be considered in the decision; (*c*) all persons who have a rightful stake in the child's progress should be allowed and encouraged to contribute to the decision.

2. *Teachers must accept the responsibility for providing learning experiences for each individual reasonably commensurate with his level*

of ability and achievement. This is essential to the concept of continuous pupil progress. If a teacher of the third grade, for instance, assumes that all pupils who enter her classroom at the beginning of the school year should be equally prepared to pursue a highly standardized program for that year, only frustration for both pupil and teacher can result. It is essential that each pupil be allowed to proceed from the point at which he is. Any other arrangement results in educational gaps that cause immediate disturbance and lead to future educational complications.

3. *Parents must understand the philosophy and policies of the school with reference to continuous progress.* The educational background of most parents is such that they have had experience only with strictly graded schools, with appraisal of the acquisition of factual subject matter. Since their own school days, they have had little opportunity to keep abreast of educational research or to become acquainted with the refinements that have been made in educational practice in the elementary schools. As a result, they find the newer proposals for regulating pupil progress rather drastic departures from what they considered generally satisfactory procedures. Members of the school staff should understand this and make every effort to interpret revised practices to parents in such a manner that they can see the primary consideration given to the child.

4. *The administration must make every effort to provide a variety of flexible teaching materials.* Teachers cannot carry on a differentiated program of learning experiences without differentiated materials of instruction. Materials of instruction should vary in both difficulty and interest. They should be such that each individual in the room can find materials suited to his achievement level. This is particularly true in curricular areas devoted to the development of skills, but it is also a necessary consideration in all aspects of the curriculum.

Ungraded Units and Pupil Progress.—One of the big problems of pupil progress is to find an administrative scheme of organization that will permit differentiated standards of educational achievement for individuals without, at the same time, penalizing them or placing a stigma on them. One of the more promising developments of recent years is the use of a lengthened cycle, rather than a single year, in organizing the work of the elementary school. Usually, this approach, where adopted, has meant that the six years of the school program have been organized on the basis of two units, or cycles—*the primary unit,* and *the advanced unit.* The former embraces the work typically done in kindergarten and the first three grades, and the latter, that done in grades four, five, and six. Within each cycle little emphasis is placed on grade levels, and pupils are assigned to rooms and teachers rather than to grades. This arrangement allows greater flexibility and encourages the organization of work around broader and richer learning experiences.

In most situations where the school is organized as a primary and an advanced unit, as described above, it is assumed that it is possible, often desirable, and even natural, for some children to remain as members of the primary unit for a year longer than others. In making such adjustments, the educational welfare of the child is foremost, and minimum emphasis is placed on his grade placement. The chief purpose of the plan is to allow him to proceed through the school program in as continuous and uninterrupted a manner as possible.

When ungraded units are adopted as the plan of organization in a school, teachers usually remain with a particular group of children throughout the cycle. This longer association with the children improves the teacher's knowledge of members of the group, and makes it easier to provide instruction to meet the particular needs of each.

Two Considerations Related to Promotion Policy

Regardless of the nature of the particular promotion plan used in a school, there are occasions when individual adjustments have to be made in the application of general policies. These occasions often involve decisions with respect to promotion or nonpromotion. It is the opinion of the author that two particular considerations have a connection with these decisions: (1) the parent's role in the decision, and (2) the terminology that is used in connection with adjustments in pupil progress. These will be discussed separately.

The Parent's Role in Promotion Decisions.—Aside from the child himself, the parent should be the person with the greatest investment in the child's life and the greatest interest in his success. Generally speaking, parents want their children to get along well and to derive the greatest possible benefit from their school experiences. This being the case, the school should make every attempt to encourage and utilize parental interest when decisions are to be made which will affect the child's entire future.

It must be remembered that nonpromotion is tantamount to taking an extra year of a child's life for purposes we deem important enough to warrant such action. Before doing so, we should be completely assured that the results will be sufficiently beneficial to justify such a move. As pointed out earlier there is considerable evidence which casts doubt on nonpromotion in most instances, and suggests caution in all decisions on the child's promotion status. Certainly it is the responsibility of the professional staff of the school to study carefully all the factors involved in the classification of children with special problems and to make recommendations regarding the placement of such children. It seems sensible, however, to rely heavily, if not entirely, on the wishes of parents in making the final decision. When children are retained at a grade level without the understanding and against the wishes of parents, the resulting resentment usually counteracts any possible benefits of the adjustment.

The Terminology Used in Connection with Nonpromotion.— Another matter of concern is the terminology that has developed in connection with pupil progress or, more particularly, in connection with nonpromotion. When a child is not promoted, he is referred to as having "failed" or "flunked." He is characterized as being "unable to do the work" or "not able to keep up with his group." When he is retained in a grade, he is constantly reminded of the fact that he is a "repeater." Perhaps these few examples are sufficient to illustrate the labels given children who learn slowly and who, therefore, are denied the blessings of normal progression from grade to grade.

The negative connotations which accompany nonpromotion may be a serious threat to the security and self-respect of a child. To complicate the matter further, the children who are likely to be subject to nonpromotion are also those who particularly need to have their morale and self-confidence strengthened. Much could be done in this respect if the unwholesome vocabulary frequently used in connection with nonpromotion could be eliminated or be replaced by terms which do not affect the feelings of the individual so adversely. Positive comments promote positive action; negative comments often aggravate an already serious problem. Teachers and administrators should remember this in all their communications with the child and about him.

EVALUATION AND PUPIL PROGRESS

Evaluation lies at the very heart of the problem of pupil progress in the elementary school. At every stage of the educational process judgments of achievement have to be made and educational success has to be defined in terms of some kind of performance. This process involves evaluation. The measures utilized to evaluate the educational growth of the child usually grow out of the concepts of pupil progress held by those who formulate and control the school program. For that reason, it is advisable to consider here some of the trends in evaluation currently emerging in the modern elementary school.

Evaluation as Distinguished from Measurement.—When the program of the elementary school was built mainly on textbooks and the memorizing of factual materials, and when the "recitation" was the chief instrument of teaching methodology, measurement assumed a natural importance. Since school marks represented success, or nonsuccess, and since there must be a basis for the marks, it was necessary to determine how much subject matter had been mastered sufficiently well to be recalled upon request. This necessity eventually led to the paper and pencil test and to other devices for revealing the quantity of achievement each child could demonstrate. Over the years educational measurement has been refined considerably and has many uses at all levels of the educational process. However, in recent years the process of appraising the effectiveness of education has been broadened far beyond the limits of measurement.

Evaluation seeks to relate educational outcomes to the child's motives. It is the process whereby a learner's attainments are judged in terms of many contributing factors, some inherent in the learner, others in the situation, and still others in the objectives which the learner seeks to realize. It requires that we measure growth to the extent of our ability to do so and that we seek to determine whether or not such growth is commensurate with the ability of the learner as he performs within existing situations. Measurement, then, is one of the processes utilized in evaluating the teaching-learning situation and its many outcomes.

Evaluation in Relation to Goals.—Change in status does not necessarily mean progress. Genuine progress involves movement toward some desirable objective. In the elementary school, some of these objectives remain relatively stable from year to year and from child to child; others differ as times change, as they also differ from child to child. Those who attempt to evaluate the changes which occur in the child as a result of his educational experiences must keep his educational goals in sharp focus. These goals arise from the values considered important for him. To determine the success he is experiencing as he moves toward such objectives is the job of evaluation. No teacher or administrator can shrink from these obligations.

Evaluation Through Many Types of Evidence.—Modern education has brought an increasing tendency to evaluate pupil progress on the basis of many factors. Both standardized and teacher-made tests continue to be useful as measuring instruments if they are constructed well, used scientifically, and interpreted wisely. In addition to these devices, actual behavior in real and hypothetical situations is increasingly being brought into the process of evaluation. Role playing and dramatizations are being developed as means through which children can be given the opportunity to demonstrate understanding. Less emphasis, at least in the elementary schools, is being placed on written forms of evaluation and correspondingly more emphasis is being attached to natural and functional forms of demonstrating educational growth.

Evaluation in Terms of Individual Ability.—In terms of the work of an individual child, evaluation is both a preliminary and an end process. Some form of evaluation is a prerequisite for differentiation of instruction. In other words, before we can provide for the needs of individual children, we must know the nature and extent of these needs. This calls for evaluation. In this sense it is a diagnostic process. In another sense, any kind of periodic or continuous evaluation is an appraisal of the child's growth up to a particular time. In either case, it is important to remember that modern evaluative practices reflect a growing feeling that educational outcomes should be appraised in terms of the capacities of the individual child. This idea is in direct opposition to the notion that the progress of all children should be measured against the same scale of uniform standards.

Evaluation by the Group.—Many aspects of evaluation are being shifted from the teacher to the group. When we consider that one of the major objectives of education is intelligent self-direction of the individual, it is encouraging to note the recent trends toward self-evaluation which can be observed at all levels of the educational ladder. Even in the primary classrooms of the elementary school, children are being encouraged to discuss and establish group standards of behavior and to appraise their own effectiveness in living up to these established standards. At the same time, pupils more and more are being made responsible for passing judgment on their own performances and progress. While the obligation of the teacher for evaluation should not be underestimated nor relinquished, it seems entirely wholesome for children to assume some responsibility for appraising their own work as far as their maturity will permit. Indeed, this is an important part of their educational growth.

Evaluation by Various Persons Involved in the Educational Process.—The preceding paragraph suggests that the evaluative function is no longer so highly concentrated in the hands of the teacher. We are coming to believe that evaluation, to be effective, must be a cooperative enterprise to which several different persons must make a contribution. Some of these are:

Pupil self-evaluation. If the purposes in a learning situation are clear to pupils, there are many points at which they can contribute to the process of evaluation. A pupil can help identify his purposes, contribute through discussion to the selection of learning experiences or units of work to achieve purposes, keep records of growth in learning skills, and help in interpreting outcomes of learning experiences in terms of determining their extent and value.

Group evaluation. Members of a group in the elementary school can usually participate in many ways in determining the progress being made toward the attainment of goals which have been cooperatively established. Particularly important is the contribution which can be made by the group in connection with growth toward responsibility, consideration for others, respect for property of others, and other aspects of social sensitivity and maturity. Members of a group can also be led to develop these skills to the point where they can be usefully applied in the constructive criticism of each other's efforts.

Teacher evaluation. The chief and final responsibility for evaluation, of course, usually rests with the teacher. The author believes that this is as it should be if the teacher is mature and wise in the fulfillment of his responsibilities. Such wisdom requires that the teacher evaluate the progress of pupils in terms of the individual abilities of each, by means of various evidences of growth as shown by appropriate evaluative devices, and on the basis of the purposes and goals of the learner. It also appears that the more closely the teacher's evaluation is related to the actual behavior traits of pupils, the more useful it is.

Parent evaluation. Continuous appraisal of the school program is being made by parents who send their children to school. It is not only desirable but imperative that the interest of parents be channeled into the evaluative process as it relates to their children. This involves frequent consultation with parents, continuous opportunities for them to observe school activities and to have such activities interpreted in the light of existing school purposes. It further involves the necessity for easy communication between school and home and for finding ways in which parents can participate in the nontechnical phases of their child's educational activities.

It should also be remembered that the community itself is continuously judging the quality of the school program. This implies the desirability of directing some effort toward helping the community understand the role and processes of the school in order that they may more accurately determine its value.

OBTAINING DATA FOR EVALUATING PUPIL PROGRESS

Before we can engage in truly effective evaluation of a child's progress we must know something of his history, his status, and his potentialities. Information regarding various aspects of the child's status and growth must come from all possible sources. It is important that the teacher explore all available possibilities for adding to his knowledge of the child before attempting to pass professional judgment on his educational progress. Some types of data are relatively common and somewhat obvious; others are less easy of access.

Cumulative records should be studied carefully by the teacher in an effort to gain as much information as possible regarding the child. From this source, the teacher usually can discover any pertinent facts regarding the physical history of the child, along with information about particular deficiencies. The records also may reveal the child's general pattern of progress in prior years of his schooling. These records are particularly valuable in that they give a continuous picture of the child's educational history.

Test data are valuable in the determination of pupil progress. In the main, the teacher will gain much insight into the child's status and progress through careful analysis of the results of at least five kinds of standardized tests, even though they cannot be classified on a completely discrete basis: (1) mental tests, (2) achievement tests, (3) readiness tests, (4) diagnostic tests, and (5) personality tests or scales. In addition, much use can be made of teacher-made tests, both for instruction and appraisal. It is the opinion of the author that each elementary school staff should cooperatively devise a general framework for a testing program for their particular school and that some attention should be given to all phases of testing as indicated above.

Observational data can provide considerable information on the daily behavior and progress of the child. The observation of the child from day to day may be done in both a casual and systematic manner. Pertinent or unusual behavior of the child is usually recorded in cumulative anecdotal records kept by the teacher. These records should ordinarily include the date each type of behavior is observed, the situation under which it occurred, and an objective, brief account of the event. Such records should be free from any sort of biased interpretation by the teacher. Each entry in such records is not entirely significant in itself, but over a period of time certain patterns of the child's behavior often are revealed through such anecdotal accounts of his activities both in the classroom and on the playground.

Inventories of interests and attitudes frequently can be useful in reflecting inner feelings which may affect the school progress of children.

While certain commercial interest and attitude scales are available if desired, many schools utilize teacher-made inventories. Such inventories can be constructed in the form of a check list or they may be formulated in such a way that more freedom is permitted the pupil in responding to the items included. Sometimes different inventories are constructed and used for different purposes. For instance, one can survey the reading interests of children, the radio programs listened to, or the kinds of hobbies children find most interesting. It is customary, however, to include several areas of interest in a single inventory. The same is true in selecting items to be used to indicate the attitudes of children toward various elements in home, school, and community life.

Information revealed by such scales and inventories as the ones mentioned above should be supplemented and verified, of course, by the knowledge which comes to the teacher from her continuous awareness of the reaction of various individual pupils to each phase of the instructional program of the school.

Casual conversations and individual conferences with pupils offer additional opportunities for the teacher to learn more about children as a basis for evaluating their progress. Often there is an opportunity before school in the morning, after school, during the recess or lunch hour, or on the playground for the teacher to visit informally with a child. It is surprising sometimes just how much pertinent information can be gained from the child during such natural and unguarded moments. Of course, conferences with parents and other teachers who work with a child are often helpful, too, in gaining insight into his behavior.

When an intensive study is made of an individual child over a period of time, it is usually referred to as a *case study*. This is admittedly a time-consuming technique for a busy teacher, but often such a study pays great dividends in furnishing leads to discovering the causes of puzzling behavior in children. All types of data are useful in making case studies and such data are usually organized according to some systematic outline. Usually included in the case study outline are such things as: (1) physical behavior and status, (2) family history and relationships, (3) educational history, (4) mental and emotional status, and (5) social relationships and problems.

Sociometric techniques have contributed much in recent years to the understanding of children by teachers and other professional personnel. The chief purpose of sociometry is to indicate the child's status as a member of his group. By asking children questions which require them to choose members of the group for some group activity, or with whom they would like to share experiences, some idea of the social acceptance of the child among children can be gained. This technique, which was suggested in an earlier chapter as one of the bases for grouping, can also be valuable in assisting the teacher to obtain complete understanding of the members of the group.

Role playing, dramatic representations, and projective techniques of various kinds are still other means of learning more about children, their capacities, their growth, and their problems. There appears to be an increasing tendency among teachers in modern schools to make use of such devices, which seems entirely compatible with the trend toward evaluating pupil growth and behavior in terms of behavioral reactions.

Action Suggestions for the Principal

1. Make a careful study, with the staff, of entrance policies of the school to determine the extent of their consistency with research in child development.

2. Always keep the emphasis on the child's progress rather than on periodic and artificial standards.

3. Remember that learning is cumulative and continuous; try to help the school develop policies for pupil progress which approach this concept as nearly as possible.

4. Evaluate pupil progress by more than one means.

5. In so far as possible, evaluate multiple factors of pupil growth in determining progress.

6. Strive to possess a thorough knowledge of research with regard to promotion and nonpromotion.

7. Encourage cooperative study by the staff of evaluation and promotional policies of the school; try to arrive at a general consensus.

8. Avoid administrative retardation of a child unless the evidence is clear that such an adjustment will make him become more successful.

9. In cases of the adjustment in the classification of an individual child, invite all persons with understanding of and interest in the child to participate in the decision.

10. In such cases of individual adjustment, make the best possible professional recommendation, then lean heavily on the parents for the final decision.

11. Keep pupil classification procedures flexible so that appropriate adjustments in pupil placement can be easily made.

12. Avoid "conditional promotions."

13. Try to move children along through school in such a manner that they remain with compatible groups.

14. Be sure that parents understand the considerations upon which pupil progress is based.

15. Make continuous progress for each child the goal of the school.

16. Provide for each teacher suitable teaching materials for children with a wide range of ability and achievement.

17. De-emphasize by any constructive means the importance of grade levels.

18. Encourage teachers to remain with a group of children through two- or three-year cycles.

19. Strive to build up a positive approach to the evaluation and reporting of pupil achievement.

20. Work to eliminate negative and unwholesome terminology in communications with and about the child.

21. Evaluate pupil progress in terms of conscious goals.

22. Practice, and encourage teachers to practice, both honesty and humaneness in discussing a pupil's progress with a parent or with the child himself.

SELECTED REFERENCES FOR EXTENDED READING

CASWELL, HOLLIS L., and FOSHAY, A. WELLESLEY. *Education in the Elementary School.* New York: American Book Co., 1950, chap. 13.

DEPARTMENT OF ELEMENTARY SCHOOL PRINCIPALS. "Reporting Pupil Progress," *The National Elementary Principal,* XXXI, No. 6 (June, 1952).

DOUGHERTY, JAMES H., GORMAN, FRANK H., and PHILLIPS, CLAUDE A. *Elementary School Organization and Management.* New York: The Macmillan Co., 1950, chap. 9.

ELSBREE, WILLARD S. *Pupil Progress in the Elementary School.* New York: Bureau of Publications, Teachers College, Columbia University, 1943.

ELSBREE, WILLARD S., and MCNALLY, HAROLD J. *Elementary School Administration and Supervision.* New York: American Book Co., 1951, chaps. 10, 11, 12.

HYMES, JAMES L. *Effective Home-School Relations.* New York: Prentice-Hall, Inc., 1953.

JACOBSON, PAUL, REAVIS, WILLIAM C., and LOGSDON, JAMES D. *Duties of School Principals.* New York: Prentice-Hall, Inc., 1950, chap. 13.

MEHL, MARIE A., MILLS, HUBERT H., and DOUGLASS, HARL R. *Teaching in Elementary School.* New York: The Ronald Press Co., 1950.

OTTO, HENRY J. *Elementary School Organization and Administration.* New York: Appleton-Century-Crofts, Inc., 1954, chap. 6.

STENDLER, CELIA BURNS. "Let's Look at Parent-Teacher Conferences," *Educational Leadership,* VI (February, 1949), 292-98.

STRANG, RUTH M. *Reporting to Parents.* New York: Bureau of Publications, Teachers College, Columbia University, 1947.

YEAGER, WILLIAM A. *Administration and the Pupil.* New York: Harper & Bros., 1949, chap. 10.

PART IV

IMPROVING THE CURRICULUM
OF THE SCHOOL

Chapter 11

IMPROVING THE CURRICULUM

The curriculum is as good as the learning it inspires

The curriculum is the moving force of the school program. It is the set of consciously devised learning experiences for which the school accepts responsibility, and through which it expects to achieve its purposes. It is true, of course, that many other factors of the school program enter into its total effectiveness. Such things as the instructional resources of the school, the special services it offers children, and the professional preparation of teachers all affect the quality of the curriculum and the learning that occurs through its use. However, it is safe to assume that the total success of the school cannot rise much above the level of educational insight with which the curriculum is conceived and implemented.

It has become popular, in recent years, to think of the curriculum of any child as being composed of all the experiences which that particular child has in his interaction with his environment. This development has tended to replace the notion of "the school's curriculum" with that of "the child's curriculum." In fact, one of the more outstanding books in the field of curriculum issued in recent years is developed around the relationship of the child to the curriculum.[1] The author wholeheartedly endorses the importance of this relationship and believes that the final test of any curricular efforts is the effect they have on individual learners. However, in order to crystallize and focus professional responsibilities in the matter, the curriculum here is considered to be those learning experiences which the school devises, guides, and utilizes in its organized efforts to provide for the needs of children.

In no aspect of the educational effort is leadership more important than in the development and maintenance of a sound curriculum through which stimulating teaching is encouraged and functional learning is assured. Certainly a major function of the educational leader is that of encouraging sound curriculum development, providing for administra-

[1] J. Murray Lee and Dorris May Lee, *The Child and His Curriculum* (New York: Appleton-Century-Crofts, Inc., 1950).

tive and instructional adaptation of the curriculum to differing needs of learners, and maintenance of a climate in which the fullest possibilities of the curriculum may be realized through the operation of high level, cooperative human relations. It is appropriate, therefore, to discuss at some length in the remainder of this chapter the role of the administrative leader of an elementary school as it relates to curriculum building and implementation.

SOME BASIC PRINCIPLES RELATED TO CURRICULUM IMPROVEMENT

The school curriculum is usually caught between the changing demands of progress and the inertia of tradition. It usually resides in a state of compromise somewhere between the positions assumed by the imaginative professional zealot and the completely uninformed, or reactionary, layman. Schools, as instruments of society, are charged with the responsibility both of preserving the values of the past and present and of predicting the demands of the future. To meet these responsibilities, schools consciously select and emphasize certain learning experiences from the array of things which might be learned from the universe about us. These learning experiences are then adapted to the maturity and needs of learners, organized and coordinated, and presented through means intellectually palatable to children. This process of selection, adaptation, and organization is the essence of curriculum development.

The curriculum of the elementary school would mean little if detached from the personal, social, economic, civic, and ethical purposes it is designed to achieve. It must always be thought of, therefore, in the context of contemporary human affairs as well as in connection with the perpetuation of valuable elements of the cultural heritage. This suggests the necessity for continuous evaluation and revision in terms of existing conditions. Creating the conditions for the continuous, thoughtful analysis of the school curriculum is one of the most stimulating challenges to the energies of the administrative leader. To meet this challenge, he must be aware of the many relationships existing between the curriculum of the school and the many other facets of human aspiration and activity. Perhaps some of these relationships can be pointed up through the brief discussion of certain guiding principles.

1. *The curriculum consists of all the learning experiences of children which the school consciously utilizes in its efforts to help these children achieve desirable goals.* The curriculum is the instructional provision for learning. It is not a course of study or even a curriculum guide, although the curriculum of the school may be indicated descriptively, or

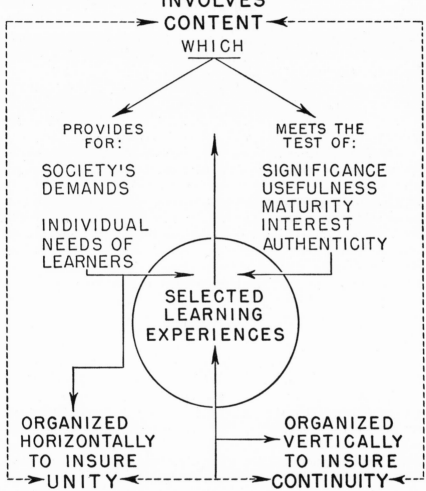

Figure 11

Some Major Aspects of the Curriculum

suggested, through a curriculum guide or through other types of printed materials. A curriculum is *what happens*; a course of study or curriculum guide indicates *what is expected to happen;* and curriculum reports or unit descriptions often reveal *what has happened.* It seems important to make this distinction clear, as the real significance of the curriculum reveals itself at the time and place of its contact with learners.

Deliberate emphasis is placed here on the assertion that the curriculum is composed of "learning experiences" which serve as steps toward the achievement of desired types of growth in children. The curriculum is more than subject matter as it is usually defined. It involves provision for functional contact with various forms of human experience and activity as well as reaction physically, intellectually, and emotionally to them.

2. *The nature of the curriculum should be determined both by the demands of contemporary society and by the needs of individuals.* The history of education provides numerous examples of differences of opinion on the proper orientation of the curriculum. Some have insisted, as some do even yet, that the curriculum should be chiefly a compact package of human experience to date; others have felt that the school curriculum should be geared largely to a preparatory function and should reflect a consideration for matters which will become important at some future date; still others contend that the curriculum should be flavored heavily with the solving of current problems, creative exploration, and actual experience with the basic processes of living.

Few would deny today that one of the primary elements of the curriculum should be an understanding and appreciation of our heritage of American life and culture, as well as an understanding and appreciation of human progress and experience in all parts of the world. It is important that children learn as much as possible about the physical and social world around them, for, in so doing, they come to understand the interrelationships that promote, or perhaps sometimes complicate, modern civilization. We have reached a stage in human affairs in which a person cannot live successfully alone. Each individual has come to expect certain benefits to himself from the corporate efforts of society, and society makes certain demands upon each individual if he is to be an efficient member of the groups in which he lives, works, and seeks recreation. These demands cannot be ignored in the formulation of the elementary school curriculum and, of course, they are not ignored in the operation of good modern elementary schools.

Society-centered goals of the school, though important, are not enough. In fact, it may be said that this approach is not even strictly American in character since it is also practiced by totalitarian systems in their use of the educational structure to accomplish political ends. The distinguishing feature of American education, as it is also the basic tenet of American democracy, is the concern and consideration for the individual. Respect for this feature, then, implies that we shall develop curricula that make provisions for differences in interest, background, ability, and purpose of individual children who attend our schools. It is essential that persons who are responsible for the curriculum of the elementary school keep in mind that we are not attempting to produce either "rugged individualists" or docile persons who will submissively conform to a great, massive, social machine with purposes and activities entirely standardized. Rather, it is the goal of modern education to help children develop in such a way that they will be both individually competent and socially effective.

3. *The curriculum should be directly related to the purposes of the school.* Presumably, all elementary schools have many objectives in common. At the same time, it must be recognized that each school may, and probably should, have certain objectives that are unique to that particular school. These may arise from differences in community life and culture, in vocational emphases, in the age and composition of the school population, or in existing ideas about what constitutes effective education for a particular group of children.

It is essential that the objectives of a school be determined clearly as a logical prerequisite to intelligent curriculum planning. If we want children to learn certain things, to become certain kinds of people, to develop special skills, or to have special attention given to unique deficiencies or handicaps, we must select and plan for the kinds of learning experiences which contribute most directly to each of these respective ends. It is for this reason that considerable emphasis is placed on the determination of objectives in an earlier part of this book in which the formulation of the school program is discussed. It does not seem possible to make an astute approach to the development of a sound curriculum without first considering the aims which are to be fulfilled.

4. *The curriculum should be the regulating factor in the nature, selection, utilization, and evaluation of school facilities.* The curriculum is the heart of the school program, but its effectiveness does not depend alone upon its own quality or soundness. The extent of its effectiveness depends also upon the quality and suitability of the facilities through which the curriculum is activated. The school site should be selected and the school plant constructed for the program to be carried out. Activity rooms are useless in an instruction program which utilizes few activities; facilities for creative work in art and construction cannot produce magic dividends in a school whose curriculum embraces no opportunities for such activities.

The furnishings and materials of instruction also should be selected and organized for the type of curriculum around which the school program is developed. The curriculum of the modern elementary school requires the accessibility of many more types of materials than was true of the more narrow curriculum of the past. This refers both to *types of materials* and to *variety of materials* within each type. A more detailed discussion of materials of instruction appears in a later section of this chapter.

5. *The curriculum of the school should be the determining factor in the organization of the school.* The chief function of school organization is that of making the instructional program operate smoothly and economically, and with optimum effectiveness. Varying approaches to the curriculum demand correspondingly different types of organization. For example, the use made of grouping in the school organization depends largely on the concept of the curriculum prevailing in a particular school. The same is true for the manner in which pupil progress is regulated in the school, or for the extent to which the instructional program is unified into broad fields or compartmentalized into subject areas.

Again, it should be noted that the first responsibility of the school staff, with whatever assistance they may gain from other sources, is to formulate the purposes the school hopes to serve in the lives of the children who attend it. The next step is to develop a curriculum that will effectively produce these results. The third step is to organize the school in such a manner that the instructional program operates with maximum efficiency. All these factors are related, and it is impossible to conceive constructive efforts to develop the organization of the school without proper prior consideration of the curriculum.

6. *The curriculum should be formulated on a cooperative basis.* Many persons have a direct and justifiable interest in the curriculum of the school. The development of the curriculum is not the sole responsibility of a state or city curriculum director, an administrator, a supervisor, or even the professional staff of a school. The resources of numerous potential contributors should go into the formulation of the curriculum. Although it is readily admitted that some person, or persons, must assume responsibility for the leadership in coordinating efforts to improve the curriculum, it is equally necessary that wide participation be encouraged in these efforts. Certainly classroom teachers, upon whose efforts and understanding the success of the curriculum really depends, must take an active part in its determination. It is similarly desirable to insure that the interests, ideas, needs, and planning of children are utilized in curriculum development.

The community-conscious school can hardly afford to ignore the potential contributions of laymen to the curriculum of the school. Not only can means be devised for the constructive participation of parents and citizens in curriculum development or revision, but such persons also can contribute directly to the instructional program of the school through participation in community excursions, sharing experiences and knowledge with children in the classroom, and through many other forms of cooperative school-community activities.

7. *The curriculum should utilize both long-range and day-to-day planning.* There are enough stabilized, common elements of the curriculum to make advance planning profitable. Teachers in the elementary school, especially if they are beginning their teaching experience, are somewhat hampered by the complete absence of a plan for the instructional program. No business would long endure if its personnel had no preconceived notions about the means whereby its products were to be created or assembled. Likewise, it is not too much to expect trained professional personnel in education to be able to conceive in advance a generally sound structure to guide the instructional program of the school. Such planning, if done thoughtfully and without finality, can avoid wasteful duplication of effort, provide necessary continuity in the learning experiences of children throughout the years of the elementary school, and create among staff members a greater understanding of the context of the work of each.

While support is being given here for the advance planning of the curriculum, this position does not imply in any way any disregard for the necessity for current day-to-day planning and adjustment of learning experiences. In fact, one of the greatest weaknesses of the state-prescribed curricula prevalent in earlier years in many states was their rigidity and lack of flexibility. Such flexibility can only be achieved through the adaptation of learning experiences to daily needs and conditions. There is probably never a truly successful school day that does not involve the teacher and children in some on-the-spot planning.

Long-range curriculum planning and development will lend stability, sense of direction, and continuity to a program of instruction in the elementary school. At the same time, flexibility and differentiation must be accomplished through continuous planning and adaptation throughout each day of the school year. Both approaches are necessary if the curriculum is to be really effective.

8. *The curriculum cannot be separated from teaching methodology.* It is essential that the curriculum of the elementary school be consistent with, and actuated by, sound methods of teaching. In the final analysis, the curriculum is only a potential until it comes into contact with learners. The results of this impact on learners are influenced greatly by the nature and quality of the methodology employed. Under the guiding hand of the expert teacher, many gaps or deficiencies in the planned program of instruction go unnoticed because the ingenuity of the teacher compen-

sates for such weaknesses; conversely a teacher unskilled in modern techniques of teaching cannot achieve the expected beneficial outcomes from even the most thoughtfully conceived curriculum. In developing local programs of curriculum improvement, therefore, it is necessary to include an analysis of procedures in the program as well as the study of desirable content for the curriculum of the school.

9. *The curriculum should be based on sound criteria for the selection of learning experiences.* There are literally millions of things to be learned in and from the universe which surrounds the learner. Obviously all of them cannot be learned by any one person. Selection must take place from the very beginning of the organized learning activities of children. This selection must be in terms of some sort of criteria, or bases. It is not sufficient justification for the inclusion of certain content in the elementary school curriculum to insist that such content has always been included as a part of elementary education. Conversely, it is no more reasonable to insist on incorporating subject matter simply because it is new. The only value in selecting particular learning experiences is that such experiences will produce certain effects in children. It is for the school to decide what these desired attainments should be. This demands thoughtful leadership by school personnel in order to coordinate the best ideas of all concerned in this process.

The criteria governing the selection of curriculum content should include the factors contributing to successful living. The formulation of these criteria requires consideration of the learner's personal, vocational, social, intellectual, emotional, and spiritual needs. These and other aspects of selecting curriculum content will be discussed in some detail in a later section of this chapter.

10. *The curriculum should be organized in terms of what is known about the learning process.* Much of what persists in the elementary school curriculum originally got its importance from a belief in psychologies of learning that since have been largely discredited. One reason that the elementary school curriculum has been so highly compartmentalized into subjects has been the assumption that the intellectual processes operate in terms of more or less isolated "faculties." In the same way, much of the rigidity of the teaching-learning situation has been related to the more mechanistic concepts of the learning process.

It is now apparent from modern research that learning is both experiential and contextual in nature. In other words, we learn much of what we learn through our own activities and through our reactions to those activities. We also learn particular things in relation to the other things and conditions which exist in the "field" around us. All acquired knowledge gets its real meaning when it is integrated, or intellectually assimilated, into the pattern of experience each of us possesses, or within which we live.

The curriculum, then, should be organized in such a manner that it encourages, rather than hinders, purposeful activities, unified integration of these activities, and the utilization of natural relationships between learning and living.

11. *The curriculum should be organized in terms of what is known about child development.* Continuity is an essential condition of growth. This applies as well to educational growth as to physical development. It is important, then, that planned learned experiences are consonant with the normal stages of development revealed by modern methods of child study. Significant contributions in this field have been made by such educators as Olson,[2] Gesell,[3] and Strang.[4] The works of these authors and their associates provide detailed information in this field.

Two aspects of vertical organization of the curriculum deserve attention. The first is the relation of the common learnings of children to the general stages of human development represented in the elementary school. For example, it is important in the skills areas, such as reading, that the sequence of materials and methods be suited to the normal interest and abilities of children at the various stages of their progress through school. In the second place, it is equally essential to provide for variations in materials and methods in establishing a continuous series of learning experiences for individual children who may vary from the so-called normal patterns of growth. Continuity must be maintained for all, but this can occur only if variations in the rate of learning in individuals are recognized and provided for. The sequence, or grade placement of learning experiences, or even the curriculum content, is not important in itself; it does become important in its relation to continuity of learning on the part of each child.

12. *The curriculum should be susceptible to continuous evaluation and revision.* The truly productive endeavors of mankind almost invariably are sensitive to changes in conditions which affect such endeavors. Business and industrial practices, professional techniques, and social services all reflect an awareness of change from year to year and, oftentimes, from day to day. Most of us assume that this is a wholesome situation. Certainly none of us desires a world of stagnation. There are those among us, however, both lay and professional, who appear to believe that what is once good in the educational field will always remain

[2] Willard C. Olson, *Child Development* (Boston: D. C. Heath & Co., 1949).

[3] Arnold Gesell and Frances Ilg, *The Child From Five to Ten* (New York: Harper & Bros., 1946).

[4] Ruth Strang, *An Introduction to Child Study*, 3d ed. (New York: The Macmillan Co., 1951).

good, and that a curriculum from which one generation profited should not be modified lest succeeding generations be deprived of their basic educational rights. Such an attitude violates common sense and tends to create a rather severe lag between *what we could do* and *what we do* for our children.

The curriculum should never be considered a finished product or a final plan. With the leadership of the principal and others, the staff should examine the program continuously, try to detect its weaknesses or capitalize on its strengths, exchange ideas on methods of teaching, search for suitable, improved subject matter as needs require, and cooperatively devise as many means as possible for the systematic appraisal of its outcomes. Attention to such matters as these can be coordinated into a continuous program of curriculum evaluation and development that will keep the educational program in step with other aspects of progress in the community (or in our total society, for that matter). Change for the sake of change is seldom desirable, but change based on thoughtful and expert evaluation is the very essence of progress in all areas of cooperative human effort, including education. The curriculum, to be genuinely useful, must continuously be subjected to such evaluation and such modification.

Major Aspects of Curriculum Improvement

The improvement of the instructional program involves several aspects of curriculum development. Any serious search of the curriculum for possibilities for improvement necessarily must include search for answers to the following questions:

1. What should be taught, or more properly, what should be learned?
2. How should these learning experiences be organized for best results?
3. In what order, or sequence, should various elements of the curriculum be presented?
4. Through what teaching methods and techniques can the full possibilities of the curriculum be realized?
5. What resources and materials for instruction are necessary for the optimum utilization of the curriculum?

These questions have a real bearing on curriculum improvement and the answers to them form a fundamental approach to the logical study of the teaching-learning situation. Each will be discussed in the following parts of this section under the following headings: (1) improving the content of the curriculum, (2) improving the continuity of the curriculum, (3) improving the unity of the curriculum, (4) improving methods of teaching, and (5) improving the instructional resources for learning.

CONTENT

Improving the Content of the Elementary School Curriculum.— Numerous bases for the selection of curriculum content have been proposed and used at various periods in the history of American education. Most people, lay and professional, agree that what we teach in our schools is important. However, there is no comparable agreement as to the underlying bases for the selection of the subject matter of the curriculum. Differences in opinion along this line are reflected in such varying terms as "the subject-matter curriculum," "the experience curriculum," the "child-centered school," the "community-centered school," or, as appears in an interesting recent volume on the teaching-learning process,[5] "the reality-centered school."

There have been several attempts to classify the procedures through which the content of the curriculum can be modified. One of these classifications was made by Alberty[6] and is illustrative of the categories into which such procedures may be divided. These procedures are:

1. *Textbook,* through which the thinking of the textbook author becomes the source of expertness which delimits the curriculum.
2. *Laissez faire, or opportunistic,* through which the curriculum is regulated very largely, if not entirely, by the individual teacher.
3. *Activity analysis,* through which the curriculum is formulated on the basis of determining the nature of activities which people normally perform in life.
4. *Social functions,* which involves the systematic formulation of functional learning experiences based on philosophically defensible objectives.
5. *Learner needs,* in which considerable emphasis is placed on the characteristics and needs of learners at various stages of educational development rather than upon anticipated adult needs.

Although this classification of procedures was originally made in relation to the secondary school curriculum, it seems to be equally applicable, with the few adaptations made by the writer, to the elementary school curriculum and to efforts to improve it.

A careful study of the various approaches to curriculum development in recent years in our schools leads to the impression that there are three chief sources from which the content of the curriculum of the elementary

[5] Nathaniel Cantor, *The Teaching-Learning Process* (New York: The Dryden Press, 1953).

[6] Adapted from H. B. Alberty, *Reorganizing the High-school Curriculum* (New York: The Macmillan Co., 1947), p. 182.

school is usually drawn. They are: (1) an analysis of the interests and needs of children as they can be best determined, (2) an analysis of the environment, and (3) an analysis of the culture. These categories are not mutually exclusive, of course, and tend toward becoming merged into a composite pattern in the integrated curriculum.

Certainly one clear impression emerges from most of the curriculum study being carried on: if the curriculum of the elementary school is to fulfill its designated purpose, it must be constructed for, and around, the child. This requires a consideration of both current and anticipated needs of the child as he grows toward adulthood. The modern functional approach to learning places the emphasis on current and existing problems and needs on the assumption that one's ability to solve the problems of the future is best developed and judged by the extent to which he utilizes opportunities to solve the problems of the present. With this consideration in mind, it seems that any intelligent approach to curriculum building must rest upon some sort of analysis of *learner needs*.

The interests of learners also exert a marked influence on the curriculum. The motivating effect of interest influences pupil achievement and should be recognized at the level of content selection and placement.

As was pointed out in an earlier part of this chapter, there is an infinite number of potential learning experiences. Any attempt to have the curriculum of the elementary school be truly representative of all areas of human knowledge and experience could lead only to educational chaos through the process of curricular dilution. The prevention of such a condition requires selection of content so that that which remains is truly significant.

Much of the selection that occurs in curriculum building concerns *the relationships of man to his physical and social environment*. Those understandings essential to the process of living a reasonably successful and enlightened life deserve inclusion in the content of the curriculum. These understandings are important for their contribution to fruitful and functional living in an ever expanding environment. Learning experiences involving such subject matter should be selected and developed so as to insure continuously broadening horizons for the learner as he views the world and as he attempts to understand the interrelationships among its various elements.

A third source of direction in choosing the content of the school curriculum is *the culture which forms the setting of the school*. Those who strive to develop an optimum program of learning experiences for twentieth-century children cannot ignore the forces of the culture which so powerfully influence contemporary concepts of "the good life." Most of the problems of the current era cannot be understood, and certainly not solved, without being viewed in the context of the culture within which they have occurred or evolved.

Learning experiences of elementary school children should be selected and organized in such a way that they reflect proper concern for the democratic way of life and for the ethical ideals upon which such a way of living must firmly rest. In this regard, attempts should be made to provide a curriculum that will serve as a suitable medium for gaining an understanding of the social, economic, political, and spiritual factors which have brought our efforts at self-government to their current level.

An appreciation of the arts and inventive genius which have marked American as well as world civilization is another facet of the culture which merits the attention of those who contribute to the task of shaping the curriculum.

Criteria for the Selection of Curriculum Content.—The first step in the wise selection of learning experiences for children is to get in mind the criteria which are to govern the choices made. This process demands time and careful thought. It is at this stage of curriculum determination that the corporate wisdom of the professional staff, parents, laymen, and curriculum experts should be sought and utilized.

Each school probably should develop its own criteria to serve as its guide in curriculum development and implementation, to be based on the school's own unique goals, if they are different in any way from those of other schools. For a start toward curriculum study, however, it may be wise for a school staff to begin with the consideration of some commonly accepted set of criteria and then work toward its adaptation for local use. For this reason some illustrative lists of criteria are included here:

CRITERIA FOR SELECTION OF CURRICULUM CONTENT

1. *The criterion of significance.* Is the subject matter of sufficient importance to warrant special attention? Will it make a major contribution to the basic fund of knowledge and understanding needed by the learner?
2. *The criterion of usefulness.* Will this learning experience contribute to the development of functional skills or knowledge? Does it represent a current need of the learner? Is there reasonable certainty that the outcome of this learning experience will be useful in the future?
3. *The criterion of maturity.* Is this learning experience geared to the developmental stage of the learner? Is it experience that has meaning for learners at their present maturity level?
4. *The criterion of interest.* Will this learning experience hold interest for the learners? Is it related to their purposes? Will it motivate them to make their best efforts?

5. *The criterion of authenticity.* Is this subject matter reliable? Is it honestly and objectively developed? Is it true? Will it be consistent with the spirit of objectivity?

These criteria have been developed in considerable detail by the writer as he has worked as a consultant with local school systems in their efforts to improve the curriculum at the elementary school level. Perhaps the summarizing headings given here will be sufficient to illustrate their general nature.

Another illustrative set of criteria in which the nature and quality of specific learning experiences are emphasized was compiled by a classroom teacher as bases for the selection of suitable learning experience for children:

BASES FOR SELECTION OF LEARNING EXPERIENCES[7]

1. Does it help the learner assume responsibility?

2. Does it give the learner an opportunity to face problems?

3. Does it give the learner opportunity to learn how to live happily with others?

4. Does it give the learner an opportunity to learn the skills necessary for individual growth and group participation?

5. Does the learning experience provide a knowledge of basic communication skills?

6. Does it give the learner a sense of satisfaction and pride in work well done?

7. Does it give the learner a chance to do what he can do?

8. Does it give the learner an opportunity to learn his own rights and the rights of others?

9. Is the learning experience important to the learner?

10. Does the learning experience show constructive interaction between teacher and children?

11. Does the learning experience allow the child to make choices and to understand and accept the results of his decisions?

12. Does the child have the opportunity to practice the behaviors indicated by the objectives of the learning experience?

13. Does the learning experience produce an atmosphere that fosters self-respect, self-reliance, respect for others, and a cooperative attitude?

CONTINUITY

Growth Continuity and Grade Placement.—A second consideration in curriculum development is that of providing a sequence of learning experiences that does not violate the continuous nature of growth.

[7] Ruth Hochstetler in an unpublished paper submitted to the writer.

In former years this problem of sequence was met chiefly through designated grade placement of materials of instruction. This approach involved the efforts of curriculum specialists and groups who developed specific courses of study for statewide use. Such materials typically specified both the content and placement of materials in the various curriculum areas.

At that time the attention given to grade placement consisted largely of deciding on the total content of the elementary school program, at least in general terms, and then chopping it into parts which appeared to be consistent with the average maturity of the children at each grade level. In many instances more consideration appeared to be given to the quantity of curriculum content than to the nature of it. Gradually through the years, however, there has developed a concern for the appropriateness of particular content and methods for each of the various grade levels.

In the modern school the key to the vertical organization of the curriculum is continuity. After elements of curriculum content to be emphasized are selected, they must be arranged in some longitudinal sequence of scope and difficulty consistent with the developing maturity and interests of the learner. Particularly, the skills of children need to be developed in a graduated manner consonant with the stages of growth through which learners develop. The same is true with respect to other types of learning, too, though probably not in so obvious a manner nor to such an apparent degree. This changing emphasis has resulted to a large degree from the studies in child development that have been made in recent years. A second factor in the change from "placement" to "continuity" has been the research of recent years concerning the effectiveness with which children learn various types of materials at various levels.

A good illustration of the effect of educational research on the curriculum has occurred in the field of arithmetic. For example, as a result of studies in this field, ideas regarding the place of drill in the development of an understanding of quantitative relationships have been almost completely revised. Whereas, in schools of an earlier day, the child first learned the symbolism of numbers, he now is given many varied opportunities to come in contact with situations in which the use of numbers is important. Then, after number meanings have been established, drill is employed to create facility in number usage. This change in approach to the understanding and use of numbers is reflected in the curriculum of the modern school as well as in textbooks in the field of arithmetic.

In studying and appraising provisions for sequential learning in the elementary school, the important consideration is not that certain things should be learned at a particular time or at a particular age or grade level, but rather that things should be learned in an order that guarantees essential continuity. Some of the ways in which such continuity may be encouraged are through:

1. A lessened emphasis on common grade standards for all children of a given age
2. Longer periods of teacher-pupil association, that is, each teacher remains with a group of children through a longer period than a semester or a single year
3. The use of a variety of instructional materials, varied in both interest and difficulty
4. Liberalized promotion policies
5. Staff cooperation and interconsultation on pupil adjustments and progress
6. Use of the unit or broad fields approach to curriculum organization
7. Provisions for individualized remedial help with particular difficulties
8. A realistic and functional record system that lends itself to the cumulative use by teachers who work with a child through each grade sequence
9. The elimination of terminology which associates either credit or stigma with a particular learning rate
10. Avoidance of both repetition and gaps in the learning sequence

The most realistic attack on the problem of continuity must be made at the classroom level. Such continuity cannot be insured either by administrative machinery or by decree.

Horizontal Organization of the Curriculum

It is not enough that defensible curriculum content be selected for children and arranged in terms of a development sequence. One of the great contributions of the more modern psychologies of learning has been the recognition of the integrative and unified character of learning. Such a concept of learning suggests that a thing acquires meaning from its organismic context as well as from its inherent nature. Meaning also comes from the association of ideas of a similar character. Many educators now feel that the essence of the learning process is the incorporation of a new means of responding into an already established experiential pattern. Of the many possible constructive outcomes from effective horizontal organization of the curriculum, three appear to be of greatest importance: (1) unity, (2) enrichment, and (3) flexibility. These three characteristic features also may be considered basic criteria for appraising curriculum organization.

The attempt to achieve a greater degree of unity, enrichment, and flexibility in the school program has brought about a movement through several stages or types of organization. They are: (1) the organization of the curriculum into rather discrete subjects with little relationship among them; (2) modification of organization through correlation of two or more subjects into a subject area; (3) the core curriculum approach which focalizes curriculum organization around a "core area"; (4) the realignment of subject areas into integrated "broad fields"; and (5) the organization of learning experiences around problem areas or functional experiences. As the horizontal organization of learning experiences moves from the "subject" emphasis toward the broader "problem" emphasis, subjects gradually lose their unique identity, and lines between subject areas become more and more flexible and often are entirely eliminated.

Unity is essential to effective integration of learning experiences. Understanding is not acquired in an additive kind of way. It appears to develop from a perspective of the manner in which elements of knowledge and experience fit together. It comes from reaction to and reconstruction of experience.

A second essential feature of good curriculum organization is the provision for *enrichment*. Learning experiences should be organized in such a way that they continuously stretch and extend the skills and horizons of the learner. Such enrichment depends for its fulfillment on the amount and nature of materials and resources, their organization, and the teaching methodology through which they are used. Some of the essential factors which help to enrich the curriculum are:

1. A variety of reading materials, differentiated in difficulty, and easily accessible to the learner at all times.
2. A variety of appropriate audio-visual materials to provide partially direct experiences.
3. Many direct experiences through the use of community resources.
4. The organization of learning experiences around broad and functional problems wherever possible. With reference to these problems, opportunities should be provided to:
   a) Pursue individual interests and to explore and use individual resources for learning.
   b) Cooperate in committee and research groups in the study of special aspects of the problem.
   c) Apply the skills of communication to good advantage.
   d) Share information with all other members of the classroom group.

e) Have an opportunity to exercise initiative and creativeness in the study of the problem.

A third major outcome of good curriculum organization is *flexibility*. Many of the same considerations essential to enrichment also are necessary for flexibility. Flexibility comes largely through either (1) differentiation or (2) adaptation, or both. The main points at which flexibility may be exercised in providing for instructional differentiation usually are related to:

1. *Purposes* of individual learners
2. Establishment of expected *standards of attainment* for different individuals
3. Types of *teaching and learning activities* with regard to such matters as
   a) Opportunities for creative and imaginative approaches to learning
   b) Proportionate use of direct and vicarious types of experiences
   c) The extent to which repetitive practice is used
   d) Proportionate use of individual and group work
4. Types and variety of *instructional materials* provided in the classroom
5. Approaches to *evaluation* of individual growth and progress

The Unit Approach to Curriculum Organization.—Recent years have brought about an increasing use of the unit of work as a means of providing enrichment, individualization, and integration of learning experiences. In the main, units have been of two general types: (1) topical or subject-matter units, and (2) activity or experience units. Of course, modifications are sometimes made in unit selection and organization which utilize elements of both of these more extreme types. Many teachers in modern elementary schools make splendid use of the activity unit. It is customary to develop such units around functional centers of interest, usually in the social studies or science area. Through teacher-pupil planning directional goals, purposes, or questions are formulated. This planning stage is usually followed by the exploration of ways by which individuals or groups can seek information about the problem through the use and development of desired skills and creative activity. Work periods are then set up along with opportunities for group sharing of ideas and problems and information. Finally, provision is made for some type of culminating activity. Ideally, the culminating activity contributes to the evaluation of outcomes of the unit through the demonstrated use of understandings gained during the course of the unit activity.

Many good statements have been formulated which set forth the characteristics of good units.[8] Most of them reflect rather common agreement on such basic features as the following:

Desirable units should:

1. Evolve around a center of interest that is important to children.
2. Be sufficiently significant to merit intensive study.
3. Be related to definite purposes which are functionally genuine.
4. Offer opportunities for many facets of educational growth.
5. Involve materials that are geared to the maturity levels of the participating children.
6. Utilize various types of learning activities.
7. Provide opportunities for both individual and group activity.
8. Involve pupil-planning at every feasible stage of development.
9. Provide for the functional integration of acquired knowledge, skills, or understandings.
10. Be susceptible to evaluation.

TEACHING METHODS AND THE CURRICULUM

The best single guarantee of desirable learning experiences for a group of children is an understanding and competent teacher. Enthusiasm of the teacher is a great motivating force for children. Sound teaching methods require a knowledge of child development, an appreciation of children's interest, a broad and interesting array of information, and the technical knowledge to organize learning activities into a well-integrated program. The teacher is the agent who is most directly responsible for implementing the curriculum. The quality of the school program is determined very largely by the composite teaching methods of those who use it.

A curriculum bulletin[9] in social studies issued recently in Wisconsin contains the following check list of rather specific items for the evaluation of teaching practices.

EVALUATION OF TEACHING PRACTICES

The following check list may well be used by teachers for evaluation of their own teaching techniques:

1. Do I use a unit organization in my work?
2. Do I list for my guidance the understandings to be developed in a unit?
3. Do I define preplanning of possible activities?
4. Do I use cooperative pupil-teacher planning?
   a) Using flexible small group instruction?
   b) Providing materials suited to the reading ability of individuals?

---

[8] For example, see J. Murray Lee and Dorris May Lee, *The Child and His Curriculum* (New York: Appleton-Century-Crofts, Inc., 1950), chap. 7.

[9] Statewide Social Studies Committee, *I Did It This Way:* Curriculum Bulletin No. 14 (Madison, Wisconsin: Wisconsin Cooperative Educational Planning Program, 1951).

    c) Using activities suited to the needs and abilities of different children?
5. Do I provide for individual differences?
6. Do I help pupils develop skill in the use of books, for example? In:
    a) Using best sources of information?
    b) Using index and table of contents?
    c) Using glossary and dictionary?
    d) Note taking?
    e) Interpreting pictures?
    f) Skimming?
    g) Outlining?
    h) Summarizing?
7. Do I see that students use those activities that will best develop understandings, attitudes, and skills desired as outcomes of a unit?
8. Do I help boys and girls in the development of skills concerning maps, globes, charts, and graphs? In:
    a) Reading them?
    b) Interpreting them?
    c) Locating them?
    d) Making them?
9. Do I make use of such activities and audio-visual aids as:
    a) Committee work?
    b) Construction?
    c) Community resources (people, places, etc.)?
    d) Demonstrations?
    e) Dramatizations?
    f) Exhibits?
    g) Experiments?
    h) Field trips?
    i) Film strips?
    j) Models?
    k) Motion pictures?
    l) Music, folk dances, poetry, and art?
    m) Phonograph?
    n) Pupils' experiences?
    o) Radio?
    p) Slides?
    q) Tape recorder?
    r) Teacher's experiences?
10. Do I help children to know of their successes and improvement through:
    a) Comparing work with standards?
    b) Criticizing [my] own work?
    c) Checking and evaluating own conclusions?
    d) Keeping individual progress charts?
    e) Getting verbal recognition by the teacher?
    f) Getting recognition by the class?
    g) Testing—when testing is good teaching or leads to it?

11. Do I help in the development of democratic ways of living in my classroom by:

a) Providing for growth in group responsibility; for example, through use of: room committees; bulletin board committees; club activities?

b) Providing for growth in individual responsibility; for example, through use of: group chairmen; class librarians; hobbies?

c) Keeping the class atmosphere one of cooperation?

INSTRUCTIONAL MATERIALS AND THE CURRICULUM

Learning involves reaction to the elements of one's environment. If learning is to be stimulated to a maximum degree, the immediate classroom environment must be rich with worth-while and varied instructional materials. Since learning is manipulative as well as abstract in nature, good materials for instruction constitute a medium through which the learner makes contact with new ideas, or through which he achieves new skills. One can hardly expect to improve the curriculum of the school without giving serious attention to the acquisition of suitable materials of all types. Indeed, the success of the more integrated modern curriculum depends very heavily upon a sufficient quantity and variety of printed, audio-visual, construction and art, and other materials necessary for the numerous activities involved in the development of a unit or problem.

Some guiding principles for selecting and using teaching materials are set forth in a recent bulletin of the Indiana State Department of Public Instruction.[10] Some of the major ideas included in that statement are as follows:

1. Any material selected as a learning aid should do the work better than any other type of material. This kind of material is not used just because it is conveniently available or because the teacher is "expected" to use it. For example, a motion picture would be more effective than still pictures in illustrating the fishing methods practiced by the Norwegians. On the other hand, for studying the natural scenery of Norway, still pictures would probably be as effective as a motion picture, and would be more economical in time and equipment.

2. Materials should be timely and purposeful. Whether used to introduce a topic, to answer specific questions, or to provide a review, materials should offer information pertinent to the immediate interests of the children. This timeliness should be particularly characteristic of free and inexpensive materials received from commercial sources. For example, in the area of air-age education, many charts and booklets are available. These materials can be effectively used only if the group is interested in the implications of our air age.

3. Materials should be suited to the needs, interests, and experiences of the

10 *Expanding Experiences in the Elementary School,* Curriculum Bulletin No. 215 (Indianapolis: State Department of Public Instruction, 1953), pp. 30-32.

children. The teacher must recognize the developmental characteristics of children nine to eleven years old, and must be aware of the interests of a particular group, and recognize that different groups vary in their interests. It must also be remembered that the personal experiences of every group are unique and that, even within a given group, individual experience is unique. A teacher should utilize all the experiences of children in order to clarify and expand the learnings of the entire group.

4. Teachers should use instructional materials from a wide variety of sources. In addition to the teaching aids and resources ordinarily found in a school, the home and community furnish many valuable materials. There are always residents of a vicinity who become valuable resources because of their special interests or experiences. Local businesses and industries should be considered because of their contributions to the community. School journeys to such firms may enrich the curriculum. A local library may provide materials not readily available elsewhere. State and federal government resources should also be employed. For example, the Department of Interior has information on mineral resources; the Department of Agriculture has helps on forestry and conservation; the State Library contains information on a wide variety of subjects. Most cities have a chamber of commerce which is willing to answer questions about the community.

5. In selection of instructional materials, children, teachers, administrators, and parents have a joint responsibility. Children will identify themselves more closely with their learning experiences if they have an opportunity to choose the materials with which they work. Parents and other lay members of a community may likewise offer helpful suggestions in selecting and acquiring materials. Those who have a part in planning the school program are more likely to support it.

6. Adequate preparation should be made for the use of all materials selected. The teacher should be familiar with the characteristics of a material and know how its use can contribute to the growth of boys and girls. This familiarity is especially important in using audio-visual materials. Children need also to see how materials selected can be of help to them. For example, a group of eleven-year-old children were interested in play-party games and dances that were enjoyed by the pioneers. Several albums of records were available for use. Both children and teacher listened to these records in order to decide which would be best suited for their purpose. Analysis of the rhythmic patterns and of the vocabulary of the calls was a factor in influencing the final selection of records.

7. Materials should be evaluated after they have been used. It is necessary for the teacher to determine the effectiveness of a particular material in meeting the educational objective for which it was selected. Both teacher and children need to evaluate the material used in terms of the extent to which it meets the needs of the group.

ORGANIZATION FOR COOPERATIVE CURRICULUM IMPROVEMENT

Curriculum improvement in a local school does not just happen. It proceeds best when most members of the staff recognize a need for study and improvement of the school program. Furthermore, a genuine cooperative effort at constructive curriculum revision requires thoughtful planning and systematic organization. The two basic elements of effective local curriculum study are: (1) the organization of the professional staff and other participants in the effort and (2) the development of the study through certain essential stages of intensive deliberation.

Organization for Curriculum Study.—Leadership is essential in a local school or school system. However, leadership alone cannot insure a successful effort. The wide participation of teachers, other staff members, and laymen is necessary if desirable outcomes are to be realized from such cooperative study. With such participation, under competent leadership, the study of the curriculum can influence very favorably the classroom practices of teachers, thus becoming a very profitable in-service activity. It must be recognized also that the chances for effective implementation of curriculum change are much better if teachers generally have participated in the formulation of such change.

Many school systems establish a central curriculum council to act as a "steering and clearing" committee in coordinating curriculum development throughout the system. Others operate on the basis of building committees or through the efforts of the staff as a whole. Sometimes "vertical" and/or "horizontal" committees are created to study not only the content of the curriculum but also its organization. In the opinion of the writer, the particular plan of organization is relatively unimportant. The greatest need is to get the cheerful involvement of the total staff in such an effort, and any reasonable plan for achieving such participation seems worth trying.

In addition to striving for a workable cooperative approach to curriculum study, school systems are increasingly seeking and using the services of one or more professional curriculum consultants to assist them in viewing their instructional program and practices as objectively as possible.

Stages of Curriculum Study.—It is usually wise to select a particular curriculum area or problem as an initial approach to curriculum improvement. Whether this is done or whether the whole program is designated for systematic examination, however, certain aspects of the school program have to be investigated and studied if improvement is to be the end result. These major aspects, though not completely sequential in nature, are closely related to the following developmental phases of curriculum study: (1) study and selection of purposes or goals; (2) selection of appropriate curriculum content; (3) study and selection of suitable types of activities for functionalizing the selected content; (4) organization of learning experiences (the contacts of children with the selected content through suitable activities) in order to promote maximum integration; (5) organization of learning experiences in such a manner as to insure optimum continuity consistent with the stages of child development; (6) adaptation of learning experiences to local needs and conditions; (7) means for evaluating teaching and learning in terms of expressed purposes.

In summarizing the various factors involved in curriculum improvement, it seems appropriate to include here a statement of major considerations which evolved from an in-service curriculum seminar with which the writer was associated.[11]

1. Effective curriculum development is based on the recognition by classroom teachers of the need for constructive change.
2. Curriculum development is effective to the extent to which persons in positions of leadership provide encouragement and assistance in analyzing the current status of the curriculum and in working toward proposed revisions.
3. The mechanics of curriculum development should be determined and understood by all persons involved in curriculum improvement.
4. Accessibility of adequate resource materials and resource persons is an essential factor in curriculum development.
5. Curriculum development must include the continuous provision for free exchange of opinions, ideas, and experiences as vital factors in the selection of content and its organization.
6. Efforts at curriculum improvement should be accomplished by recognition of the nature and needs of the immediate school community.
7. The direction curriculum development takes should be determined largely by the needs and interests of the students involved.
8. The effectiveness of curriculum change within a school system is dependent upon adequate methods of communication.
9. Curriculum change should be gradual enough to keep good relations within the school system and to promote understanding between the school system and the public.
10. Teachers should recognize that curriculum improvement actually occurs in the classroom.
11. Effective curriculum development involves a variety of approaches and activities both experimental and judgmental. Both the methods of the individual and society should be considered in curriculum development.
12. Effective curriculum development appears to proceed from broad considerations and problems to more specific applications in the school and classroom.

[11] Compiled by Hanne J. Hicks and R. L. Springer from materials submitted by members of an In-Service Curriculum Seminar, Indianapolis Public Schools, 1952.

13. Effective curriculum development should include some provision for utilizing the ideas and participation of laymen.

14. Both the curriculum and acceptance of curriculum revision seemed to bear direct relationship to the number of teachers within the school system participating in the program.

15. One of the basic considerations in curriculum development should be a consideration of the nature of child growth and development.

16. Efforts at curriculum revision should represent continuous progress toward a curriculum that:

   a) Is adaptable to meeting the needs of children and youth

   b) Recognizes and supplements the child's total educational environment

   c) Provides content that is varied in interest and difficulty

   d) Encourages effective work habits and skills as well as positive attitudes toward further learning

   e) Is organized in terms of the best that is known about the way learning takes place

   f) Utilizes the social setting as an integral part of the learning situation.

A truly effective curriculum in the elementary school can be achieved only through competent leadership, interested and effective participation of teachers and parents, and a genuine desire on the part of all concerned to keep curriculum content, teaching methods, and instructional materials in step with the progress made in other community endeavors. To do less is to short-change the only really important customers of the school—the children.

ACTION SUGGESTIONS FOR THE PRINCIPAL

1. Get a clear idea as to what the curriculum of the school is expected to accomplish.

2. Work with the professional staff and parents in exploring ideas as to the areas of the curriculum to be emphasized.

3. Develop machinery for easy sharing of successful teaching ideas among the members of the teaching staff.

4. Encourage the cooperative development of essential curriculum guides or statements of philosophy and purposes of the school.

5. Create a professional atmosphere which encourages the spirit of research in better ways of teaching.

6. Provide leadership in the study of the curriculum in relation to community conditions and needs.

7. Encourage teachers to make a record of resource units or other useful approaches to the organization of learning experiences in the classroom.

8. Attempt to provide for "clinical discussions" of the various curriculum areas in group meetings of the staff.

9. Provide occasional opportunities in the school day for particular groups of teachers, such as primary teachers, to get together informally to

discuss the continuity of the curriculum and other related problems of curricular organization.

10. Strive to make the organization of the school support and strengthen the instructional program of the school rather than interfere with it.

11. Collect and keep an up-to-date collection of curriculum literature and materials as a part of the professional library of the school.

12. Develop with the staff criteria for the selection of desirable learning experiences.

13. Invite members of the teaching staff, on a rotation basis, to lead discussions of such matters as unit organization or the findings of recent research in child development for groups of teachers and/or parents.

14. Involve as many members as possible in curriculum development and in the selection of textbooks and other teaching materials.

15. Make an occasional inventory of children's interests as a clue to better ways to motivate desirable learning in the school.

16. Encourage teachers to keep a file of community resources which can be used for direct learning experiences and for enriching the curriculum.

17. Make follow-up studies of pupils who leave the school as one means of discovering strengths and weaknesses of the curriculum.

18. Make a conscious effort to develop in the school definite and systematic provisions for the continuous evaluation of the instructional program.

19. Try to provide a great variety of teaching materials in each classroom suitable for the varied interests and abilities of the individuals in the group.

20. Encourage all constructive attempts by teachers to unify and integrate learning experiences into broader and more meaningful instructional units.

21. Encourage teachers and children to utilize actual school conditions and problems as functional learning experiences wherever feasible.

22. Work for the coordination of the instructional program of the school but avoid insistence on uniformity of curriculum organization or teaching policies from classroom to classroom. Encourage teacher creativeness and initiative.

23. Encourage teachers to develop and use means for the self-evaluation of teaching performance.

24. Keep in mind that curriculum content or organization is good not necessarily because it is old or new but because it accomplishes its purposes in the best possible manner.

25. Learn everything possible about modern curriculum research and literature in order to serve as a leader with rich resources for teachers, pupils, and parents who want to work for improved learning experiences.

SELECTED REFERENCES FOR EXTENDED READING

ADAMS, FAY. *Educating America's Children: Elementary School Curriculum and Methods* (rev.). New York: The Ronald Press Co., 1954.

ASSOCIATION FOR SUPERVISION AND CURRICULUM DEVELOPMENT. *Action for Curriculum Improvement.* 1951 Yearbook. Washington, D. C.: National Education Association, 1951.

———. *The Three R's in the Elementary School.* Washington, D. C.: National Education Association, 1952.

———. *Forces Affecting American Education.* 1953 Yearbook. Washington, D. C.: National Education Association, 1953.

BAXTER, BERNICE, LEWIS, GERTRUDE M., and CROSS, GERTRUDE M. *The Role of Elementary Education.* Boston: D. C. Heath & Co., 1952.

BECK, ROBERT H., COOK, WALTER W., and KEARNEY, NOLAN C. *Curriculum in the Modern Elementary School.* New York: Prentice-Hall, Inc., 1953.

CASWELL, HOLLIS L., and ASSOCIATES. *Curriculum Improvement in Public School Systems.* New York: Teachers College, Columbia University, 1950.

CASWELL, HOLLIS L., and FOSHAY, A. WELLESLEY. *Education in the Elementary School.* New York: American Book Co., 1950.

DEPARTMENT OF ELEMENTARY SCHOOL PRINCIPALS. *Bases for Effective Learning: Thirty-First Yearbook.* Washington, D. C.: National Education Association, 1952.

HARAP, HENRY. "What's New in Curriculum?" *NEA Journal,* XLIII (January, 1954), pp. 37-38.

INDIANA STATE DEPARTMENT OF PUBLIC INSTRUCTION. *Expanding Experience in the Elementary School.* Bulletin No. 215. Indianapolis, Indiana: State Department of Public Instruction, 1953.

KRUG, EDWARD A. *Curriculum Planning.* New York: Harper & Bros., 1950.

LEE, J. MURRAY, and LEE, DORRIS MAY. *The Child and His Curriculum.* New York: Appleton-Century-Crofts, Inc., 1950.

MEHL, MARIE A., MILLS, HUBERT H., and DOUGLASS, HARL R. *Teaching in Elementary School.* New York: The Ronald Press Co., 1950.

OTTO, HENRY J. *Elementary School Organization and Administration.* New York: Appleton-Century-Crofts, Inc., 1954, chaps. 3 and 7.

RAGAN, WILLIAM B. *Modern Elementary Curriculum.* New York: The Dryden Press, 1953.

REAVIS, WILLIAM C., PIERCE, PAUL R., STULLKEN, EDWARD H., and SMITH, BERTRAND L. *Administering the Elementary School.* New York: Prentice-Hall, Inc., 1953, chaps. 5 and 6.

SHANE, HAROLD G., and McSWAIN, E. T. *Evaluation and the Elementary Curriculum.* New York: Henry Holt & Co., 1951.

SMITH, B. OTHANIEL, STANLEY, WILLIAM O., and SHORES, J. HARLAN. *Fundamentals of Curriculum Development.* Yonkers, N. Y.: World Book Co., 1950.

SPEARS, HAROLD. *The Teacher and Curriculum Planning.* New York: Prentice-Hall, Inc., 1951.

STRATEMEYER, FLORENCE B. *Guide to a Curriculum for Modern Living.* New York: Teachers College, Columbia University, 1952.

Chapter 12

ADJUSTING THE CURRICULUM TO THE NEEDS OF CHILDREN

Fitness for freedom is not mass produced—Education Policies Commission

The curriculum of the school becomes an educational agent at the point and time of contact with the learner. Prior to this interaction between the child and the elements of the curriculum which stimulate him to thought and action in terms of his own experiences, even the most carefully devised teaching plans bear few results. It is not enough, therefore, that the learning experiences planned for, and with, children are arranged in a logical sequence. In some instances, of course, this is important. However, of greater importance is the guarantee that the conditions surrounding the learning situation are such that maximum results are achieved when the curriculum makes its impact on the child.

It is important to keep reminding ourselves that the curriculum exists to serve children, not vice versa. The acceptance of this principle carries with it the necessity for curriculum adjustment. If children are all different, as we say and know they are, and if the curriculum exists to serve children, then we cannot justifiably take the position that the same set of learning experiences is sufficient for all. We must rather attempt to analyze the needs of children as thoughtfully and scientifically as possible and then to provide learning experiences that are designed to meet these needs.

This chapter includes a discussion of a few broad principles underlying curriculum adjustment, some of the general and specific adjustments to be made in the elementary school, and some of the requirements for the successful adaptation of learning experiences to particular needs of children.

Some Basic Principles of Curriculum Adjustment

Curriculum adjustment based on whim or unjustified impressions is often more damaging than none at all. It is necessary, therefore, to preface attempts at curriculum adaptation with a careful consideration of the chief factors involved.

1. *The curriculum should be considered a servant of the educational process.* There is no magic in the curriculum itself. As suggested earlier, it becomes alive when it involves the experiences and purposes of the learner. It is true that the curriculum of the school must reflect a recognition of the intentions and aspirations of society as well as the needs of individual learners; this fact does not, however, justify a standardized curriculum or the resistance to change and adaptation that have appeared to characterize the curriculum of many public schools even to this day.

It is important that we refrain from attaching to the conventional school curriculum an inviolate, if not almost sacred, character which it does not merit and which its true purposes do not support. The real function of the curriculum is to aid and abet learning through the guidance and stimulation which well-chosen experiences and activities can provide. It is a *good curriculum* when it provides *good learning* for children; it gets its value from the effect it produces on learners. Obviously, with children differing as they do, certain adaptations are required if the curriculum is to serve them well. As pointed out in the preceding chapter, it is essential that each child be provided a curriculum that establishes unity, continuity, and as much enrichment as possible in his learning pattern. The strength of the curriculum lies more in its usefulness along these lines than in the respectability attributed to it in terms of uniformity and antiquity.

2. *Curriculum adjustment should be preceded by careful analysis and evaluation of educational needs.* There is little virtue in curriculum change itself, but when changes or adaptations are made to serve purposes which otherwise could not be served, they are not only valuable but essential to good education. In general, all change should be based on careful evaluation. Certainly revisions in the instructional program designed to meet particular needs of individual children cannot be either clearly conceived or formulated without a preliminary and exhaustive study of the needs to be met. It is folly to assume that specific needs of learners can be met by generalized adjustments in instructional content and practice. The means employed in such cases must be as specialized in many instances as the needs they are expected to serve.

3. *Curriculum adjustments should differ as individual and group needs differ.* This may be considered a corollary of the preceding principle. Children differ in their physical needs and deviations, in the level of their emotional stability, and in many other ways which represent variations and combinations of these factors. When we are seeking

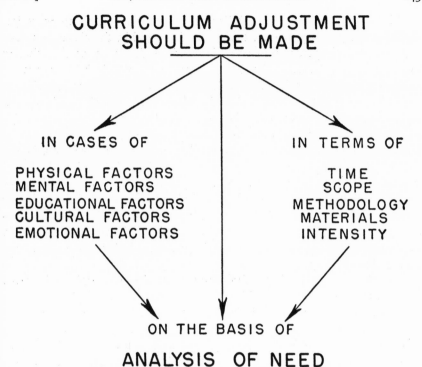

CURRICULUM ADJUSTMENT
SHOULD BE MADE

IN CASES OF

PHYSICAL FACTORS
MENTAL FACTORS
EDUCATIONAL FACTORS
CULTURAL FACTORS
EMOTIONAL FACTORS

IN TERMS OF

TIME
SCOPE
METHODOLOGY
MATERIALS
INTENSITY

ON THE BASIS OF

ANALYSIS OF NEED
ADAPTATION OF RESOURCES
CONTINUOUS EVALUATION

Figure 12

Some Basic Elements in Curriculum Adjustment

means whereby effective learning experiences may be provided for children with these several types of differences, we must assume that standardized adaptations of the program may not be enough to accomplish the task. Each type of problem, or difference, must be studied carefully as a basis for making whatever adjustments are feasible in terms of the problem and the available facilities for meeting it.

In some cases, it is necessary to make adjustments in the extent and nature of content of the curriculum; in others, change may be desirable in the instructional methods and activities employed in the teaching-learning process; in still others, the factors and physical conditions surrounding the learning situation may need to be altered in terms of particular needs or deficiencies.

4. *Curriculum adjustment is closely related to the teaching process.*

Good teaching requires the ability to differentiate teaching materials and methods as they are used with children within the classroom. No more condemning statement could be made with respect to a teacher in the modern elementary school than that he treats all children exactly alike. Common sense, in addition to a great body of supporting evidence regarding the nature of children and how they develop, demands adjustments in the day-to-day activities of children as they progress through the various levels of the elementary school program.

Some of these adjustments will be related to the variation in the rate of learning among children. Some will be concerned with differences in backgrounds and some will be used as a means to provide areas of enrichment for particular children because of special deficiencies or unusual abilities. The important thing to emphasize is that the effectiveness of administrative provisions for curriculum adjustment depends, in the final analysis, upon understanding and skillful adaptation at the teaching level.

5. *Effective curriculum adjustment depends upon rich and varied instructional resources.* Aside from specialized physical equipment needed by many exceptional children who attend elementary schools, numerous other kinds of resources are necessary for genuinely successful differentiation of the instructional program. Not only are various types of materials and facilities needed, manipulative, reading, audio-visual, etc., but there must be variation within each type. For instance, reading materials should cover many wide fields of interest and, at the same time, be graded in difficulty so that they are usable by individual members of the group. This is equally true in a regular heterogeneous classroom group or with an ungraded group in a special class for educationally retarded children. More will be said about instructional resources for use with exceptional children in a later part of this chapter.

6. *Curriculum adjustment should be multidimensional in character.* The curriculum should be administered in such a way that flexibility is possible in several directions. Instructional demands made upon learners may be differentiated in terms of time, scope, or thoroughness. Actually, attempts to regulate pupil progress through nonpromotion or acceleration, unfruitful as they have often been, are efforts to adjust the curriculum through manipulation of the time element. In a similar way, extension of resources and methods beyond the textbook and classroom through individualized activity and group projects also represents an attempt to adjust the curriculum to children through variation in the scope and nature of the learning experiences encountered. In other limited ways, attempts have also been made to adjust the curriculum to children with varying abilities through varying the intensity with

which individual children pursue particular learning activities. A later part of this chapter will treat this aspect of curriculum adjustment a bit more fully.

7. *Curriculum adjustment should be provided on the basis of specific needs and total well-being of children.* Specific problems of children often affect their total outlook on life and on their own school experiences. It is not enough to provide for only a single predominant need of a child; it is essential also to consider the social and emotional effects of the problem and to provide adjustments which relieve, rather than aggravate, any negative attitudes which may attend the principal problem. For example, the physically handicapped child, or the slow-learning child, may feel socially inferior to his fellows if his situation does not provide opportunities for normal interaction with other children. The same situation may exist when children are singled out for remedial instruction. Such provisions should be established in such a manner as to avoid social stigma or self-pity on the part of participants. This is merely to suggest that we look beyond the immediate problem of a child when attempting to adjust the curriculum to his needs.

8. *Provisions for curriculum adjustment should be based on human considerations rather than on administrative expedience.* It may seem trite and wholly unnecessary to state such a principle as a guide for personnel of the modern elementary school. However, when one observes the bases, or lack of them, upon which children are frequently assigned to special classes, or when he is sensitive to the great pressure which increasing numbers of school children are currently exerting on school facilities, he cannot avoid concern about the proportionate weight administrative considerations may carry in such matters. Educational wisdom seems to demand that we first determine the kinds of needs that exist, decide as scientifically as possible what provisions ought to be made, and then seek to establish or adapt facilities in accordance with these findings. It should be remembered that people are more important than things, and that the facilities are to serve the people, not the converse.

9. *As in any other aspect of educational endeavor, curriculum adjustment should be susceptible to continuous evaluation.* When the curriculum of the school is revised or adapted to special purposes or to particular people, it is expected that it will thereby be more effective than otherwise would be possible. This assumption carries with it the responsibility for evaluating what is done in order to establish the extent to which this hope is being achieved. This calls for the use of as many techniques of evaluation as possible. It means that individual cases should be studied carefully to determine aspects and extent of growth

occurring in particular children. Experimental approaches to the comparison of methods and materials employed in various situations may shed additional light on the effectiveness of our adjustment efforts. Certainly it will mean that all efforts to differentiate instruction will be characterized by the continuous recognition of particular purposes and by the continuously present question of how well these purposes are being met.

SOME GENERAL TYPES OF CURRICULUM ADJUSTMENT

The typical elementary school classroom group will reflect a great range of ability and background among the children who compose it. Such a group will likely contain a few slow-learning children; some unusually bright or gifted children; some whose educational backgrounds have been either inadequate or interrupted; and one or more children with physical, emotional, or mental deviations of sufficient magnitude to require highly specialized treatment. It appears safe to assume that at least half of the children in many classrooms deviate sufficiently in some manner as to require rather marked curricular adjustments in both content and method. It is necessary, therefore, to explore some of the elements of the school program which lend themselves to adjustment, and over which reasonable control can be exercised.

As pointed out earlier, three types of adjustment seem to offer possibilities for differentiating instruction within the classroom for a great many cases. They are: (1) adjustment in time, (2) adjustment in scope, and (3) adjustment in depth and thoroughness. Each of these seems to merit further discussion at this point.

Differentiation Through Adjustments in Time.—Since children differ so notably in the rates at which they learn, it is reasonable to assume that, if common tasks are demanded of them, more time should be allowed for some children to complete the tasks than for others. It has been mentioned that nonpromotion and acceleration have sometimes been justified as meeting the need for such time adjustment. To some extent, perhaps, they have served such a purpose. However, their contributions have been diminished considerably by their ill effects and by the manner in which they have been administered, with undue emphasis on "failure" and "repeating." In practice they have not guaranteed the continuous progress essential to effective learning.

In spite of the limitations of administrative policies as means for obtaining useful differentiation in the instruction program, some desirable practices are related to certain administrative considerations. It is held by many that the organization of the elementary school into fewer "graded segments" offers a partial solution to the problem of curriculum adjustment. This trend is most often found in schools organized in terms of a "primary unit" and "advanced unit," as described in Chapter 9. In these instances, little emphasis is placed on grade levels but a great effort is expended to insure as great continuity as possible in the development of each child. Under such plans it is possible for one child to spend four years in the primary phase of the program while others may spend only three, although this is not necessarily common practice nor one of the most essential features of such an approach. At any rate, this type of organization does seem to minimize rigid year by year standards for all and, to that extent at least, to alleviate some of the restrictive structure of the typical school program.

Another way in which time adjustments may be obtained is through the use of greater *flexibility in scheduling*. Through utilizing broader blocks of time within the school day and the school week, greater opportunity will be created for individualized work and for differentiating instruction within the class setup. It is generally conceded that the greater the number of separate class periods within the school day, the less the likelihood that any marked differentiation will occur in the instructional program as it is carried on from day to day. As independent activities of the children are encouraged, the teacher is freed to give special attention to children who really need it. Broader blocks of work within the school day also permit more individualized approaches to evaluation than would otherwise be afforded, since the bases for judging progress are broader and more varied. It appears that the thoughtful administrator would do well to explore the advantages of flexible scheduling and to encourage its use as far as conditions permit.

Grouping and group work within the classroom permit variations in the amount of time given to development of skills through practice and application. Such grouping helps to utilize differentiated instructional materials—both basic and independent work materials—in establishing desired skills and in alleviating deficiencies. This approach to organization also allows individual children to locate sources of information in keeping with their own abilities and interests and yet to make a worthwhile contribution through sharing their findings with others.

Use of the *free or individualized work period* is another manner in which individual abilities can be met constructively. During such periods the special interests and aptitudes of children can be identified and their problems and deficiencies can be noted. Sometimes such a period is used in connection with the development of units of work and at other times—less frequently perhaps—it is set aside as a part of the school day in which children may pursue any aspect of their work they desire.

Recognition of differing rates and kinds of learning among members of the group should result in the use of evaluative devices which reflect various types of growth. In this connection, it is well to avoid the exclusive use of timed tests and evaluative instruments since they tend to penalize children who work at slower rates. Undoubtedly, some emphasis should be put on the ability to work at a reasonably efficient rate, but it seems unnecessary to carry this emphasis to the point of constant use of timed devices.

Some extension of time can conceivably be gained for some children through the judicious use of homework. If children are asked to do homework, it should be in connection with concepts already understood and should be free from the pressure of "extra work."

Differentiation Through Adjustment in Scope of the Curriculum. —It is possible to make further adjustments in the curriculum through expansion and control of its content and through variation in the types of activities used to develop understanding of the content. This type of adjustment can be accomplished in numerous ways. Perhaps a few of the most important approaches can be mentioned as illustrations of the direction such efforts should take.

The use made of *supplementary* and *independent reading activities* has a very genuine bearing on the adaptation of the curriculum to individuals. If all are required to read exactly the same materials and in turn have their performances adjudged against uniform standards, it is obvious that little concern for the individuals is involved. On the other hand, when children are permitted to read materials that conform to their reading ability level and to select materials on many occasions on the basis of individual interest, greater motivation results and greater achievement can be expected. For more rapid learners particularly it seems unfortunate to restrict reading activities to certain basic books when so many wonderful books are available through the use of which understanding can be extended and horizons be broadened. One of the ways, then, of extending the scope of the curriculum is to make full use of a variety of reading materials at varying levels of difficulty.

It is equally important to seek *variety in the kinds of activities* children may engage in as they develop an understanding of various components of the curriculum. For example, if they are studying pioneer life in this nation, there are many ways of gaining understanding of the ways in which people of an earlier day lived. Some of these activities will involve reading; some, perhaps, the use of geographical and map skills; and still others, the use of manipulative skills in constructing miniature reproductions of houses of pioneer villages.

The use of *community resources, audio-visual materials,* and *home and club activities* as extensions through which the curriculum can be varied and enriched have been found to pay real educational dividends. They add to the number of possibilities for guaranteeing flexibility in the instructional program as they tend to utilize special interests of learners. In addition, the use of resources other than those purely literary in nature contributes to broader understanding and to acquaintance with more functional aspects of things being learned.

Unit organization of learning experiences, particularly in the so-called content fields such as science and social studies, in itself can contribute materially to differentiation of instruction. Such units form the focal core or problem around which particular children can make contributions to group study on the basis of individual abilities and interests. At the same time, unit organization provides opportunities for developing skills of group work, research skills, and skill in self and group evaluation.

Even in more formalized types of school organization the *flexible assignment* can be utilized to good advantage in meeting the challenge of individual differences. This can be accomplished simply through providing for all children a minimum assignment and then providing opportunities for some of them to go beyond the common assignment. An even better way to use the same idea is to formulate a list of possible activities related to the day's work and let the children choose the ones they feel they should do. With skillful guidance from the teacher this can be a very helpful technique for getting desired participation from pupils in the areas of their greatest need.

In summarizing, it may be said that the curriculum of the school should be varied enough and rich enough to permit considerable selectivity by pupils as they perform their school tasks. In such selectivity lies one of the hopes for more intelligent adaptation of learning experiences to the actual needs and growth patterns of individual learners.

Differentiation Through Adjustment in the Intensity Dimension of the Learning Experience.—Professional educators have demonstrated far more skill in adjusting the time and scope elements of the instructional program than in providing means whereby the thoroughness and depth of learning experiences can be advantageously controlled and utilized. This, however, does not negate the desirability of such an approach. In fact, this appears to be an area which should challenge the ingenuity of teachers and administrators alike as they hope to furnish for their pupils a truly flexible curriculum.

Much of such control is related to both subject matter and method. For example, it is probably agreed that nearly all children should learn to read but it does not follow that all children should reach the same level of reading ability nor read the same materials. For some children, with limited intellectual capacities and thus with restricted vocational possibilities, the reading of directions and signs may be a highly valuable pursuit well within their academic proficiencies. For such children, the reading of abstract and philosophical matter is not useful. The intellectually gifted child, however, needs to be provided with opportunities to read widely and penetratingly and to be able to extend thereby his vision and imagination. A similar situation exists with reference to number skills and to other areas of the curriculum. Certainly the backgrounds, abilities, interests, and aptitudes of a child should do much to govern the extent to which his experiences with various elements of the curriculum are superficial, or exhaustive, or neither.

As a general rule, concrete and direct experience is more helpful to the learning process for children who learn more slowly than for the gifted. Conversely, the gifted child should be freed from a continuous round of monotonous repetition or drill and from the simplicity of direct kinds of experiences which he has previously engaged in to a great extent.

Curriculum Adjustments for Exceptional Children

The person who is average or "normal" in every respect is indeed rare. The population is made up of people who differ in height, weight, visual acuity, hearing acuity, intellectual ability, emotional stability, and in many other ways. Indeed, as stated earlier, part of the strength of the democratic process lies in the fact that those who participate in it are different rather than alike. At the same time, it is often difficult to cope with the self-conscious stigma that may accompany the realization that one is different from others. This condition may be alleviated somewhat if we remember that most of us deviate from average status and behavior in one or more respects, at least to some degree.

Some of the changes in the structure of the public elementary schools have been discussed in an earlier part of this book. It is enough at this point to reiterate that only in recent years has the population of schools at this level approached heterogeneity. In earlier periods, when the values of education were not so universally recognized, many children dropped out of school at very early ages, or at the time when they could become useful workers on the farm or in the father's business. Currently, elementary schools are serving a very large percentage of the children of all the people—some gifted, some mentally retarded, some orthopedically handicapped, and many others, each one possessing individual characteristics which distinguish him from all others. As a result of this change in consumer, schools have found it necessary to make marked adjustments in their programs in order to serve the best interests of all types of children who attend school.

The following paragraphs point out some of the types of exceptional children and suggest some of the basic considerations in providing program adjustments for each type.

Operational Problems of Exceptional Children.—Children often deviate from normal in ways which impede or preclude typical child behavior, or which hinder regular participation in school activities. For example, the child who is orthopedically afflicted is frequently not able to move about in his pursuit of the day's activities in the manner in which other children do. The child with severe visual difficulty cannot read materials which others can read. Those with hearing losses miss a great deal of the communication which occurs in the course of the day. Mentally deficient children cannot bring to the problem-solving situations of the school day the same intellectual insights that others have to offer.

One of the great challenges to teachers and administrators is that of creating a setting for education in which exceptional children can perform with a maximum of educational efficiency. This often means a rethinking of classroom organization and routines, careful selection of instructional materials, a flexible curriculum, and highly individualized methods of instruction. Exceptional children must be provided with materials they can use, be asked to do things they can do without frustrating disappointments, and be helped to gain the general satisfactions of life from the things which they can do. In some instances, these things may be done within the regular classroom; in others, a special class type of organization offers the better solution. The particular advantages of each approach will be discussed in connection with each of the general types of deviation represented among exceptional children.

Of course, exceptional children are not all handicapped. Indeed, mentally gifted children, for example, are often exceptional. In all cases, however, it is essential to provide learning experiences commensurate with the resources of the learners involved.

Social and Psychological Problems of Exceptional Children.—
Particular disabilities are often accompanied by the development of

certain social and psychological problems. At certain stages of development, it is important to the child to be like other children. The fact that some illness or accident has left a child in a condition which makes him different from others is often a hard situation for him to face. As a result, he may indulge in self-pity, become an extreme introvert, or perhaps even develop feelings of resentment which lead to aggressive actions, verbal or otherwise. The correlation between being exceptional and personality distortion seems to be sufficient to require careful provisions for dealing with this phase of the child's development. If possible, it is desirable to maintain many normal social contacts for children who have handicaps. Such children should be kept in touch with current activities and happenings so that they will not get a feeling of social detachment from the world, community, school, or family.

It may be said, then, that a twofold task faces the school in its attempts to provide a suitable program for exceptional children. The first is the necessity for *dealing with the operational problem involved,* through the provision of an educational setting in which a child's learning is affected minimally by his particular deficiency or handicap. The second involves the *creation of provisions whereby the development of negative social and psychological effects of the problem may be prevented.*

Some Emerging Views Toward the Education of Exceptional Children.—As education in America has increasingly become the rightful heritage of all children, more and more attention has been given to the education of the exceptional child. This interest has been expressed in many ways by different agencies. For example, the various states increasingly have contributed to the education of exceptional children through direct financial aid, maintenance of residential schools and institutions, and through provision of special consultant services from the state agency. Although state support of special schools came into being in the early part of the nineteenth century, recent years have seen a great expansion in state support for such efforts; today all states make some type of contribution to the education of exceptional children.

Local communities and school districts, too, have increased their efforts to provide for exceptional children. In many instances, these efforts have led to the establishment of special classes and schools operated within the administrative framework of the local school system. Often regular appropriations for such schools are supplemented by funds provided by community agencies and private subsidies of various kinds.

Educators are coming more and more to the belief that the purposes of education for handicapped children are not materially different from those for other children. Education for such children must create conditions which consider the capacities of the children, which make available suitable and varied materials, and which provide highly individualized means for achieving goals within the reach of these children. It is the opinion of the author that children should not be segregated for instructional purposes if the proper adjustments can be made for them in the regular classroom. Undoubtedly, if all teachers were sympathetically inclined toward, and adequately trained in, the techniques of individualized instruction and, in addition, if classroom groups were sufficiently small, there would be a minimum need for special classes for most types of exceptional children. However, these conditions do not exist in a great many situations and until they do come to pass, the special class or special school will probably continue to serve a very real and important need.

In the establishment of the special class, there is a danger resulting from the tendency to make such a class, or school, a convenient "dumping ground" for all problem cases which teachers encounter in their regular classrooms. Obviously, children should be assigned to such classes or schools only after careful testing and analysis, and after it has been determined that they require the specialized facilities of the special class or school.

The modern approach to the education of exceptional children involves three possible adjustments: (1) instructional adjustments within the regular classroom, (2) the establishment and maintenance of special classes, and (3) provisions for instruction of children within their homes or wherever they reside. These approaches will be discussed in relation to each of several types of exceptional children frequently found in public schools.

Some General Types of Exceptional Children

Five general types of exceptional children are found frequently in the public schools. They are: (1) the physically handicapped, (2) the mentally deviant, (3) the educationally retarded, (4) the culturally deprived, and (5) the socially and emotionally immature. Each type of deviant must be studied in terms of his particular condition so that educational provisions can be made accordingly.

The Physically Handicapped.—Conservative estimates indicate that more than five per cent of the children of elementary and secondary school age in this country suffer from some type of physical impairment sufficient to classify them as exceptional children. This means that in each classroom in the country one might expect to find at least one or two children with physical disabilities sufficiently serious to interfere with regular classroom work and activity unless adjustments are made for them.

Among the physically handicapped children, those with *impaired hearing* are found relatively frequently in classrooms of elementary schools. The hearing losses sustained by such children may range from only a slight loss to complete deafness and should be provided for in terms of their degree of seriousness and the extent to which the loss interferes with normal school activity. Losses up to 20 decibels usually present no critical educational problems for the child. Usually they can be compensated for by the use of common-sense measures in the classroom, such as seating the child in an advantageous position in the room where he can have a maximum chance of hearing what is said. Children with slightly greater loss probably should be equipped with hearing aids. They also should have the opportunity for special training in lip reading if the loss is sufficiently great for them to be classified as hard-of-hearing children. Children whose impairment of hearing approaches complete deafness probably should not be expected to respond effectively to the instructional program of the regular classroom but rather should be assigned to a special class where specialized facilities are available.

Teachers and administrators should be alert to such symptoms as inattention to directions, frequent requests for repeating statements, or habitual turning of the head, as these may represent the efforts of a hard-of-hearing child to compensate for his handicap in the classroom. If such indications persist, screening tests should be administered; and the parents should be asked to seek professional advice from a hearing specialist.

Though they occur somewhat less frequently than the deaf and hard-of-hearing, *blind and partially seeing children* constitute another group of physically exceptional children who require special adaptations of the school program if they are to derive benefit from it. Blind children, usually considered to be those who possess a visual acuity of no more than 20/200 in the better eye even after correction, are usually assigned to special schools for instruction and, at present, this appears to be the best solution for such cases.

It is an unresolved question as to whether or not partially seeing children can best be served in the special class. Many informed educators believe, and the author agrees, that the all-round welfare of such children can be better guaranteed through association with regular class groups throughout part of the school day, at least, with specialized instruction during part of the day with the use of sight-saving materials and under the guidance of a special teacher. At any rate, some sort of combined use of the regular classroom and special facilities and personnel seems best in these cases.

Many schools are now making special provisions for dealing with the *speech problems of children*. Although such problems are not always physical in nature, they do often bear some relationship to physical development. Some speech problems are directly attributable to organic conditions such as those associated with harelip or cerebral palsy; others result from imitation of incorrect patterns, lack of voice control and quality, or from emotional tensions and pressures.

Although the alleviation of some speech disorders can be brought about only through surgery or other medical treatment, parents and teachers can do a number of things to create favorable conditions for preventing and dealing with speech problems of children. Some of these are:

1. Setting proper examples of voice control and modulation before the child at all times.
2. Exemplifying acceptable patterns of enunciation and pronounciation.
3. Acquiring knowledge about the speech and language development of children so that the speech demands and expectations placed on children are not beyond those which should reasonably be expected.
4. Creating a friendly conversational atmosphere in the home and school, free from emotional tensions and fears.
5. Providing for, and cooperatively utilizing, the services of speech therapists in the speech development of children.
6. Using the services of other professional specialists in cases requiring such assistance.

The *orthopedic handicaps* of children range from very mild deformities to almost complete incapacity. There is little reason to exclude from the regular classroom those whose disabilities do not seriously interfere with normal activity. They will require understanding on the part of the teacher and their associates, but they can usually participate in most activities with little difficulty.

The more seriously crippled child, on the other hand, will be greatly handicapped in the typical classroom. He requires therapeutic treatment, rest, and specialized care and instruction that can best be given in a special situation where the necessary technical facilities and assistance are available to him.

Children with *lowered vitality* caused by disease or infection also need special consideration in the school program. Provisions for rest and freedom from climbing stairs and from other types of physical exertion are essential for these children. It is also important to find ways in which such pupils can gain recognition among their fellows, since they are usually deprived of the opportunity to participate in athletic contests and other competitive endeavor.

In some instances, special teachers are provided for periodic visits to hospital-bound or home-bound children. This arrangement, wherever it is possible, has two advantages: (1) it provides essential instruction and (2) it keeps the isolated child in touch with his school world, with positive psychological effects. A few schools have experimented with the use of communication systems which allow the child at home to participate in the discussions of the group at school. Although such practices are not yet widespread, their effectiveness seems to warrant the prediction that they will come into much greater use as the years go by.

The Mentally Retarded.—Mental deviation occurs in two opposite directions: the mentally deficient and the mentally gifted. The former includes a wide range of intellectual deficiency dispersed along a mental scale extending from the "slow learner" down to the idiot. As a general rule, however, children with I.Q.'s below 50 are considered to be un-educable and are usually not found in public schools. They are usually either institutionalized or cared for at home.

In most instances, children with I.Q.'s ranging between 50 or 60 and about 75 are considered to be in the *mentally retarded* group—educable but requiring rather drastic departures from the program provided in the regular classroom. Special classes are the most common plan for meeting the needs of this group. Such classes are free from grade standards, usually are relatively small in size, and utilize highly individualized methods and facilities. It is not only customary, but desirable, in such classes to emphasize social and vocational aspects of the program for these children, but there appears to be a diminishing tendency to condemn the members of special classes to a constant round of simple handicrafts. The trend in this respect appears to be a commendable development.

Mental retardation in children is often accompanied by physical or sensory defects and, in a considerable number of cases, by social maladjustment. According to Baker,[1] they lack powers of self-criticism, associational ability, and reasoning to any notable extent and tend to have greater ability to deal with concrete situations than with abstract ideas.

It may be stated in a general way, then, that mentally retarded children require the kind of attention that can be given in a good special class, while the slow learner, possessing slightly higher mental facility,

[1] Harry J. Baker, *Introduction to Exceptional Children* (New York: The Macmillan Co., 1947). All quotations by permission of the publisher.

may receive instruction to advantage in the regular classroom if sufficient adjustments are made in the curriculum and in teaching methods. Unfortunately, not only slow-learning children continue to be a part of the regular classroom structure of the typical school, but also a great majority of the mentally retarded, since special classes are scarce except in the larger city school systems. One of the responsibilities of administrative leaders is to learn everything possible about resources for meeting the needs of these children and then furnishing leadership in obtaining proper facilities for carrying this knowledge into appropriate action.

Curriculum adjustment for the mentally retarded has many facets. Kelly and Stevens[2] mention five aspects of curriculum adaptation related to the mentally retarded, as follows:

The first is concerned with the curriculum itself, which contains carefully chosen experiences in order to meet the needs of the mentally retarded learner. This should be characteristic of the curriculum for all mentally retarded children from the youngest to the oldest, because the scope of experiences must fit the social age of this type of pupil while the understanding of those experiences are brought within his mental grasp.

The second problem pertains to curriculum adjustment as indicated by the length of the individual school-life span in relation to pupil capacity. This problem governs three aspects: the age of enrollment of the pupil in a special class; the mental capacity of the enrollee; and the type of program to be offered the mentally retarded pupil during his years in school. Since the average age of referral and grade placement is eight or nine, it probably means that only eight school years may be available for educational guidance. Therefore, not only must expediency be served in planning what can be offered in the allotted time but also the offerings must be continually adjusted to the mental capacity of the pupil and to his evolving social needs.

The third problem involves curriculum offerings as governed by class organization. Since the social-age grouping of the pupils of the special elementary class is usually wide, ranging in some instances from six to twelve, the opportunity for teacher emphasis on a wide scope of curriculum materials and for pupil assimilation and consolidation of acquired knowledge and skills will be limited. However, it should be possible to formulate what is offered according to a plan which makes the total offering both balanced and complete.

For those mentally retarded pupils who remain with one teacher for two or more years, every effort should be made to blot out situations which make for boredom or ennui. This is accomplished by a well-conceived plan of organization which includes a wide variety of experiences, so arranged that they will permit a continuous flow of pupil developments. This approach may be employed for the individual who enters late or is just passing through, as well as

[2] Elizabeth M. Kelly and Harvey A. Stevens, "Special Education for the Mentally Handicapped," *Forty-Ninth Yearbook of the National Society for the Study of Education*, Part II (Chicago: University of Chicago Press, 1950), pp. 251-52.

for those who may remain in the same class organization the full span of school years.

The fourth problem centers around the essentials of curriculum offerings and the determination of the depth and breadth of what will constitute the essence. The limitations of time and pupil handicaps dictate a curriculum content that can be made realistic and consumable for the mentally retarded. At the same time, it is important to include in the list of essences, cultural phases dealing with the humanities, and those offering opportunity for the expression and development of aesthetic ideas and attitudes which will be reflected in the personality of the individual.

A fifth problem has to do with the securing of materials to implement curriculum content. Though there is still a meager supply of generalized educational material suitable for the mentally retarded pupil, some materials designed for extension of the scope of experiences provided for normal children are helpful to some degree. Progressive school systems in metropolitan areas with a large concentration of special classes have been developing their own materials for the mentally handicapped or adapting for use those used with the regular groups. Supplementary educational materials are being developed from the units of experience organized especially for the mentally retarded. These are particularly valuable since the vocabulary involved in them is suitable for the mentally retarded. The materials generally found in regular grade-school reading materials are not commensurable with the social interests of pupils of this classification.

Obviously, the problem of providing adequate instruction for mentally retarded children is not one which can be met exclusively and completely through local efforts and resources. Several promising cooperative efforts offer considerable hope for more constructive efforts in behalf of such children. These developments include[3] :

1. Provisions for guidance, consultant, and technical services by state departments of instruction.
2. Establishment of special classes and schools on a regional basis through the cooperation of local schools.
3. Transportation of mentally retarded children to special class centers or schools.
4. Development of programs of in-service training in the field of special education for regular teaching and administrative personnel.
5. Use of special supervisors in the field of special education for the mentally retarded.
6. Use of clinical and consultant services of state colleges and universities and other available agencies.

There is considerable support for the use of kinesthetic aids in the instructional activities of children with limited mental ability. Such approaches, along with the use of varied forms of audio-visual materials,

3 Adapted from Kelly and Stevens, *op. cit.*, p. 253.

are valuable, particularly in providing additional motivation for such children.

The Mentally Gifted.—Those deviating mentally from the average in the opposite direction are the *mentally gifted*. Since these children tend to get along satisfactorily without special attention, considerably less emphasis has been placed on special provisions for them than for mentally retarded children, even though about two per cent of the school population may be classified in the gifted category.

Mentally gifted children learn more rapidly than other children, an ability evidenced rather generally by superior reading ability and unusual competence in problem solving and other activities involving abstract processes. Such children usually excel in the ability to see relationships and to generalize from specific sets of facts. They are often imaginative and creative, and tend to rebel against excessive drill and repetition or monotonous routines and unvaried activities.

Almost from the earliest days of organized education, there has been some concern over what should constitute a suitable program for the gifted child. Throughout the years the attempts to meet this challenge have varied, but two approaches have emerged. The first is to care for the unusually rapid progress of the mentally gifted through the administrative device of *acceleration*. It is maintained by the advocates of this plan that acceleration places brighter pupils in a more challenging situation and motivates them to greater educational endeavor. Others maintain that this approach to the problem may alleviate some curriculum problems but will create social maladjustments at the same time.

A second approach is *enrichment*. Proponents of this approach are usually divided into two camps; one contends that such enrichment can best occur in the regular classroom through individualized assignments and activities, while the other believes that enrichment can be best provided for in special classes for the gifted in which the whole program is geared to the characteristics and needs of these childdren. It is obvious that arguments can be marshalled to support each view. Much depends, of course, on the nature of the enrichment and whether it is adapted to the capacities of the gifted child. The important thing is to provide genuine curriculum enrichment for these children; how it is to be done can best be determined by local school personnel after study of the evidence available, including their own experimentation with curriculum adaptations for the rapid-learning child.

There is some fear among parents and educators that the designation of certain children as "gifted" may, in itself, contribute to feelings of superiority and social insensitivity. In some schools, notably Cleveland

and Detroit, the classes set up for these children are known as "major-work classes." Baker[4] cites ten factors used in the Detroit schools for selecting candidates for "major-work classes." They are:

1. General behavior
2. Effort as related to ability
3. Group intelligence rating
4. Rating of age for grade
5. Height ratio for age
6. Weight ratio for age
7. Rating for comprehension in reading
8. Rating on recent scholastic marks
9. Rating on number of permanently erupted teeth
10. Rating for participation in school activities

Sumption, Norris, and Terman,[5] in a general discussion of the possible provisions for the gifted, suggest that acceleration and enrichment should complement each other in the best educational program. They further summarize their thinking regarding such a program as follows:

1. For centuries society has recognized the value of providing exceptional educational opportunities to gifted youth, but for the most part such provisions have been sporadic and inadequate.

2. Equality of opportunity demands that each child be given the type of education which best meets his needs and capacities. This principle is violated when a gifted child is forced to accept an education which does not take into account his superior ability and give him an opportunity to develop it.

3. In terms of social welfare, the effective education of gifted youth is imperative. It is folly for society to fail to utilize its most able human resources.

4. In general, gifted children do not cause trouble in school. Perhaps, unfortunately, they tend to adjust to the program set up for the normal child and work along with a minimum amount of effort and little opportunity to develop their full powers. Probably this is one factor contributing to the greatest neglect of this type of child as compared to the mentally retarded, the speech defective, and the socially delinquent.

5. The objectives in the education of gifted are the same as for other children. The difference lies in the greater emphasis placed on creative effort, intellectual initiative, critical thinking, social adjustment, social responsibility, and the development of unselfish qualities of leadership.

6. The first problem for educators is to discover gifted children. This may not always be an easy task. At present a combination of standardized tests, teachers' judgments, and classroom performance probably offers the best means of finding them.

7. The second step, that of providing an enriched educational program for the gifted, is more difficult than discovering them. Yet it is essential that these

[4] Harry J. Baker, op. cit., p. 283.
[5] Merle R. Sumption, Dorothy Norris, and Lewis Terman, "Special Education for the Gifted Child," The Education of Exceptional Children, Forty-Ninth Yearbook of the National Society for the Study of Education, Part II (Chicago: University of Chicago Press, 1950), pp. 278-79.

children have sufficient opportunities to develop their abilities above and beyond what is called for in the normal school program.

8. Enrichment may be serviced through special schools, special classes, or individual attention as the demands of different situations dictate. The authors of this chapter recommend that wherever possible special classes be organized for the education of gifted children. In cases where the individual instruction plan is adopted, a specially trained supervising teacher is recommended.

9. Moderate acceleration, particularly in high school and college, is not inadvisable when the individual is socially and physically mature for his age. Especially is this true where there are no enrichment opportunities for the gifted child. It is quite possible and desirable to save one or two or even three years of the individual's educational life when he is well advanced in social and physical maturity. Except in unusual cases, such acceleration should probably take place in the latter part of the educational program.

10. No program of education for any type of exceptional child offers greater possibilities for the social welfare than does an effective educational program for the child with superior mental ability.

The Educationally Retarded.—Mental retardation is sometimes attributed to children who are only *educationally* retarded. That is, they have the necessary ability to learn normally but have been deprived, for some reason, of the opportunity for a sufficiently adequate educational program for them to achieve what might be expected from them. Sometimes such children are members of transient families, moving so frequently that anything resembling continuity in their educational experiences is virtually impossible. A long history of illness sometimes results in an educational experience for a child so sporadic that he cannot achieve up to the levels of his fellows of similar chronological age, even though he may have the inherent ability for doing so. Undoubtedly, some educational retardation is the result of poor educational background involving questionable methods, inadequate materials, or undue pressures which have resulted in emotional reactions against school. Whatever the reasons for their condition, children whose educational achievement is notably below the norm ought to be studied carefully and dealt with in a sympathetic and wise manner, so that proper motivation can be regained.

Children whose ability levels are considerably above their achievement levels may be considered *remedial* cases. This is as true of a child actually performing above the group norms or national norms as of the child whose achievement ranks at the bottom of the group. Remedial instruction is suggested not by the level of performance but by the size of the *educational gap* between ability and performance.

This definition of a remedial case suggests four important steps in providing for the needs of educationally retarded children:

1. Use all suitable and available methods for establishing an *expectancy* level as a standard of performance for such children. This will require determination of the intellectual capacity of the child as well as an appraisal of his general pattern of growth and physical vigor. In such cases it is advisable to administer at least two mental tests, one of which should be individually administered by a person trained in the use of such instruments. It is also desirable to test both the language and non-language factors of mental proficiency in order to determine any differences that may exist.

2. Attempt to get as complete a picture as possible of the child's *performance level.* This effort requires more than the administration of an achievement test, although, of course, such tests are useful in this connection. The determination of this level for the child should involve a study of his educational performance—verbal, written, and manipulative. It is particularly important to note the reading level at which the child is reasonably proficient, since much of his school activity depends on his ability to read.

3. Seek as complete diagnoses as possible in order to determine the operational factors hindering the child from experiencing greater success. This may be achieved in many ways. Among the methods usually employed are the use of diagnostic scales, charts, and tests, teacher observation and analysis of the child's behavior and work, screening tests for possible detection of physical barriers to success, interviews with the child and his parents, sociometric techniques, and the study of the child's family and school history.

4. Provide a good program of action designed to: (*a*) generate maximum motivation, (*b*) remove physical and emotional barriers to learning, (*c*) furnish effective basic instruction beginning at the points of "educational breakdown" in the child's background. This will involve considerable attention to the development of needed skills, the alleviation of specific deficiencies, and the continuous measurement of success.

In the opinion of the author, remedial instruction does not differ materially from generally effective teaching procedures. It does require from the teacher a high degree of sympathy and understanding, highly individualized activities for the learner, and provisions for maximum motivation. Mehl, Mills, and Douglass[6] have suggested seven conditions essential to the success of remedial work as follows:

1. The child must be aware of the fact that improvement is needed.
2. The child must understand the need for remedial work.

6 Marie A. Mehl, Hubert H. Mills, and Harl R. Douglass, *Teaching in the Elementary School* (New York: The Ronald Press Co., 1950), p. 395.

3. The child must be interested in wanting to improve.
4. The child must assume the responsibility to do something about it.
5. The child must know what the correct pattern of response must be.
6. The child must know how to go about making the needed correction.
7. The child must experience improvement.

The educationally retarded child needs the security and interaction of the regular classroom. While it is possible for such a child to benefit substantially from being assigned to a special teacher for particular help and guidance during a period or part of the school day, his educational salvation does not lie in his assignment to a special class on a full-time basis. It does lie in a secure, happy, and satisfying association with an understanding and skillful classroom teacher.

The Culturally Exceptional.—Variation in cultural background may show itself in many ways among school children. The great disparity of experience enjoyed by children during their preschool years has a marked effect on subsequent school progress. This is shown not only in their readiness for reading but in many other ways as well.

Children also differ considerably in their language backgrounds. Those who come from homes where the level and quality of the spoken language is limited naturally are not able to demonstrate the language adeptness desired for children as they develop. Even more of a problem is that often experienced by the child who attends an English-speaking school but who comes from a home in which some other language is spoken. In either case, the teacher should demonstrate genuine understanding; and, in the latter case, he should, if possible, capitalize on the situation and attempt to help the child understand that it can be a distinct asset for him to know something about another language. The important thing is to avoid a situation in which the child feels any kind of stigma because his language or accent is different from that of other children.

Children with limited, or highly different, cultural backgrounds need the experience of mingling with children of their own age in a regular classroom situation. Care should be exercised so that their lack of experiential background is not mistakenly assumed to be mental retardation, leading to assignment to a special class. This does not appear to be the answer in such cases.

The Socially and Emotionally Maladjusted.—The personality deviations in elementary school children cover a wide range in nature and degree. For example, antisocial feelings may be expressed in one child through serious withdrawal tendencies, while another with similar feelings may show completely aggressive overt behavior. Because the scale of social behavior is complex, it is easy for the teacher with limited understanding to misconstrue the natural expressions of exuberance of children as being abnormal behavior. For this reason, it is essential that all who work with children should go beyond superficial behavior itself and strive to analyze the conditions and attitudes which prompt it. Herein lies the chief distinction between normal and abnormal social behavior, as well as the only channel through which undesirable behavior can be improved.

The school has a dual responsibility in meeting the problem of social maladjustment in children. In the first place, conditions conducive to wholesome social development of children should be established and maintained in the school. The concept of discipline which prevades the school, the interest manifest in the individual child, the opportunities for children to achieve status and recognition among their fellows, and the degree of mutual understanding and interaction between home and school are all contributing factors to this end.

In spite of commendable preventive conditions, however, some cases of rather acute social maladjustment and emotional instability seem destined to occur. These children often have attended numerous schools, may have been rejected at home, have experienced lack of success and unusual frustration in school work, and have, accordingly, developed a distinct and active dislike for school and all that it represents. Such children present a real challenge to teachers and administrators and demand a maximum of patience, understanding, and ingenuity.

The welfare not only of the individual child but also of the other children who compose a school group must be considered in deciding on the most suitable provisions for the socially maladjusted child. For this reason, it is impossible to set forth any specific proposals for dealing with this problem. Such decisions must involve a consideration of the particular characteristics of the child and the facilities available. Some guidance in this direction is given by Stullken,[7] who proposed a set of twelve principles which underlie the development of special educational provisions for this class of pupils. They are:

1. Socially maladjusted children are entitled to the advantage of a special educational program that will permit them to develop to the limit of their capacities.
2. Segregation as commonly defined is not a necessary concomitant of the education of socially maladjusted children.
3. In organizing and administering a program of special education for the

[7] Edward H. Stullken, "Special Schools and Classes for the Socially Maladjusted," *The Education of Exceptional Children, Forty-Ninth Yearbook of the National Society for the Study of Education* (Chicago: University of Chicago Press, 1950), pp. 299-301.

socially maladjusted, school administrators must maintain a balance between the interests of pupils needing placement in special groups and the interests of the great majority of the school population.

4. The school administrator should be the final authority in the transfer of children to a special group or to a special program for socially maladjusted individuals.

5. Schools must recognize the fact that a socially maladjusted child is one who may be normal within himself but yet be exceptional because of antisocial home and community influences.

6. The special-education program for socially maladjusted children should be a part of and not apart from the general educational program.

7. School systems should provide for early identification and early diagnosis of children who are maladjusted.

8. The education of socially maladjusted children requires a broader basis than that of mere intellectual development.

9. Any program of education for the socially maladjusted will be conditioned by the selection of properly qualified and trained personnel.

10. No program for socially maladjusted children is sound unless it recognizes the fact that the behavior of such children is symptomatic and purposive.

11. Socially maladjusted children differ from normal children more in degree than in kind.

12. Teachers, school administrators, and social workers should not initiate programs for educating or treating socially maladjusted children without first making a survey to determine the extent and nature of the local problem.

ACTION SUGGESTIONS FOR THE PRINCIPAL

1. Allocate some of the meetings of faculty groups to the study of how to adjust the curriculum to individuals.

2. Consult teacher-educating institutions and the state department of public instruction for curriculum bulletins or other materials which may be shared with faculty members.

3. Encourage teachers to visit nearby schools which have records of providing unusually good programs for exceptional children.

4. Remember, and help teachers to realize, that a curriculum is no good until a child can use it.

5. Precede curriculum adjustments by careful study and analysis of the needs to be met.

6. In evaluation of the school program, include some attention to the study of the growth of individuals as well as group norms.

7. Encourage teachers to use a variety of teaching methods to meet the needs of children with varying abilities.

8. Provide differentiated and varied instructional materials for classroom use.

9. Wherever possible, attempt to provide for the specific remedial needs of children without seriously disturbing their social relationships.

10. Explore as many ways as possible of providing for needed classroom adjustments of deviant children.

11. Arrange for the staff to become acquainted with modern equipment and materials for screening and alleviating educational disabilities.

12. Provide flexibility in the scheduling of classes and activities wherever feasible.

13. Encourage the organization of classroom activities in such a manner that each child can contribute at his own level.

14. Utilize the talents of gifted children in leadership roles in the school activities.

15. Integrate exceptional children into the over-all school population in as many ways as possible without interfering with their specialized instruction.

16. Avoid unfavorable terminology in connection with special classes or schools.

17. Refrain from overdramatizing the handicaps of children.

18. Get acquainted with all the available community and state agencies from which help for exceptional children can be gained.

19. Provide a school environment that emphasizes *success* rather than *failure* and work toward a curriculum that allows each child to succeed to the limits of his ability.

20. Encourage teachers to think in terms of individual objectives as well as group objectives.

21. Work with teachers in making comparative studies of the abilities and the achievement levels of children.

22. Use case studies in analyzing the needs of individual pupils.

23. Try to visit and work with the parents of individual children, particularly those with special educational problems.

24. Provide for the pooling of teacher resources in providing a suitable program of experiences for individuals.

25. Create a school program that allows each child to remain important.

SELECTED REFERENCES FOR EXTENDED READING

BAKER, HARRY J. *Introduction to Exceptional Children* (rev.). New York: The Macmillan Co., 1953.

BURTON, WILLIAM H. *The Guidance of Learning Activities.* New York: Appleton-Century-Crofts, Inc., 1944, chap. 17.

ELSBREE, WILLARD S., and MCNALLY, HAROLD J. *Elementary School Administration and Supervision.* New York: American Book Co., 1951, chap. 9.

GARRISON, KARL C. *The Psychology of Exceptional Children.* New York: The Ronald Press Co., 1950.

HECK, ARCH O. *The Education of Exceptional Children.* New York: McGraw-Hill Book Co., 1953.

KIRK, SAMUEL A., and JOHNSON, G. ORVILLE. *Educating the Retarded Child.* Boston: Houghton-Mifflin Co., 1951.

MEHL, MARIE A., MILLS, HUBERT H., and DOUGLASS, HARL R. *Teaching in Elementary School.* New York: The Ronald Press Co., 1950, chap. 19.

MICHAELIS, JOHN U., and GRIM, PAUL R. *The Student Teacher in the Elementary School*. New York: Prentice-Hall, Inc., 1953.

NATIONAL ELEMENTARY PRINCIPAL. *Meeting Special Needs of the Individual Child: Nineteenth Yearbook*, XIX, No. 6. Washington, D. C.: Department of Elementary Principals, National Education Association, 1940.

NATIONAL SOCIETY FOR THE STUDY OF EDUCATION. *The Education of Exceptional Children: Forty-Ninth Yearbook*. Chicago: University of Chicago Press, 1950.

OTTO, HENRY J. *Elementary School Organization and Administration*. New York: Appleton-Century-Crofts, Inc., 1954, chap. 12.

WILES, KIMBALL. *Teaching for Better Schools*. New York: Prentice-Hall, Inc., 1952, chaps. 11 and 12.

WITTY, PAUL A. (ed.). *The Gifted Child*. Boston: D. C. Heath & Co., 1951.

PART V
IMPROVING THE SERVICES OF THE SCHOOL

Chapter 13

IMPROVING THE HEALTH AND SAFETY PROGRAM
OF THE SCHOOL

Education for living cannot ignore education for health

A very real relationship exists between the physical vigor of a child and his total educational development. Particularly in recent years, schools have begun to accept their share of the responsibility for the physical development and well-being of children. This has been a natural outgrowth of the more modern concepts of psychology which emphasize the organismic and integrated characteristics of the child's nature, and which assume learning to involve the unified development of many interrelated facets of the child's resources. From this view of learning, it follows that the intellectual development of a child cannot be considered, or promoted, apart from a corresponding consideration of other components of the learner's total being. It seems hardly possible, then, to discuss the organization of the modern elementary school without giving careful attention to provisions for improving and maintaining the personal well-being of the children who attend school.

Positive efforts to guarantee maximum results from the health program of the school involve many areas of activity. The personal well-being of children is affected by the physical plant of the school, the quality of the custodial services of the school, the nature of the program of health instruction, the attention given to mental hygiene, the health services provided, and many other facets of the school program. It is certainly a duty of educational leadership to coordinate these efforts into a composite program that will yield definite, constructive results in this very important aspect of the child's development.

The ensuing discussion of the health and safety program of the modern elementary school is organized in relation to: (1) some principles underlying a good health and safety program, (2) the most important aspects of an effective health program, (3) some provisions for mental and emotional health which the school should make, (4) some important considerations affecting the safety of children, and (5) meeting the nutritional needs of children through the school lunch program.

Principles Underlying the Health and Safety Program

The activities of the personnnel of the school in the selection and operation of health facilities should reflect a knowledge of child development and should be consistent with the objectives of the school. In other words, the specialized efforts to prevent, or to cope with, the health problems—physical, mental, and emotional—of children should be consistent with the general educational endeavors of the school.[1] Sometimes the formulation of guiding principles gives direction and scope to such efforts. For that reason, the following principles are included here to form a framework for the subsequent discussion of these problems.

1. *The personal well-being of each child should be a matter of primary concern to the school and to those who administer its program.* The more functional approaches to health and health instruction only recently have become respected and integral parts of the business of the school. For this reason, as well as others, this aspect of the child's development frequently has been considered a necessary, though not always desirable, appendage somewhat loosely connected with the curriculum proper. Progress is being made in eliminating this unfortunate restriction upon the health program, but many schools, even yet, evidence lack of understanding and even greater lack of facilities in meeting the challenge of this aspect of the program. It is essential that the personal well-being of children should be considered of first importance, rather than tangential to the school program.

2. *The personal well-being of children involves many facets of human development and adjustment.* It is unrealistic to think of personal well-being only in terms of physical vigor and freedom from disease; well-rounded development of children involves their mental health and emotional stability as well. Recognition of this fact requires that provisions be made in the school program for the development of all aspects of self-realization for the child. These provisions should include proper attention to the educational environment, the quality of human relationships within the school, and the special guidance and assistance that can be given to children with physical, mental, or emotional health problems.

3. *The program of the school should provide for the effective integration of the various facets of the health and safety program.* The health and safety program of the school has as its major purpose the development

---

[1] William A. Yeager, *Administration and the Pupil* (New York: Harper & Bros., 1949), chap. 17; American Association of School Administrators, *Health in Schools, Twentieth Yearbook* (Washington, D. C.: National Education Association, 1942).

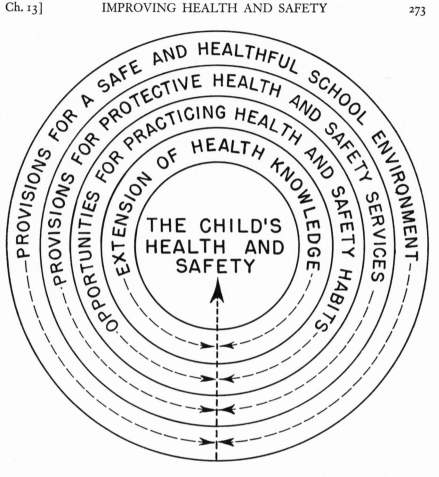

Figure 13

Providing for the Health and Safety of Children

of happy, hearty, healthy individuals who can function efficiently as they meet the demands of daily living. This objective is achieved in many ways. It involves the acquisition of knowledge, the development of understanding, the formulation of habits, and the emergence of a pride in personal and community wholesomeness. The program of the school should be so coordinated that all components of healthful living are merged in the child's pattern of behavior. Health instruction, physical education, administration of the health services, control of communicable disease, standards of cleanliness maintained in the school, and operation of the school lunch program should be related. Unless the child is aware of a relationship between each of these and his own welfare, the over-all health program will fall far short of yielding its maximum benefit in achieving desired goals of self-realization.

4. *The physical environment should be conducive to healthful and safe living.* The construction and maintenance of the physical plant bears a very direct relationship to the physical, mental, and emotional well-being of children who inhabit it. The type of construction, provisions for ventilation, heating, and acoustic control, as well as the specialized facilities needed for health services, all contribute to the well-being of children. In addition, attention should be given to toilet and lavatory facilities, fire protection, and provisions for proper custodial care of the plant so that dirt and dust are not allowed to accumulate. Such care not only guarantees better protection against possible disease, but also helps children to develop a pride in clean and orderly surroundings.

5. *Good teaching in health and safety involves example as well as instruction.* Children develop many of their impressions about health and safety habits from their associations with adults. It is important for teachers, administrators, and parents to demonstrate the kinds of behavior they desire for children with whom they work. This suggests that such adults should exercise care in posture, in their degree of recklessness when crossing the street, and in their attitudes toward desirable health habits, such as care of the teeth, skin, and hair. Children in the elementary school are rather impressionable and tend to identify themselves with teachers and other adults whom they admire. The proper example on the part of these adults can be a very potent factor in the health education of their younger associates.

The self-control and mannerisms of the teacher are important to the development of emotional stability in children. The well-mannered teacher, free from outbursts of anger or recrimination, who demonstrates the kind of relationships with children he expects them to show in their reactions to one another, is a most constructive force in the fostering of good mental health throughout the school in which he works.

6. *The various health services of the school should be considered as part of the educative experiences of children.* It is not enough that the routine health examinations and immunization services be administered to children periodically. They should be done in such a manner that the participation of children can be a genuinely educative experience designed to extend their understanding of health problems and to help them develop positive attitudes toward preventive measures against possible disease or infection. These salutary outcomes can be brought about through discussion prior to the administration of such services

and through common sense approaches by classroom teachers and specialized medical personnel who are interested in children and skilled in working with them.

7. *An effective health program involves pleasant working relationships with parents and community agencies.* The school cannot possibly administer a completely successful health program alone. Such a program requires the interest and cooperation of parents and other individuals and agencies in the community. The school should exercise initiative in securing this type of needed assistance from sources outside the school. Beginning with the annual health roundup of preschool children which many schools sponsor, there is need for continued supplementation of the school's services throughout the entire sequence of the elementary school and beyond. The interest and cooperation of parents can often be obtained through health study groups, follow-up conferences, and letters related to the results of health examinations, or through rotating parent participation in some phase of the health services of the school.

The administrator and teaching personnel of the school should attempt to develop an acquaintance with health officials in the community and to make intelligent use of various community agencies in alleviating the health problems in the school. If the efforts of all concerned can be coordinated effectively through the school program, then maximum benefits are likely to accrue for the children involved.

8. *Specialized personnel and facilities should be provided if the school expects to render adequate health service.* Although many aspects of the health program of the school depend upon the efforts of the regular staff of teaching and administrative personnel, the specialized technical and medical services to children cannot, and should not, be attempted without qualified personnel. Such specialists include the doctor of medicine, the nurse, the dentist, the dental hygienist, and the trained psychologist or guidance worker. Even though it is not feasible for small schools to employ full-time health personnel, they can often secure such services on a part-time or rotating basis in cooperation with other schools of a city or county system. A description of some of the important health facilities of the school was given in Chapter 7.

9. *The health program and services should be evaluated periodically with a view toward improvement.* There should be provisions, within the framework of curriculum study by the staff and other interested persons, for the periodic appraisal of the health and safety program of the school. As services become routine after a number of years, or as new demands seem to be made on the school in relation to the health of children, it is necessary to re-think and re-examine the methods being

employed to gain the desired objectives in this area. Such study should involve the participation of professional staff, health and safety specialists, parents, representatives of community and state agencies, and others who have a legitimate stake in the health problem. From such cooperative efforts can come a renewed appreciation of the current program as well as the identification of aspects needing improvement.

Promoting Physical Health in the Elementary School

The school health program should embrace three major areas of concern: (1) provisions for a healthful school environment that is conducive to wholesome living, (2) a functionally designed program for the development of knowledge, attitudes, and habits in the field of health and physical education, and (3) suitable health services. If one is anxious to develop a fully functioning program of health services in the elementary school, careful attention to all three of these aspects of the program is essential. Some of the specific characteristics of each will be discussed in the following paragraphs.

A Healthful School Environment.—The pride and interest with which children view health matters usually rises a little higher than the standards of health and cleanliness to which they have been accustomed. This stresses the importance of the physical environment which the school affords the child from day to day, and of good housekeeping in the promotion of sound concepts and habits of healthful living.

As mentioned earlier, it is essential that the environment of the school be kept free from health hazards. Aside from eliminating, as far as possible, situations which might lead to the injury of children, there are many other aspects of school maintenance and custodial care which directly affect the health of children. Water fountains and lavatory facilities need continuous care if they are to be kept in a safe condition for use. School lunch and kitchen facilities may be sources of trouble if they do not receive suitable attention; and, of course, there must be proper provisions for the disposal of garbage and waste materials so that their accumulation does not create a health hazard.

Another important aspect of the school environment is the control of physical conditions within the classroom. Careful attention must be given to such matters as the regulation of heat, light, ventilation, and noise. While many elementary schools now have thermostatic control of heat, a health problem still exists for those who do not enjoy the benefits of such facilities. Irregular heat and poor ventilation contribute to a high incidence of the common cold and, undoubtedly, to the spread of other types of infections and communicable diseases. Part of the problem of maintaining proper regulation of heat in the classroom is related to the fact that the basal metabolism rate differs somewhat between girls and boys and between children and adults. This often means that a room well regulated for boys and girls who are active will seem too cold for a teacher. This presents something of a problem, since the regulation of the temperature and ventilation in many cases is based on the sensory comfort of the teacher rather than that of the children.

Modern building trends have reflected great progress in lighting classrooms, but a very large proportion of classrooms still are inadequately lighted. Adequate lighting includes attention to quality, quantity, and distribution of light. It involves some suitable means for controlling the sunlight as well as providing necessary artificial lighting. Means for modifying the lighting of the room during different parts of the day, or on days alternately sunny and cloudy, also are essential. More and more attention is being given in modern schools to the interior decoration of classrooms, since it has been established that surrounding colors are not only related to proper light distribution throughout the classroom, but also have a psychological effect on the inhabitants of the room.

Acoustic construction materials have made a great contribution to the physical comfort and emotional tone of modern elementary classrooms. By subduing the natural noise which accompanies the activities of a group of busy children, communication becomes easier and less strained and the normal functions of the classroom can be carried on in an atmosphere conducive to pleasant living and efficient learning. Control of sound is particularly important in parts of the building used by large groups of children simultaneously, such as the cafeteria, activity rooms, or auditorium.

The Instructional Program in Health and Physical Education.— Although there are many casual and incidental opportunities for children to learn about health and the functioning of their bodies, instruction in this basic area of human well-being should not be left to chance. To a degree, at least, sound health practices depend on an understanding of the functioning of the body and the kind of care which keeps it operating with maximum efficiency. This assumption calls for a carefully designed program of instruction through which recognized health objectives may be achieved. Such a program should emphasize healthful living rather than physiological technicalities, and should be formulated on the basis of prevailing personal and community health problems, needs, and interests, as well as on the growth characteristics of children as they progress through the various levels of the elementary school.

An effective program of instruction emphasizes the translation of health knowledge into the children's habits of action. This is another way of saying that healthful living cannot be learned during a health period alone but must be an integral part of the daily activities of boys and girls. This is not to refute the value of health knowledge as a basis for intelligent action, but it does suggest the major importance of the applied phases of learning in the area of health. The routines of the school day, the housekeeping which children engage in, and the continuous emphasis on good health habits all are a part of the program of health instruction.

Another important phase of the program is physical education. The modern physical education program utilizes many different types of activities to achieve its objectives of physical fitness, relaxation, social development, recreational interests, and character development.

In the elementary school physical education is usually taught by the regular classroom teacher with whatever help is available from members of the physical education staff. This is especially true in schools with self-contained classrooms, and at the primary levels in nearly all schools.

The program usually includes opportunities for free play, which may be supervised but which is largely undirected. Such activities provide an excellent outlet for the pentup emotions of children, as well as a suitable means for their physical development. Rhythmic activities also constitute an integral part of the program, especially for younger children. These activities for children at the upper levels of the elementary school often take the form of folk dancing.

A third important activity of the physical education program is that of team games, usually introduced in the upper grades at the time when the activities of boys and girls may begin to differ noticeably. Such games are excellent means for training in sportsmanship and teamwork, but they should be kept free from the extreme emphasis on competition which sometimes unhappily prevails even at the elementary school levels.

Ideally, a school should have specialized personnel and facilities for corrective physical education, geared to the particular needs of certain children. In any case, the physical education should be so conceived and operated that provisions can be made for the participation of all children, each at his own level of growth and physical proficiency. This will require the differentiation of the program just as is desirable with every other phase of the school curriculum. Such a program can be most effective if it is cooperatively designed, functionally and realistically operated, and continuously evaluated.

The Health Services of the School.—Provisions for health services to school children, and frequently to preschool children, have become an integral part of the structure and facilities of the modern elementary school. Such services include provisions for: (1) first aid in cases of injury or sudden illness, (2) the control of communicable disease or infection, and (3) screening tests and examinations with appropriate follow-up procedures.

It is well to remember that schools have a responsibility to render appropriate immediate aid in case of illness or injury at school, but that they have an equally strong responsibility to render no more than first aid. The school is usually held to be responsible for only the emergency handling of such cases and not for any subsequent treatment. Some aspects of the handling of such circumstances, however, stand out as being so important that perhaps they should be mentioned specifically:

1. At least one member of the school staff with specialized training in first-aid measures should be on the school premises at all times.
2. The school should be equipped with first-aid kits containing the necessary supplies for dealing with emergency conditions.
3. All teachers and members of the school staff should have, and understand clearly, instructions for guiding their actions in cases of emergency.
4. The possibility of immediate contact with the school nurse or doctor should be maintained as fully as possible at all hours of the school day.
5. School records should contain all information necessary for contacting a child's parents and/or family doctor.
6. The school should maintain proper rest quarters for children who are injured or who become ill at school.
7. Children who are sent home because of injury or illness should always be accompanied.

If a high level of health is to prevail among the population of the elementary school, teachers and administrators, as well as specialized personnel, must fulfill certain responsibilities in the control of illness and communicable disease, which must go beyond the traditional concept and practice of the routine of daily inspection. They must have authentic information regarding the symptomatic indications of abnormal health conditions and must be continuously sensitive to the presence of these symptoms in children throughout the school day. This continuing, careful observation of children also can guide teachers in their work with children and can furnish the bases for conferences with parents or for referrals to health officials for diagnosis and possible treatment.

Children with symptoms suggesting something other than very minor illness should be identified and excluded from school as soon as possible after the onset of the symptoms. This insures earlier and more complete treatment for the child and minimizes the danger of the spread of the condition to other children. Immediate action in this regard is justified not only for the health of the individual child, but also for general attendance, since epidemics which spread throughout classrooms, or even throughout the school and community, obviously have a very disastrous effect on attendance.

The school should have definite measures and procedures for the exclusion of suspected health cases from school, for transportation to their homes, and for the notification of parents. In addition, there should be just as sound procedures for re-admitting children to their classrooms after having been absent with a communicable disease. Both aspects of school organization are necessary if the health of all children is to be fully protected. In both cases, the services and professional advice of the school nurse or health official are highly desirable and should be provided, if at all possible.

The health needs and problems of many children can be identified through well-organized physical examinations of various types. It is the practice in many school systems now to provide general examinations, inoculations, and vaccinations of children even before they enter the elementary school and to continue to administer periodic screening examinations throughout the years the child remains in the elementary school. Through such examinations, it is possible for questionable health conditions to be identified sufficiently early to prevent more serious developments.

General examinations are usually conducted by the school physician, by personnel from the city, county, or state health agency, or through arrangements with private physicians in the school community. In addition to giving attention to such general health factors as height, weight, posture, and skin condition, such examinations also are usually directed toward the detection of respiratory or cardiac difficulties. The amount of good to be accomplished through these examinations depends to a very large degree on the effectiveness of follow-up procedures and on the interest and cooperation which the school is able to generate in parents.

School examinations may also include tests to determine the vision and hearing status of the children. Such tests should be given regularly and fairly frequently in order to detect any sudden change or impairment in vision or hearing of children; certainly they should occur at least once annually and, in addition, facilities should be available for the testing of any particular child at any time there is reasonable doubt concerning his sight or hearing. The methods and facilities employed should be up to date and as thorough as possible.

There are differences of opinion, each view supported to some degree by research, as to the most effective instruments for screening out children who should be referred to eye specialists because of imperfect vision. Local conditions and facilities, of course, are usually the greatest determining factor in checking the vision of children.

The most common check of acuity of vision is by the use of the Snellen Charts, with which most teachers and administrators are familiar. This device, though ordinarily valuable and inexpensive, is limited by the possibility of malfeasance by those who respond to it, since there is no way of actually determining the authenticity of responses. It is also limited in the number of elements of the visual process which can be examined through its use since it is constructed mainly to determine general visual acuity of each eye operating independently of the other.

A number of schools are now using such devices as the Keystone Telebinocular in the administration of screening tests for vision. Research has cast some doubt upon the theory that such devices actually are more accurate in the identification of cases of vision needing professional attention than are simpler and less expensive means such as the Snellen Chart. Be that as it may, the telebinocular test is much more inclusive in the number of aspects of vision measured and appears to include at least some checks on inaccurate responses. With this type of instrument it is possible to check astigmatism, color-blindness, and muscular imbalance, as well as the individual acuity of vision of each eye. Another advantage of this instrument is that either eye can be examined without the necessity of covering the other.

Whatever devices are used for screening tests of vision, it is important that they be available to and usable by classroom teachers in their efforts to identify pupils who need the attention of eye specialists. The complete function of the screening program is identification; diagnosis and treatment must be left to those specially qualified to render these services.

Screening tests of hearing are prompted by the same general considerations that underlie adequate tests of vision. The whisper test and the watch tick test are simple screening devices that can be used without special training on the part of classroom teachers. However, an increasing number of schools are purchasing either the 4-A Audiometer for group testing or the 2-A Audiometer for individual testing. Though these instruments are relatively expensive, they seem to offer better possibilities for screening, particularly if schools have sound-proof quarters in which such tests can be administered. As in the case of vision, one of the most important facets of the auditory screening is the provision made for following up the findings to insure indicated examination and treatment for children whose hearing does not measure up to expected standards.

Promoting Mental Health in the Elementary School

Maintenance of good mental and emotional health of children ranks with care of physical health as a basic objective of the elementary school, and demands a many-sided program. There is reason to believe that it is more nearly accomplished through wholesome environment and favorable human relationships which the child enjoys than through direct processes of instruction. It is possible to include here only a few of the considerations which underlie a constructive approach to the maintenance of good mental health.

Good mental health involves self-respect. When a child is discredited in his own eyes, or when he comes to doubt his ability to cope with the ordinary tasks of daily living, or when he constantly feels inferior to his associates, he cannot experience good mental health nor can he face effectively the realities of daily living.

In a similar manner, possession of respect and esteem of others is an essential ingredient of a healthy mental attitude. It is imperative, therefore, for schools to provide learning experiences that offer each individual the opportunity for reasonable success and for the occasional recognition of his fellows.

One of the basic conditions for good mental health is the maintenance of a reasonable balance between the resources one possesses and the demands that are made upon him. This often reveals itself in the cases of children with physical limitations or mental incapacity, and even those with limited socioeconomic backgrounds. They may come to feel that life has cheated them out of the normal equipment for living happily and successfully, and as a result, they may withdraw, become overly aggressive and resentful, or evince other forms of emotional disturbance.

It is a major responsibility of the school to fit its program to children and to guarantee enough flexibility in the program so that each child can be engaged in tasks which he is able to perform through his own efforts. This is not to imply that children always should be engaged in activities which are easy for them; it is rather to assert that it is educationally both unwise and inhumane to demand of children things which they cannot possibly do. Such demands can lead only to frustration at best and, at worst, to serious emotional and social maladjustment. It will be recalled that a more detailed discussion of curriculum adjustment for such children was given in Chapter 11.

Provisions for the social integration of children into the groups to which they are assigned have a direct influence on the level of mental health maintained in a school. School activities should be sufficiently varied to permit each child to participate on an equal basis with his associates and to gain satisfactions from such participation.

The concept of discipline which pervades the atmosphere and organization of the school the child attends is another vital aspect of mental health. Harsh punishments, rigid controls, and lack of understanding on the part of teachers all contribute to the creation, rather than the alleviation, of problems of mental health. Sympathetic and interested guidance, fair and humane treatment, and the demonstration of self-control, patience, and good humor, are valuable assets of the skillful teacher in establishing the conditions for wholesome living relationships in the school.

In summing up the role of the school in relation to mental health Thorpe[2] emphasizes eight important phases of the mental hygiene program: (1) a democratic philosophy of education; (2) attention to physical health and growth; (3) a comprehensive program of activities; (4) effective methods of study and work; (5) adjustment of tasks to maturity levels; (6) development of a wholesome attitude toward sex; (7) a consistent and intelligent program of discipline; (8) the presence of one or more adults in whom the child can confide.

Many emotional problems of children are caused, or aggravated, by conditions outside the school. Even though the school is not responsible for these conditions, every legitimate effort should be made to alleviate them through securing the interest and cooperation of parents in the child's welfare. Some of the home conditions which frequently produce unfavorable effects on children are parental tensions and bickering, sibling rivalry, rejection by parents, domination by others, overprotection, overindulgence of the whims of the child, and the persistent presence of unpleasant issues regarding eating and sleep habits. These and many other influences produce negative attitudes within the child which he carries over into his school life. All suitable channels of home-school interaction should be explored in order to develop a program of consistent action designed to foster in each child the best possible attitudes toward himself and toward others with whom he lives, plays, and works.

[2] Louis P. Thorpe, *The Psychology of Mental Health* (New York: The Ronald Press Co., 1950), pp. 584-85.

PROMOTING SAFETY IN THE ELEMENTARY SCHOOL

The school has a responsibility for the safety of children. It must be met through provisions for the immediate safety of children as they attend school and, in addition, through a program for the development of proper habits of safety which will persist throughout life.

Safety in the School Plant.—One of the first obligations of the school for safety is to provide the safest possible plant to house the activities of children. Construction should be sound, fireproof, and free from all types of hazards. Many modern buildings are so constructed that sharp corners are eliminated in corridors, and such facilities as water fountains and display cases are recessed into the wall for safety. Floors should be constructed of such materials, and maintained in such a manner, that they are not slippery. In buildings of more than one story, stairs should be equipped with guard rails and other features necessary fully to protect the children who use them. Frequent examination and continuous maintenance of the school plant and site are necessary so that existing hazards may be removed as quickly as possible. Broken windows or defective door-stops are common occurrences that demand immediate attention if the premises are to be kept safe.

Care should be exercised in the selection, use, and maintenance of such playground equipment as swings, merry-go-rounds, and teeter-boards. Defective equipment can result in serious accidents to school children. Children should be taught the proper use of facilities and necessary supervision should be provided to establish safety-conscious practices by children, especially as new equipment becomes less novel.

Patrols and Other Organizations.—Although statistics show that children of elementary school age suffer fewer fatal accidents than children of any other age level, it still remains important to reduce the incidence of accidents as far as possible. This concern for the safety of children has extended even beyond the school premises and has resulted in the formation of school patrols in numerous communities. Such organizations, usually composed of boys from the upper grades, not only protect children from some of the hazards of traffic in going to and from school, but also develop responsibility in members of the patrol. Police departments, civic and service clubs, automobile and travel associations, and many other civic-minded groups are often glad to cooperate in the formation and activities of such school patrols.

Development of Safety Habits.—There is some doubt of any one best approach to the teaching of habits of safety to children or, for that matter, to adults. There is general agreement that a program designed for such purposes must go far beyond the mere scheduling of a class in safety. Undoubtedly, the methods and materials employed must differ at different ages. Audio-visual materials seem to be valuable in dramatizing important safety principles. Facsimilies of traffic signs and lights are often used to good advantage, particularly with young children who are getting their initial experiences with crossing busy streets to and from school. Dramatic activities and participation in art projects involving safety themes can help to develop safety consciousness in children. Occasional discussion and evaluation of behavior involving unnecessary risks may be another avenue of approach. It is important, in connection with these and other acceptable means, to give recognition for safe conduct rather than to reserve most of the attention for those who appear to be oblivious to safety. It is the desirable behavior that should be glamorized if children are to be safety-conscious.

NUTRITIONAL NEEDS OF CHILDREN AND THE SCHOOL LUNCH PROGRAM

Only in recent years have the contributions of the school lunch to the health and education of children been generally recognized. In former years, children carried lunches to school, only because of their inability to travel the necessary distance home for lunch and not from any educational considerations. Proper attention to the over-all aspects of the health program for children demands the interest of the school in the child's nutritional needs and in the provisions of the home and school for meeting them.

The modern school lunch program got its greatest impetus during the depression years, when agencies of the federal government sought to supplement the lunches of children through the distribution of surplus food commodities. Later this method of assistance was replaced by cash reimbursements to schools furnishing approved types of school lunch programs. During these years other legislation was passed which affected the purchase and distribution of various types of commodities. Typical of such developments was the provision made for the distribution of milk to school children at greatly reduced prices. In 1946 the National School Lunch Act was passed which provides both for financial subsidies and for furnishing certain commodities to schools, the schools paying only transportation costs. Reimbursements are made through the state agencies responsible for the supervision of lunch programs.

Considerable evidence has been accumulated in recent years to establish a very real relationship between the adequacy of a child's meals and his school attendance and progress. If children, then, are to achieve desired outcomes from their school experiences, they must be provided with an adequate diet. The school lunch program can make a direct contribution in this direction. Even children who live near enough to the school to enable them to go home for lunch often eat hurriedly, or alone, where the mother is employed outside the home during the day. In such cases, it is probably better for the child to eat at school.

One of the major concerns of the school in providing school lunches is the adequacy of the menu. The Type A lunch, approved under the program of reimbursement, is a well-balanced lunch designed to meet all of the basic nutritional needs of children and, at the same time, to provide enough variety to avoid undue monotony of diet.

School cafeterias should be managed on a businesslike basis and be operated by responsible and competent persons who, in addition, have a genuine interest in children. The importance of clean and attractive surroundings have been mentioned elsewhere in this volume, but it is reiterated here for emphasis. Of all places in the whole school, none exists where the standards of cleanliness should be higher than in the lunch room and kitchen.

It is altogether proper that the school emphasize the importance of furnishing nutritious meals to large numbers of children in an expeditious and efficient manner. One of the objectives of the school lunch program is thereby met. However, the lunch activities of children should be educational as well as nutritious. The lunch room should be so attractive and so well managed that children develop social insights and competence through eating with their associates.

In order to obtain proper social outcomes attention to several aspects of the lunch room setting is required. In the first place, the lunch room should not be overcrowded with more children than facilities can reasonably be expected to accommodate. Often large numbers of diners can be cared for by scheduling more than a single lunch period and by "staggering" the periods.

Another requisite is that the lunch room have provisions for acoustic control. Ceilings and walls of acoustic tile or other noise-controlling construction will do much to provide a pleasant atmosphere for conversation in the lunch room or for music during lunch if the school can provide radios or record-players for this purpose. Music appears to have a salutary effect on boisterous and raucous voices and tends to create a pleasant atmosphere.

Finally, it is desirable that children gain lessons in courtesy and dining etiquette from their experiences in the school lunchroom. In fact, the whole school lunch program should be thought of as an integral part of the total investment which the school is making in good health and good education.

ACTION SUGGESTIONS FOR THE PRINCIPAL

1. Work for a school environment that is safe and healthful.

2. Consider the personal welfare of each child a basic responsibility of the school.

3. Work for a health program that gives attention to all facets of health.

4. Strive to make the organization of the school contribute to effective coordination of health services and instruction.

5. Give proper emphasis to custodial care of the building as an element of the health program.

6. Serve as an example of good physical and mental health and encourage teachers to do so.

7. Glamorize wholesome living in all constructive ways.

8. Make periodic and systematic inspections of the school premises for safety hazards.

9. Work with the staff in developing an understanding of proper ventilation and lighting in the classroom.

10. Strive for the functional integration of health and physical education with the total program of the school.

11. Work with teachers and pupils to develop appropriate standards for housekeeping in the school.

12. Provide flexibility in the physical education program to care for differences in children.

13. Provide desirable rest facilities.

14. Develop a clear and complete understanding with the staff as to the proper steps to be taken in case of injuries to children at school.

15. Maintain complete health records of children.

16. Work closely with parents and medical officials on special health problems of particular children.

17. Provide suitable first aid facilities at the school at all times.

18. Develop sensible but systematic provisions for excluding and readmitting children with communicable diseases.

19. Furnish all teachers with information regarding symptoms of various childhood diseases.

20. Provide the best possible personnel and equipment for screening examinations.

21. Provide administrative machinery for the prompt and immediate follow-up on results of health examinations.

22. Study with the staff the relation of school discipline to the mental health of children.

23. Work for a businesslike but cheerful tone throughout the school.

24. Adjust the demands made upon teachers and pupils to the resources they possess.

25. Be willing to work with medical and social agencies outside the school on the physical and emotional problems of children.

26. Provide necessary safety precautions and supervision on the playground of the school.

27. Work in every way possible to make the school lunch have both physical and social value.

28. Invite parents and citizens to help evaluate the health and safety program of the school.

SELECTED REFERENCES FOR EXTENDED READING

AMERICAN ASSOCIATION OF SCHOOL ADMINISTRATORS. *Safety Education: Eighteenth Yearbook.* Washington, D. C.: The Association, 1940.

——. *Health in Schools: Twentieth Yearbook.* Washington, D. C.: The Association, 1942.

CHENOWITH, LAURENCE B., and SELKIRK, THEODORE K. *School Health Problems.* New York: Appleton-Century-Crofts, Inc., 1947.

COOPS, HELEN L. *Health Education in Elementary Schools.* New York: The Ronald Press Co., 1950.

CROMWELL, GERTRUDE E. *The Health of the School Child.* Philadelphia: W. B. Saunders Co., 1946.

GROUT, RUTH E. *Health Teaching in Schools.* Philadelphia: W. B. Saunders Co., 1948.

OBERTENFFER, DELBERT. *School Health Education.* New York: Harper & Bros., 1949.

OTTO, HENRY J. *Elementary School Organization and Administration.* New York: Appleton-Century-Crofts, Inc., 1954, chap. 11.

TURNER, C. E. *School Health and Health Education.* St. Louis: C. V. Mosby Co., 1947.

WALKER, HERBERT. *Health in the Elementary School.* New York: The Ronald Press Co., 1955.

WILLIAMS, JESSE F., and ABERNATHY, RUTH. *Health Education in Schools.* New York: The Ronald Press Co., 1949.

YEAGER, WILLIAM A. *Administration and the Pupil.* New York: Harper & Bros., 1949, chap. 17.

Chapter 14

IMPROVING THE LIBRARY SERVICES OF THE ELEMENTARY SCHOOL

*Books are magic carpets which take us into the enchanted regions
of the world—and of the mind*

Library services are a basic resource of the modern elementary school. In earlier years when a single textbook provided the information for the study of a major area of the curriculum and when the day's schedule was overcrowded and highly compartmentalized, little thought was directed toward the need for extended library services. Today, as schools are placing increasing emphasis on broad approaches to unified, functional problems of living, it is essential that rich and varied instructional resources be provided as an integral part of the educational process.

For the purposes of this discussion, library services will be interpreted very broadly to include various types of instructional resources which children and teachers use to supplement and enhance the regular teacher-learner processes. These resources include not only numerous types of printed materials but also audio-visual materials and equipment.

Great disparity is noted in the provisions for library service from school to school and from community to community. The more modern schools have sensed the significance of this aspect of the school program and have usually included in their programs some means for library service, even though frequently on a limited basis. However, since the advent of the school library is a relatively recent innovation among elementary schools, it has been easy for less progressive schools to neglect the development of this phase of the school structure. Sometimes this lag has been the result of a lack of vision; in other cases, lack of financial support undoubtedly has been the limiting factor.

Metropolitan schools have tended to develop much better library services than those in rural areas but, even among city schools, a large percentage do not have adequate library facilities at the elementary school levels. Among rural schools the problem appears to be even more acute. There is some indication that awareness of this problem is increasing and that schools are sensing the necessity, to a greater degree than heretofore, for adequate library facilities. At any rate, the establishment of adequate and functional library service in the elementary schools is one of today's basic problems in education and is a goal toward whose achievement educational leaders should devote their best efforts. Certainly, it is a goal that is far from being reached at present. This lack represents one of the major handicaps to genuine educational improvement.

This chapter is devoted to a discussion of the role of library service in the modern elementary school and of the important components of that service. For the sake of emphasis, the discussion is divided as follows: (1) some basic principles underlying good library service, (2) the comparative merits of centralized and decentralized collections of materials, (3) the necessary conditions for good library service, (4) essential aspects of good library service, (5) essential types of instructional resources, and (6) some guiding considerations in the selection of instructional materials.

Principles Underlying Good Library Service

Effective library service does not automatically happen with the purchase of books or with the building of a library. It is an essential part of the total structure, organization, and processes of the school. As such it bears many interrelationships with other aspects of the school program if it is to function effectively. Perhaps some of these relationships are best indicated through a consideration of certain broad principles which seem to provide some guidance, at least, in conceiving clearly the basic character and comprehensiveness of effective library service in the modern elementary school.

1. *The modern concept of the curriculum requires adequate library service for its effective implementation.* Modern approaches to curriculum organization utilize a variety of teaching methods, activities, and sources of information. Flexibility is maintained both in scope and difficulty of materials used in the learning process. Interests of children are utilized through differentiated assignments and through organization of learning experiences around problem areas or units. Emphasis is placed on independent research activities as well as on group and committee work. Facility in locating and evaluating information is increasingly considered one of the basic skills of learning. It is obvious to the thoughtful person that the success of a program of instruction based on

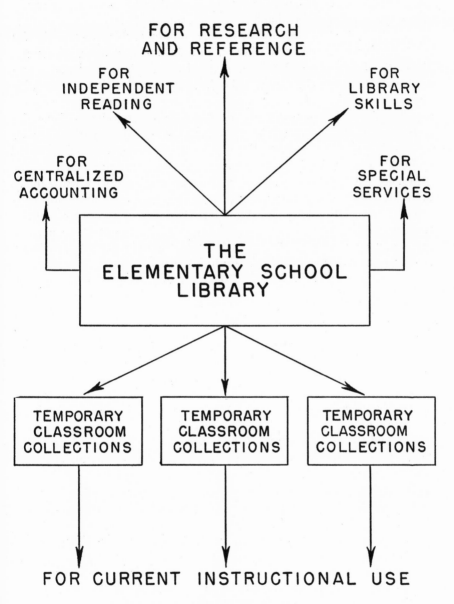

Figure 14

The Library in the Elementary School

varied types of activity will be commensurate with the adequacy of the resources and services available to teachers and pupils.

2. *The importance of library service should be sufficient to justify a reasonable investment in physical and human resources.* Since the adequacy of instructional resources largely determines the breadth and quality of the curriculum of the school, it is imperative that a reasonable proportion of the school's investment be used for providing such resources. Schools often attempt economy in the purchase of supplementary and library materials, as if assuming that these particular aids to learning are optional. Such an assumption is unwarranted. Adequate library service is so necessary to a good program that the provision for such service should be a matter of high priority when funds are allocated for facilities and for personnel. Otherwise, the whole program of instruction suffers from the lack of sufficient resources to make it genuinely operative. Since library service is important to a good modern program of elementary education, schools should be willing to make the necessary investment for high quality.

3. *The nature and functions of the library services offered should be consistent with the educational objectives of the school.* Library services should be of sufficient scope and offered in such a manner that the primary objectives of the school will be served. For example, one of the generally accepted aims of the modern school is to provide children with the skills needed for finding authentic information in an efficient manner. It is readily seen that this is a type of learning to which good library services can make a substantial contribution. Similarly, another of the goals of modern education is to give learners the knowledge and appreciation of ways in which each can enrich his own life through reading, music, and the arts, or through the cultivation of hobbies. Again, this is an area which can be developed fully only through the availability and use of rich library resources. In these and many other ways, the educational leader should be aware of the relationship between the realization of the legitimate aims of education and the quality of instructional resources provided for the school.

4. *Library services should support the total instructional program of the school.* It is a mistake to conceive of library services as a sort of department of the school program; neither is the main function of the library a teaching function. The chief justification for library services lies in its support and enrichment of the instructional program of the school. Its main contribution is the assistance afforded in helping teachers teach better and in helping learners learn better. Therefore, the quality and success of the library services of a school must be evaluated in terms of the extent to which they make a contribution to

the constructive educational processes that are the business of the school. Such services should contribute not only to the knowledge acquired by children who use them but to the development of habits, skills, and aesthetic appreciations as well.

5. *Library services should be comprehensive in purpose and scope.* If the total purposes of the school are to be served as seems desirable, the library services provided necessarily must vary also in order to contribute to the many facets of the school program. Some services will be primarily designed to serve children directly; others will be expected to serve children in an indirect way through offering assistance and resources to teachers in the preparation of instructional plans and materials. Services also should vary in nature to accommodate children of various age groups within the school. Circulation methods, operational regulations, and book accounting all need to be flexible enough to be useful in dealing with the various persons who use the elementary school library. On different occasions, library resources can be used for teaching, for guidance, or for the development of wise ways for the use of leisure. All these and many other functions can be performed through library services that are sufficiently flexible and varied to meet the multinatured demands of the school day.

6. *Library resources should be representative in character and balanced in quantity.* A great deal of the value of the library depends upon the scope of its resources. The educational purposes of the school are not served by a library which offers an extensive volume of materials in one particular area of the curriculum and little or nothing in others. All major areas of human experience appropriate for use in the elementary school should be represented in the stock of resources maintained, and getting materials from several reputable sources or authors is to be preferred over an abundance of materials by a single author to the general exclusion of others. As a rule, it is better also to have fewer copies of a great many materials which are circulated well than to purchase a great number of copies of books and other materials only to have a few of them used at any one time.

7. *In providing good library services, emphasis should be placed on improving the accessibility and utilization of instructional resources.* Large inventories of books and instructional materials, though suggesting a rich and expansive educational program, are not virtues in themselves. How many books are purchased, housed, or protected from loss are matters of importance but are not the primary concern in providing maximum library services. The matter of greatest importance is that of bringing adequate and appropriate materials into contact with learners so that their education may thereby be broadened. Although

the acquisition of instructional materials is a necessary prerequisite to their use, the basic functions of library service are not fulfilled until effective means for distribution and utilization of these materials are established and maintained. One of the important tasks of leadership in the school is to improve these aspects of library service.

8. *Library services should utilize the contributions of many persons interested in the educational process.* Specialized personnel with training in both teaching and library techniques naturally must furnish much of the leadership if improvement is made and maintained in this important area of the school program. However, if these services are to be properly integrated with the pattern of school operation, the contributions of many other persons must be sought and utilized. These include administrators, supervisors, teachers, pupils, and parents. It will have to be determined in each case just how various participants can make their best contributions, but many schools find it possible and helpful to utilize the judgments and ideas of various school personnel in such matters as selection of materials, routine accession and circulation of materials, and in the subsequent evaluation of their use. The attitudes and skills of the school principal as a leader will do much to determine how effectively the efforts of various interested persons can be coordinated to create the optimum situation for library service.

9. *The selection of materials should be based on both the corporate interests of the school and the individual needs and interests of children.* Valuable guidance in the selection of library materials can be gained through intelligent survey and analysis of children's interests. This approach should be utilized as fully as possible in building an appropriate inventory of materials. This is particularly important since one of the purposes of the elementary school library service is to stimulate and encourage independent reading habits of children. In order to be highly motivated toward reading, children must have access to materials that interest them.

It is advisable to consider also the over-all objectives and program of the school, as well as the character of the groups it serves from time to time, in setting up and applying the criteria for the selection of instructional and independent reading materials. Both the common and the specific needs of the children who attend school can be met with a reasonable outlay if wisdom and leadership are exercised in selection.

10. *The library services of the school should include resources for professional staff and parents as well as children.* There can be little doubt that the primary obligation of good library services is to the pupils who attend school. In all aspects of the school program, this primary obligation should be remembered. Naturally, then, the first concern in select-

ing and using instructional resources should be the effect such materials will have on children. However, it must be recognized that children can sometimes be benefited indirectly as well as directly. By including among library resources professional books for teachers and educational books for parents, much can often be accomplished to improve the level of educational experiences for the child. Materials in the field of child development, descriptions of acceptable play equipment and situations for children, or listings of desirable inexpensive reading materials that can be purchased for children to read in their leisure hours may be included. Possibilities are many and varied, as will be recognized by those who explore them.

Establishing the Conditions for Good Library Services

Certain facilities and conditions are necessary if good library services are to be provided. Like any other aspect of human endeavor, harvests cannot be expected unless the effort is made to prepare the ground and sow the seed. Some of these requisites for good library service relate to physical facilities, others to the amount and quality of personnel available, and still others to competence in conception and execution of the plan. Some of these requisites for effective library service are discussed in the following paragraphs.

A Sound Philosophy of Library Service.—As is true of other aspects of the educational program, what is done in the name of library service is largely determined by the beliefs held by the persons responsible for it. Among modern educators there is little dissent from the idea that effective library services are desirable for a good elementary school. The differences appear at the point of decision as to how such library service is to be best guaranteed and most economically achieved. Some of these differences of opinion are reflected in the planning of school plants, the hiring of personnel, and in the allocation of funds in the school budget. It is imperative that administrative leaders work with their associates in the careful study of school objectives and the contributions which good library service can make to their realization. In turn, then, these professional groups should utilize all available sources of information to determine the conditions and methods through which this service can be made most effective.

One of the more persistent issues in library service is the relative merit of centralized and decentralized organization. The modern curriculum brought with it a greater emphasis on the need for immediately accessible reading materials in the classroom. This development, profitable though it has been, unfortunately has been interpreted by some to indicate the desirability of housing all library resources in classroom collections.

As mentioned in an earlier discussion of school plant and facilities, good library service requires both a centralized library and provisions for temporary classroom collections. The one possible exception to this general rule is the extremely small school unit where it might conceivably be preferable to operate without a centralized library. Even here, however, some provisions should be made for the sharing of library resources and for maintaining a pool of such resources for the school as a whole.

The centralized library offers many advantages. It creates more favorable means for making materials available to persons throughout the whole school. It minimizes the tendency toward possessiveness of teachers who acquire and use classroom materials, and thus the central library contributes to the development of a spirit of teamwork and sharing essential to a good program of instruction. Centralization of library resources also helps to eliminate useless and wasteful duplication of materials by making it possible for the same materials to be used by various persons at different periods of the school year.

Children gain many benefits directly from the centralized library. It offers them opportunities for learning useful library skills and for gaining practice in the selection of books suited to their interests and purposes. A good elementary school library is an excellent place for children to learn habits of considerateness and courtesy and to put into practice the individual and group research skills essential to organization of learning experiences in the modern classroom.

The establishment of a centralized library should help provide, rather than hinder, adequate and up-to-date classroom collections. This implies the necessity for sensible means of distributing and rotating materials among various classrooms. Simple and businesslike plans should be devised so that teachers may easily transfer sets of materials from the library to their classrooms to be used in connection with the development of particular units of work or for other special purposes. Such arrangements are assumed to be an essential part of the functioning of a central library in the school.

Physical Facilities and Library Service.—The general features which should characterize the library quarters of the school have been described briefly in Chapter 7 in connection with the planning of the school plant. As noted there, the part of the plant allocated to library services should be easily accessible, well lighted, airy, generally pleasant, and functionally designed to fulfill the purposes for which it exists. In addition, these quarters should be as free from building and street noises as it is possible to make them. In every way they should be conducive to comfort and to concentration.

One of the more essential features of a good library is adequate space. Library quarters should include a large circulation and reading room with sufficient space to accommodate a regular classroom group of pupils at the same time regular circulation activities are being carried on. At least 25 square feet per reader has generally been recommended in planning the size of such reading rooms. In addition to this general library room, a work room and at least one small conference room should be included. In schools where audio-visual materials such as slides, filmstrips, and record collections are housed in the library, there should be a room equipped visually and acoustically for the viewing and audition of these materials.

The amount of shelving and seating space required depends on the enrollment of the school and the size of the collection of materials to be housed in the library. Shelving should be adjusted to the various kinds of materials and, in height, to the pupils who use the materials. Obviously, placing materials on high shelves which children cannot easily reach will discourage browsing and individual book selection. Similarly, tables and chairs should vary in size to accommodate children of all sizes and ages as well as adults. It is important that the furnishings of the school library be durable, attractive, and of sufficient flexibility to accommodate various types of activities and groups which the library serves.

Professional Staff and Library Service.—The need for the services of professional personnel specially trained in library service will vary with the size of the school. In elementary schools of moderate size, at least one full-time librarian should be employed; in larger schools additional personnel will be needed; in small school units it is often found to be desirable to employ a teacher-librarian who can devote at least half time to library service in the school. In any school large enough to have multiple classrooms, it is desirable to have some person with experience, interest, and training to be responsible for the library. In any of these cases, it is advisable for the person assigned to library duties to be fully acquainted both with library skills and with the teaching-learning process. For the elementary school, it may be even more important for such a person to have a sound and comprehensive view of elementary education than to possess highly specialized library skills, desirable as these may be, if one is forced to make such a choice.

Under competent leadership and guidance it is often possible to utilize the part-time services of pupils and parents to supplement the work of the library staff. In fact, many parents welcome the opportunity to assist with recording, accession, and book-mending. It gives them the satisfaction of rendering service to the school, and, at the same time, affords the opportunity to improve their knowledge of children's materials and to have greater contact with the operation of the school.

Children often enjoy helping with routine tasks necessary in the successful administration of library services when these tasks are within their ability. In assigning such responsibilities to pupils care should be exercised to prevent too much time being taken away from their other school activities. It is well to remember, with either parents or children, that they should be asked only to assist and not to assume responsibility for professional services.

Adequate Funds for Library Materials.—It is clear that none of the conditions previously described as desirable can prevail without a reasonable financial investment. Provisions must be made for the initial outlay of plant, personnel services, and materials as well as for the upkeep, maintenance, and replacement of books. It is usually recommended that the book collection of a library contain five to ten times as many titles as there are children enrolled in the school. This depends, of course, upon the size of the school. The ratio will logically decrease with the increasing size of the school. In order to sustain a collection in good condition and to replace volumes that become worn beyond the state of usability, the school should plan on an expenditure of not less than $2.00 per pupil enrolled, as recommended by authoritative educational organizations.[1]

Cooperation by Members of the Staff.—In discussing the essential conditions for good library service, one cannot omit consideration of the necessity for teamwork by members of the staff. It is true that the school librarian must play a leadership role in the administration and improvement of library services and must render specialized technical and professional services which others are not prepared to offer. However, the quality and effectiveness of the services of the librarian are not guaranteed by his competence alone. They depend upon the attitudes of administrators and teachers toward the services, the extent to which services are used, the willingness to share materials, the cooperative approaches which can be made to book selection, and the degree of efficiency developed and maintained in scheduling the use

---

[1] See pamphlet issued by Joint Committee of the American Library Association and the National Education Association, *The Price of Wisdom* (Washington, D. C.: National Education Association, 1949).

of library quarters. Effective communication and pleasant and mutually satisfying working relations must be maintained between those who administer the library services and members of the teaching staff if productive service is to result. The more the library services are integrated with the total program of the school, the greater the likelihood that such cooperation will be achieved.

IMPORTANT ELEMENTS OF LIBRARY SERVICE IN THE SCHOOL

The library is the center for many types of activities during the school day. It does not seem necessary to enumerate all of them here but rather to suggest only that the components of good library service are numerous and varied. Three of these elements, however, tend to serve as focal points of the library function and, therefore, are discussed briefly at this point.

Accounting for and Maintenance of Materials.—This is one of the less glamorous, though none the less essential aspects of library service. The school must provide in some manner for the selection, accession, accounting, inventory, binding, and repairing of books and materials. Such tasks normally become the responsibility of the school librarian if one is employed. In schools where full-time library personnel are not employed, it becomes a problem to provide these services in a systematic and efficient way. As a result, there is considerable waste through depreciation and loss that otherwise might be prevented.

Specific criteria and techniques for acceptable library practice can be procured from state library agencies, state departments of public instruction, and from library education divisions of institutions of higher learning. While there is no need for imposing a highly technical system on a very small school, it is always desirable to make sound and systematic plans for book accounting. In spite of this service, some book loss will naturally occur, and should be expected, if books are being used. While such losses should not be condoned to the point where carelessness is encouraged, it is well to avoid making unpleasant issues about such losses or imposing penalties so excessive as to discourage the use of library books. Such practices can have an extremely negative effect on the attitudes children develop toward books and reading. A good librarian will be both human and businesslike.

Circulation of Materials.—The manner through which materials are brought into contact with consumers is of high educational importance. There is little or no virtue in a large collection of materials if such materials are never used. Effective circulation is the agent through which physical materials are translated into educational possibilities. As such, circulation is a valuable part of the total library service.

The writer recalls an experience with a school survey which revealed an almost complete absence of reading materials for the children of the school. Naturally, one of the results of the survey was the recommendation for the acquisition of a substantial supply of supplementary and recreational reading materials. A return visit to the school two years later disclosed that the recommendations of the survey team had been followed to the extent of spending several thousand dollars for needed books. The unfortunate part of the situation, however, was that, after being acquired, the books were stored in a dark corner of a hallway and there was very little evidence that they were ever disturbed except on rare occasions. Educational benefits cannot be expected to accrue from the mere purchase of materials unless appropriate means are sought and found for getting the materials used.

Circulation methods should include two possibilities for getting library books and other materials distributed; the first is the provision for teachers to be able to take whole sets of materials to the classroom for use over a period of time. The other is a plan whereby children can check out books directly from the library for their own individual use. In either case the circulation methods should be systematic but should be simple to use.

The Function of Library Service in Instruction.—By far the most important function of library service is that of improving teaching and learning. In fact, the major justification for library service in the elementary school is that such service will motivate and enrich the learning processes going on in the school. These aims are achieved in a number of ways. Some methods involve direct teaching; others are more casual and incidental.

The elementary school library may be used to teach children the basic skills of effective library use. They learn to use card catalogs and to locate materials. Such activities help to develop simple research skills and to instill appreciation for books and periodicals as sources of information. Through contacts with books under skillful guidance, children learn respect for books and how to care for them properly. The library can also make a valuable contribution in helping children learn to work and study effectively together, with proper consideration for each other and for other users of the library. Another direct outcome of library use is that of developing in children the ability to evaluate materials in terms of their own interests, purposes, and abilities.

The librarian's broad knowledge of materials is thus a very valuable source of help to the teacher who has a genuine desire to enrich the work of his classroom. The librarian often can assist the classroom teacher directly in locating materials to be used in connection with particular units of work or for special purposes. Many useful teaching aids and pamphlets come to the attention of the librarian, who is usually glad to make them available to teachers. It is a fortunate situation if the librarian has sufficient knowledge of the school program to know where materials will be most useful. This mutually beneficial working relationship can be achieved only by a staff that has learned to live and work together successfully. Much responsibility for this kind of relationship rests with the administrative leader of the school.

The extent to which the elementary school library aids learning depends on the policies which govern its use. The major objective of the library staff, as well as of the instruction and administration staff, should be the wide use of materials from the library. Policies which encourage children to borrow books for use at school or to read at home can do much to shape and motivate the reading practices and tastes of children. The friendliness of the librarian, liberal schedules for checking out books, and reasonable measures for controlling circulation are all factors which affect the operation of such policies. Classroom teachers should help develop in children a sense of responsibility in caring for books and in observing necessary and sensible regulations designed to provide for efficient circulation and use of materials.

In schools where the library is actually a materials center, many types of materials and services can be provided other than those which involve books. In such a center, for example, where audio-visual materials and equipment are provided, instruction and guidance are sometimes provided in the selection and use of such materials. Such services demand broad training on the part of the librarian.

A few schools use their libraries as a resource for parent education. Under the leadership of the librarian or an interested and competent teacher, study groups can be formed in which parents have an opportunity to examine various types of desirable reading materials for children and to develop criteria for the selection of suitable materials for children at various age levels.

Essential Types of Materials Needed for Good Library Service

The effectiveness of library service depends greatly on the quality and variety of materials the library can provide to complement and support the school's program of instruction. Roughly, the collection of resources needed for an adequate instruction materials center may be classified in three major divisions: (1) books, (2) periodicals, and (3) audio-visual and other graphic materials and devices. The more common types of resources under each of these headings are discussed in the following paragraphs.

Books and Pamphlets.—There are three major uses of books and other reading materials in the typical school library. The first is for *reference*. While suitable reference materials should be a part of the resources of each classroom, it is impossible to provide each room with all that is necessary and desirable. Therefore, it is essential that the library collection contain sets of approved encyclopedias suitable for use by different age groups. Atlases and dictionaries should also be available in the library. As for dictionaries, at least one unabridged edition should be provided, along with multiple copies of more simplified editions suitable for the use of younger children who are just learning dictionary skills.

Printed library materials are also used for *supplementary reading*. Through their use children are able to enrich and extend their information in various areas of the curriculum beyond the limitations of basal text materials. Some such materials are used for group work and some, of course, are used mainly by individuals. If a modern unit or problem approach to the curriculum is used in the school, it is imperative that ample materials of a supplementary nature be available to children as they pursue the study of selected centers of interest. Collections of supplementary materials, as suggested earlier in another connection, should be representative of the various major areas of the curriculum, graded in difficulty, and consistent with children's interests.

A third use for library materials is *recreational reading*. It is important that children have an opportunity to select and read some books *merely because they enjoy them*. In this way they simultaneously create a taste for reading, improve their reading skills through use, broaden their horizons of knowledge and experience, and engage in wholesome leisure activity. Such opportunities for children also carry over into their reading habits at home and usually stimulate them to utilize public library resources during vacation periods and even later in adult life. Obviously, these desirable outcomes of independent reading opportunities in school can be brought about only if reasonable facilities are provided for such reading.

Periodicals.—A good library does not consist of books alone. Provisions must be made for the inclusion of such current materials as newspapers and magazines. News materials should be varied in difficulty so that children of all ages can develop habits of news reading without the discouragement that comes from trying to read the standard daily newspaper without being able to do so. Magazines also should be varied in format, vocabulary difficulty, and content. It is advisable, if resources permit, to provide some materials which offer general news coverage and others which appeal to particular interests of boys and girls. In addition to creating an interest in current affairs through the reading of periodicals, much valuable information can be gained through this particular means.

In some schools where money for subscriptions to periodicals is limited, a plan is developed whereby children bring appropriate magazines from home to be used in the reading room or classroom. In this way, many materials which would otherwise be discarded can be put to good use in the school. In such instances, of course, there should be careful guidance in the selection of material donated. While such a plan cannot possibly be considered a wholly satisfactory substitute for adequate library procurement of such materials, it does offer some possibility for the enrichment of the supply of materials in schools with lack of sufficient funds.

Audio-visual Materials.—The modern elementary school utilizes a great variety of audio-visual devices and materials. Such materials bring a vivid impact of personal involvement to the learner that is difficult to secure from printed materials. As a result, they not only lend variety to the methods of instruction, but also can produce a high degree of motivation. Hence audio-visual materials have become a part of the educational outlay of the modern school.

The types of audio-visual materials used in the elementary school range from the very simple to the more technical, which require a considerable investment of mechanized equipment. As in the case of book collections, schools should exercise care in selecting materials and equipment so that a balanced program can be provided, adapted to the size and character of the school.

A valuable asset to the elementary school is a well-kept *picture and clipping file*. Pictures can be valuable for instruction by creating visual images of processes, or in portraying comparisons or contrasts between two or more conditions or situations. Many teachers wish to build picture files to accompany certain units of study. When the collections of individual teachers can be pooled in the library, they create a valuable source for enlivening instruction throughout the whole school. The school librarian can be helpful in clipping and mounting pertinent pictures or other current materials for possible use by teachers and pupils.

Files of these materials should be made available to both children and teachers if they are to fulfill their greatest purposes. One of the important considerations with regard to the usefulness of such files is the provision for continuous evaluation and revision of various pieces in the collection. Obsolete and misleading materials can do more damage than good. There is considerable value in providing opportunities for teachers to work cooperatively with the librarian in establishing criteria for the selection of both the materials and the centers of interest around which they may be classified.

Modern teaching methods can make many different uses of *slides, filmstrips,* and *motion picture films.* Since films are relatively more expensive than other types of projection materials and film rental agencies render services to schools at nominal cost, usually only the larger school systems find it profitable to purchase large collections of films. This is not true of slides and filmstrips, since many schools and teachers develop their own materials of this type. This trend results partly from the increased interest in photography as a hobby and partly from a growing recognition of the value of such materials for educational use. In addition, another contributing factor undoubtedly has been the increasing number of teachers who are gaining an understanding of audio-visual materials as a part of their professional preparation for teaching.

Because they can be produced to meet certain needs in a specific way, slides are a very flexible medium for teaching. Through their use pictures can be projected on a screen for group use, and such materials as musical scales, word lists, outlines, or maps can be suitably enlarged and projected for instruction. Filmstrips can usually be purchased commercially more cheaply than slides and serve somewhat the same general purposes, except that they may not have an equal degree of adaptability to classroom use.

Motion pictures, especially those with sound track, have been demonstrated to be the best known substitute for direct experience. Their effectiveness is enhanced considerably by their emotional impact and the continuity of action which this medium permits. There are two limitations to their use not present to the same degree in other audio-visual materials: their projection requires at least a minimum amount of technical skill and knowledge of projection equipment which not all teachers possess, and it is sometimes difficult to get a particular film at the time it would be most useful in the classroom. In spite of these limitations, however, films are increasingly becoming an accepted part of the educational resources of the modern elementary school.

Recording equipment is another educational facility which is becoming increasingly common in good elementary schools. Through the use of recorders children can have an opportunity to evaluate their own speech and reading performances. Recorders can be used also for reproducing musical numbers or programs, radio programs of interest, or for making records of group discussions. The multiplicity of uses of such equipment has contributed to the growing willingness of school officials to consider these facilities as justifiable school equipment.

Maps, globes, charts, and *graphs* are other forms of instructional resources essential to a good school program. It is desirable for each classroom to be equipped with such materials, which will be used frequently if not daily. However, distribution of such facilities through the library or materials center can help avoid needless duplication and thus make a wider range of supplies available with a minimum expenditure.

Models, specimens, and *dioramas* are other materials frequently found to be a useful part of the school's collection. Collections of specimens are most commonly found in connection with science, while models and diorama exhibits often are used to portray places, objects, or peoples of historic or geographic importance. By capitalizing on the natural interests of children, many such collections and materials can be provided by the children themselves with proper encouragement and guidance.

The educational use of *radio* and *television* affords much variation and enrichment for certain phases of the school program. Viewing and listening to important public events can have a very significant impact upon children as a means of developing an understanding and appreciation of the American way of life. Although the ideal situation demands that these facilities be available in the classroom, most schools have not found it feasible to invest to that extent. It is desirable, however, for each school to have one or more radio and television receivers.

SELECTION OF BOOKS AND LIBRARY MATERIALS

The first step in the selection of library materials is the careful study of the school program and the establishment of the criteria for selection in terms of the purposes and population of the school. This must be a cooperative undertaking, but its chances of success are much greater when the responsibility for leadership is assumed by the school principal with the specialized technical assistance that can be provided by the library staff.

Aside from the valuable guidance that can be furnished by the school librarian in the selection of materials, excellent bibliographies of materials suitable for all ages can be obtained from various library organizations and agencies as well as from reliable distributors of children's materials. Books should be selected for representativeness and quality and in such quantities that the processes of the school can be served to best advantage. It is a good policy in purchasing materials to buy only those books which have the approval of recognized and competent agencies. For information about books one can usually consult such publications as bibliographies and reviews issued by the American Library Association, The National Education Association, The National Council of Teachers of English, or The Association for Childhood Education. A similar policy should govern the selection of other instructional materials, such as film and filmstrips. Lists and descriptions of these materials can usually be furnished by appropriate agencies.[2]

ACTION SUGGESTIONS FOR THE PRINCIPAL

1. Build up the concept of *library service* rather than a library collection.

2. Work for complete understanding by the whole staff of the library service.

3. Strive to make the library service an integrated part of the total program of the school.

4. Try to provide specialized personnel to render professional library service but include children, teachers, and parents in its processes.

5. Place the library where many constructive purposes are served and maximum use is possible.

6. Keep library resources varied in nature and representing a wide range of vocabulary difficulty.

7. Encourage small group and individual use of the library.

8. Cooperate with libraries in other buildings and with the public library in sharing resources.

9. Simplify procedures for transferring sets of materials from library to classroom for use in instruction.

10. Emphasize use and accessibility of materials.

11. Encourage librarians and/or teachers to build picture files and other nonbook resources for classroom use.

12. Make provisions for teaching simple library skills through actual use of the library.

13. Include a professional library of materials for teachers as a part of the library services of the school.

14. Provide a parents' corner or section of the library.

15. Strive to make the library one of the most pleasant places in the whole building.

16. Encourage children to browse.

[2] See such publications as Margaret Rufsvold, *Audio-Visual School Library Service: A Handbook for Librarians* (Chicago: American Library Association, 1949), and *Educational Film Guide* (New York: H. W. Wilson Co.), published quarterly.

17. Support an adequate budget for library service as one of the most essential parts of the school program.

18. Interest teachers in the selection of materials.

19. Make inventories of children's interests as guides to selection of materials.

20. Provide a library that offers all types of reading.

21. Provide a workroom for accession and repair of materials.

22. If possible, provide a conference room for the use of small discussion or research groups.

23. Include various types of audio-visual materials as a part of the instructional resources of the school.

24. Adjust furniture and shelving to heights suitable for elementary school users.

25. Consider it one of the main functions of the library to create in children a desire to read, and love and respect for books.

Selected References for Extended Reading

DALE, EDGAR. *Audio-Visual Methods in Teaching.* New York: The Dryden Press, 1946.

DEPARTMENT OF ELEMENTARY SCHOOL PRINCIPALS, *Elementary School Libraries Today: Thirtieth Yearbook.* Washington, D. C.: National Education Association, 1951.

DOUGLAS, MARY PEACOCK. *School Libraries for Today and Tomorrow.* Chicago: American Library Association, 1945.

——. *The Teacher-Librarian's Handbook.* Chicago: American Library Association, 1945.

ELSBREE, WILLARD S., and MCNALLY, HAROLD J. *Elementary School Administration and Supervision.* New York: American Book Co., 1951, chaps. 18 and 19.

GARDINER, JEWEL, and BAISDEN, LEO B. *Administering Library Service in the Elementary School.* Chicago: American Library Association, 1941.

LEE, J. MURRAY, and LEE, DORRIS MAY. *The Child and His Curriculum.* New York: Appleton-Century-Crofts, Inc., 1950, chap. 18.

OTTO, HENRY J. *Elementary-School Organization and Administration.* New York: Appleton-Century-Crofts, Inc., 1954, chap. 10.

RUFSVOLD, MARGARET I. *Audio-Visual School Library Service: A Handbook for Librarians.* Chicago: American Library Association, 1949.

WALRAVEN, MARGARET K., and HALL-QUEST, ALFRED L. *Teaching Through the Elementary School Library.* New York: H. W. Wilson Co., 1948.

Chapter 15

IMPROVING PUPIL PERSONNEL AND GUIDANCE SERVICES

A good example and a sympathetic ear are the first requisites of those who would guide

In the broadest sense, all education is guidance and all processes of the school which are related to the status and well-being of the individual child are pupil personnel measures. However, to view them in such a general way fails to recognize the importance of the specialized contribution made in recent years by these particular fields of education. A concern for the adjustment of the individual pupil is a very natural outgrowth of modern educational developments, which stress individual patterns of growth and rates of learning. Such a concern is also implied in one of the basic tenets of our democratic process—a respect for each individual and his rights.

The facets of pupil personnel are far too numerous to be treated in detail in such a volume as this. However, some aspects of pupil personnel services are so basically a part of the total structure and organization of the modern elementary school that they require consideration in any attempt to evaluate and improve the program of such a school. They include such matters as: (1) school census, (2) pupil attendance, and (3) child guidance. (Another phase of pupil welfare, health and safety, was treated in considerable detail in a previous chapter.) Though not mutually exclusive, each of these three aspects of pupil personnel will be discussed specifically after a brief enumeration of some of the basic principles related to the modern point of view toward the welfare and guidance of pupils in the elementary school.

Principles Underlying Pupil Personnel and Guidance Services

Adjustment is a two-way process. As stated earlier, it is a primary responsibility of the elementary school to adjust its offerings and services to the needs of the children it serves, and it is commendable that many schools are entering into serious study of curriculum adaptation and revision in order to meet this obligation more fully. However, a second, and perhaps just as important, responsibility of the school is to assist children in making proper adjustments. Individual children must learn to adjust to themselves, their families, their social groups, and to the common social and vocational demands of school and of life. If both of these obligations of the school are to be met in an adequate manner, those in leadership positions should consider the purposes of pupil personnel and guidance services as clearly and broadly as possible. A few important considerations follow.

1. *The unit of the school should be the child.* In the modern school the yardstick by which success must be measured is the extent to which the child has been constructively affected by the activities of the school. The application of such a scale indicates that a school which has more failures than successes among its clientele is in itself a failure. One of the primary jobs of the modern school is to help each child adjust to and take advantage of his resources and environment in such a way that maximum results, both immediate and long range, are achieved. The guidance point of view which permeates the program of the good elementary school places the child first in importance and often is willing to subordinate *things* to human values. For example, absence from school may and should demand attention but is not, in itself, as important as the *conditions* and *causes* of continuous absence. The first concern must be what is happening to the child. That is the justification and the most worthy goal of the school.

2. *School attendance is a means for bringing a child into favorable contact with opportunities for growth.* There is no great virtue in school attendance as such. Its importance is derived from the assumption that, when children attend school, something worth while happens to them. When greater comparative emphasis is placed on attendance than on the welfare of the child, the accompanying positive results are likely to be diminished. This is another way of saying that an uninterrupted attendance record is more nearly a reflection of an abiding interest and suitable conditions for learning than it is a desired educational end. On the other hand, it must be recognized that a very real relationship exists between school attendance and educational achievement—a relationship implied in the provisions of legislation regarding both *compulsory education* and *compulsory school attendance* in this country. Both developments, even though they occurred slightly more than a hundred years apart, were based on the assumption that, in order to gain the benefits from education, children should be provided schools and be required to attend them. Modern schools accept the importance of school attendance

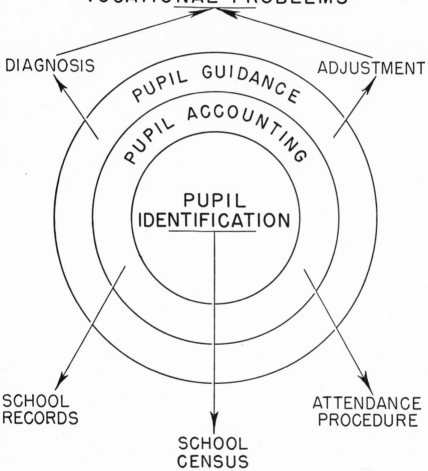

Figure 15

Pupil Personnel Activities in the Elementary School

but deal with problems of nonattendance much more sympathetically and clinically than has been generally true in the past.

3. *Schools should have adequate provisions for knowing who should be attending school as well as who is attending.* A complete attendance

picture cannot be gained from the establishment of class rolls and subsequent checks on daily attendance. An equally important element of pupil accounting is the *school enumeration*. This is the process through which children of school age throughout the territory served by the school unit are identified and entered upon the school records. Specific details of the school census will be discussed in a later part of this chapter. It is sufficient at this point to emphasize that such a census represents an integral part of the pupil accounting system of the school and has many educational as well as legal implications for the operation of the school.

4. *Pupil accounting procedures should provide adequate bases both for future planning and for necessary follow-up of pupils.* It is obvious that administrators, teachers, and special personnel should know as much as possible about the children who are attending the elementary school at any particular time. It is equally important, though not so obvious to many, for them to know something about the size and nature of the school population that will appear in future years. This function of the school census provides some reasonable base for projecting educational plans of the school. In order for it to serve this purpose adequately, the school census should be continuous. The continuing school census is becoming a most valuable, though not yet common, part of the total program of pupil personnel in elementary schools.

Another element of good pupil accounting is the provision for following up pupils who transfer from one school to another, and for maintaining records of pupils for a reasonable number of years after they leave school.

5. *In all problems of pupil personnel and guidance, schools should establish means for studying symptoms and for working on causes.* Problems of maladjustment of pupils are not easily ignored if they are evidenced in such ways as nonattendance or antisocial behavior by pupils. In such cases, administrators and teachers are rightfully concerned that such conditions interfere with the personal development and social acceptance of pupils to a very acute degree. The unfortunate part of such a situation is that all too often the steps taken by the school are directed to the symptoms of maladjustment rather than toward the alleviation of its causes. A school staff should utilize all sources of information, pool information regarding problem cases, and then establish a wholesome group approach to a remedy for the existing problem. This requires suitable records, effective and cooperative working relationships among members of the staff, and intelligent use of specialized assistance of qualified agencies outside the school.

6. *Child guidance is closely related to good teaching.* Though the

specialized nature and function of guidance in education does not permit the term to be used synonymously with teaching, the two processes do involve some identical elements and are closely related to each other. Teachers, therefore, cannot legitimately assume that all guidance must come from a source outside their classrooms. When a teacher in the first grade discovers some physical or emotional difficulty of a child that hinders him from normal progress in learning to read and takes appropriate steps to alleviate such a barrier to normal development, that teacher is practicing guidance.

The genuine concern of teachers for children as individuals is the heart of successful guidance. Many examples can be cited to show numerous ways in which good teaching employs the spirit and processes of guidance. While one recognizes this close relationship, he should not, by so doing, allow himself to adopt the fallacious philosophy that all guidance activities should be the responsibility of the classroom teacher. To take such a position is to deprive the classroom teacher of invaluable supplementary resources for assistance with problems which require technical knowledge.

7. *Guidance services should be more preventive in nature than corrective.* The old adage, "an ounce of prevention is worth a pound of cure," can be as aptly applied to the personal, educational, and social problems of children as to other aspects of human experience. One of the primary purposes of guidance and personnel services is to identify and alleviate minor problems of children before they reach major proportions. In order to locate and treat these minor maladjustments before they have a chance to become serious, teachers must be highly sensitive to the conduct and reactions of children and to the implications of those symptomatic expressions. Special guidance workers and school psychologists can be useful too in the preventive phases of the guidance program as in the more serious cases of maladjustment.

8. *Guidance is largely individual in nature.* Notwithstanding the fact that "group guidance" techniques are sometimes used to clarify and direct the thinking of persons with a common cause or problem, guidance functions at the elementary school levels are largely individual in character. Since the experiential background, the mental and emotional set, and the engaging problems of each pupil are different from those of all others, the diagnosis and subsequent consideration of his particular case must be specifically approached on an individual basis. Of course, individual consideration does not, and should not, preclude the use of data with respect to group behavior or performance, or the necessary analysis of the child's relationships with his peers. These and many

other kinds of information must be secured if the child is to receive the individual guidance that he needs.

9. *Guidance involves many types of service to children.* Since the major purpose of guidance in the elementary school is to foster adjustment, the types of service that may be involved in such a process are almost as varied as the possible number of difficulties children may experience in adjusting to their environment. For that reason, guidance must be considered as being achieved through coordinated, though flexible, efforts to understand individual children, to set up the best possible conditions for optimum adjustment, and to eliminate, as far as possible, those conditions which hinder growth and progress. In dealing with the problems of children, teachers, administrators, and guidance workers will find certain common needs which serve at least as avenues of exploration in trying to assist these children. Some of these may be thought of as specific aspects of child guidance although, of course, they are not at all mutually exclusive.

10. *Guidance involves assistance with perspective.* Many children with problems appear to exist in a maze of confusion. They are not clear as to what is expected of them and life seems to be made up of a multitude of complicating factors. One of the services that can be rendered to children is to help them see clearly through tasks to be achieved, to recognize and marshal their resources for working toward the established goal, and to evaluate and face up to their own strengths and weaknesses in a realistic manner. This necessarily must be a gradual process, with ample evidence of progress, if it is to be successful; but it is an essential prerequisite to the alleviation of children's problems and frustrations. Before one can perform in an acceptable way, he must know what constitutes successful performance for him and why it is considered acceptable. This seems not only an educational truism but the essence of common sense as well.

11. *Guidance involves the establishment of directional goals that are realistic for the individual concerned.* A person with a problem of adjustment cannot solve his problem through blind and scattered efforts. His efforts must be directed toward some immediate goal which is within his possible reach. Such goals should be directly related to the problem at hand and should, through their achievement, create a sense of personal satisfaction. Often children at the elementary school levels need considerable help in identifying their aims so that they are both related to their major problem and yet meaningful to the child. Such help is one of the obligations of guidance services.

12. *Guidance involves the maintenance or restoration of self-esteem and personal confidence.* Children with problems are often plagued by

feelings of inferiority. Before their satisfactory adjustment can be assured, they must have sufficient opportunities to succeed and to earn the approval of others to build within them a feeling of worthwhileness. Sympathetic teachers, administrators, and guidance workers can find many ways through which a feeling of self-assurance can be established. It is important to see that such children get immediate recognition for accomplishments or improvement, but it is equally essential to avoid a condescending attitude in giving such recognition.

13. *Guidance involves social adjustment.* Many of the behavior problems of children stem from their efforts to gain the attention or approbation of those around them. Such children may just lack proper knowledge of and experience with acceptable behavior, or they may actually devise attention-getting modes of conduct. It is not enough, therefore, that children with problems gain self-satisfaction from their efforts; they must be helped to conduct themselves in such a manner that they win social approval and acceptance from their fellows. Assistance in gaining social proficiency is thus one of the real contributions which guidance services can make to children lacking in this respect.

14. *Guidance often involves help in systematizing work habits.* A wholesome attitude toward one's responsibilities is one of the attributes of the well-adjusted person. Conversely, maladjusted persons, including children, often approach their responsibilities in a negative and disconnected manner. They gain few satisfactions from the jobs they do, or from the completion of tasks undertaken. They sometimes become frustrated by certain elements of work or study and carry these frustrations over into other aspects of their work. Proper budgeting of time or the elimination of wasteful diversions of effort are aspects of guidance in this area which will pay dividends with the pupil who is experiencing difficulty in approaching his work in a productive manner.

ESTABLISHING THE SCHOOL CENSUS

The first step in the successful development of a systematic program of pupil accounting and personnel is the establishment of provisions for accurate census records of children of school age. Although nearly all states provide for such a census, there is considerable variation in the inclusive ages applied from state to state. The most common practice is to seek records on all children between the ages of six and twenty-one, though recent years seem to have brought a trend toward including younger children in the census.

Purposes and Characteristics.—The school census serves many different purposes. Some of its more important values are in providing:

(1) information as to the size of forthcoming groups which enter school, (2) information useful in planning for the use or expansion of school facilities, (3) a list of pupils against which enrollment and attendance may be checked, (4) advance information about needs for transportation of pupils, and (5) help in identifying special educational problems in the community. In addition, the school census often reveals many of the causes of nonattendance and can be helpful in improving school-community relationships.

In order to be wholly useful, the school census must have certain characteristics. It must be: (1) *inclusive,* covering all children of the school community; (2) *accurate* in all information gathered and recorded; (3) *continuous,* containing cumulative information about all children from birth to the established upper age limit for the district; and (4) *skillfully administered* in collecting, maintaining, and interpreting data. In larger school systems, of course, specially trained attendance personnel are usually available to administer the census; but in smaller school districts, census data are often gathered by parents, teachers, or other appointed persons. Actually, there is considerable value in having teachers assist with the canvass of the community to secure data regarding children. Through this process they learn about home and community conditions and may be able to discover community resources which might be used in the program of the school. If regular teaching or clerical personnel are used for this purpose, they should be given the necessary prior training to accomplish the task in an efficient manner.

Various supplementary sources of data are sometimes used to extend the information gained from the community canvass. These may include existing school records, questionnaires, or records furnished by private schools and community agencies.

Census Data.—Information on all children from birth to twenty-one years of age should be kept in the central census file of the school system under the supervision of the appropriate school official. It is usually more convenient to keep such data on filing cards designed to meet the needs of the local school. Such cards ordinarily contain the name of the child, the names of the parents or guardian, the date of birth, school attended, and any other pertinent information which the school needs to identify the child properly.

The school should maintain an *active* card file for all children currently within the census ages and an *inactive* file for those who have been removed. The active file, to be useful, must be kept up to date by adding the cards of new pupils, removing transfers, and making necessary revisions in data from year to year.

In addition to the central census of the school system, most principals find it desirable to keep a "school census" with data on children residing within the territory served by the particular elementary school. This information is valuable in school planning and in community analysis necessary for a live educational program.

Extensions of the School Census.—Complete school census information contributes materially to the development of wholesome working relationships between the school and the home. Two aspects of these relationships deserve more than passing mention. The first is the contact of the school with the child and family new to the school community. Many schools have found it profitable to send a brochure of welcome and information about the school to the family just arrived in the community. Others carry this effort still further by arranging a call by the principal, a teacher, or a committee of teachers or parents, or a combination of both. An early contact, however it is made, is of great value in making new pupils and parents feel welcome and in getting children into school promptly after their arrival in the neighborhood.

Another valuable contact of the school is that made with the parents of new-born children in the neighborhood. By sending a note of congratulations and inviting the parents to use the resources of the school during the preschool development of the child, the school principal can make a substantial contribution to potential parent-school relations. The following letter is a sample of what might be done in this respect.

Friendlytown School
March 1, 19—

Dear Mr. and Mrs. _____

Congratulations on the arrival of your new son (or daughter)! All of us here at Friendlytown School extend best wishes to him for a long, healthy, happy and successful life. We shall look forward to the school year of 1960-61 when he will be eligible to enroll officially in the school. In the meantime we hope you will feel free to use any resources of the school that might be helpful to the development of your child. We call your particular attention to the following:

Our study groups for preschool mothers which meet regularly each month.

The school readiness materials for preschool children which are circulated at the request of parents.

Our library on child development which we are happy to have parents use. It includes authentic materials on child care, physical growth, speech development of children, and many other matters related to the wholesome growth of children.

Our booklists of materials suitable for reading to very young children.

We are enclosing complete information about some of these activities and materials and we hope you will contact the school for any further information you desire.

Sincerely,

_____

Principal

With such early initial contacts with the home, and with intermittent opportunities for the preschool child to come to the school for various activities, his entrance into the organized program of the school can be accomplished smoothly and effectively.

IMPROVING THE ATTENDANCE SERVICES OF THE SCHOOL

The system of free public education in America has been based on the assumption that all children should receive a basic education as a means of maintaining an enlightened citizenry with the ability to govern themselves. This assumption was forcibly dramatized by the early enactment of compulsory education laws and by the later enactment of compulsory attendance laws to compel parents to take advantage of public education for their children. Since 1918 all states have had in effect compulsory attendance laws, although they differ considerably in the ages covered and the conditions for exemptions.

Aside from the legal significance of school attendance, its educational importance must be considered, since it bears a direct relationship to the effectiveness of the school program. In the first place, reasonably regular school attendance is essential to the efficient functioning of school organization. It obviously is not feasible, and certainly not economical, to organize the elementary school on a completely individual basis. Since it must be organized on a group basis in most respects, the stability of groups in terms of attendance is an ever present factor of school operation and regulation.

Another reason for the importance of school attendance is related to the element of continuity in the curriculum of the school. As most instructional programs are administered, absences from school create troublesome gaps in the developmental phases of the curriculum. This is particularly true in the skills areas, in which sequential development of competency is needed for achievement.

School attendance is important for a third very practical reason. In many situations the allocation of state money for the support of schools is determined on the basis of some formula involving school attendance. Under such provisions, a child in attendance brings money into the school treasury; in the same way, an absence diminishes the amount received by the school. This arrangement often causes a very understandable concern on the part of school administrators with regard to serious attendance problems in a community. However, it should be pointed out that in some instances a disproportionate concern for attendance may result in having children come to school when they should remain at home because of colds or slight illnesses or other legitimate causes.

Attendance services of the school include two major categories: (1) the enrollment of children in the school who are eligible for admission, and (2) keeping these children in school at all times when they should be in school.

Enrollment.—The initial step in accounting for pupils is the process of getting them officially enrolled in the school. Enrollment procedures vary from school to school, largely in terms of school size. As a rule, the smaller the school the simpler the process of getting a child entered upon the records as an official member of the student body. This may naturally be expected, since much of the desired information about children can be gained by the teacher at first hand in the very small schools. In large city schools, however, the records and procedures used in enrollment may be very elaborate and detailed. In all cases certain basic considerations should govern enrollment procedures. Some of these considerations are:

1. Provisions for time-consuming processes and special problems to be cared for in advance of the opening of school. Both school personnel and parents suffer frustration from long lines of children and parents who wait for attention while the special problems of a few persons are discussed at great length.

2. Adequate advance information to parents regarding the opening of school and the enrollment procedures to be employed. Some schools issue splendid bulletins for this purpose.

3. Completeness of enrollment information. As nearly as possible all needed information about children should be obtained at the time of their enrollment in school. This may include educational history, health information, and personal data needed by the school.

4. Lack of duplication in records and information. Parents may become irked at requests for the same information over and over as their child proceeds through school. Provisions for cumulative organization and utilization of data will eliminate the necessity for information being gathered each year.

Attendance Records.—One important phase of administering school attendance is the maintenance of accurate records. While many commercial forms are available for recording information about attendance or absences, most schools find it advisable to select or develop standardized forms suitable for local use. Some of the information involved in complete attendance records is: (1) cumulative data regarding each child's attendance during the school month or year, (2) information regarding tardiness, (3) information regarding the causes of absences or tardiness, (4) forms or information for re-admitting children to classes after absences, and (5) information on children transferred from one school to another.

Early in the year the principal should provide the opportunity for all new teachers to receive complete instructions and explanations as to the procedures for carrying out their responsibilities in connection with school attendance. Clear understanding should be sought with regard to the admission of children to school and the procedures for eliminating from the classroom children who, for health or other reasons, should not be in school.

In all cases, records should be sufficiently complete to allow school personnel to verify past records of attendance or action taken in connection with attendance problems or procedures. Furthermore, since attendance records are often the basis upon which state school support is allocated, accuracy in the development and maintenance of records becomes a legal responsibility.

Improving Attendance.—The major purpose of working on attendance is not to have perfect attendance by all pupils each day of the year. If such a situation were possible, it is doubtful whether it would be desirable under typical conditions. As pointed out earlier, there are many times when a child should remain at home for his own safety and that of others. The real purpose of effective school attendance procedures, then, is to guarantee that children who should be in school are in school. Moreover, in the better schools this is achieved in ways consistent with good education and effective human relations. Efficient attendance procedures of the school must be based on: (1) a clear notion of educational objectives of the school by all members of the school staff and by parents, (2) a clear definition of what constitutes absence or tardiness, (3) clear understanding of how absences are to be explained and excused, (4) a clear understanding of the responsibility of school personnel in attendance procedures, and (5) close working relationships with parents in such matters as health problems of children.

Six areas must be considered in attempts to improve school attendance. They are:

1. *Improving the personal responsibility of children.* One of the prime purposes of the school program is the development of a sense of personal responsibility. If children become self-directive and see real purpose in their days spent at school, there will be a diminishing tendency to avoid school through unnecessary absence. Children cannot be drawn to school because it is important to someone else; they will be drawn toward it if they feel it is important to them.

2. *Improving the child's curriculum.* Children, like adults, tend to avoid things which lead only to frustration, or things which have no meaning for them. Often children have only one escape from a curriculum which is wholly unsuited to them—they stay away from school. If a school makes a genuine attempt to provide profitable and interesting learning experiences for children, it is, at the same time, taking very significant steps toward reducing unnecessary absence from school.

3. *Improving health conditions for children.* Obviously, there is a very clear relationship between health problems and attendance problems. Successful efforts to control the spread of communicable disease or to improve the health habits of children have a very favorable effect on school attendance. Provision for the identification of illness in its early stages is also important in reducing instances in which health problems result in serious and widespread attendance problems.

4. *Improving the community environment.* The presence and operation of distracting, unwholesome "hangouts" and activities in school neighborhoods is a real threat to school attendance. While it is not the legal business of the school to pass judgment on the operation of local businesses, it is the responsibility of school personnel to seek the cooperation of all for the benefit and welfare of the children who attend school and to try to develop a community pride in providing worth-while leisure activities for children and youth.

5. *Improving economic conditions.* Sometimes children are absent from school simply because they do not have clothes to wear, or do not have money to participate in activities with other children. In such cases, where demonstrated need exists, means can usually be found whereby such conditions can be alleviated. In many such cases, the principal can work with local welfare agencies in such a manner that the situation can be much improved.

6. *Improving the understanding of parents.* The greater the degree of understanding about the program of the school and its importance, the less likelihood there is that parents will keep their children from school unnecessarily. Group meetings of parents and school personnel can be

very helpful in bringing about such understanding and in developing "ground rules" for school attendance.

TRANSPORTATION SERVICES OF THE SCHOOL

School Attendance and Transportation.—Closely related to school attendance are the problems of transportation of children to and from school. Although the transportation of pupils has been an important administrative problem at the secondary school level for some time, it has been only recently that elementary schools have been affected to any substantial degree by this phase of school operation. As the consolidation of smaller school units into larger ones has been increasingly achieved, however, the development of organized means for transporting pupils has become a necessity in many situations. This is particularly true in sparsely populated areas in which children live long distances from established schools.

Elementary school pupils frequently are transported in buses operated for the school system as a whole. These buses may be owned and operated by the school district itself, or they may be privately owned and operated for the school on a contract basis. The specific arrangements for transportation of the pupils in any school must depend upon the structure and size of the community served by the school and the relative proportions of pupils living at considerable distances from the school.

School transportation is not an isolated administrative problem. It is closely related to such matters as school schedules, extra-school activities of children, supervision and management, and the provisions for exceptional children. Therefore, provisions for the transportation of children should be worked out as efficiently as possible to serve the educational program of the school.

Two major considerations in transporting pupils are safety and economy. No system of transportation for children can be justified unless it represents the maximum of safety for those being transported. At the same time, economy of time, money, and effort are also important factors in the efficient management of transportation.

Safety in Transportation.—Three aspects of safety in transportation deserve the careful attention of the administrator of the school. They are: (1) the safe condition of equipment, (2) the qualifications of the driver, and (3) the safety of children during loading and unloading. The *safe condition of equipment* can be guaranteed only if buses are structurally and operationally sound and provisions are made for prompt repairs when they become necessary. Brakes, motor, and the signal system must be kept in good order if maximum safety is to be guaranteed. Provisions must be made for the periodic check of equipment to see that it is maintained in a workable condition at all times when being used. In many instances, the administrator will need to make regular checks to insure that these conditions are being met and that all state and school regulations are being observed in the operation and maintenance of school buses.

The *bus driver* is the real key to safe transportation of school children. In spite of well maintained equipment, the greatest factor in safety is the driver himself. Certain qualifications are absolutely necessary if he is to perform his work successfully. The more important are: (1) punctuality, (2) soberness and reliability, (3) a liking for children, (4) good morals and habits, and (5) necessary technical skills for operating the bus in a highly competent manner.

The third most important safety factor is that of providing needed supervision for children on the bus and during periods when they are loading or unloading. Definite responsibilities of the driver for the management of children on the bus should be worked out by the principal, the driver, and any others who have direct obligations in the administration of transportation for the school. Plans for supervising children as they wait for buses also are important elements in the over-all functioning of transportation facilities and services.

Other Considerations.—School bus routes should be established in such manner as to avoid keeping children on the bus for an unduly long time. Young children tire easily and it is important for them not to have to arise too early or to spend too much time on the bus during trips to and from the school. This problem is not acute except in some few situations in which large territories are being served with a minimum number of buses or without due regard for the problems involved.

A few schools are buying small shelters or other inexpensive buildings along the bus routes for the use of children who must wait for buses in cold or inclement weather. This seems to be a favorable development with a great deal to recommend it, especially in areas where weather is severe or in situations where bus routes are unusually long and schedules rather indefinite. In such instances, it seems advisable to arrange for such properties to be occupied by tenants, perhaps rent-free, who could supervise the children during these waiting periods to insure their complete safety.

Many elementary schools are now operating at least one bus for educational purposes during the school day. Such a vehicle, available at all times, can make educational excursions safer and more profitable. When such buses are operated, the same precautions as those mentioned previously should apply to them and their operators.

GUIDANCE SERVICES IN THE ELEMENTARY SCHOOL

There has been a distinct difference in the concepts of guidance held in secondary schools and elementary schools. Guidance has become an important and integral part of the modern secondary school, with an identity of its own. On the other hand, elementary schools have been reluctant to accept guidance as being composed of services uniquely different from regular teaching processes employed by competent teachers.[1] These varying points of view are understandable in terms of the structure of the schools at the two levels. While the secondary school has remained almost completely departmentalized, the elementary school has in recent years moved toward the unified, self-contained classroom as an expression of modern theories of child development. Many modern elementary schools are approaching the matter of guidance, however, in what appears to be a professionally sensible manner. They are (1) applying many of the techniques of modern guidance in the regular instructional and pupil personnel procedures of the school, and (2) they are utilizing available guidance workers and counselors for specialized help with acute problems.

The Principal and Guidance.—The administrative leader of the elementary school sets the stage for effective guidance procedures. The extent to which the school is permeated with the spirit of friendliness and respect for the individual is a factor in providing and using opportunities for guiding children through the developmental stages of the elementary school. The kinds of control and the concepts of discipline which prevail also affect the extent to which effective guidance techniques can be employed. Moon and Dickinson, in discussing the building of favorable conditions for guidance, mention ten aspects in which the administrator is the architect of the school's guidance services.[2] They are:

1. The general atmosphere he creates, whether he has an open- or closed-door policy, and whether he places emphasis on perfection or upon growth.
2. The pattern he sets by his example.
3. The type of organization he sets up—autocratic or democratic.
4. The basis on which he selects his staff.

[1] See Henry J. Otto, *Elementary School Organization and Administration* (New York: Appleton-Century-Crofts, Inc., 1954), pp. 396-401.
[2] James V. Moon and Ruth A. Dickinson, "The Administrator as the Architect of the School Guidance Program," *Guidance for Today's Children: Thirty-Third Yearbook of the Department of Elementary School Principals* (Washington, D. C.: National Education Association, 1954), pp. 30-34.

5. The values demonstrated in the budget that he prepares.
6. The school program.
7. The educational techniques emphasized.
8. The materials used.
9. Home-school cooperation.
10. Interpretation of the school's needs, activities, and purposes to the community.

The principal not only helps to create the climate for effective guidance and provide for the kinds of organizational conditions necessary, but he also has many direct opportunities to employ guidance techniques. In this respect his role is varied—F. M. Maxwell suggests that these varied activities make it necessary for him to assume at least ten differing roles. They are: (1) observer, (2) contributor, (3) inventor, (4) discoverer, (5) coach, (6) referee, (7) challenger, (8) friend, (9) example, and (10) counselor.[3] Certainly his direct contacts with children, as well as with members of the staff and with parents, are opportunities for guidance.

Another responsibility of the principal in the guidance services of the school is that of providing opportunities for teachers to learn more about modern approaches to child guidance. They may need in-service activities designed to acquaint them with sociometric and psychometric materials and techniques, or they may wish to learn more about successful counseling techniques for use in their conferences with children and parents. By carefully planned activities, these needs can be met and greater consistency can be developed among teachers in their attitudes toward children and in the methods they employ in dealing with children's problems.

The principal can render still another guidance service by maintaining and sharing information regarding agencies and services available to the school staff as they work with children. He should have a complete knowledge of social and psychiatric services available in the community or through state agencies or institutions. The next best thing to actually providing a direct service is to know where the service can be obtained.

The Teacher and Guidance.—Most of the actual guidance in the elementary school is the work of classroom teachers. This is in part because they spend most of the school day with children and, as a result, have many more opportunities for guiding children than do other members of the school staff. It is true also because of the close relationship between teaching and guidance mentioned earlier in this discussion.

[3] *Ibid.*, pp. 25-29.

Some of the points at which the teacher may employ guidance materials, procedures, or advice from specialists are in:

1. Grouping children for various instructional and social activities.
2. Working on the problem of social acceptance of children by their peers through such means as sociometry.
3. Developing effective means for self-direction and discipline.
4. Identifying emotional and personality problems of children.
5. Developing personal case studies and educational histories of children.
6. Making special provisions for children with physical and health problems.
7. Keeping anecdotal records of significant pupil behavior.
8. Interviewing parents regarding the progress and problems of their children.
9. Using diagnostic tests and inventories.
10. Developing broadened means for evaluating growth of children in all areas of behavior.

Another important guidance responsibility of the teacher is the kind of orientation provided for pupils new to the school. No one can be so effective in making a new person feel at home as the teacher in the classroom. This applies to all pupils at the beginning of a new school year and, as well, to pupils transferred from other schools at various times during the school year.

The Counselor and Guidance.—Even though heavy responsibility for guidance in the elementary school rests on the principal and teaching staff, the school which can boast the services of special guidance workers is indeed fortunate. Such guidance specialists, or counselors, can render valuable direct service in dealing with special problems of individual children and, furthermore, can be a valuable advisory resource for classroom teachers who need supplementary assistance in meeting certain needs of children in their classrooms.

The role of the counselor is outlined by Hildreth Lambert in a descriptive statement of the development of guidance in the elementary schools of Baltimore, Maryland. The following compilation is made from the monthy reports of the activities of the counselors as they carried out their responsibilities.[4]

I. Counselor holds group meetings:
   A. With pupils, by grade, or by groups having a common interest or need regardless of grade placement
   B. With parents, by class groups, or on common problems of youngsters—social, educational, or emotional

4 *Ibid.,* pp. 227-30.

C. With pupils and parents to visit opportunity, shop center, and occupational classes as well as general vocational and junior high schools (The counselor accompanies parents and pupils on such visits to interpret the programs to them.)

D. With teachers, doctors, nurses, home visitors, school social workers, agency social workers, and principals to discuss the problems of individual pupils or groups of pupils

E. With groups of pupils who have been scheduled for special testing, either aptitude tests or individual intelligence tests

II. Counselor interviews:

A. Pupils

    1. Pupils who are new in the school, except those entering the kindergarten or first grade at the regular time

    2. Pupils who can be adjusted in the regular elementary-school program

       a) Pupils who need remedial work

       b) Pupils who need special schedules

       c) Pupils who need special programs because of a physical handicap

       d) Pupils who are maladjusted in the present class and probably need a transfer to another regular class

    3. Pupils who can be adjusted in other classes or schools

       a) Opportunity classes

       b) Shop center classes

       c) Physically handicapped classes or schools

       d) Occupational classes or schools

       (With the principal's permission the counselor refers pupils classified under (*a*) and (*c*) to the Division of Special Education for testing and recommendation; pupils classified under (*b*) and (*d*) to the Department of Aptitude Testing for testing and recommendation.)

    4. Pupils who are emotionally or socially maladjusted and need to be referred to the Division of Special Services

    5. Other maladjusted pupils—the counselor studies class analysis charts and consults with the principal and the teacher for possible cases of:

       a) Pupils of limited mental ability performing below grade level

       b) Pupils of normal mental ability performing below grade level

       c) Pupils who are more than one term over age for the grade

       d) Pupils of superior ability not performing to capacity

       e) Pupils of superior ability performing above grade level and presenting adjustment problems

    6. Pupils in Grade VI-A who present some problem as to their next educational step

       a) Pupils of superior ability who should be accelerated

       b) Pupils who, with profit to themselves, should repeat

    c) Pupils who should be promoted to occupational classes or general vocational schools

  7. Pupils who are referred to the counselor by the classroom teacher or the principal

  8. Pupils who have special talents or abilities

  9. Pupils who have failed a grade

 10. Pupils who are well adjusted and proceeding at the normal rate through the grades

 B. Adults who can aid in pupil adjustment

  1. Parents

  2. Teachers

  3. Physicians and nurses

  4. Home visitors

  5. School social workers

  6. Other counselors

  7. Administrative officers of the school

  8. Directors and supervisors of the school system

  9. Agency social workers

 10. Officers of the police and fire departments

 11. Members of the community

 C. Parents in the home

  1. Parents of every pupil in Grade VI-A

  2. Parents of pupils who are considered eligible for placement in opportunity, shop center, or occupational classes and in general vocational schools

  3. Parents of pupils with special problems

III. Counselor observes pupils:

At the request of the teacher the counselor observes and records the behavior of individual pupils in classrooms, the halls, the playground, and other situations

IV. Counselor tests pupils or refers pupils for testing:

 A. Administers, scores, and records the intelligence and achievement tests of pupils who are new in the school or who have not been tested at the regularly scheduled periods

 B. Refers pupils for aptitude testing; interprets the results to teachers, pupils, and parents; and places the test results in the cumulative record

 C. Refers pupils for individual intelligence testing for admission to the reading clinics or for other reasons

V. Counselor collects and disseminates information:

 A. Literature that will aid teachers and parents in understanding the educational, emotional, and social needs of children

 B. Bulletins and catalogs that give information to teachers and parents about health, welfare, recreational, educational, and vocational opportunities

VI. Counselor uses, makes, and studies records:
   A. Pupil's cumulative record
      1. Studies the record as a basis for the interview
      2. Adds an elementary-school guidance record for each pupil interview
      3. Records salient facts of each interview
   B. Writes case histories of individual pupils when needed
   C. Studies class analysis charts
   D. Makes a class study when the whole group needs to be analyzed
   E. Compiles data for the application forms of pupils referred to the Division of Special Services, to the Division of Special Education, and to the Division of Aptitude Testing
   F. Secures the signature of the parent for transfer to occupational or opportunity classes
   G. Keeps daily records and prepares semi-annual reports for the central office
      1. Adult interviews
      2. Class observations and visits
      3. Contact with outside agencies
      4. Home visits
      5. Other counselor contacts
      6. Placements and adjustment in other classes or schools
      7. Pupil interviews
      8. Referrals to the Department of Aptitude Testing
      9. Referrals to the Division of Special Services and to the Division of Special Education
     10. Referrals for special testing
     11. Tests administered
     12. Visits of parents and pupils to other schools
VII. Counselor follows up:
   A. Pupils transferred to opportunity, shop center, and occupational schools or classes
   B. Pupils promoted to the junior high school

GUIDING CHILDREN'S EFFORTS TO OVERCOME EDUCATIONAL DIFFICULTIES

Much of the emphasis on guidance in the elementary school should be related to the maintenance of conditions which prevent problems and difficulties from arising. In spite of this stress on prevention, however, certain educational problems are sure to be present in any typical school situation. The child who for some unknown reason is not achieving in the manner which might reasonably be expected presents a real challenge to teachers, principal, and guidance worker alike.

The diagnosis of learning difficulties involves several questions to which answers must be found if improvement is to be expected. Some of them are:

1. *Is there a physical cause for the learning difficulty?* The answer to this question in the case of each child must be sought from his health history, conferences with parents, use of screening tests, or referral to medical specialists.

2. *Is there an intellectual basis for the difficulty?* To get information in this area, it is necessary to administer tests of ability and tests of performance or achievement and compare the results of the two to determine whether there exists a gap between the child's ability to perform and his actual performance.

3. *Is there an emotional problem involved in the situation?* Interviews with child and parents or the use of certain projective techniques can be useful in this area of the child's response to the school situation. Anecdotal records also are often valuable at this point.

4. *Are social problems related to the child's difficulty?* Sociometric techniques and interviews and casual conversation sometimes will yield information in this regard.

5. *Does the child have the necessary background of experience for successful achievement?* Case studies and analyses of the past home and school history of the child are usually helpful in discovering whether or not this is an important factor in the problem.

6. *Does the child have the necessary skills for successful achievement?* Oral reading under controlled conditions of rate and vocabulary, diagnostic tests in skills areas of the curriculum, and observation of actual performance of the child from day to day furnish useful clues to points at which he may need to develop additional skills.

In working with the child who is experiencing serious difficulty, improvement must be brought about through motivating means. Some important factors in such improvements are: (1) being pleasantly honest and frank with the child in discussing the nature of his problem and how he may improve; (2) helping the child develop the necessary skills for achieving at a higher level; (3) providing the child with suitable materials which he can use independently with success; (4) giving the child immediate knowledge of his improvements; (5) removing the unpleasant emotional factors which previously attended his unsuccessful attempts to learn; (6) helping the child see purpose for his activities.

DISCIPLINE AS GUIDANCE IN THE ELEMENTARY SCHOOL

A major purpose of the school is the development in children of the power of intelligent self-direction and self-control, because both individual freedom and social restraint are important in the maintenance of our social structure. A child should have an opportunity to exercise his initiative and to explore his environment in his efforts to extend his understanding of the world about him. He must learn at the same time, however, that society places certain restraints upon him to prevent his conduct from coming into conflict with the rights of those about him. Therefore, it is the responsibility of those who determine the nature of the organization of the school to set up conditions conducive to the development of this recognition by children and to positive growth in the direction of self-government.

The history of school discipline borders on barbarism at many points. In the earlier elementary schools of this country, the emphasis was on the teacher's *control* rather than on the development of *self-control* by the pupil. Since the important thing was complete regulation and control, any means which accomplished this end seemed justified. As a result, school discipline has emerged through at least four stages or combinations thereof. They are: (1) control through physical force, (2) control through the force of a strong and dominating personality of the teacher, (3) control through social pressures and opinion, and (4) self-control under guidance. Although schools of the modern era may employ combinations of all four in regulating pupil conduct in the elementary school, the trend has been away from physical punishment toward guiding children in their development of self-direction.

If the elementary school is to provide a fertile ground for the growth of children in their powers of self-direction and in their consideration for their associates, certain approaches seem to have considerable merit in the establishment of favorable conditions for guiding children's behavior:

1. Work toward a common and consistent philosophy of discipline for children, staff, and parents.
2. Dramatize desired types of behavior rather than instances of undesirable behavior.
3. Strive to keep children busy at interesting and profitable tasks which they can do.
4. In instances of behavior problems, strive to protect the self-respect of all concerned with the problem.
5. Distinguish between the symptoms and causes in cases of behavior problems.
6. Develop clinical procedures for dealing with serious individual problems.
7. Make use of all appropriate referral agencies in helping children overcome personal problems.
8. Utilize school standards and pride in establishing desired modes of school conduct.

9. Plan school organization and routine activities in a business-like and efficient manner.

10. Encourage the staff to exemplify the kind of behavior desired for boys and girls in the school.

11. Adapt standards of conduct to purposes and conditions in the school.

12. When punishments are necessary, let them be the natural consequences of the undesirable behavior if possible.

Action Suggestions for the Principal

1. Encourage teachers to try to obtain complete information on each child, including all aspects of his growth.

2. Use varied diagnostic techniques in the school such as tests, scales, inventories, projective techniques, observation, sociometry, and screening examinations for physical defects.

3. Search for causes of unusual behavior rather than dealing exclusively with symptoms.

4. Develop cumulative records that contain all pertinent information about each child.

5. Strive to develop school pride in punctuality.

6. Develop case studies on pupils with serious attendance problems.

7. Early in the year make sure that parents, teachers, and children all understand procedures for reporting nonattendance and for maintaining pupil accounting records.

8. Strive to help teachers develop a guidance point of view.

9. Develop and keep a file of the health and psychological agencies from which the school might get assistance in working with individual guidance problems.

10. Help children establish positive goals.

11. Keep a continuing census of all pupils in the school community from birth to completion of the secondary school.

12. Develop simple and effective procedures for the follow-up of pupils who leave the school either through transfer or otherwise.

13. Use census data to anticipate building and personnel needs well in advance and submit these needs to the proper administrative officials in writing.

14. Develop and maintain contacts with parents of preschool children who ultimately will attend the school.

15. Provide for the orientation of pupils new to the school.

16. Provide leisurely opportunities for parents to discuss individual problems of their children prior to the opening of the school year.

17. Organize study groups of parents and teachers to discuss such problems as attendance or health.

18. Work with the staff in developing a curriculum so suited to the needs of children as to make truancy unnecessary.

19. Arrange "clinical sessions" with members of the staff to discuss individual children who need specialized guidance.

20. Cooperate with community agencies interested in the health and welfare of children.

21. Help create a climate in which people can be comfortable even though different.

22. Use available help from guidance workers and specialists to supplement the guidance efforts of teachers.

23. Provide remedial help for children who have been absent from school for a long period of time.

24. Always seek to help each child achieve to his level of ability.

25. Help teachers solve the behavior problems of children in a constructive manner.

26. Realize that a child who creates a problem for others probably has a greater problem of his own.

27. Seek to develop cooperatively with the staff a school organization that guarantees each child a maximum chance to succeed.

SELECTED REFERENCES FOR EXTENDED READING

CASWELL, HOLLIS L., and FOSHAY, A. WELLESLEY. *Education in the Elementary School.* New York: American Book Co., 1950, chap. 11.

DEPARTMENT OF ELEMENTARY SCHOOL PRINCIPALS. *Guidance for Today's Children: Thirty-Third Yearbook.* Washington, D. C.: National Education Association, 1954.

DETJEN, ERVIN W., and DETJEN, MARY FORD. *Elementary School Guidance.* New York: McGraw-Hill Book Co., Inc., 1952.

LEE, J. MURRAY, and LEE, DORRIS MAY. *The Child and His Curriculum.* New York: Appleton-Century-Crofts, Inc., 1950.

MEHL, MARIE, MILLS, HUBERT H., and DOUGLASS, HARL R. *Teaching in Elementary School.* New York: The Ronald Press Co., 1950, chaps. 19 and 20.

OTTO, HENRY J. *Elementary-School Organization and Administration.* New York: Appleton-Century-Crofts, Inc., 1954, chap. 9.

STRANG, RUTH. *An Introduction to Child Study.* New York: The Macmillan Co., 1951.

THORPE, LOUIS P. *The Psychology of Mental Health.* New York: The Ronald Press Co., 1950.

WILES, KIMBALL. *Teaching for Better Schools.* New York: Prentice-Hall, Inc., 1952, chaps. 11 and 12.

WILLEY, ROY DE VERL. *Guidance in Elementary Education.* New York: Harper & Bros., 1952.

YEAGER, WILLIAM A. *Administration and the Pupil.* New York: Harper & Bros., 1949.

PART VI

IMPROVING PROFESSIONAL RELATIONSHIPS
IN THE SCHOOL

Chapter 16

IMPROVING PROFESSIONAL RELATIONSHIPS
IN THE SCHOOL

He who would educate must first learn to cooperate

The school is a social institution. This is to say that its effectiveness depends upon the type and quality of human relationships that exist among the individuals involved in its processes. Indeed, education itself is largely a matter of human interaction. Thus, if one wishes to improve the quality of education in any particular situation, at least one approach is to work for improved person-to-person relationships among the personnel who staff the school.

The educational effort of the modern elementary school depends upon effective teamwork. Cooperative efforts strengthen the organization and methodology of the school while conditions of conflict often paralyze group effort completely, leaving little or no semblance of the strength that comes from unity.

Both size and functions of the typical modern elementary school demand a coordinated approach by members of the professional staff. Responsibilities have to be shared, group decisions have to be made, and special interests and abilities should be utilized. All these necessitate mutual concern and interaction among administrators, supervisors, teachers, and children.

The elementary school teacher in the modern school cannot succeed in terms of the rugged individualism exhibited by his counterpart of an earlier day. In many one-room schools of the past generation, and undoubtedly in a considerable number even today, a single teacher performed virtually all the functions of school operation, including custodial duties. Today the members of the staff have become much more interdependent in discharging their respective obligations. Because of the necessity for this interdependence, the lack of wholesome working relationships within the school can hamper immeasurably the total quality of the school program and the adequacy of its outcomes.

Although some persons appear to maintain the most cordial type of human relationships with their fellows without any visible sign of effort, it must be said that competence in human relations is a social skill that has to be developed or learned. The very young child is a highly egocentric individual until he learns, through experience, how to manage his relations with others in an acceptable and mutually advantageous manner. In much the same way, members of a school staff do not possess inherently "good" or "poor" human relations which they cannot modify, although it must be admitted that a long history or pattern of social behavior tends to become inflexible. However, in spite of the inroads which an attitude of intolerant individualism may make on one's personality over the years, it is often surprising to find how drastically a person may alter his uncooperative tendencies if given the proper opportunities, environment, encouragement, and guidance.

This chapter is devoted to the discussion of working relationships among the professional staff of the school, the effect of these relationships upon children, and how they may be improved. Specifically, attention will be given to: (1) some basic principles of human relations, (2) improving relationships between the principal and the teaching staff, (3) improving relationships among teachers, (4) improving relationships with supervisory personnel, and (5) improving relationships with children. In subsequent chapters relationships with nonteaching personnel and school-community relations will be discussed.

Principles Underlying Wholesome Professional Relationships

Good human relations seem simple for those who possess and practice them and difficult for those who do not. They can be as complicated as human emotions and as simple as common sense. The difficulty of reducing human behavior to a pattern of clear-cut steps to insure desirable professional relationships is so obvious that it will not be attempted in this volume. However, some facts and principles are clearly related to the problem of developing optimum relationships among members of the school staff and they should be pondered carefully by the administrative leader of the school.

1. *The type of professional relationships found in a school is related to the prevailing concept of leadership in the school.* Autocratic leadership does not foster the highest quality of professional relationships among members of the professional team of the school. Under such leadership the lines of communication and responsibility run directly from the leader to each member of the staff or vice versa. There is little need or opportunity for interaction among members of the staff in regard to development of policies or in working on solutions to common problems.

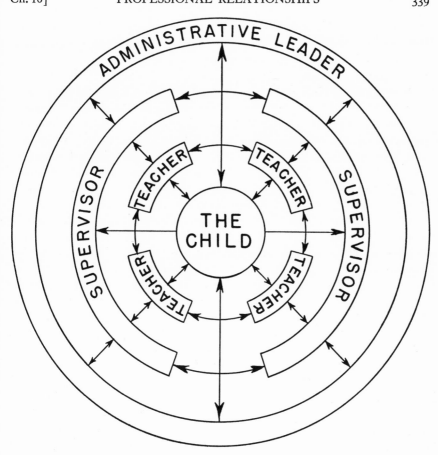

Figure 16

**The Pattern of Professional Relationships
in the Elementary School**

A second respect in which autocratic leadership affects professional relationships adversely is that "leadership by decree" tends to create an atmosphere of suspicion. Under such a concept of leadership, individual staff members may be accused, either justly or falsely, of seeking administrative favor at the expense of their fellows. In such an atmosphere of distrust, free and easy communication among teachers is stifled and the spirit of sharing and cooperative endeavor is soon snuffed out.

Democratic leadership, on the other hand, creates a situation that is fertile with opportunities for growth in the skills of working together harmoniously. Such a situation is essential for true professional endeavor.

2. *Effective professional relationships are based on attitudes of mutual respect.* It is relatively easy for persons who respect each other to work together, but it is difficult to establish the necessary conditions for harmonious endeavor in a situation in which individuals do not respect each other. If staff members are competent, conscientious, and courteous, they are likely to command the respect of their fellows. Conversely, if some members shirk their responsibilities or allow their personal ambitions to interfere with their normal relations with their associates, they are likely to affect adversely the total pattern of human relations in the school.

An administrative leader can do much to create the conditions for mutual respect among staff members. Through such approaches as the rotation of responsibilities, giving proper credit for the various contributions of all members of the staff, and exercising a sensible professional impartiality, he can strengthen the esteem which each staff member holds for other members of the professional team. Such an esteem not only creates a more pleasant social climate in the school but also establishes a sound social structure for working effectively on group responsibilities and problems.

3. *Effective professional relationships are based on the conscious possession of common purposes.* People are more likely to be favorably disposed toward matters in which they share a common concern. Common needs promote common interests and common purposes often are forerunners of cooperative effort to achieve them. An essential part of democratic organization in the elementary school is the pooling of resources and ingenuity toward the solution of problems of mutual concern. When teachers are encouraged to participate in the study and solution of their own problems such as discipline, relations with parents, salary schedules, scheduling of classes and activities, or whatever they may be, they are thereby promoting a common cause through cooperative effort. Such opportunities, fully utilized, can serve as the very foundation for improved working relationships among professional staff members. At the same time, through combined wisdom and ideas, better solutions to the problems are likely to result.

4. *Effective professional relationships are based on a feeling of reasonable security.* Unhappy people are seldom either productive or cooperative. They are likely to carry their tensions into the school day, into their relationships and activities with children, and into their contacts with their teaching associates. Since much personal tension may be attributed to insecurity of one kind or another, it is important

that administrators make every effort to remove causes of unnecessary worry or frustration. Indeed, a major contribution of a good leader to improved educational performance of the staff is the upgrading of morale. This can be done in many ways. It involves attention to individuals as individuals, concern for their problems, credit for their accomplishments, a reasonable guarantee of tenure, freedom from an overemphasis on rating, sincere compliments where they are deserved, and an appreciation of the uniqueness of each person. Administrators should realize that comfortable people are more productive than others, and accordingly should act to promote security in all constructive ways.

5. *Effective professional relationships depend upon good physical and mental health.* Both personality and social competence are influenced very directly by the level of physical and mental health enjoyed by a person. Teachers with health and emotional problems usually become hypersensitive, hypercritical, and irritable. Often such persons indulge in self-pity or tend to withdraw socially from the rest of the professional group. In many instances, they find themselves in conflict with other members of the staff over trivial matters. Any or all of these conditions hamper the professional relationships necessary for carrying on the work of the school.

Teachers with health problems merit the earnest attention and sympathy of their administrative leader. Sometimes an adjustment in assignment, a vacation, or a leave of absence is the only solution. In less serious cases, appropriate medical attention plus sympathetic understanding and assistance usually will improve the situation greatly. At any rate, anything the principal, or others, can do to provide a healthful environment and to promote physical health and positive attitudes on the part of staff members will pay great dividends as a contribution to the general working climate of the school.

6. *Effective professional relationships depend upon the professional attitudes of personnel.* Being a member of a profession lays an obligation upon a teacher or administrator. Such membership implies a concern for others. The effective orientation of new teachers and the types of opportunities provided for them to grow in their professional stature and attitudes through service are essential to good relations among members. The development of a professional group conscience toward children and toward the responsibility that education thrusts upon members of the profession is necessary to effective group effort. Administrators ought to use every appropriate opportunity to impress upon members of the staff their importance and the significance of the work they are doing. This positive approach not only causes people to work better, but to work together better as well.

7. Effective professional relationships are directly related to the physical and social environment of the school. The wholesomeness of the physical and social environment of the school has a profound influence on the persons who inhabit it. The attractiveness of the building, the cleanliness of the surroundings, the homelike quality of the classrooms, and even the color of the walls, all have their effect upon the personalities of teachers as they pursue their responsibilities within the school environment.

Personal feelings, in turn, have a favorable effect on the interaction of the various individuals who compose the staff of the school. A friendly, comfortable, and cheerful environment reflects itself in friendly relations. Such an atmosphere is a good investment in personal motivation that pays off in better teaching.

8. Effective professional relationships depend upon good facilities for communication. The cooperative approach to democratic school organization rests heavily on the presence of opportunities for the sharing of ideas and opinions. This interchange of ideas, in turn, can occur only through communication.

Effective communication in the school program is dependent, of course, on administrative provisions for transmitting information from one member to another. However, the problem of communication goes much deeper than that. Genuinely adequate communication can result only when the various members of the staff have worked together sufficiently to arrive at some common denominators in educational concepts. Group discussion of school problems and educational issues can do much to remove the fuzziness of the definitions and concepts of the teachers. Just as children learn through doing, so teachers learn to communicate effectively through the processes of discussion and group activity.

9. Effective professional relationships are developed through opportunities for cooperative endeavor. This statement is closely related to the preceding one but is a bit more inclusive in its application. Good human relations in the school, like any other form of human proficiency, can deteriorate or even die from lack of exercise. The more people work together, the more efficient their group processes usually become, the more sympathetic they become toward each other's problems, and the more resourceful each member becomes. Good working relationships cannot be created magically as in a vacuum; they are the result of refined practice and sincere mutual effort.

If teachers are given opportunities to help make decisions that affect the direction and operation of the school program, along with provisions for continuous communication regarding the activities of the school, they can become fully as skilled in human relations as they are in the technical aspects of classroom teaching.

10. *Effective human relations are contagious and cumulative.* Good will fosters more good will; pleasant relations tend to multiply in their effects upon people. The quality of human relations enjoyed among members of the staff can be felt among associates, children, and parents, and even the casual visitor to the school often senses immediately the feeling of friendliness, cordiality, and cooperation that permeates the atmosphere of the school. On the other hand, children and others are adept in recognizing differences among teachers, or conflict between a teacher and the principal. By emphasizing the positive attitudes of staff members, and by offering real leadership through his own example, the principal can often initiate a climate of professional friendliness that will soon grow and develop to a very desirable proportion.

IMPROVING RELATIONS BETWEEN THE PRINCIPAL AND THE PROFESSIONAL STAFF

There are many avenues through which a principal may create desirable working relationships with the members of the teaching staff. Some of the approaches to improved relations depend chiefly upon the attitudes and actions of the principal as a person, whereas others are more closely related to the actual organizational machinery of the school. Some of the professional attributes and activities which successful principals have found effective in building good relations with members of the staff merit detailed discussion at this point. They are: (1) improving morale, (2) improving communication, (3) creating favorable employment conditions, (4) recognizing the achievements of staff members, (5) defining responsibilities, and (6) rotating opportunities for leadership.

Maintaining and Improving the Morale of Teachers.—Good morale is the state of mind and spirit which keeps a person favorably disposed toward his responsibilities. It is a form of inner personal and professional enthusiasm which keeps one operating on a relatively high plane of satisfaction. It is impossible to isolate or cite all the essential components of good morale. Such factors are sometimes vague, and often intermingled and overlapping. However, it is possible to enumerate a few elements which seem to have been demonstrated to have positive effects on the morale of professional people.

There is no substitute for *kindness* as an essential ingredient of pleasant human relations. The kind and considerate principal already possesses a strong resource for developing good working relations with the staff. Willingness to be inconvenienced for the benefit of an associate and the little favors which can be bestowed from day to day often will be remembered long after one's technical competence and managerial abilities are forgotten.

Another important attribute of the administrative leader in maintaining the respect and morale of the staff is *honesty*. A principal can be frank without being undiplomatic, thoughtless, or brutal; staff members gradually come to respect a leader who is kindly, yet straightforward and dependable. On the other hand, teachers usually dislike subterfuge, evasion, and misrepresentation of facts or conditions. Such tendencies on the part of the principal, however well-intentioned, usually do not solve the problem of the moment; and, furthermore, they tend to impair the principal's future effectiveness in working with the staff.

Closely related to professional honesty is the matter of *keeping promises*. Teachers have every right to expect action from their professional leader once such action has been promised. If he commits himself to some particular action, he should make every effort to carry through his commitments or, if such action becomes impossible or impractical, he should explain to the persons involved the reasons for the change in his course of action. If a principal persists in forgetting about his professional promises, he cannot long expect to maintain the highest type of respect among his associates.

Promptness of action is almost as important as certainty of action if the administrative leader is to keep the morale of his teaching staff at a high level. Nothing is more exasperating to teachers or more devastating to their morale than the necessity of waiting for an important decision in a matter which remains on a principal's desk for days or weeks. Such delay breeds an impatience not conducive to the development of effective relations. Action by the principal should not be impulsive, but it should be reasonably prompt.

Another important factor in the successful building of staff morale is a *minimum of administrative regulation*. Teachers like to have enough directions to give them needed guidance in the performance of their duties, but they do not like to feel as if their leader considers it necessary to control their activities completely. Over-regulation tends to destroy self-respect and precludes the likelihood of growth in self-direction. The wise principal usually refrains from issuing frequent rules concerning trivial matters. He has learned that greater dividends accrue from the development of broader policies within the framework of which individuals may exercise their own initiative in specific matters.

In the final analysis, nothing can have greater effect on the morale of teachers than a *demonstrated faith* in their motives and efforts.

Teachers like to be appreciated as intelligent beings with reasonably sound judgment. Even more, they will exert their greatest efforts to justify the faith of their leader in them. Such faith is a great morale builder and a powerful motivating influence.

Working for Improved Communication.—The ease with which teachers can communicate with their principal about important aspects of their work is a rather reliable index of the quality of their working relationship with him. If teachers are reluctant to discuss their problems with their educational leader, it is often because they are doubtful or fearful about his probable reaction. They may fear that he will construe the discussion as an indication of weakness and will lower his estimate of the competence of a teacher who is frank to admit he is experiencing problem situations in the classroom. Such reluctance on the part of teachers is an indication of poor human relations. If a principal senses a chronic tenseness in teachers who confer with him, it is probably a sign that he should examine his person-to-person relations with the staff.

The manner in which an administrator issues announcements and instructions is an important part of his communication with the members of the teaching staff. Necessary directions should be clear and concise, but they need not be authoritarian in wording or spirit; neither should they reflect a condescending attitude or a feeling of superwisdom.

If it is prepared well, the school bulletin can be a valuable administrative device for communicating information to teachers. In a recent publication Farley suggests seven characteristics of good bulletins. He says they should be: (1) short, (2) to the point, (3) simple, (4) prepared in attractive form, (5) clear in purpose, (6) friendly in tone, and (7) timely.[1]

Mysterious announcements or communications strain the relations between an administrator and his associates. A summons issued to a teacher in the morning to come to the principal's office after school for a conference can only puzzle and worry the teacher who receives it unless it includes an explanation of the reason for the conference, couched in the tone of a friendly invitation.

The principal can make another valuable contribution to good human relations with the staff by keeping them fully informed about developments and policies which may affect them. Withholding from teachers information regarding the policies and plans of school officials is naturally interpreted by interested teachers as evidence of distrust. On

---

[1] Adapted from Edgar S. Farley, "Not 'Deathless Prose' But Good," in *Time for the Job: Reprinted Sections of the National Elementary Principal for 1953-54* (Washington, D. C.: Department of Elementary School Principals, National Education Association, 1954).

the other hand, bringing members of the staff into the early stages of discussion about school matters does a great deal to give them the feeling of being genuine partners in the educational enterprise.

Promoting Teacher Welfare.—Teachers are likely to cooperate fully with an administrative leader who demonstrates a sincere, active interest in their welfare. This interest may be shown in numerous ways. Creating more favorable working conditions in the school is always a good starting point for the principal who wishes to gain the appreciation of teachers. Such matters as providing adequate restrooms for teachers, needed clerical services, or an adequate place for parking their cars, are closely related to good teacher morale.

A respect for teacher load is another way the principal can contribute to the welfare of teachers. It does a great deal for the spirit of a tired teacher for the principal to offer occasionally to teach her group of children while she visits in another school or catches up on planning for some special project for which she is responsible. Fairness in assigning routine responsibilities for supervision of the lunchroom or playground is also important to the feelings of teachers.

Working for better salaries for teachers is another concrete evidence of the principal's interest in their welfare. He should be among the first to support salary schedules commensurate with the value of teachers to the school and community. He also should support and promote, wherever possible, provisions for sick leave for teachers and for other benefits which they have every right to expect as professional workers.

Methods of evaluating teacher performance are related to the comfort and security of teachers. Rigid check lists and overuse of classroom visits that are obviously inspections tend to destroy, rather than promote, friendly rapport between an administrator and the teachers in a school. Teachers *feel better* and *do better* when they are invited to participate in the evaluation of their work.

Recognizing Teachers' Efforts.—Teachers, in general, want to succeed in their work. Furthermore, they want others to know that they are being successful. The principal who notes the extra efforts of individual teachers or comments on successful innovations which the teacher has introduced into classroom practice is contributing to good morale. In addition, he is motivating the teacher to even greater effort.

Some means for sharing the ingenuity of individual teachers can be a very productive in-service device for staff morale and improvement. Regular bulletins which describe creative activities of teachers, or informal discussion groups at which teachers share experiences, often are useful in this respect. The nature of the means for acquainting members of the staff with each other's activities is relatively unimportant; the significant thing is to provide some appropriate way in which this type of sharing and recognition may be realized.

The principal should give proper recognition to others for their ideas as well as for their efforts. Nothing seems to demoralize a staff more quickly than repeated situations in which an administrator uses the ideas of staff members but reserves the credit for himself. Such a practice by the principal soon destroys every vestige of professional imagination and inventiveness in staff members and creates an attitude of distrust toward him. The wise principal will realize that special recognition which comes to a member of the staff is an indirect tribute to his leadership as well as a direct compliment to the teacher.

Defining Responsibilities Clearly.—Teachers work best, and are happier, when they have a clear notion about what is expected of them. Vague lines of responsibility often lead to professional conflicts among staff members as they perform their duties. Every teacher has a right to know the nature of his professional duties and the criteria upon which his performance will be appraised, as long as they are not too detailed or restrictive. It is the principal's obligation to guarantee that the teachers in a school have an opportunity to learn their responsibilities in the operation of the over-all school program as well as in their own classrooms.

Rotating Opportunities for Leadership.—Nothing appears to be more effective in creating respect for a leader than the rotation of leadership among members of a group. At the same time, assumption of the responsibility for leadership by members of the teaching staff is an effective instrument for promoting professional growth.

Obviously, a principal should not relinquish the responsibilities of his office, nor foist administrative problems upon teachers who are already overworked in carrying out their own classroom duties. There are numerous opportunities in the organization and operation of an elementary school, however, for teachers to assume the role of leader for the group. Curriculum study and development, playground problems, teacher-parent relations, and the building of a professional library are areas of concern in which teacher leadership might be used to great advantage.

Improving Professional Relationships Among Teachers

It is obvious that the chief responsibility for harmony among professional staff members lies with the teachers themselves. Laudable personal characteristics of teachers show up in their relations with their associates. In a similar manner, their frustrations and tensions inhibit the development of smooth working relations with others. In spite of these facts, however, the administrative leader, by his own actions and attitudes, can do much to insure that teachers work well with each other. Some of the important aspects of principal-teacher relationships discussed in the previous section, of course, apply also to the development of desirable relationships among the teachers themselves. However, a few additional approaches used by successful principals are included for further discussion. If the administrative leader wishes to create the conditions most favorable to group harmony among the professional staff he will attempt to:

Set an example of courtesy and consideration toward others. One of the best ways of influencing the behavior of others in a positive manner is to demonstrate the virtues we wish to cultivate. Common courtesy, friendliness, and genuinely humane consideration of the problems of others tends to set a standard of professional conduct for the whole school. Cheerful acceptance of group decisions, even though they are counter to the personal wishes and ideas of the leader, can do much to develop a feeling of tolerance and good will among staff members. A grouchy, complaining, or whining principal can expect his dyspeptic attitudes to cast a shadow over the whole pattern of human relations in the school; but the balance, common sense, and human graciousness of the competent leader will lessen chances for conflict and inspire the best professional behavior from others with whom he works.

Avoid unwarranted favoritism to particular teachers. The writer does not wish to suggest that all teachers should receive identical treatment by the principal. Such an approach suggests no thoughtful personnel practices at all. Teachers should be treated as individuals with differing abilities and problems just as they, in turn, must consider the children they teach as individuals. However, there is a marked distinction between differentiation and favoritism in personnel practices. When a particular teacher is consistently assigned the lightest load of responsibility in the school organization, or is chronically and noticeably absent when there are extra jobs to be done in the school, fellow teachers build a hostile attitude toward both the offending teacher and the principal who presumably approves her actions. Such conditions tend to undermine any spirit of cooperation which otherwise is being developed in the school.

Be cautious about confidential agreements with teachers. Closely akin to the above situation is that in which the principal enters into secret pacts with individual teachers regarding their responsibilities in the operation of the school. There will be times, of course, when teachers will have problems which need not and should not be known to the other members of the staff. However, as a general rule, the policies governing personnel matters should be known and understood by all teachers and should be applied in an equitable manner. This should apply in such matters as the amount of pay a teacher is to receive during periods of absence or leave, or the requirements through which teachers qualify for higher positions on the existing salary schedule for the school. In cases where teacher councils or faculty groups participate in the formulation of personnel policies, the principal is in a sounder professional position if he has the prior approval of such a group for whatever adjustments might become necessary for individuals.

Keep group meetings of the staff informal. Social, physical, and emotional comforts are assets to joint understanding and cooperative effort. Highly organized and formal staff meetings are not conducive to group interaction. For that reason, many principals are encouraging teachers to serve simple refreshments at their meetings as a means of breaking down social barriers. In addition, it helps to create an atmosphere for effective work together if the physical quarters where teachers meet are comfortable and informal. It does little for the spirit of good fellowship if a teacher, after a strenuous day of teaching, has to force herself into a classroom chair that is too small and uncomfortable and remain there throughout the proceedings of a boresome faculty meeting. Wise principals will exert every effort to prevent such conditions and will give serious attention to providing quarters that are harmonious with the cheerful and friendly relationships they wish to cultivate in the staff.

Help build status for each teacher. An insecure teacher is usually uncomfortable in the presence of others. Sometimes this personal insecurity comes from being on temporary appointment, from being a substitute teacher, from having less than the average or required amount of professional preparation, from being inexperienced, or from some emotionally disturbing personal problem. Regardless of the source of such personal feelings of inadequacy, it is the obligation of the administrative leader to help such a teacher establish and maintain status with the other members of the group. He can contribute to this end by casual, sincere comments and by giving such a teacher opportunities to do the kinds of things for and with the group in which she can demonstrate success. Unless the insecure feelings of such a person are alleviated, they tend to result in the isolation of the person from the rest of the group, thus affecting the structure and processes of the entire group. Efforts to prevent such an event pay great dividends.

Provide varied opportunities for group decisions. Many decisions with respect to school policies as they affect the welfare of teachers can be formulated through the cooperative study of the whole staff. When teachers have mutual interests and have the privilege of helping promote these interests, they build among themselves a feeling of corporate interdependence. They can begin to see that they profit from the pooling of resources and that they can contribute to their own well-being, as well as their effectiveness, by working together on common problems. By permitting and encouraging teachers to take an active part in policy development, a principal can make a valuable contribution to staff unity.

Emphasize the positive in all school activities. The principal who places major emphasis on wholesome behavior helps set an emotional tone for desirable staff relationships. Such a tone can be fostered in many ways. Teachers can be encouraged to emphasize the desirable traits and achievements of children rather than those that are undesirable. Parents can be given credit for their help in providing good learning experiences for their children. Bulletins and newsletters can be prepared in such a manner that they invoke wholesome reactions. Teachers can be given credit for the extra things that they do to improve the school program. Discipline problems and staff conflicts can be treated objectively and fairly with a minimum of fanfare and publicity. Once the personnel of the school establish the tendency to look for the best in others rather than the worst, a major step has been taken toward wholesome staff relationships.

Apply the basic convictions of democratic leadership. Earlier in this volume some of the essential elements of democratic leadership were explored and discussed as they concern the total educational enterprise. However, some of the basic tenets of the democratic approach seem to have such a direct bearing on professional relationships that they are cited here. At a meeting of professors of school administration held to explore the obligations of administrative leadership and ways to improve it, a list of some of these basic tenets was clearly stated:[2]

1. The welfare of the group is assured by the welfare of each individual.
2. Decisions reached through the cooperative use of intelligence are, in total, more valid than decisions made by individuals. A group can take into account more completely than an individual the various considerations which are relevant to the problem at hand. In resolving the conflicts between various points of view, the group can see new relationships and develop a synthesis which is greater than its component ideas.
3. Every idea is entitled to a fair hearing. An idea is to be examined on its

[2] National Conference of Professors of Educational Administration, *Providing and Improving Administrative Leadership for America's Schools: Fourth Report* (New York: Bureau of Publications, Teachers College, Columbia University, 1951), pp. 19-20.

merits rather than on the basis of who proposed it. When it is examined by free informed citizens, there is nothing to fear.
4. Every person can make a unique and important contribution. Individuality rather than uniformity extends the comprehensiveness of problem exploration.
5. Growth comes from within the group rather than from without. People must be allowed to discover things for themselves. They take less initiative when they are told what to do than when they have a part in determining the course of action.
6. Democracy is a way of living. Democratic systems are not perfected systems, but bettering ones. Democratic means are essential for the attainment of democratic ends.
7. Democratic methods are efficient methods. Democracy creates the best plan of action. It helps individuals develop creative power. It helps the group use all its resources to solve its problems. It commits the members of the group to the success of the plan.
8. Individuals are dependable. The instances of untrustworthiness are small compared with the total number of occasions on which reliance was placed upon individuals. If examined closely even those instances are likely to represent misunderstanding rather than bad faith.
9. Persons merit love. Tender and devout love for all men is the essential component of great personal leadership in a democratic society.

Develop with the staff a high sense of ethics toward their associates and their profession. The professionalizing of teaching has been a long and gradual process. Even to this day it is difficult to get all teachers to accept the obligations that accompany membership in a true profession. One of the responsibilities of leadership, therefore, seems to be that of assisting teachers in establishing for themselves high standards of professional ethics. Through sincere adherence to such standards, teachers establish ground rules for themselves to prevent thoughtless or unscrupulous members from trampling upon the rights of others. Such a sense of ethics carries over into the relationships which prevail at the local school level.

An unwritten code of ethics probably prevails in many modern elementary schools. It seems profitable, however, for the members of the staff of every school to be aware of some of the written codes which members of their profession have formulated to help guarantee a high professional level among teachers. The most common example of such a code is that issued by the National Education Association. It follows:[3]

CODE OF ETHICS

BELIEVING: That true democracy can best be achieved by a process of free public education made available to all the children of all the people;

[3] National Education Association. *NEA Handbook* (Washington, D. C.: National Education Association, 1949-1950), pp. 397-400.

That the teachers in the United States have a large and inescapable responsibility in fashioning the ideals of children and youth;

That such responsibility requires the services of men and women of high ideals, broad education, and profound human understanding; and, in order that the aims of democratic education may be realized more fully, that the welfare of the teaching profession may be promoted; and,

That teachers may observe proper standards of conduct in their professional relations, the National Education Association of the United States proposes the code of ethics for its members.

The term "teacher" as used in this code shall include all persons directly engaged in education work, whether in a teaching, an administrative, or a supervisory capacity.

Article I—Relations to Pupils and the Home

Section 1—It is the duty of the teacher to be just, courteous, and professional in all his relations with pupils. He should consider their individual differences, needs, interests, temperaments, aptitudes, and environments.

Section 2—He should refrain from tutoring pupils of his classes for pay, and from referring such pupils to any member of his immediate family for tutoring.

Section 3—The professional relations of a teacher with his pupils demand the same scrupulous care that is required in the confidential relations of one teacher with another. A teacher, therefore, should not disclose any information obtained confidentially from his pupils, unless it is for the best interest of the child and the public.

Section 4—A teacher should seek to establish friendly and intelligent cooperation between home and school, ever keeping in mind the dignity of his profession and the welfare of the pupils. He should do or say nothing that would undermine the confidence and respect of his pupils for their parents. He should inform the pupils and parents regarding the importance, purposes, accomplishments, and needs of the schools.

Article II—Relations to Civic Affairs

Section 1—It is the obligation of every teacher to inculcate in his pupils an appreciation of the principles of democracy. He should direct full and free discussion of appropriate controversial issues with the expectation that comparisons, contrasts, and interpretations will lead to an understanding, appreciation, acceptance, and practice of the principles of democracy. A teacher should refrain from using his classroom privileges and prestige to promote partisan politics, sectarian religious views, or selfish propaganda of any kind.

Section 2—A teacher should recognize and perform all the duties of citizenship. He should subordinate his personal desires to the best interests of the public good. He should be loyal to the school system, the state, and the nation, but should exercise his right to give constructive criticisms.

Section 3—A teacher's life should show that education makes people better citizens and better neighbors. His personal conduct should not needlessly offend the accepted pattern of behavior of the community in which he serves.

Article III—Relations to the Profession

Section 1—Each member of the teaching profession should dignify his calling on all occasions and should uphold the importance of his services to society. On the other hand, he should not indulge in personal exploitation.

Section 2—A teacher should encourage able and sincere individuals to enter the teaching profession and discourage those who plan to use this profession merely as a stepping-stone to some other vocation.

Section 3—It is the duty of the teacher to maintain his own efficiency by study, by travel, and by other means which keep him abreast of the trends in education and the world in which he lives.

Section 4—Every teacher should have membership in his local, state, and national professional organizations, and should participate actively and unselfishly in them. Professional growth and personality development are the natural product of such professional activity. Teachers should avoid the promotion of organization rivalry and divisive competition which weaken the cause of education.

Section 5—While not limiting their services by reason of small salary, teachers should insist upon a salary scale commensurate with the social demands laid upon them by society. They should not knowingly underbid a rival or agree to accept a salary lower than that provided by a recognized schedule. They should not apply for positions for the sole purpose of forcing an increase in salary in their present position; correspondingly, school officials should not refuse to give deserved salary increases to efficient employees until offers from other school authorities have forced them to do so.

Section 6—A teacher should not apply for a specific position currently held by another teacher. Unless the rules of the school system otherwise prescribe, he should file his application with the chief executive officer.

Section 7—Since qualification should be the sole determining factor in appointment and promotion, the use of pressure on school officials to secure a position or to obtain other favors is unethical.

Section 8—Testimonials regarding teachers should be truthful and confidential, and should be treated as confidential information by the school authorities receiving them.

Section 9—A contract, once signed, should be faithfully adhered to until it is dissolved by mutual consent. Ample notification should be given by both school officials and teachers in case a change in position is to be made.

Section 10—Democratic procedures should be practiced by members of the teaching profession. Cooperation should be predicated upon the recognition of the worth and the dignity of individual personality. All teachers should observe the professional courtesy of transacting official business with the properly designated authority.

Section 11—School officials should encourage and nurture the professional growth of all teachers by promotion or by other appropriate methods of recognition. School officials who fail to recommend a worthy teacher for a better position outside their school system because they do not desire to lose his services are acting unethically.

Section 12—A teacher should avoid unfavorable criticism of other teachers except that formally presented to a school official for the welfare of the school. It is unethical to fail to report to the duly constituted authority any matters which are detrimental to the welfare of the school.

Section 13—Except when called upon for counsel or other assistance, a teacher should not interfere in any matter between another teacher and a pupil.

Section 14—A teacher should not act as an agent, or accept a commission, royalty, or other compensation, for endorsing books or other school materials in the selection or purchase of which he can exert influence, or concerning which he can exercise the right of decision; nor should he accept a commission or other compensation for helping another to secure a position.

Improving Relationships with Special Supervisory Personnel

The quality of the professional relations existing between a supervisor and the personnel of a local school has a direct effect on the services such a supervisor can provide in the school. This general observation appears to apply equally well to the work of so-called general supervisors or of supervisors in such special fields as music and art. As was indicated in an earlier chapter on curriculum, classrooms in modern elementary schools are becoming more and more self-contained in the sense that a single teacher is responsible for the major part of the day's instructional activities. However, this trend does not minimize the importance and usefulness of special supervisors and consultants who work directly with teachers in improving instruction in their classrooms.

Much of the effectiveness of a supervisor depends upon the rapport that is established with teachers and administrators. Friendly relations and the sense of being co-workers are essential to beneficial supervisory activities in the local school. Supervisors should consider themselves as "service personnel" rather than "directors" or "inspectors." Most teachers wish to do a satisfactory job of teaching and welcome supervisory help if it is given in a friendly and competent manner.

There is no set formula of action through which proper relations with supervisory staff can be guaranteed. However, there are some ways in which improved relationships usually may be developed and maintained.

Work for a clear and complete understanding of the specific responsibilities of each supervisor who regularly works with teachers. If the supervisor, or consultant, is responsible to the principal of a building in which he works, that fact should be known and accepted by all. If one of the duties of the supervisor is to help teachers acquire instructional materials, all personnel should be aware of this obligation. Whatever the situation, it is important for both teachers and supervisor to know what one has a right to expect from the other.

Work with the supervisor cooperatively in determining his schedule of activities in a school. The administrative leader cannot expect to promote good relations with a supervisor by imposing a schedule upon him without his consent. On the other hand, if the supervisor works on some basis other than on call, his schedule should be worked out with demonstrated concern for the convenience of both supervisor and the teaching staff. Disregard for the preferences of the supervisor can only have a negative effect on his attitude toward a particular school and the personnel who are responsible for its operation.

Build positive attitudes in the school toward consultant and supervisory services. If the services of special supervisors are genuinely helpful to teachers, a favorable attitude toward such assistance will soon be established. The principal can help to build teacher acceptance of supervisory service by his own attitudes toward it. By his casual remarks about supervisory personnel, he affects the feeling of teachers about them. If he appears to consider supervisors in the category of necessary evils, then teachers are likely to absorb some of this feeling; if, on the other hand, he obviously appreciates the specialized help to be gained from the visits and contributions of supervisors, teachers also are more likely to develop positive attitudes toward them.

There is another advantage to the positive approach in working with supervisors. The supervisor, himself, is almost sure to sense the degree of cordiality with which he is received in a particular school. If teachers and principal evince an eagerness to avail themselves of his special help, the supervisor in turn will be likely to exert his very best efforts to merit their respect and favor.

Much of the responsibility for mutually profitable and pleasant relationships lies with the supervisor. Even though he may be more experienced and more highly trained than the teachers with whom he works, he should avoid any semblance of superiority in manner or deed. Treating teachers in a manner that indicates that they are intelligent and important is essential if the desired type of relations are to be developed between them.

The manner in which a supervisor makes a classroom visit can promote or destroy the feeling of partnership which he may desire to foster with teachers. He should know the rules of the school and adapt his visit to them. He should always make his presence in the building known to the principal upon entering. His entrance into classrooms should be quiet and unobtrusive rather than dramatic, but not to the extent of sneaking into the room without the knowledge of the teacher. Common courtesy demands that the teacher should be aware of any visitor who enters the room. The supervisor should feel free to mingle among the children as they pursue their work but should be careful not to upset the general plan of work being followed. When leaving the classroom, the supervisor should comment on some of the outstanding activities or methods observed. It is also well to plan for an individual conference with the teacher, so that the day's activities may be reviewed or problems can be discussed. The main thing is to keep all aspects of the visit on a positive plane as far as possible.

Include supervisory personnel in staff affairs. Supervisors often find themselves without a professional home base. Often the location of a supervisor's office is such that he is somewhat isolated from the schools in which he renders most of his services. He is too often a fringe member of all groups and a full-fledged member of none. It shows both courtesy and foresight for a principal to include special personnel in as many activities of the school as possible. Supervisors can be invited to attend staff meetings as well as social affairs of the group. Such interaction allows teachers to become better acquainted with the supervisor as a person and thus tends to break down any professional barriers which may exist between them. In addition, by gaining greater knowledge of the personnel and program of the school, the supervisor can be more intelligent about his own activities by tailoring them to the nature and needs of particular situations.

IMPROVING THE ADMINISTRATOR'S RELATIONSHIPS WITH CHILDREN

The elementary school principal has two types of relationships with children: (1) those which are direct person-to-person relationships and (2) indirect relationships through teachers or parents. The impressions children gain about their administrative leader in the school have a strong effect on their general attitudes toward the school as a whole. Both the principal's philosophy of education and his personal behavior bear directly on his relationships with children as well as on the way in which the school is organized and administered. If the principal is to derive personal and professional satisfactions from his relationships with pupils, certain simple, but important, suggestions need to be followed.

Get to know children personally as individuals if possible. It helps to establish good relations with a child if the principal knows him. It gives the ego of a boy or girl a lift to have the principal call him by name on the street, in the grocery store, or even on the playground. Short conversations and casual comments that include some reference to a child's family or his special hobby do much to build a bridge of effective relations. It is wholly desirable for children to realize that their principal is entirely natural and human.

Build up favorable attitudes toward the principal's office. The principal's office should be considered the administrative headquarters of the school and should be respected as such. It is unfortunate, however, in many schools that the concepts of the office are closely allied with disciplinary judgments and penal actions. When children shrink with horror at the thought of visiting the principal's office, they are not likely to consider its occupant a friend. A principal can move to dispel such notions by being accessible to children who bring matters to his attention and by treating all children justly and kindly.

Seek children's opinions about appropriate school matters. Participation usually improves responsibility, and this is particularly true when the children of an elementary school are considered. By inviting the student council, class committees, or even individual children to come to his office to give their opinions, the principal can test the pulse of the school, create favorable attitudes toward his office and, simultaneously, develop in the participating children a genuine feeling of belongingness in the school. It is also possible to receive some very valuable ideas from children regarding some aspects of the school program.

Participate occasionally in the free activities of children. Children are usually pleased to have the principal join them in their activities. For the principal to join one of their team games on the playground as one of their equals does much to create an impression of him as a "regular fellow" and usually moves him just a bit closer to the confidence and respect of the children. Having lunch with a group of children in the school cafeteria or lunchroom on occasions is another way of accomplishing the same result.

Avoid violation of the confidence of children. Children of elementary school age often are prone to confide in persons whom they consider their friends. When children give information to the principal on a confidential basis, they are grieved if the principal teases them or discusses the information in the presence of parents or teachers. The principal also should be careful about needlessly spreading information about a child's family activities, often furnished innocently by the casual conversation of young children.

Be firm but fair in dealing with disciplinary problems. On the whole children have a rather keen sense of justice. They are quick to detect weakness, indecision, or outright injustice. In general, they do not rebel against accepting the consequences of their unwise acts; but they do object, inwardly at least, to unreasonable and discriminative punishments. If the principal is unemotional about disciplinary problems, remains calm and friendly, and yet metes out judgments and suggestions in a firm, impersonal manner, his relationships with children will not suffer as a result. In fact, handling the behavior problems of children judiciously is likely to add to his stature in the eyes of the school population.

The personality, attitudes, and professional behavior of the administrative leader is an important factor in establishing, maintaining, and strengthening his relations with teachers, supervisors, and children. In all his contacts, he can do no better than to remember and practice the rule of treating others as he would like to be treated. This admonition, simple as it sounds, is the first principle in human relations.

ACTION SUGGESTIONS FOR THE PRINCIPAL

1. Make frequent friendly visits to classrooms.
2. Encourage intervisiting by teachers, both locally and in other schools.
3. Assume the classroom responsibilities of teachers occasionally.
4. Provide definite means for the effective orientation of new teachers.
5. Provide clerical service for teachers.
6. Remain accessible to teachers.
7. Emphasize the importance of teachers and the work they do.
8. Try to give teachers frequent compliments regarding the things they are doing well.
9. Keep teachers informed about policies and plans of the school system.
10. Solve as many school problems as possible through group study and action.
11. Practice placing the kindest construction on the comments of associates.
12. Allow for differences of professional opinion among staff members and treat such differences impersonally and objectively.
13. Keep promises which are made to teachers and pupils.
14. Be prompt in following through on promised action.
15. Avoid trivial and restrictive rules concerning the activities of teachers.
16. Encourage teachers to participate in the evaluation of their teaching performances.
17. Encourage teachers and children to contribute ideas for the improvement of the school.
18. Be sure that each person on the staff clearly understands the extent and nature of his responsibilities.
19. Provide easy means for teachers to share and pool their ideas.
20. Keep staff meetings informal.
21. Encourage teachers to assume leadership in studying matters of vital importance to them.
22. Practice the Golden Rule.
23. Attempt to make a success of each teacher and pupil in the school; do not accept failure as inevitable.

24. Cooperate with supervisors in the definition and allocation of responsibilities.

25. Make supervisors feel at home in the school.

26. Be ethical in dealing with confidential information about teachers and children.

27. Keep a sense of humor.

SELECTED REFERENCES FOR EXTENDED READING

ADAMS, HAROLD P., and DICKEY, FRANK G. *Basic Principles of Supervision.* New York American Book Co., 1953.

CAMPBELL, CLYDE M. (ed.). *Practical Applications of Democratic Administration.* New York: Harper & Bros., 1952, chap. 8.

CHAMBERLAIN, LEO M., and KINDRED, LESLIE W. *The Teacher and School Organization.* New York: Prentice-Hall, Inc., 1949.

CHAMBERLAIN, LEO M., and REUTTER, E. EDMUND, JR. *Staff Personnel in the Public Schools.* New York: Prentice-Hall, Inc., 1954.

HAND, HAROLD C. "What Makes for High Teacher Morale?" *Educational Leadership,* V (January, 1948), pp. 279-80.

JACOBSON, PAUL B., REAVIS, WILLIAM C., and LOGSDON, JAMES D. *Duties of School Principals.* New York: Prentice-Hall, Inc., 1950, chap. 14.

KYTE, GEORGE C. *The Principal at Work.* Boston: Ginn & Co., 1952, chaps. 10, 15, and 17.

McNERNEY, CHESTER T. *Educational Supervision.* New York: McGraw-Hill Book Co., Inc., 1951, chap. 7.

NATIONAL CONFERENCE OF PROFESSORS OF EDUCATIONAL ADMINISTRATION. *Providing and Improving Administrative Leadership for America's Schools, A Fourth Report.* New York: Bureau of Publications, Teachers College, Columbia University, 1951.

SHANE, HAROLD G., and YAUCH, WILBUR A. *Creative School Administration.* New York: Henry Holt & Co., 1954, chap. 14.

WEBER, CLARENCE A. *Personnel Problems of School Administrators.* New York: McGraw-Hill Book Co., Inc., 1954.

WILES, KIMBALL. *Supervision for Better Schools.* New York: Prentice-Hall, Inc., 1950.

YAUCH, WILBUR A. *Improving Human Relations in School Administration.* New York: Harper & Bros., 1949.

YEAGER, WILLIAM A. *Administration and the Teacher.* New York: Harper & Bros., 1954.

Chapter 17

IMPROVING RELATIONSHIPS WITH NONTEACHING PERSONNEL

One partner may be worth many workers

In a sense, all members of the school staff are educators. Even though professional workers must bear most of the responsibility for planning and operating the educational program, nonteaching personnel make a substantial contribution to the routine processes and environment of the school. Each member of such a staff is uniquely important as a member of the total school team. Much of the smooth operation and pleasant atmosphere of good elementary schools is attributable to the understanding and technical skills of noncertificated workers.

A good service staff affects the well-being of the school at many points and in many ways. These workers have many contacts with children, which provide numerous opportunities for them to influence their attitudes and personal well-being. The work of the custodian, the cafeteria worker, and the bus driver is closely related to the personal comfort and health of children who attend the school.

The services which nonteaching workers provide for teachers contribute very materially to good morale and to the over-all effectiveness of the instructional program. A clean classroom, a good lunch, and needed clerical service are conditions which keep teachers going about their duties in a cheerful manner.

Parents also feel the influence of a good service staff. School secretaries are usually the first members of the staff to greet visitors to the school. A pleasant reception by such workers or the appearance of a well-kept building tends to create a favorable first impression of the school that may be invaluable in terms of community relations.

The work of the nonteaching staff is probably more difficult to coordinate and to integrate with the total program of the school than that of the professional staff. The curriculum of the school tends to serve as a unifying force for the latter, whereas the work of the school custodian, the cafeteria manager, or the bus driver appears to have little in common except that they all perform their services for children. This situation presents a real challenge to personnel leadership in the school and makes it even more important for the principal to know and practice constructive ways for establishing good relationships with and among nonteaching employees of the school.

This chapter is devoted to an exploration of some of the factors which affect the quality of relationships involving nonteaching personnel. The discussion is organized around the following major considerations: (1) some basic principles to guide relationships with nonteaching personnel, (2) some approaches to improved services of nonteaching personnel, and (3) some basic functions of key service personnel with suggestions for improvement.

PRINCIPLES UNDERLYING RELATIONSHIPS WITH NONTEACHING PERSONNEL

Obtaining the best possible services from nonteaching personnel is too vital to a good educational program to be ignored. The administrative leader who minimizes the role of such personnel in the educational process is thereby hindering the professional staff and the children in the school from accomplishing all that might be achieved under more favorable conditions. Custodial, clerical, health, and food services are so closely allied with the basic job of the school that certain principles seem to apply to all of them if they are to make their optimum contribution to the total program.

1. *Nonteaching personnel should be considered as members of the educational team.* All members of the school staff have an impact on the children who attend school. The teaching staff assumes major responsibility for the motivation and administration of learning; at the same time, members of the service staff very largely provide the quality of environment which exists. Who is to say that the work of the teacher who assists a child in learning to read is more important than that of the school nurse who protects his health? Is not the work of the custodian who provides a clean and hazard-free environment very important also? These services, whether professional or otherwise, cannot be reduced to common denominators and therefore cannot be compared in importance. It is enough, however, to recognize that each service employee makes his own peculiar contribution to the total welfare of the school—a contribution without which the effectiveness of the school program suffers.

Workers who sense their relation to a team effort usually respond in a positive way. Awareness of this relationship lends dignity and significance to the jobs they perform and tends to give their morale a boost. The wise administrative leader will search for ways in which service person-

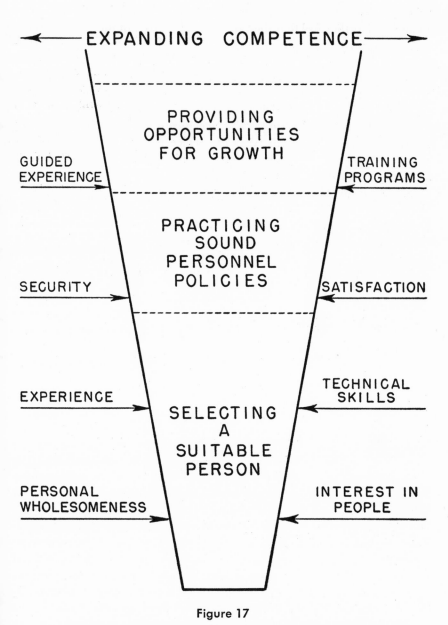

Figure 17

Steps in Building an Effective Nonteaching Staff

nel can be brought into the planning and operation of the school in such a manner that they feel that they are an integral part of the enterprise.

2. *Nonteaching personnel should be selected on the basis of appropriate and established criteria.* While considerable control is exercised over the qualifications of teaching personnel through licenses and certification requirements, nonteaching personnel are too frequently selected on the basis of considerations which have little, if any, connection with their qualifications for the job they seek. Specifications should be formulated to guide the selection of all types of service personnel in terms of the kind of person needed, the experience required, and the technical skills necessary for carrying out the responsibilities of the position.

3. *The duties of each member of the nonteaching staff should be clearly defined and understood.* It is not enough to select competent workers as members of the service staff. The building of an effective educational team requires a clear understanding on the part of all of the staff as to the specific obligations to be performed by each staff member. Otherwise, important services are left undone, efforts are likely to be duplicated at some points, and workers are thereby encouraged to perform their duties in a slipshod manner. A staff member may possess the basic skills necessary for performing his duties but he needs and deserves a certain amount of orientation to the particular position he accepts in the school. Even if he is an experienced worker, conditions differ from school to school sufficiently that each new position may require a redefinition of responsibilities, hours, and conditions of work.

4. *Relations with various other members of the staff and with children should be clearly defined and understood.* Confusion and conflict often result from vague notions of lines of responsibility as they involve the relations of nonteaching personnel with other individuals and school groups. For example, it is frequently a matter of considerable concern as to the extent of disciplinary responsibility cafeteria workers or school custodians are expected to exercise over children in the lunchroom or corridors of the building. In a similar manner, the question often arises as to the proper way for teachers to file complaints regarding such things as custodial care of the classroom, or to request special services from members of the service staff. These things may seem trivial to the casual observer, but the tendency for such misunderstandings to develop into major issues in the school attaches to them more than nominal importance. This is the type of case in which "an ounce of prevention is *indeed* worth a pound of cure."

5. *Nonteaching personnel should be recognized as front-line public relations agents of the school.* As indicated in the introductory part of this chapter, the first contacts of parents and other visitors with the

school usually involve nonteaching personnel. A person coming to the school is likely to be greeted by the school secretary or clerk. If he spends any time in the school, he cannot fail to note how clean the floors are kept, how sanitary the fountains appear to be, or how disreputable has become the condition of the restrooms. All these factors influence the attitudes of citizens toward their schools either favorably or otherwise, depending on the competency of the members of the school staff who are responsible for the existing conditions. Such workers, by the very nature of their positions, have an opportunity to say favorable things about the school or, conversely, to arouse suspicion regarding it.

As a rule, parents are vitally interested in the health problems of their children. The competence and attitudes of the school nurse, dental hygienist, or school doctor or dentist in caring for the health needs of children can make lasting impressions on parents. The sympathetic understanding shown by the school nurse, or some other member of the school staff, in visiting parents in their homes, or in transporting ill children from school to their homes, can be a real factor in the establishment of favorable attitudes toward the school, its staff, and its program.

The services provided when parent groups and other community groups hold meetings at school are important to public relations. Having rooms previously arranged or food service provided contributes to the success of such meetings and thus tends to build up wholesome relationships outside the school.

Though the major obligation of service personnel is to the children attending the school, their influence on community relations should not be underestimated.

6. *Opportunities for training in service should be provided for nonteaching personnel.* It is just as essential to provide opportunities for growth and improvement in service of nonteaching personnel as members of the professional staff. Some types of nonteaching positions do not actually require that any certain standard of qualifications or technical skill be met as a condition of employment. When this is the case, as is often true with cafeteria workers or custodial employees, it is doubly important that such personnel receive guidance and training on the job. Some of this training can be given through the tactful guidance and suggestions of the school administrator, but other agencies should not be overlooked as possibilities for contributing to the task of helping these workers grow on the job.

7. *Nonteaching personnel should have appropriate opportunity for participating in the formulation of school policy.* It is important that persons who are responsible for the operation of certain policies in the

school should have a voice in the formulation of these policies.[1] This does not mean that all staff members necessarily should assume equal responsibility for the development of school policies; it does suggest, however, that each staff member should have an opportunity to express his opinions about matters which directly affect him and the performance of his duties. As administrative leaders become more ingenious in their utilization of the ideas of people with varying interests and responsibilities, they find that the burden of implementing policies in the school becomes correspondingly lighter.

8. *Nonteaching personnel who work in a school should be directly responsible to the principal of that school.* It is difficult for a staff member to identify himself with the educational team of the school if his administrative allegiance rests outside the school. When such workers are directly responsible to the Board of Education, they tend to develop an independence of action that hampers cooperation in the school. In addition, such an arrangement easily can result in conflicting directions regarding the discharge of duties. Such a condition can be expected to have a negative effect on staff rapport and on the effectiveness of the services rendered.

In large school systems maintenance workers and other nonteaching personnel are frequently responsible to a director in the central administrative offices of the school system. Viewed strictly from the angle of business administration, there is little doubt that such an arrangement has merit. However, from an educational point of view, it seems somewhat inconsistent with modern concepts of elementary school organization and operation. Some schools have effected a compromise by regulating such personnel matters as hours of work, salary scale, and sick leaves through a central agency and, at the same time, making the worker responsible to the principal of the school in all matters relating to the performance of his duties.

9. *All suitable agencies should be utilized in helping nonteaching personnel perform their duties well.* Genuine competence of nonteaching personnel gains the respect and appreciation of the whole school and community. This appreciation, in turn, tends to motivate the worker to even greater efforts to please his associates. Thus, any means through which workers can improve their competencies will have an effect on school relationships. Administrative leaders should be alert to the possibilities of utilizing such types of aids as materials, workshops, or consultant services of community and state agencies and institutions for this purpose.

[1] See Harold G. Shane and Wilbur A. Yauch, *Creative School Administration* (New York: Henry Holt & Co., 1954), pp. 448-52.

10. *The services of nonteaching personnel should be evaluated largely on the basis of the educational purposes they serve.* Technical proficiency is not enough to recommend the services of a school staff member. Workers who dislike children or who have little understanding or respect for what the school is attempting to achieve are almost sure to be unsuccessful in their jobs. On the other hand, a cheerful willingness to contribute wherever possible to the program of the school, or to assist teachers in planning and preparing for activities or special projects, is a major criterion of success for nonteaching staff members. When the services of various members of the staff are evaluated, any effective appraisal must include some attention to the objectives of the school and the extent to which workers contribute to the realization of these goals.

Some Approaches to Improved Relationships with Nonteaching Personnel

People are much alike in the general nature of their reactions to others. The same types of consideration which help the principal establish good working relationships with teachers are also essential to good relationships with nonteaching personnel. Therefore, much of what was said in the previous chapter about creating favorable conditions for effective professional relationships will apply equally well to members of the nonteaching staff.

The traditional tendency for people to attach proportionately greater importance and prestige to managerial and professional pursuits than to those involving manual labor has persisted in the minds of many even to the present day.[2] This prevailing notion makes it even more important for the principal to do everything possible to assign proper educational importance to nonteaching services. This can be done in such a way that improved relationships will result from the process. Some of the approaches which successful administrative leaders have found effective are as follows:

Let workers know that their services are essential to the effectiveness of the school program. Many school employees, such as custodial and maintenance workers, perform their services without having any intimate knowledge of or connection with actual school processes. Their work is often done in the boiler room, school kitchen, or in some other place somewhat remote from the main centers of educational activity. Even further detachment from the school program results because much of their work is done during the early morning or after-school hours.

[2] Clarence A. Weber, *Personnel Problems of School Administrators* (New York: McGraw-Hill Book Co., Inc., 1954), pp. 229-30.

All these conditions make it important to attach educational value to the efforts of such workers and to let them know that such values are recognized by others.

Workers should be told of the importance of their contributions, but it is also necessary to tell them *why* they are important. The principal and members of the teaching staff should use every suitable occasion for helping service personnel learn more about the school, the way it is organized, and how the program of instruction is supported by the various services of the school. The more thoroughly workers understand the relationships between the various activities of members of the staff, the more they will come to see their own roles in the light of a corporate effort rather than as isolated and meaningless activities for which they are paid a certain amount per day. These staff members, like all other normal people, like to feel that *their* efforts are *needed* and *wanted*.

Let workers know that their services are appreciated. It is not enough for members of the service staff to see the value of their efforts in the total school program, important as this knowledge is to their morale and motivation. It is desirable also that they have the feeling of personal appreciation by members of the professional staff—particularly the administrative leader. Such appreciation can be shown in numerous ways. Comments of gratefulness for the little extra efforts of staff members, compliments on the manner in which work is consistently done, little remembrances on special occasions, the inclusion of staff members in social affairs of the faculty and little memos of thanks for helping with particular projects, all help to convey to service personnel the appreciation others feel for their work.

The writer recalls a visit to an elementary school in the company of some visiting educators from another country. The school building was an old one but its floors and walls were unusually clean and attractive. During the course of the visit the principal sent for the school custodian in order that he might meet the school visitors. The comments made in his presence about the splendid care of the building, as well as the recognition being accorded him by the principal, brought a smile of satisfaction to the face of the custodian. Obviously such continuous treatment by that principal had been a definite factor in the competence of the custodian and in creating the great pride he felt in his work. This is a single example of many ways in which a person can be shown, as well as told, that he is appreciated. As a rule, any kind of favorable recognition contributes to this end; being slighted or ignored usually can be depended upon to have the opposite effect.

Let workers know when their services are improving. The old adage that "nothing succeeds like success itself" is as applicable to the nonteaching staff as to any group of people anywhere. Many workers of this group enter upon their duties without the benefit of any substantial prior training. It is only natural that they will experience some problems and difficulties in the early stages of their employment. As their competencies are developed on the job, it is highly desirable that they be informed of their successes. Often the principal can make a suggestion which, if followed through successfully, can be made the basis for complimenting the worker on his efforts. Sometimes a principal may suggest that the superintendent of schools send a note to members of the staff calling attention to the excellent manner in which they have developed into highly competent members of the educational team. However it is done in a particular situation, some means of letting staff members know of their progress on the job is essential to good morale and to further growth.

Ask the advice of nonteaching members of the staff about matters in their respective realms of competence. Staff workers should be recognized in planning changes and activities which affect them. If the cafeteria kitchen is to be remodeled, the lunchroom supervisor and her staff certainly should contribute their ideas to the solution of the problem. On occasions when it is necessary to rearrange the offices of the school, the school secretary may have some very practical and worth-while opinions as to how it might be done best. If the problem involving the health and safety of children is being considered, the school nurse should be one of the leading contributors to whatever solution emerges. Asking the advice of workers can result in two major benefits: (1) valuable ideas may thus be derived and (2) relationships with the nonteaching staff members are strengthened.

Capitalize on the initiative of staff members. Members of the school staff should be given as much responsibility and as much freedom from regulation as they can use successfully. Each staff member differs in his enthusiasm, his attitudes, and in his willingness and ability to accept responsibility. Certainly, many workers in the service areas need careful guidance and direction and should be given as much as they need for fulfilling their obligations in a satisfactory manner. Often, a staff member shows a spark of unusual enthusiasm for his work. He is obviously willing to expend extra effort and thought in the hope of performing his duties better. Such an individual should not have his spirit of service stifled by restrictions on his activities. It is better to allow such a person to use his own judgment as often as possible than to bind him to a set of rigid instructions. This approach whets his energies and keeps him from falling victim to boredom.

Be systematic in providing necessary instructions and guidance for nonteaching personnel. Workers need to know what is expected of them and how it is to be accomplished. This is particularly true of workers new to their positions. Necessary instructions and regulations should be as few and simple and as clear as possible. They should be consistent, so that routines can be readily established by workers as they engage in the performance of their respective duties. All members of the staff deserve to be notified well in advance of any changes in schedule which will affect them and their work. They need to have prior knowledge of special events and programs which require extra services from them. Such consideration on the part of the principal is no more than common courtesy to his associates, but a violation of this courtesy can bring havoc to existing relationships with members of the staff.

Show a sincere interest in the personal problems of members of the nonteaching staff. The day-to-day contacts which the principal naturally has with members of the teaching staff offer numerous opportunities for him to keep in touch with their fortunes and problems. It is relatively easy for him to keep informed about such things as the health of members of their families or their transportation problems in getting to school. There are numerous opportunities for him to express concern for them in the problems they face. Such is not the case with members of the nonteaching staff. As a general rule (with the exception of the school secretary, and possibly of the school nurse) opportunities for inquiries of this type are considerably fewer. It thus becomes easy for the principal to neglect to express interest in the personal problems which such workers sometimes face.

Financial stress, health problems, or domestic troubles definitely affect the work of a staff member. The principal should not be unduly inquisitive about such matters, but when given the opportunity, he can demonstrate a sympathetic understanding and perhaps even be able to offer needed advice. By so doing he will show the interest which contributes to friendly relations and, at the same time, indirectly contributes to the regaining of the efficiency of the worker on his job.

Matters brought to the attention of the principal by service workers should receive the same prompt consideration as those brought by anyone else. The satisfaction that comes with having such matters treated with dispatch and dignity lends added strength to the loyalty such a worker feels toward the school.

Provide effective means for the consideration of grievances and dissatisfactions of staff members. In spite of the very best efforts of the principal as an administrative leader, staff members will experience some dissatisfactions and conflicts in carrying on their work from day to day. A few such workers may be chronic complainers, but on many occasions workers are disturbed for very justifiable reasons. Whether the grievance is real or imagined, justified or unjustified, opportunity must be provided for its fair and prompt handling. If discussion about complaints is avoided or deferred unduly, such complaints tend to accumulate and become more acute as time passes. It is usually wise to bring such matters into the open as soon as possible, to establish the facts, and to deal with the problem in a just manner.

Considerable study and research concerning personnel relations have emanated from the industrial world. From these activities have come many practices and recommendations that well can be applied to members of a staff in a school. For example, Enion[3] has suggested three important measures for humanizing relationships with workers. They are:

1. Use the *why* approach rather than the *blame* approach when handling a personnel problem.
2. Learn to listen to workers.
3. Encourage worker participation in the business.

It is important that the tone of the conference between a disgruntled worker and the principal be kept as pleasant and as objective as possible. However, it is equally important for the worker to have a complete opportunity to get his grievance "off his chest."

Functions and Problems of Key Members of the Nonteaching Staff

Schools differ considerably in the nature and size of the staff they employ to operate the program of the school. These differences tend to be based on the size of the school, its financial resources, its geographical location, and the modern or traditional character of its program. As a result of these variations, it is impossible to describe a typical or standard school staff. In small schools the only nonteaching employee may be the custodian. At the other end of the scale will be found schools with a full complement of custodial workers, clerical workers, medical and health staff, and supervisors of the food and transportation services, as well as others. In this discussion will be included personnel whose services seem essential to a good elementary school. If a school is so small that these services cannot be provided justifiably, then it is hoped that such services might be provided on a part-time basis or through a sharing of personnel with other schools of similar size.

The following seem to be so important to the operation of the modern elementary school that they merit considerable emphasis: (1) the school

[3] Richard A. Enion, "Three Ways to Humanize Your Handling of Workers," *Personnel Journal*, XXXIII, No. 2 (June, 1954), p. 62.

secretary, (2) the custodial workers, (3) the cafeteria manager, (4) the school nurse, and (5) bus drivers.

The School Secretary.—The services rendered by the secretaries and clerks employed in the office of the modern elementary school are essential to the total functioning of the school. Some schools are of sufficient size and have adequate resources to justify a clerical staff of several members. This is a rare situation, however, and most schools employ no more than one or two clerical workers. Obviously this varies by schools, by communities, and by states.

The school secretary, by the very nature of her position, must have a complete knowledge of the school and its activities. She is not only the secretary to the principal, but she is a receptionist who continuously must be depended upon to issue all types of information promptly and accurately. At the same time she is usually the custodian of school records, the compiler of data for reports, and the person who most often is responsible for getting out notices, announcements, and bulletins to parents and citizens. All of these varied responsibilities, and many others not named, demand a person of skill, personality, and integrity. At the salaries which typically are paid for the services of school secretaries, it is difficult, if not impossible, to secure the high degree of competence actually required in such a position.

The fact that the secretary necessarily must know what is going on in the school, or what is being planned, sometimes creates a situation not completely conducive to good relationships with the professional staff. This is especially true in occasional instances when such knowledge, as well as proximity to administrative activities in the school, develops in the secretary an overabundance of officiousness and a condescending attitude toward teachers and other members of the staff.[4]

In recent years school secretaries have attempted to work toward professionalizing themselves and their work, and undoubtedly they are making considerable progress in this respect. Good secretaries are so necessary to the activities of the school that they are beginning to receive the credit they deserve, though their salaries are not always commensurate with those received by persons of equal competence in some other fields of work.

In an article by Luck,[5] six essentials for gaining professional status are given. They are:

1. Preliminary and in-service training that imparts skills and that is intelligent in character as well.

---

[4] See Weber, *op. cit.*, p. 230.

[5] Martha S. Luck, "Professional Training and Status for the Administrator's Secretary," *Nation's Schools*, XLVII, No. 4 (April, 1951), p. 41.

2. A motivation that shows a desire to serve others.
3. A willingness to improve continually even if it means sacrifices.
4. Living and working by the educational secretaries' code of ethics.
5. Helping recruit replacements for educational secretaries who retire or withdraw.
6. Working with the professional organizations for educational secretaries to set up standards for members of the group.

Certain traits and competencies are indispensable to the school secretary who would be an outstanding success in her work. Some of the most important are:

1. *A pleasing personality* with the ability to meet people in a friendly and cordial manner. Good grooming and suitable taste in dress and manner are important to the effectiveness of the secretary. Her manner must be businesslike but cordial.

2. *A liking for people* that adds zest to her work. Since most of the duties of the secretary bring her into contact with people, it is necessary for her to have a favorable attitude toward them.

3. *An interest in children* that gives meaning to the processes of the school and the office. While the secretary has no direct responsibility for children, she has innumerable daily associations with them which require sympathetic understanding and interest.

4. *An interest in education* which keeps her from becoming bored with her technical duties. The genuinely competent secretary usually likes to feel that she is an important cog in the educational machinery of the school and enjoys identifying herself with it.

5. *The technical skills* needed for handling necessary clerical tasks in a proficient manner. A secretary who is unreliable, incompetent, and inaccurate is more of a liability than an asset to the school.

6. *Keen judgment and tact* in dealing with the problems brought to the office and in handling information which passes through the office.

7. *Wholesome character* which equips her to be a suitable example of successful living.

As indicated in an earlier part of this chapter, the school secretary is one of the school's most valuable public relations agents if she performs her obligations well. Her telephone manner, the way in which she receives visitors, or her patience in dealing with a distraught parent or teacher all are opportunities for creating favorable attitudes toward the school. The in-service training and guidance of the secretary should seek to develop these competencies if they are not already possessed by her.

In his relationships with the school secretary, the principal should avoid extreme attitudes. He should not assume an aloof and overbusinesslike manner, for such an attitude disturbs the air of pleasant friendliness and informality that should prevail throughout the school. On the other hand, he should be equally careful to avoid turning office procedures and relationships into a continuous and merry round of conviviality. It is possible for the principal to maintain a friendly and pleasant atmosphere in the office without sacrificing the maintenance of a reasonable degree of dignity in his relationship with office personnel.

The wise administrator will delegate many of the office routines and duties to the secretary. He should exercise proper caution, however, about overburdening her with too many unpleasant chores or requiring her to handle professional personnel problems. He should also be sure of the dependability of the secretary before he entrusts to her care highly confidential data about personnel. Common sense is the best key to effective relations with the secretary. If she exercises good judgment in handling some office details and referring others more important to the principal and if he, in return, delegates office tasks judiciously, there will be little cause for conflict between them.

The School Custodian.—It is difficult to overestimate the importance of the work done by the custodial force of the modern elementary school. The quality of their work determines the whole school atmosphere and the standards of cleanliness in the building, and influences the whole program of the school in numerous indirect ways. In spite of the importance of the custodian as a member of the educational team of the school, the job has carried little prestige in many communities and typically has commanded a relatively low salary. In many schools the work of the custodian is spread over long hours; and he enjoys little security in terms of tenure, salary schedule, or retirement benefits.

All these conditions have combined to make the task of selecting a school custodian a difficult one. Many persons of the type needed for custodial duties in a school either have their own farms or businesses or can make better wages as factory workers or technicians of some sort. In spite of these conditions, many schools do manage to employ and retain capable custodians who perform their duties well and serve as genuine assets to the schools they serve.

Several steps can be taken to improve the services of the custodial staff and to establish conditions conducive to effective and pleasant relationships within the school. The first is related to the manner in which the custodian is selected. If he is to become truly a member of the staff of the school and is expected to cooperate in the general school effort, the staff of the school should have a voice in his selection. Although the principal sometimes is consulted in the choice of custodian for a particular school, the opportunity for other professional staff members to participate in the selective process is rather uncommon at the present time.

A second step that can be taken to improve the custodian's service to the school and his relationships with the members of the staff is to make him directly responsible to the principal of the school. As pointed out in an earlier discussion of staff relationships, the allegiance of the custodian is divided when he is administratively responsible to someone outside the school in which he works. Such an arrangement often breeds conflict and, what is probably worse, indifference to duty. In a recent study of one hundred fifty school systems in Indiana[6] it is interesting to note the variation among schools as to the fixing of responsibility of custodial help. Based on the one hundred fifty cases the following data were obtained:

1. The custodian is responsible to:

Building principal	42
Superintendent and principal	33
Superintendent or assistant	30
Superintendent of buildings and grounds	12
Principal and superintendent of buildings and grounds	3
Head custodian and others	10

2. The custodian's work is approved by:

Principal and superintendent	40
Superintendent	38
Principal	15
Principal and superintendent of buildings and grounds	11
Superintendent and board	5
Superintendent of buildings and grounds	4
Others	13

A third means for the improvement of custodial services is through provisions for the in-service training of school custodians. Aside from the guidance that can be furnished by the principal, there are other more systematized approaches to this problem of training. Supply houses now have available materials on the care of floors, proper cleaning procedures, and building maintenance. These can be brought to the attention of the custodian as one means of helping him acquire improved technical skills on the job. Some state agencies and institutions regularly conduct workshops and training programs for school custodians. The principal not only should encourage the custodian's participation in such workshops but should also make sure that, by attending, the custodian will increase

[6] John E. Baker, "Administration of Custodial Services in Indiana," *The Hoosier School Board Journal,* I, No. 2 (February, 1955); p. 8.

his own prestige. It seems altogether desirable for a school to assist with the expenses of custodians who are willing to improve their own efficiency through attendance at such workshops and conferences. If a school system is sufficiently large, of course, the wise procedure is to develop its own workshops for such training locally.

Perhaps the most important approach to the development of proper working relationships with the custodian is that of attempting to establish the principle of school-wide responsibility for good housekeeping in the building and a universal interest and pride in keeping the school environment clean and attractive. As pointed out in an earlier chapter, teachers and children should be sensitive to their obligations for maintaining reasonable standards of orderliness and cleanliness in the classroom and throughout the school plant. Children should not be permitted to clutter their rooms unnecessarily or throw paper towels on the restroom floors. Such thoughtless actions tend to develop poor habits in the children and, at the same time, place an undue burden on the custodial staff.

While many aspects of the custodian's responsibility were discussed in Chapter 7 in connection with the school plant, it may be desirable to reiterate some of the functions he may be expected to assume in the modern elementary school. The custodian should recognize his obligation to assist teachers by making simple repairs to window shades or furniture, by moving equipment and furnishings, or by helping with simple carpenter work involved in the preparations for a particular room project. However, he should be protected from becoming the victim of the occasional teacher who persistently demands his services in connection with minor housekeeping chores in the classroom. Such problems should be sensed and dealt with by the principal before they erupt into serious staff conflicts. Most schools of substantial size require requests for special services from the custodian to be submitted to the office in writing. This practice tends to make it possible for the custodian to distribute his efforts more equitably throughout the building.

Many schools of moderate size find it desirable to employ a woman as the second member of the custodial staff. While women should not be expected to assume the heavy maintenance work of the school, they can be valuable in its housekeeping activities.

Clear policies should be developed in the school governing the custodian's responsibilities for night meetings, games, and other occasions on which his presence is required. These policies also should provide for the amount of extra pay, if any, he is to receive and how, and by whom, it is to be paid. Such matters appear somewhat trivial but, unless a clear understanding is developed regarding them, they offer a fertile field for disgruntled attitudes and unfavorable working relationships.

Food Service Personnel.—The value and efficiency of the school lunch program rest on the workers most directly responsible for its operation. The task of directing or supervising the school cafeteria or lunchroom requires a happy combination of human relations, technical knowledge of food preparation and nutrition, and managerial ability. Fortunate are the staff and pupils of a school which boasts a cafeteria manager of such caliber.

Since the food service of a school is closely allied with the health and well-being of children, it is impossible to attach too much importance to the role of cafeteria personnel. The relations of cafeteria workers with the principal and teaching staff should be such that an understanding of the relationship of the food service to health instruction, the development of health habits, and other aspects of the total school program is fostered. Such workers should be encouraged to place as much emphasis as possible on the educational aspects of the lunch hour.

As pointed out in Chapter 7, the physical setting of the school lunch program is very important; providing a peaceful atmosphere where children can chat pleasantly and naturally is a primary need. In addition, opportunities for learning proper eating habits and for practicing simple rules of table etiquette should be included in the objectives to be achieved through children's participation in the lunch program.

Cafeteria workers, like custodians, often have little prior training for their work in the school. This places an obligation on the principal to encourage such workers to avail themselves of opportunities for extending their knowledge of the job to be done. Workshops in nutrition and food preparation are often held on the campuses of colleges, or are sponsored in various communities by either public or private agencies, and can be useful to cafeteria personnel in improving their skills and understanding.

Since cafeteria workers often come to work at mid-morning and leave before school dismissal in the afternoon, they usually do not acquire a feeling of close identity with the total program of the school. These workers, even more than many others in the school, need to have special attention devoted to means whereby they may be integrated with the corporate effort of the school. An occasional invitation to attend informal meetings of the staff or to discuss eating habits with children as a part of their study of health will encourage closer relationships. The resourceful administrative leader will discover many other avenues to the solution of this problem.

The School Nurse.—The school nurse invariably deals with matters important to children, teachers, and parents. The health of the child is of paramount importance to the parent, and the manner in which it is protected and preserved bears directly on the attitudes of both child and parent toward the school. In this connection, the writer recalls a school nurse who, though technically proficient in the performance of her duties, often brought children to tears through her brusque manner, disturbed parents with her communications couched in commanding terms, and occasionally created considerable anxiety on the part of teachers and administrator in the school. Needless to say, such a person is a liability to the development of wholesome relations within the school and between the school and community. Fortunately, such an example is the exception rather than the rule. In general, school nurses render vital service in a cheerful and willing manner and enjoy pleasant relations with children, teachers, and parents.

The relationship between the principal and the school nurse is somewhat different from those existing with custodial or cafeteria workers. The school nurse is a professionally trained person with highly specialized knowledge which the principal himself may not be expected to possess. Therefore, he must rely on her judgment explicitly in problems concerning health in the school. While the nurse should be administratively responsible to him while she works in the local building, she has other professional loyalties and obligations to such persons as the director of health services, the school physician, and the community. The principal, therefore, should attempt to develop cordial working relations but should refrain from imposing restrictions on the activities of the nurse which might inhibit her professional effectiveness.

The location of the school nurse should be known to the principal and to the school secretary throughout the school day. In cases of injury or illness, the nurse should be consulted if at all possible before further steps are taken unless, of course, by so doing needed medical attention is unduly delayed.

The principal should encourage the school nurse to work closely with community health agencies and with local doctors and dentists in providing the best possible health care for children of the school. Her services should be used in an advisory manner in purchasing health equipment and facilities. She should be encouraged also to participate in the program of health instruction in the school in all appropriate ways.

A clear understanding should exist between the school nurse and teachers in regard to the processes through which children with symptoms of disease are to be excluded from the classroom as well as the manner in which they are subsequently to be readmitted. Inconsistencies in these practices often lead to unnecessary staff conflicts.

School Bus Drivers.—The safety of children is in the hands of the school bus driver twice daily throughout the school year. It is, therefore, vitally important that such drivers be selected with care. They need to be skilled bus operators with the expert knowledge necessary for driving on various types of roads and under various kinds of weather conditions. They should have good health and should be morally above reproach in every respect. They must be responsible, dependable, and punctual. Even more important, perhaps, is that they should possess an inherent interest in children and have sufficient knowledge of children to know what to expect from them.

The bus driver is probably the most "detached" member of the service staff of the school. His duties are performed before school opens in the morning and again after the close of school in the afternoon. He has few opportunities for actual contacts with the daily processes of the school.

The principal and teachers should make an effort to include the bus driver in a reasonable number of school activities. He should be invited to such events as the holiday parties of the total school staff and should be encouraged to participate in the programs and activities of the P.T.A. or other school-community groups. His knowledge can be used in the development of instructional units on safety or in other types of school activities.

If effective working relations are to be maintained with bus drivers, they must understand clearly just what their responsibilities are in connection with the disciplining of children while they are on the bus. Clear policies in this respect should be developed by the school, and these policies should be understood by children, parents, and members of the school staff.

Other Nonteaching Personnel.—The total effectiveness of the school is enhanced by contributions of many persons not mentioned in the preceding paragraphs. The school doctor, dentist, and dental hygienist assist with the maintenance of children's health in a vital way; and members of the school staff should work with them in a cooperative and mutually beneficial manner.

The school librarian is important to the school's program of instruction. Library personnel, though not always certificated as teachers, actually perform a teaching function and should be considered as such in terms of the relationships they develop and enjoy with other members of the staff; guidance workers and school psychologists often render valuable special service to children and assist teachers in working out solutions to existing problems of individual children.

All these people play integral and strategic parts in the truly modern elementary school. The principal's realization of the importance of these services is best demonstrated by the quality of relationships he seeks to develop with and among the various members of the school team.

Action Suggestions for the Principal

1. Look for the best in workers and capitalize on their strengths.
2. Strive to demonstrate the kind of attitudes desired in others.
3. Define responsibilities clearly.
4. Try to develop with the staff an understanding of the goals of the school.
5. Avoid statements or comments that contribute to the insecurity of staff members.
6. Give immediate recognition to workers who make unique contributions.
7. Create a school environment that emphasizes the positive.
8. Work to improve communication with nonteaching members of the staff.
9. Provide frequent opportunities for including nonteaching staff members in school affairs.
10. Keep workers informed of school-wide policies or plans.
11. Be cautious about making quick promises and be sure to keep the ones that are made.
12. Handle personal problems and requests promptly.
13. Avoid over-regulation of workers.
14. Provide opportunities for nonteaching staff members to submit ideas for school improvement.
15. Give the ideas of workers a fair hearing.
16. Emphasize by example a high level of personal and professional ethics.
17. Assume responsibility for helping workers improve through in-service opportunities.
18. Evaluate the work of the nonteaching staff in terms of the educational purposes their activities serve.
19. Give nonteaching workers a sense of importance in the total school program.
20. Point out immediately areas of improvement achieved by workers.
21. Ask the advice of members of the service staff occasionally on problems related to their fields of activity.
22. Show a sympathetic interest in the personal problems of staff members.
23. Help each staff member feel he is a member of the educational team.

SELECTED REFERENCES FOR EXTENDED READING

BAKER, JOHN E. "Administration of Custodial Services in Indiana," *The Hoosier School Board Journal,* I, No. 2 (February, 1955).

ELSBREE, WILLARD S., and MCNALLY, HAROLD J. *Elementary School Administration and Supervision.* New York: American Book Co., 1951, chaps. 16 and 20.

ELSBREE, WILLARD S., and REUTTER, E. EDMUND, JR. *Staff Personnel in the Public Schools.* New York: Prentice-Hall, Inc., 1954.

ENION, RICHARD. "Three Ways to Humanize Your Handling of Workers," *Personnel Journal,* XXXIII, No. 2 (June, 1954).

KYTE, GEORGE C. *The Principal at Work.* Boston: Ginn & Co., 1952, chap. 26.

LUCK, MARTHA S. "Professional Training and Status for the Administrator's Secretary," *Nation's Schools,* XLVII, No. 4 (April, 1951).

REAVIS, WILLIAM C., PIERCE, PAUL, STULLKEN, EDWARD H., and SMITH, BERTRAND L. *Administering the Elementary School.* New York: Prentice-Hall, Inc., 1953, chap. 17.

SHANE, HAROLD G., and YAUCH, WILBUR A. *Creative School Administration.* New York: Henry Holt & Co., 1954, chap. 14.

VILES, N. E. *The School Janitor.* Nashville: George Peabody College for Teachers, 1939.

WALTERS, J. E. *Personnel Relations.* New York: The Ronald Press Co., 1945.

WEBER, CLARENCE A. *Personnel Problems of School Administrators.* New York: McGraw-Hill Book Co., Inc., 1954, chap. 13.

WILES, KIMBALL. *Supervision for Better Schools.* New York: Prentice-Hall, Inc., 1950.

YAUCH, WILBUR A. *Improving Human Relations in School Administration.* New York: Harper & Bros., 1949.

Chapter 18

IMPROVING SCHOOL-COMMUNITY RELATIONSHIPS

An interested community is the richest laboratory a school can have

The principal of a surburban school of a metropolitan community sat at his desk one morning as a middle-aged woman and two boys—ages five and eight—were shown into the office. The woman was plainly dressed, though neat in appearance, and obviously uneducated. After a welcome to the school by the principal came a brief conversation about the weather. Then the woman began a discussion of the older child by relating a saga of educational disappointment. The boy had attended several different schools and usually became involved in behavior difficulties sufficiently serious to bring forth a recommendation that he be taken from school and referred to a "correctional" institution. Even though the pattern of the boy's lack of adjustment had been repeated in a number of schools, this unlearned mother was still seeking a school where he might succeed. That was the purpose of her present visit to the principal's office. In her own words her hope was "to find a school that would learn him to be a good boy."

This incident from the earlier professional life of the writer has flashed across his mind many times over the years as he has developed an appreciation of the faith accorded public education and the great responsibility which such faith places on the educator. It is another instance, among many, that suggests that public education is one of humanity's greatest hopes and, therefore, one of its strongest obligations to current and future generations.

The relationship of education to society has brought about an increasing awareness of the interdependence of the school and the community it serves. As American public elementary schools in particular have become the "schools for all the children of all the people," this recognition of the necessity for school-community interaction has gradually developed.

The modern educator recognizes that the school is only one of the educational agencies which affect the lives of children and youth. Seven days a week, community forces outside the school are leaving their impressions on the attitudes and behavior of these individuals. Many of these influences fortunately are positive in nature; others are not so salutary from an educational standpoint. The modern school must capitalize on opportunities for utilizing the constructive resources of community life to supplement its own program of organized learning experiences. Only in this manner can the truly functional nature of education be established and the best possible education be provided.

Neither educators nor laymen need to be apologetic, or even on the defensive, with respect to the quality of the educational program that has been developed in the better elementary schools of America. Though they do not approach perfection by any means, there is sufficient evidence to indicate that public schools have achieved commendable, if not almost miraculous, results in many areas of learning. Perhaps laymen and educators should feel some shame at the amount of support given to education as compared with the nation's expenditures for other less vital activities. Undoubtedly, also, only a limited amount of pride is justified in the extent to which integration of educational effort has been achieved in most communities.

This chapter sets forth certain attitudes toward school-community relations and explores and suggests some approaches to the implementation of cooperation. The discussions which follow are organized around the following areas of emphasis: (1) some basic principles underlying effective school-community relations, (2) stages of growth in school-community relations, (3) improving relations with parents, (4) improving interpretation of the school program, and (5) meeting criticisms of the school.

Principles Underlying Effective School-Community Relations

The administrative leader who expects to work effectively with the staff of the elementary school in promoting profitable working relations with the community must be aware of the basic considerations upon which such relations are built; some of them are discussed in the following paragraphs.

1. *Effective school-community relations are based on a mutual recognition of the importance and purposes of the school program.* The first element in effective school-community relations is a mutual faith in education as an instrument for human improvement. Parents and other citizens who see no real need for education cannot be easily enlisted as supporters of the school. Even greater obstacles to community cooperation in educational matters are created by the occasional teacher or principal who inwardly suspects that educational processes are not very

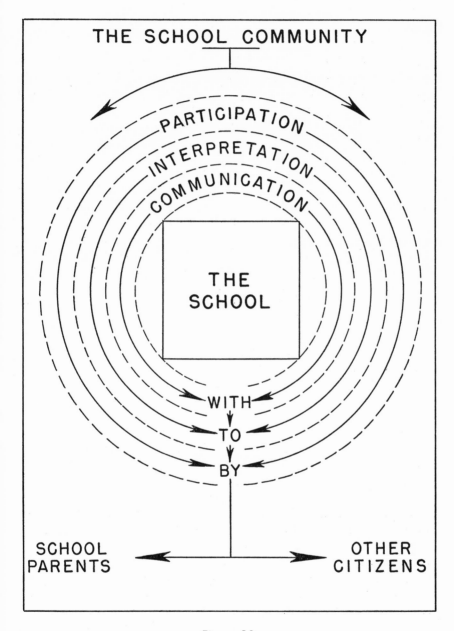

Figure 18

Steps Toward Effective School-Community Relations

effective after all. Professional educators and laymen alike must believe in the school if they are to help it accomplish its broadest and most noble purposes.

2. *Effective school-community relations depend upon the concept of partnership in education.* Before useful working relations can be established between the professional staff of the school and the individuals and agencies of the community, there must be a common recognition that education is a continuous process extending into many phases of home and community life. The assumption that the school is an isolated agency, with sole responsibility for what children learn, seriously impairs the chances for anything more than nominal contacts between the home and the school. The home and the school, as well as other constructive agencies in the community, must each supplement and reinforce the efforts of the other if optimum growth is to be achieved for the children who attend school.

3. *The common denominator of effective school-community relations is the child.* The best test of the quality of the school-community relations in any particular situation is their effect on children. Parents and citizens, though serving society as well, support schools for the benefit of children; teachers teach with the hope of satisfaction in helping children. In the final analysis, the meeting ground of all educational effort is the welfare of the child. This observation emphasizes the necessity of interpreting school activities in terms of what they are expected to do for children and the desirability of soliciting support for schools in terms of the benefits that can be provided for children as a result of adequate support. Administrators and teachers should remember always that, in the mind of each parent, the one thing that is most important in the whole school operation is the child of that parent. Consideration for children, therefore, is the key to opportunities for teachers and laymen to work together for better education.

4. *Effective school-community relations require clear and continuous communication.* People who cannot *talk* together about education cannot expect to *work* together in its behalf. If school personnel and citizens of the community are to engage in a cooperative effort on behalf of the school, they must be able to communicate and exchange ideas. Professional educators, like members of other professions, have developed technical terminology for use in communicating among themselves. This has been a by-product of the professionalizing of education and, as such, is a commendable development. Care must be exercised, however, to prevent this professional language from developing into a verbal wall which tends to hinder easy communication and thus to isolate the school from the community. This precaution should apply both for

written communications issued from the school and for oral communication between the school and the public.

5. *Effective school-community relations are achieved best through positive approaches.* Positive thinking tends to affect the behavior of the person so thinking, and to influence those with whom he comes in contact. Human nature is such that people seem to be attracted to those things which affect them favorably and, conversely, to avoid those things with an unpleasant effect. As mentioned earlier, the language of the teacher can be a potent factor in his relations with parents. Such words as "failure," "lazy," and "dumb" deter rather than nurture the development of good working relations with parents. On the other hand, a skillful teacher can use words to very great advantage in stimulating the efforts of children and in enlisting the respect and support of parents.

6. *Effective school-community relations are built on common understanding.* It is not enough to expect citizens to have a blind faith in education, nor should the professional staff of a school congratulate themselves for having the passive approval of the community with regard to the school program. Citizens generally, and parents in particular, need to learn more about the *processes* of the school as well as its *purposes.* This understanding is developed best through varied approaches. School publicity through announcements, bulletins, and newspapers is useful, but cannot serve as the sole means for interpreting the school program. There must be opportunities, not only to *hear about the school,* but to *see it in operation* and to *participate in its processes.* Educators who subscribe to the value of experience in learning should find little difficulty in justifying parent participation in developing an understanding of the school program.

7. *Effective school-community relations emerge from a belief in the democratic process.* Faith in the ability of each citizen to contribute in some manner to the shaping of his own destiny and to the improvement of society is a tenet of the American way of life. Education, as one of the concrete instruments of society for its own improvement, should also reflect such faith. School administrators who feel that only professional personnel can make valuable contributions to the educational process have little hope of generating much community enthusiasm for the school program. In turn, this lack of enthusiasm is often reflected in the lack of financial support for the school.

Some Stages of Growth in School-Community Relations

Varying degrees of school-community relations in some form have been an integral part of the development of elementary education in the

United States. Some of the earlier schools were held on plantations or, as in the case of the "dame" schools, in the household of the teacher. For many years teachers in rural schools were often "boarded around" at different homes in the community. In many sections of the country, the custom of the teacher visiting overnight in the homes of the children attending school has persisted to the present generation. School programs, box suppers, pie suppers, and ice cream "socials" are types of community entertainment and fund-raising activities that have commonly been held in schools, particularly in the rural areas.

In spite of the historical existence of so many occasions for the mingling of teachers and parents, these relationships, for the most part, have been social, and have not been extended to cooperative educational endeavors. Indeed, teachers, though not often enjoying any marked degree of financial or social prestige, historically have been held in awe by parents. It seems only fair to state also that teachers too frequently have appeared to cherish their detachment from parents in the educational process.

Notwithstanding these conditions, the emergence of a general professional consciousness of the necessity for and the educational possibilities of effective school-community relations has been a modern development. Six stages of this development, whether considered compositely or in terms of a particular school, seem noteworthy. They are: (1) isolation, (2) information, (3) communication, (4) interpretation, (5) participation, and (6) integration.

Isolation.—Some schools appear to be operated on the assumption that they have a unique function which cannot be realized if they are disturbed by forces outside the walls of the school. Considerable justification for this point of view could be mustered if, and when, education is considered a special privilege rather than a common right. It is neither a sound nor a logical attitude for the educator who is committed to the democratic processes of our society. The modern elementary school with its rich and varied program of learning experiences, its use of community resources, and its emphasis on living can never be developed through a devotion to professional isolationism.

Information.—The first concrete step in the direction of developing useful contacts between home and school has been the establishment of means for issuing information about the school and its activities. This effort has evolved largely around school publicity. These attempts to furnish information to parents and other citizens of the community have taken many forms, ranging from informal notes to radio and television programs. The chief limitation of this concept of public relations is that it is often considered to be, or becomes, a one-way process from school to home.

Communication.—A step beyond the mere issuance of school publicity is communication. This concept implies a two-way process through which useful ideas can be exchanged in an effective manner. It further involves the presence of certain common denominators of understanding and experience, so that the basis for accurate transmission of ideas can be established. Effective communication cannot be limited to verbal forms, but must include some opportunity for interaction in other ways.

Interpretation.—Good public relations require even more than the effective interchange of information and ideas. Communication between teachers and parents, or between school and community, must be interpreted in the light of the technical aspects of education, the declared purposes of the school, changing methods, and local community emphasis. Modern schools carry on a continuous search for effective ways of explaining the "why" of the school and its methods as well as the "what," to make possible sufficient understanding to assure intelligent cooperation and reasonable singleness of purpose.

Participation.—This volume is replete with suggestions regarding the role and importance of experience in learning. Here it should be emphasized that experience is fully as significant in developing a true understanding of the school program among parents as it is in its connection with the learning of children in the classroom. Resourceful school leaders have discovered suitable means whereby parents can participate constructively in the education of their children. This is not to suggest that they should assume the professional role of teachers; it does mean that they very profitably can participate in the formulation of general school policies, provide supplementary resources for learning in the home, and assist with nontechnical tasks in the school. Without some active sharing in the school enterprise, there is little likelihood of developing a functional kind of interest among parents and citizens in regard to the program of the school.

Integration.—A great many elementary schools have given considerable attention to the development of effective means of communication with lay members of the community, with very favorable results. Better schools also have found ways for parents and other citizens to participate at some stage in the school program. The greatest challenge to leadership in the field of school-community relations is that of achieving a workable integration of the efforts of all the people and agencies who can, and should, contribute to the school program. This is not easy but some suggestions for its accomplishment will be made later in this chapter.

IMPROVING RELATIONSHIPS WITH PARENTS

Good working relations between the school and the home do not just happen; they are earned. In this process, school personnel are largely responsible for the development of conditions which foster favorable relations with parents. Two types of awareness in teachers and administrators are prerequisite to any intelligent approach to an improvement of relations with the home: (1) they must remember at all times that most parents love their children very much, and (2) they must recognize the necessity of analyzing the ways in which parents form their impressions of the school.

Because parents do love their children, they applaud their successes and good fortune and they suffer with them in their misfortunes. Parents identify themselves closely with their children. They suffer at physical pain their children undergo, and unkind words about their children cut deeply into their own sensitivities. To carry the matter a step further, persons who bring happiness to children are likely to be heroes in the minds of parents; those who make them unhappy are not likely to engender much parental affection. Parents are not always able to remain objective in matters involving their children and frequently are inclined to become somewhat overemotional about their problems. It is imperative that school personnel recognize this close bond of affection between parents and children and capitalize on it, wherever possible, for the strengthening of school-home ties.

Parents get their impressions of the school in several different ways.[1] Some of the most notable of these are: (1) from their own experiences in school, (2) from their personal associations with school personnel, (3) from their children, (4) from casual observations of school activities, and (5) from written communications from the school. If these channels of good or ill will are recognized by school personnel and used effectively, favorable relations should develop. Other specific ways of creating the good will of parents follow:

Do thoughtful things for children. The regular day-to-day experiences of children are potent factors in public relations. When they succeed or do unusually interesting things at school, they are likely to carry their exuberance home with them; by the same token, unpleasant happenings at school tend to have the opposite effect. Unusually important

[1] See James L. Hymes, Jr., *Effective Home-School Relations* (New York: Prentice-Hall, Inc., 1953).

in the establishment of favorable relations with parents are the little personal favors which teachers perform for children. A demonstrated interest in a child's family or hobby, or special care given to a child when he becomes ill or is injured, can have a very marked effect on the feelings of a parent toward the school.

Maintain clear and positive channels of communication with parents. An effort should be made to remove any existing barriers to easy communication between parents and school personnel. Face-to-face conferences should be friendly and informal. Teachers often find it desirable to have conferences with parents over a cup of tea or coffee if facilities and time permit.

Written communications should be friendly, simple, clear, and to the point. Long bulletins and duplicated letters are so impersonal that they sometimes do not get the attention expected.

Even more important than the form of written communications is the tone they convey. Words used in notes to parents or in comments which are a part of pupil progress reports should be selected carefully. Some words seem to convey the flavor of good will; others, by their very nature, inhibit good relations. In a recent publication of the National School Public Relations Association[2] the varying shades of meaning that can be conveyed through the choice of words are illustrated in reports from schools concerned about the problem. They follow:

Telling Stories—About Us

When narrative report cards are used classroom teachers have to be especially careful. The written word, if ill-chosen, can build up in a minute more resentment than years of pleasant experiences with schools can eradicate.

A principal of a school using narrative report cards reads every card before it is issued. "I have to," she says, "because of the dangers that lie in emotionally colored words and expressions."

If she finds a poorly phrased thought, she consults the classroom teacher so that together they can agree upon words telling the same story but not provoking parental ire.

For example, when a teacher reported that "Yesterday John *stole* a book from the library," she suggested that the sentence read, "Yesterday John took a book from the library without the librarian's permission."

The sentence, "John is *lazy* and is failing because of his laziness," was changed to "John puts forth no effort and, therefore, cannot expect to earn a passing grade."

Other examples were: "John is a *liar*," which was changed to "When involved in trouble, John often fails to tell the truth"; and "John is a *vicious* boy and is not *fit* to associate with good boys," changed to "John has many bad

2 National School Public Relations Association, *It Starts in the Classroom* (Washington, D. C.: National Education Association, 1951), pp. 36–38.

habits which make the boys with whom he should associate avoid his company."

"I don't know why we often are so blunt with parents," declared that principal. "As educated people we ought to be outstandingly skilled at wording reports so as to encourage objective and dispassionate thinking, rather than to inspire the desire for retaliation."

Words Can Hurt—Us

In another school, because of their experience, the faculty agreed that the following words, among others, should be banned from their oral and written vocabularies in talking to and about children:

mean	worthless	dumbbell
lie	idiot	nuisance
stupid	cowardly	moron
dirty	bully	cheat
smells	dishonest	dishonorable
delinquent	dumb	thief

Narrative reports also have other dangers such as poor sentence construction, misspellings, and incorrect punctuation. A literate enemy of the school in some instances can almost crucify teachers on the evidence of their own written communications.

Words Can Help—Us

Well-written notes to parents can secure parent-teacher cooperation and create goodwill toward the school. Here are some supplementary notes to report cards which parents have appreciated. One teacher wrote:

Carl has been improving steadily in his work. He works hard and aims to please. It is a pleasure to work with him.

Mother's answer:

I'm so happy Carl is doing so much better in school. He seems to be much more interested. Thank you so much.

And another teacher wrote:

Bonnie has improved very much in reading. Please encourage her to read a lot at home so that she will keep on improving. Thank you for your fine cooperation.

Encourage parents to observe school activities. Too often the visits of parents to school are limited to such occasions as the opening day of school and the Christmas program staged by the boys and girls. These visits, of course, should not have their importance belittled; but the opportunities for parents to visit the school should extend far beyond these particular events. If an understanding of the school program is to be encouraged, there must be opportunities for parents to observe the regular day-to-day activities of the school.

One very skillful teacher with whom the writer was once associated invited small groups of parents to visit the classroom for an afternoon each month. After the visit, simple refreshments were served and an opportunity was afforded for each parent to discuss the progress of his own child with the teacher. While such group visits have very definite value, they cannot replace a standing welcome to parents to visit the classroom at times most convenient for them.

Invite the active participation of parents in the education of their children. The active participation of parents in the achievement of the educational purposes of the school can be provided at three points: (1) in the policy-forming bodies of the school, (2) in the nonteaching services, and (3) by home supplementing of the program of instruction.

School councils should always include representatives from parent groups in their membership. Curriculum study groups offer possibilities for the participation of parents. School questionnaires are sometimes sent to parents in order to get their opinions about school processes. However it is done, some useful form of parent participation in the development of school policy is desirable and highly conducive to the development of a genuine understanding of the school program.

There are many ways in which parents can assist with activities right in the school. Teachers are usually glad to have parents help with field trips and educational excursions, and parents often gain a broader understanding of the modern curriculum by doing so. They also can assist with such activities as the cataloging of new library books, staging special programs and projects, and assisting with clerical duties. These services, though seemingly menial, can do much to give parents a feeling of belongingness in their connection with the school.

Research has indicated that one of the greatest factors in the development of emotional stability and good mental health in children is the consistency of their associations with their elders. For this reason, it becomes doubly important for the school and home to work together in shaping and executing the learning experiences of children. Schools often issue bulletins[3] in which they suggest appropriate ways in which parents may reinforce and supplement the learning of children in school. One good example of such a bulletin lists the following for the consideration of parents:

How May Parents Help in the Broad School Program?

There are many ways in which you as a parent may help in the school program. It is necessary that you share with the school the responsibility of your child's total development.

You may help the school in the physical development of your child if you will:

[3] Mary Browning and Associates, *Your Child Starts to School in Louisville* (Louisville: Louisville Public Schools, 1949), pp. 23-24.

1. Remember the child who is happy and successful in his work is usually the well child.

2. See that the child has a physical examination before he enters school.

3. Follow the physical examination with the necessary corrective treatment before the opening of school: dental work, new glasses, tonsillectomy.

4. Give immunizations before school begins in order that any reaction may not cause absence.

5. See that your child has nourishing and well-balanced meals, proper habits of elimination, proper outdoor exercise, and enough rest and sleep.

6. See that your child is not over-stimulated by engaging in too many activities, such as music and dancing lessons, if they crowd out afternoon rest and play during the school term.

7. Teach and practice simple safety rules. The best method of teaching safety is by example. Know the safest and best route to school.

8. Examine your child each morning and keep him home if he shows signs of illness.

You may help the school secure the social development of your child if you will:

1. Build a happy attitude toward his going to school and toward the school, the teachers, and the things he will do at school. It is a mistake to frighten your child with threats of what will happen to him when he goes to school and what the teacher will do.

2. Provide opportunities for your child to know, play with, and share with children of his own age, and to meet and associate with adults other than those of his own family. These broadening experiences will help the child to fit more readily and happily into the school group.

3. Teach personal and social attitudes and habits which will help your child be more independent and happy in the group. These include: dressing and undressing himself, caring for his own clothing, caring for himself in the toilet, eating correctly, handling and putting away his own materials, responding promptly and courteously to directions, being courteous and considerate of others, speaking distinctly.

4. Encourage and teach by example love, appreciation, and respect for others.

You may help the school promote the desirable emotional development of your child if you will:

1. Give your child a home where he feels love, kindness, security, and understanding. Give him a home where disappointments and sorrows are faced with courage and where unnecessary fears and threats are avoided.

2. Help your child to meet situations calmly and fearlessly.

3. Help your child to learn to solve his own problems by helping himself or by cooperating with others who can help him. Teach him that crying will not solve anything.

4. Check carefully the radio programs your child hears and the movies he sees. Remember they must not be too exciting or too frightening. Procure from the Radio Council their monthly listings.

5. Share with your child's teacher any happy or unhappy experiences in the home which may affect him emotionally.

You may help the school determine the quality of your child's intellectual development if you will:

1. Have confidence in your child's teacher. Remember that she has spent years in securing the necessary professional training to teach your child just as your physician has spent years in preparing to help your child to develop physically. She is an expert in the most difficult and technical of all professions. Consult her and respect her judgment as to what is best for your child, and cooperate.

2. Talk with your child, using the correct names for things. For example, a train is not a choo-choo; a cow is not a moo-cow; a dog is not a bow-wow.

3. Listen to what your child has to say, train him to listen well, and to express his ideas clearly.

4. Try to answer all good questions intelligently. If you do not know the right answer have the courage to say, "I do not know the answer, but together we will find it."

5. Encourage your child to use every available means, including his five senses, as well as his privilege of asking others who may know.

6. Arouse intellectual curiosity by means of pictures, books, and actual experiences.

7. Give many experiences through trips, such as seeing rivers, boats, bridges, trains, buses, airports, pet shops, animals, and farms. Discuss the experiences with your child, thus making him alert, observant, and interested in talking about the things he has seen and heard.

8. Tell and read to your child well-selected stories. If you wish, the teacher or the librarian will help in the selection. Use the Parents' Service at Main Library.

9. Look at and discuss pictures with your child.

10. Send to school anything that may interest the class, such as flowers, leaves, nuts, seeds, unusual rocks, shells, cocoons, frogs, or tadpoles.

11. Offer to visit the classroom and share with the children any knowledge or experience or curios that may help with a class project.

12. Teach your child the alphabet if you wish, but teach it in an informal and incidental manner, through the use of nested blocks, alphabet songs, and the practice of answering children's questions about the alphabet.

Give parents a significant role in the development and functioning of the processes used for reporting the progress of children in school. One of the points at which relations with the home are strained is the reporting of pupil progress, and here the school has at least three obligations. They are: (1) to help parents understand some of the trends in evaluation and reporting of pupil progress and their underlying reasoning, (2) to seek and use the contributions of parents in the development of effective means for reporting, and (3) to use the most effective means possible for conveying important information about the progress of the child.

In relation to the first of these obligations, some trends that can be noted are:

1. The use of informal letters from the teacher to replace or supplement the report card.
2. The use of children's own evaluations and samples of their work.
3. The use of the teacher-parent conference.
4. The changing nature of report cards and written reports with respect to:
    a) Greater use of descriptive statements rather than symbols to indicate extent and nature of growth.
    b) Tendency toward evaluating a child's growth in terms of his individual ability and resources.
    c) The inclusion of all aspects of child growth rather than academic progress alone.
    d) Supplementation of symbols, when used, by comments by the teacher.

Actually, the teacher is the person least affected by the nature of the process used for reporting pupil progress. It is true that some instruments used for this purpose are more time-consuming than others, but, even so, the child and the parent are the persons for whom reports are designed. This being true, it is only logical to assume that parents should have some voice in determining the nature of these reports.

Some schools have employed many types of individual devices to supplement their regular system of reporting to parents, some of which seem to have a very favorable effect on parents. A survey of one school revealed a whole series of devices used by individual teachers for this purpose.[4] Some of the favorite techniques mentioned were:

1. Telephone calls, especially for comment.
2. Office hour appointments at night for the special convenience of fathers.
3. Photographs of individual children in action, sent on the pupils' birthdays to parents with the compliments of the teacher.
4. Letters of congratulation on pupil progress.
5. Test papers sent home to parents, with written teacher commendation.
6. Invitations to individual parents to come and see their children performing effectively in unit summarization or some phase of instruction.
7. News articles of pupil achievement.

[4] National School Public Relations Association, *It Starts in the Classroom, op. cit.,* p. 41.

8. Mimeographed compilations of pupil poetry and composition work.
9. "Before and after" exercises sent to homes to show pupil improvement.
10. Individual letters written by pupils explaining what they have learned.
11. A monthly newsletter written by individual teachers interpreting work and progress, filled with pupils' names.

Earn a reputation for understanding. One of the quickest ways a principal or teacher can make a friend of a parent is to demonstrate sympathy and understanding in the little crises that occur in the life of the child from day to day. The child may forget his lunch money, or the deadline for the purchase of the required gym shoes may fall before payday, or illness in the family may upset the child's whole routine, leaving no time for homework. Such occasions as these afford school personnel the opportunity to demonstrate that they are human and sympathetic. Such seemingly trivial things may loom large in the life of the child, and the help given him in meeting such situations is the stuff of which cordial relations are made.

Improving Community Interpretation of the Schools

The interaction of community elements is so essential to the development of a good, modern school program that it cannot be left to chance and hope. Most competent administrative leaders actively engage in the continuous study of ways to improve this interaction for the welfare of the school and the community. The manner of interpretation of the program of the schools to the public clearly affects this interaction. Some of the more successful means for effective interpretation are discussed briefly in the following paragraphs.

Direct Publicity.—Many larger elementary schools issue their own newspapers or have a page or more allocated for school news in the local newspaper. Smaller schools often issue small duplicated newssheets and bulletins. Classroom groups of children frequently send a "special newspaper" home to their parents as a part of their work in the language arts. Varied means for keeping a flow of interesting news going into the community are essential elements of a program of interpretation.

Sometimes handbooks and reports sent out from the central office are useful in suggesting ways in which citizens of the community may become better informed about their schools. One such report[5] lists ten ways citizens can help their schools. They are:

[5] Harold S. Vincent and Associates, *Growing in Milwaukee: Annual Report of the Superintendent of Schools* (Milwaukee: Board of Education, 1953).

1. Get to know them. Get to know personally some members of the school staff. Pay an occasional visit to your neighborhood school.
2. Join the P.T.A. and take an active part.
3. Follow school business as reported in the press, in periodicals, and over the air.
4. Attend a school board meeting. Follow the proceedings of the board.
5. After you have carefully informed yourselves on the issues involved, be sure to vote on school board matters.
6. You have fine schools—schools of which to be proud. Have faith in them, and give them your wholehearted support.
7. Take advantage of opportunities such as lay meetings, conferences, open house, workshops to gain knowledge of what your schools are trying to do, and by what methods.
8. Keep informed about school practices. Knowledge of the facts will help you understand what your schools are trying to do.
9. Help children learn to respect schools. Teach them that school is their most important business.
10. Understand and stress the importance of good schools and much schooling to happy, successful personal living, and to the progress and safety of the American way of life.

Radio and television programs have come into prominence in recent years as additional media, along with pictures and films depicting school life, which are effective in revealing and explaining important aspects of the school program.

School Activities.—Parents participate in many school activities which bring them into contact with school personnel and facilities. Health round-ups, school festivals, concerts, holiday programs, and athletic games are but few of the events which bring parents to the school. Parents and other laymen often form rather definite opinions about the school as a result of these contacts. It is important that they be handled in such a manner as to create a favorable impression of the school.

Social affairs including both parents and teachers are valuable in destroying the barriers that sometimes exist between the two groups. Family affairs at which both parents and children come to school tend to develop good relations between family and school.

Organized Groups.—Such organizations as the Parent Teacher Association, Mothers' Club, and Fathers' Club can contribute to the process of interpreting the school to the community. In addition, committees of citizens and school personnel working on school or community problems related to children can be useful for creating common understandings about important aspects of education.

Administrative leaders in a number of modern elementary schools have encouraged the formation of School Councils. Such a council is usually composed of teaching and nonteaching personnel, parents, health officials, welfare workers, and other representatives of important community agencies and groups. Such a council can be very helpful as an advisory group and can, at the same time, serve as a medium through which the school may be reliably interpreted to the community as a whole.

Meeting Criticisms of the School

Criticisms of the school can be either blessings or deadly instruments of destruction, depending upon their nature and the motives and power of those who initiate and perpetuate them. At the mid-point of the twentieth century two facts stand out: (1) schools are faced with some of the greatest problems in their history, shortages of teachers and lack of building and classroom facilities, and (2) greater interest in education is being shown by the public. The latter condition brings the hope that greater understanding will be developed among the nation's citizens, with the result that more adequate support for education will be forthcoming. Unfortunately, this increased interest in education is not all on the positive side. Recent years have brought many unfavorable criticisms of public education. The wise administrative leader will study the sources and underlying reasons for these criticisms carefully so that he and his staff may meet them in a constructive manner.

A recent workshop for leadership training of members of the Parent Teacher Association of Indiana considered this problem rather carefully. The report[6] of the workshop summarizes their conclusions as follows:

Criticisms arise for several reasons:
1. Honest desire to secure the best in education.
2. Lack of understanding.
3. Dissatisfactions.
4. Personal gains.
5. Selfish desires.
6. Unwillingness to pay for schools.
7. Vested interest groups.
8. Subversion.

How can we meet these criticisms?
1. Seek out the facts.

[6] Sixth Annual Leadership Training Workshop, *The P.T.A. Studies Crucial School Needs* (Bloomington, Indiana: Indiana University and The Indiana Congress of Parents and Teachers, July, 1954).

2. Agree on the desirable outcomes of education.
3. Respect the opinions of others.
4. Deal with differences honestly, fairly, and with consideration.
5. Keep an open mind.
6. Avoid pressure tactics, emotional action, jumping to conclusions.
7. Seek correction through proper lines of authority.
8. Support school authorities actively and intelligently.

Although certain critics of education attack public schools and educators in a loud, persistent, and wholly destructive manner, they are relatively few and generally ineffective. Of greater number are those critics, scattered throughout most communities, who in good faith feel that they have legitimate complaints against the school and its operation. This type of criticism should be met objectively and quietly, rather than emotionally and defensively, with the full awareness that it is probably caused by confusion and lack of understanding. People find it easy to criticise those things which they do not fully comprehend. Such is often the case with the school program.

Not only in contests is a good offense the best defense. This oft-quoted statement is good advice to the administrator who wishes to counteract the effects of criticism. The best policy is to provide a good school program, seek intelligent and united effort by the school staff, and provide all possible means for developing in the community an informed, interested, and participating public.

Action Suggestions for the Principal

1. Make the child the common denominator of school-community interaction.
2. Encourage parent participation in policy development.
3. Keep parents informed about school policies.
4. Interpret school activity in terms laymen can understand.
5. Encourage teacher-parent conferences.
6. Find ways in which parents can help with school routines or with special activities and excursions.
7. Work toward the development of the "community-school" concept.
8. Emphasize the strong points of the school program.
9. Use a variety of means to publicize the program of the school.
10. Encourage parent visits.
11. Send children home happy at the end of the school day.
12. Make news bulletins brief and attractive.
13. Encourage teachers to use simple and friendly language in communications with parents and on reports of children's progress.
14. Suggest that teachers spend a few minutes before afternoon dismissal to evaluate worth-while activities of the day.

15. Make occasional community surveys.

16. Discuss with parents ways in which they can help their children succeed in school.

17. Always allow a parent to discuss his grievances until he gets the matter "completely off his chest."

18. Encourage children to write letters of self-evaluation to their parents.

19. Invite parents to culminating activities of units of study.

20. Bring parents into the planning stage of prospective changes in school operation or policy.

21. Provide a library of suitable materials for parents.

22. Invite parents to school to discuss special aptitudes or achievements of their children.

23. Let children prepare periodic "room newspapers."

24. Include some parents and other laymen on the school advisory council.

SELECTED REFERENCES FOR EXTENDED READING

AMERICAN ASSOCIATION OF SCHOOL ADMINISTRATORS. *Public Relations for America's Schools: Twenty-eighth Yearbook.* Washington, D. C.: The American Association of School Administrators, 1950.

BROWNING, MARY, and ASSOCIATES. *Your Child Starts to School in Louisville.* Louisville: Bulletin of Louisville Public Schools, 1949.

DEPARTMENT OF ELEMENTARY SCHOOL PRINCIPALS. *The Public and the Elementary School: Twenty-eighth Yearbook.* Washington, D. C.: National Education Association, 1949.

——. *Bases for Effective Learning: Thirty-first Yearbook,* Washington, D. C.: National Education Association, 1952.

ELSBREE, WILLARD S., and MCNALLY, HAROLD J. *Elementary School Administration and Supervision.* New York: American Book Co., 1951, chaps. 24 and 25.

GRANT, EVA H. *Parents and Teachers as Partners.* Chicago: Science Research Associates, Inc., 1952.

HYMES, JAMES L., JR. *Effective Home-School Relations.* New York: Prentice-Hall, Inc., 1953.

NATIONAL SCHOOL PUBLIC RELATIONS ASSOCIATION. *It Starts in the Classroom.* Washington, D. C.: National Education Association, 1951.

OLSEN, EDWARD G. (ed.). *School and Community Programs.* New York: Prentice-Hall, Inc., 1949.

——. *The Modern Community School.* New York: Appleton-Century-Crofts, Inc., 1953.

OLSEN, EDWARD G., and OTHERS. *School and Community.* New York: Prentice-Hall, Inc., 1945.

OTTO, HENRY J. *Elementary School Organization and Administration.* New York: Appleton-Century-Crofts, Inc., 1954, chap. 13.

VINCENT, HAROLD S., and ASSOCIATES. *Growing in Milwaukee: Annual Report of the Superintendent of Schools.* Milwaukee: Board of Education, 1953.

YEAGER, WILLIAM A. *School-Community Relations.* New York: The Dryden Press, 1951.

PART VII

EVALUATING THE EFFECTIVENESS
OF THE SCHOOL

Chapter 19

EVALUATING THE PROGRAM OF THE SCHOOL

*Education must be judged not so much by what it is as by what
it does*

The chief administrative official of a school system was paying a visit to one of the elementary schools of the city. He had heard some rumblings of criticism from parents about the program of that particular school. During the conversation with the principal, he asked, "Is this a good school?" The principal answered without a moment's hesitation, "Yes, indeed, it is my opinion that this is a fine school." The visiting official paused thoughtfully and then inquired, "How do we know it is?" It was at that point that the principal was troubled, for he was not the kind of leader who is concerned with the systematic appraisal of the school program.

Let us assume that this particular principal represents the exception rather than the rule. However, there is a need at the present time in a great many schools for greater attention to intelligent, cooperative evaluation of the program being provided for children. This need is based on at least three important considerations. They are: (1) evidence of quality gained through evaluative processes is the best advertising a school can enjoy and the best defense against criticism, (2) continuous emphasis on evaluation keeps the program dynamic and the people who operate it professionally alive, and (3) effective evaluation is an essential prerequisite to constructive change or improvement.

No human enterprise deserves support unless there is some form of demonstrated evidence of its value in the achievement of worth-while purposes. Since the school is a direct instrument of society depending largely upon public support, it is particularly imperative that educators engage in systematic educational inventories which will reveal the nature and degree of the school's success.

It will be recalled that a discussion of the evaluation of pupil progress was presented in Chapter 10. The current chapter is concerned with the appraisal of the total school program with some attention to its several components. The discussion is organized around the following areas of emphasis: (1) principles of evaluation of the school program, (2) some essential functions of the evaluative process, and (3) the evaluation of important aspects of the school program.

Principles Underlying Evaluation of the Elementary School Program

Under the authoritarian concept of leadership, the process of evaluation is simple. It involves basically the opinion of the person "in charge." Under this concept, the appraisal, though subjective, is final and infallible. Quite the contrary is true in situations where democratic leadership is present. Evaluation is then recognized to be a comprehensive and complicated process requiring the best cooperative efforts and judgments of a great many different persons and groups. Because the modern approach to the evaluation of the school program is broad and sometimes vague in the minds of administrators and teachers, it seems important to establish certain guide-lines which may help to characterize it. For this purpose the following principles may be helpful.

1. *Evaluation precedes improvement.* There is no virtue in change alone unless such change contributes to a betterment of existing conditions. A traveler who is lost and does not know his present location finds it impossible to chart a reliable course toward his objective. He must first know where he is before his choice of routes has any meaning for him. The same is true of the school program. The first step in the improvement of objectives, the curriculum, or teaching methods is careful study and analysis of existing conditions and status. The practitioner of medicine does not prescribe treatment or medication until he surveys the patient's condition. The educator, too, must assume that prior study is the only sound basis for action. The ramifications of educational change are too important and too long-range to be considered lightly in terms of superficial whims or "hunches." The only wholly reliable hope for improvement in the educational processes of the school lies in careful, intelligent, evaluative study.

2. *All major aspects of the school program should be included in its appraisal.* Evaluation requires the examination of many facets of the school program, since many different factors contribute to the achievement of the school's objectives. Some of the resources of the school are human; others are classified as physical facilities; still others are organized plans and services. If a serious, productive study of the school is to be made, attention must be focused on such things as the nature of the curriculum, the adequacy of instructional materials, the competency of teachers and, most important of all, the growth of children. All these

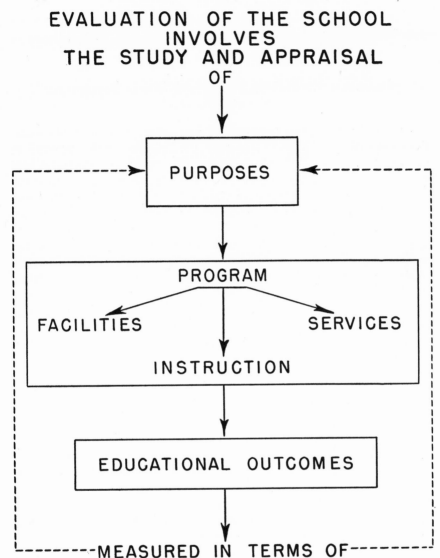

EVALUATION OF THE SCHOOL INVOLVES
THE STUDY AND APPRAISAL
OF

Figure 19

Basic Aspects of School Evaluation

factors are interrelated to such an extent that it is impossible to achieve any true appraisal of one without giving consideration to all the others.

3. *Evaluation involves both subjective and objective methods.* Evaluation involves the qualitative analysis of the school program as well as

the quantitative measurement of its outcomes. Because values are the very basis of the evaluative process, it becomes impossible to reduce its functions solely to objective devices. This does not mean that so-called objective instruments of appraisal should be avoided but rather that they must be considered a part of the broader deliberative process of evaluation.

4. *Evaluation of the school program should be continuous and cumulative.* Learning is the chief commodity of the school and continuous, cumulative appraisal of learning is a functional part of the growth process. It is only through consistent and continuous processes that selected goals can be tested, processes validated, or outcomes appraised. If a school expects to build on its successes it must develop concrete evidence regarding its cumulative strengths; in the same manner, if its weaknesses are to be eliminated or alleviated, they must be diagnosed through careful continuous evaluation. Education is a continuous, largely longitudinal process; any intelligent appraisal of such a process must have some provisions for continuity also.

5. *Evaluation of the school program requires the cooperative efforts of many people.* As was pointed out in an earlier chapter, evaluation is no longer the sole responsibility of the administrator or supervisor. A steady shift has been noted from a highly centralized evaluation to a more cooperative, group approach. Bringing more people into the evaluative process broadens the base of judgment and tends to eliminate or reduce the effect of the prejudiced point of view. Moreover, participation in the evaluative process is a means whereby broadened understanding can be functionally achieved on the part of children, parents, and teachers. Though the major responsibility rests with the professional staff of the school, parents and other laymen can make very effective contributions to the study of the school's objectives. Children can be brought into the process of evaluation at the classroom level through opportunities for exercising critical judgment through self-evaluation, and through participation in planning group activities. Evaluation of the school program can no longer be considered the domain of any one person, but it is rather the obligation of all.

6. *The evaluation of the school program requires many techniques and processes.* There is no single criterion for determining the quality of the school program and there exists no inclusive technique for its analysis. Implicit faith in any one method of study or examination limits the validity of evaluative efforts and demonstrates a lack of understanding of the true meaning and comprehensiveness of evaluation. All proved means for gathering useful data should be employed in the appraisal of the school and its activities. Measuring instruments such as

tests are useful for specific purposes but should not be construed to be, in themselves, a program of evaluation. The same can be said for any other single device. Comprehensive evaluation can be achieved only through the intelligent use of all available means—both quantitative and qualitative—for rendering valid judgments about the school program.

7. *Evaluation of the school program should be locally adaptive.* Conditions differ from community to community and from school to school. The cultural structure of one village or city may differ noticeably from that of another, even in the same state. This suggests that, although there are a great many generalized objectives and methods in education, some adaptation is usually required if each school is to meet the needs and conditions of its own particular community. Furthermore, the distinctive nature of each local school community may well help determine the points that are to be emphasized as attempts are made to evaluate the effectiveness of the school program. This is not to suggest the elimination of all common standards; it is rather to propose that we avoid insistence on complete uniformity in all communities—even in the evaluative process.

8. *Evaluation of the school program assumes the existence of professional standards and objectives.* Some administrators and teachers may have the tendency to interpret the modern emphasis on the localized group approach to evaluation as an indication that little attention need be given to common objectives and professional standards in the appraisal of the school program. Such an interpretation would be a gross mistake. It is true that evaluative study in each school must proceed from the level at which that school is currently operating; its own specific objectives should be formulated, and its own needs should be the chief determinant of program development. However, there are many points in the evaluative process at which general objectives and professional standards can and should be applied. For example, if a school is studying the adequacy of its school plant and facilities, it is difficult, if not impossible, to make any enlightened appraisal of existing conditions without an awareness of standards which have been developed by experts in that area. School personnel, and citizens of a community for that matter, need to have some means for broadening their educational horizons and stretching their understanding of good education. Research studies, statements of purpose, and evaluative scales often serve such a purpose.

THE EVALUATION PROCESS

There are at least four essential aspects of evaluation which should be applied in the appraisal of the total school program. They are: (1)

philosophic, (2) measurement, (3) judgmental, and (4) diagnostic. Each of these important components has its proper place in the study of a school system with a view toward its improvement.

The Philosophic Aspect of Evaluation.—When one is attempting to gather evidence regarding the quality of the school program, he must start with the objectives of the school. The first question that must be asked is: what is this school expected to accomplish? Unless that question can be answered there is little hope of arriving at a very revealing appraisal of its outcomes. How can one determine the success of an enterprise unless he first knows what it should be achieving?

There is no magic formula for planning a school program. Although, as indicated earlier, there are many common purposes of education that well may apply to all schools, it still is necessary for each school community to determine the characteristics of its own program of education. This phase of program development must be achieved largely through intellectual processes allowing for the interchange and critical appraisal of ideas. The opinions of any rational person can be valuable in the determination of objectives—in deciding on the job of the school. It is an important task of leadership to provide means for sifting these ideas and for bringing sound professional judgments to bear on their acceptance, modification, or disapproval. Comparative values must be tested by enlightened discussion and deliberative judgment to the point where a selection of major purposes of the school can be achieved. Important considerations in this process are: (1) participation of all persons who have a legitimate stake in the school and a constructive contribution to make; (2) analysis of the local community; (3) study of the needs of children; (4) consideration of the persistent demands of society; and (5) recognition of the nature, interests, and maturity levels of children of elementary school age.

After an interested group of educators, and others, have carefully weighed the values of our culture which should be emphasized and activated through the elementary school, they are then in a position to translate these values into objectives or expected outcomes. These are merely statements of the tasks which the school expects or wishes to accomplish. The third step in carrying out the philosophic phase of evaluation is to break these outcomes into the specific kinds of conditions, performance, or behavior desired.

The Measurement Aspect of Evaluation.—After the goals of a school have been clearly established, the next task is to seek a reliable quantitative estimate of the position of the school in relation to these outcomes or the extent of its progress toward their realization. If the objectives have been stated in such a way that they are understandable and achievable, there is a strong likelihood that they will also be measurable.

Tests or other instruments for measurement should be selected or developed carefully in terms of the kind of change they are expected to measure. Their selection should be preceded by the application of such criteria as those of: (1) validity, (2) reliability, (3) objectivity, (4) ease of administration, (5) ease of scoring, (6) susceptibility to interpretation, and (7) economy. The main thing to consider is the appropriateness of the instrument for the specific attainment that is to be measured. Tests sometimes valuable for one purpose are useless for another.

Information on many types of standardized tests can be obtained by consulting the Mental Measurements Yearbooks,[1] by reading the catalogs and manuals furnished by test publishing companies, or by examining the tests themselves.

There are many valuable devices, other than tests, for measuring status or progress toward an educational goal. Anecdotal records and scales, sociometric techniques, coded records of observations, self-rating check lists, and informal teacher-made quizzes are all useful in measuring certain phases of behavior or progress. A good evaluation program utilizes as many different instruments as possible in forming composite judgments concerning the school's effectiveness.

In the first phase of the evaluative process—that of the formulation of objectives—the major task is to determine what is to be accomplished through the program of the school. In the measurement phase, the chief concern is to discover to *what extent* these objectives are being achieved.

The Judgmental Aspect of Evaluation.—Test scores and other similar measurement indexes are not very revealing in themselves. There is little value in the results of measurement until the third step in the evaluative process is taken. This step requires the application of judgments to these results in terms of initial objectives and attending conditions. For example, a grade score of 4.2 on a standardized test in silent reading means very little in itself. Is it a good score? It is impossible to determine what kind of performance such a score indicates until one knows more about the child who took the test and the conditions which accompanied its administration. The age of the child, his educational background, his health, his school attendance, and the score he made on a similar test previously—all may be factors which would help interpret the score. So it is with many types of measurement. If their

[1] Oscar K. Buros, *Mental Measurements Yearbooks* (New Brunswick: Rutgers University Press, 1938, 1941, 1949, and 1953).

results are to be beneficial, they must be appraised carefully in the light of the factors surrounding the situation.

The Diagnostic Phase of Evaluation.—In evaluating the quality of the school program it is not enough to formulate sound and clear objectives, measure progress, and interpret the results. One further aspect of evaluation is the identification of conditions and processes which need improvement. In this regard, the evaluative process assumes a relationship to guidance in the elementary school. Strengths and weaknesses of individual performance, of teaching methodology, of the curriculum, and of the facilities used in the educational program can be detected through effective evaluation. Improvement comes more quickly in schools which have identified problem areas that should receive attention. Working on particular problems has two specific advantages: (1) more assurance of concrete progress is possible, and (2) teachers and staff members have the motivating satisfaction of working on a problem which has meaning and value to them.

The Improvement Aspect of Evaluation.—The cycle of the evaluative process is not complete until plans or proposals for improvement are formulated. As indicated above, such plans should emerge from a careful diagnostic analysis of the school program. When the areas which are to receive conscious attention toward improvement are selected, the major tasks then become those of defining the steps through which action should be taken, how group efforts should be organized, and how responsibilities can be allocated in the most effective and economical manner to produce the best possible results.

Just as in the other phases of the evaluative cycle, the school objectives should be kept clearly in mind as programs of improvement are organized. Otherwise, it is possible, and often easy, for the efforts of teachers, administrators, and parents to be diverted into some more expedient but somewhat less important channel.

EVALUATING THE GROWTH OF CHILDREN

The basic purpose of the school is to contribute to the growth of children. Therefore, the beginning point for any rational program of evaluation is the appraisal of the extent and nature of the growth that is occurring in the children who attend the school. Although the relation of evaluation to pupil progress was discussed in Chapter 10, it seems important at this point to give further attention to this important phase of evaluation.

If the appraisal of child growth is to be functionally meaningful, all aspects of growth must be evaluated in so far as possible. The modern elementary school is concerned with all forms of growth rather than with academic achievement alone. The administrator and the school staff should search for effective instruments for gathering data regarding the various components of development.

Evaluating Physical Growth.—Since all aspects of growth are heavily dependent on physical health and vigor, it is essential that teachers and administrators determine as far as possible whether or not a child is growing according to a satisfactory pattern and rate. Several devices are useful in this regard. A basic approach is that of administering *health examinations.* If such examinations are administered periodically and reasonably often, much information can be gained concerning the way the child is developing physically. In addition, health problems can be identified for treatment and correction.

Another useful device for gathering data about the physical status and growth of a child is the *parent conference.* When good rapport is established between parents and the teacher, administrator, or health official, much information can be gained which would be impossible to secure in other ways. Such conferences, based on a sincere common concern, can accomplish much for the health of the child.

The use of *pupil questionnaires* and *health histories* are other approaches which have merit in the evaluation of the physical growth of the child. These forms of information often furnish clues to problems which can be analyzed further once they are identified. *Home visits* and the *observation of children* in the classroom and on the playground sometimes are revealing with regard to the health of the child.

Three essentials for effective evaluation of the physical growth of children are: (1) adequate and varied instruments for collecting information about the physical condition of the child at various stages of growth, (2) complete records of all pertinent data with respect to physical growth, and (3) sufficient interaction with parents and health officials to guarantee a common interpretation of conditions and a unified approach to indicated improvement.

While it is not within the scope of this volume to present completely exhaustive criteria against which the physical growth of children may be measured, it may be helpful to illustrate some of the things which might be involved. Some of the questions to be answered regarding the physical growth of the children attending an elementary school are:

I. *To what extent is this child:*
   Showing an increasing interest in the importance of personal health?
   Developing a set of sound and regular health habits?

Showing a concern for personal cleanliness?
Keeping within a reasonable range of weight and height?
Practicing desirable eating habits?
Participating in wholesome outdoor play activity?
Developing good posture?
Keeping free from communicable disease or infection?
Developing a concern for a safe and healthful environment?

II. *To what extent is this school:*
Providing a safe and healthful environment for children?
Providing functional instruction in health?
Adjusting facilities to the physical needs of children—seating, lighting, special equipment, etc.?
Keeping regular height and weight records of children?
Obtaining a complete health history of each child?
Providing playground equipment and other facilities for the development of physical fitness in each child?
Helping personnel to become sensitive to the symptoms of maladjustments in physical development of each child?
Promoting good health habits?
Providing health services for the children who attend school?
Utilizing the services of outside agencies who might well contribute to the physical development of children?
Providing proper nutritional facilities?
Working with parents with regard to the physical development of their children?

Evaluating Social Growth.—Social relationships and skills must be learned by children through opportunities for interaction with their peers and associates. It is a complicated process for children to progress from the stage of being strongly egocentric to that of consideration for others. One of the basic responsibilities of the school is to provide optimum conditions and experiences for this development. This responsibility carries with it the necessity for continuous evaluation of the program as it affects the gradual achievement of social competence.

It is not a simple matter to evaluate growth in social skills and sensitivity. They do not lend themselves to the kinds of measurements that can be applied to the weight of a child, or even to the development of a skill such as reading or arithmetic. Yet the outcomes, though somewhat less tangible, are just as real if the means for their identification and evaluation can be found. Some progress has been made in this respect in recent years.

Much can be determined about the social growth of a child through *talking with him* and through *observing his behavior* among other children. Little casual conferences before and after school, incidental conversation on the playground or at lunchtime, or brief visits to the home can be very revealing of the social growth of the child. *Inventories of pupil interest* and *questionnaires* sometimes provide clues to this aspect of growth.

The *anecdotal record* is one of the more valuable evaluative instruments for determining the extent and quality of social growth of children. When such records, or behavior logs, are utilized by teachers, care should be exercised to keep them objective. There is a strong tendency for teachers to use such records for interpretive purposes or for documenting and dignifying their own personal prejudices toward a child. Such records should contain only simple statements of facts that are significant in the growth of a child. The following statements illustrate some types of comments that may become useful in the evaluative process:

Joe had a fight on the playground to-day. This is the third fight for Joe this week.

Bill spent most of his lunch period today alone reading in the library. This afternoon he asked if he might go to the workroom to study where it would be more quiet.

Arthur contributed a joke to our sharing period today. He is shy and this is his first voluntary contribution to group discussion since he came to our school last week.

Sue had a temper tantrum this morning on the playground when she was not allowed to take three successive "turns" on the swing while other children waited for it.

Jill suggested today that our group save the money we spend to exchange gifts this year so that we may contribute it to some fund for refugees.

Charles acted as our room host today when we had several visitors and did a fine job of it.

The *analysis of written statements* and compositions of children often provides considerable information with regard to their interest in and acceptance by others. For example, when a child expresses himself on such a matter as "My Greatest Wish" or "The Three Most Important Things in the World to Me," much is usually revealed about his social maturity level.

One of the more helpful devices in the area of social relations of children is the *sociogram*. The techniques of sociometry have been mentioned earlier in connection with the study and grouping of children. This approach has much value in these areas but it is also effective as an evaluative process. By repeatedly administering sociometric tests with a group of children, a teacher can begin to accumulate data which show growth from isolation to acceptance on the part of individual children.

Social "isolates" can be identified and watched carefully with a view toward improvement; on the other end of the scale the social "stars" can be discovered, and social "chains" and "cliques" can be noted. The skillful teacher, or administrator, can gain much evidence about social acceptance and growth through the use of sociometry.

Evaluating Growth in Basic Skills.—The only true test of skills is the actual performance of them. Numerical skills and understanding can best be judged by how well a person solves problems; reading skills must be appraised by the effectiveness with which a person actually reads. This sounds simple. On the contrary, it is impossible to evaluate completely the *actual performance* of skills used by children from day to day. This process alone would require the full time of the teacher and many other persons in addition. The next best approach is to evaluate skills through testing and observing *sample performance*. This approach is the basis for most testing devices and programs. By careful selection of sample items of performance, one can get relatively accurate data with respect to the performance level of the individual being tested.

An effort should be made in the elementary school to determine the extent and quality of growth occurring in relation to skills of communication, number skills, and skills of critical thinking. Much reliable information about growth in these areas can be secured through the direct observations of the teacher. Such observations are subjective, however, and should be supplemented wherever possible by other systematic means of appraisal appropriate to the skills area and to the development level of the children whose growth is being evaluated.

Oral checks, written projects, and teacher-made tests are some of the more common devices used by many teachers to get information about the achievement of children in the skills area. When used, such devices must be as closely related as possible to the functional use of the skill to be evaluated.

Standardized achievement tests are used in a great many schools as an organized means of determining achievement of pupils in the skills areas. While the use of such tests is open to abuses of misinterpretation or overemphasis, nevertheless they can be valuable in the hands of understanding professional people.

Some of the tests commonly used to measure achievement in skills areas are as follows:[2]

---

[2] For a more inclusive list, see Theodore L. Torgerson and Georgia Sachs Adams, *Measurement and Evaluation for the Elementary School Teacher* (New York: The Dryden Press, 1954), pp. 462-67.

Test batteries which include several skills areas:

Metropolitan Achievement	World Book Company
Modern School Achievement	Bureau of Publications, Teachers College, Columbia University
Stanford Achievement	World Book Company

Arithmetic:

Buswell-John Diagnostic Test	Public School Publishing Company
Compass Diagnostic Tests	Scott, Foresman & Co.
Iowa Every-Pupil Tests of Basic Arithmetic Skills	Houghton Mifflin Co.

Handwriting:

Ayres Handwriting Scales	Bureau of Educational Research and Service, Extension Division, The State University of Iowa
Conrad Manuscript Writing Standards	

Language:

Iowa Every-Pupil Test	Bureau of Educational Research and Service, Extension Division, The State University of Iowa
Iowa Language Abilities Test	

Reading:

Durrell Analysis of Reading Difficulty	World Book Company
Gates Reading Diagnostic Tests	Bureau of Publications, Teachers College, Columbia University
Gray's Oral Reading Paragraphs	Public School Publishing Company
Gates Basic Reading Tests	Bureau of Publications, Teachers College, Columbia University
Iowa Silent Reading Test	World Book Company
Nelson Silent Reading Test	Houghton Mifflin Company
Sangren-Woody Silent Reading Test	World Book Company

Spelling:

Ayres Spelling Scale	Bureau of Publications, Teachers College, Columbia University
Buckingham Extension of the Ayres Spelling Scale	Public School Publishing Company
Morrison-McCall Spelling Scale	World Book Company

Evaluating Growth in Understanding.—The modern elementary school is concerned with producing people who possess efficient skills for living and for further learning. However, it has obligations beyond the development of these skills. One of the chief of these obligations is that of developing an understanding of the physical and social environment. The focal effort of this task is related to the sciences and social studies in the elementary school, but it has concomitants which cut completely across the curriculum and beyond. Understanding, like social sensitivity, is not easy to evaluate. It does not reflect itself in the types of concrete manifestations that are easily measured. A relatively recent yearbook in this field has made a genuine contribution to the thinking of professional people about the problem and contains some guides to improving this aspect of evaluation.[3] It is a useful source for the administrator or teacher who is struggling to find better ways of appraising growth in understanding.

Again, as in the case of the evaluation of skills, standardized and teacher-made tests are used in the appraisal of growth in the so-called "content" areas of the curriculum. Any good battery of achievement tests usually includes subtests in these areas. However, it is no longer desirable, or necessary, to use tests as the *sole* evaluative instruments in these fields. Some of the other ways growth in understanding of the environment may be evidenced are:

> Teacher conferences with pupils and parents.
> Observation of reading habits and work-study skills of pupils.
> Analysis of samples of work such as stories, maps, and notebooks or scrapbooks.
> Discussion panels and individual and group reports.
> Dramatic presentations and role playing.

Some evidence regarding the extent to which the elementary school program is giving children an optimum situation for the development of growth in understanding can be obtained through seeking answers to such questions as:

> Are definite goals and purposes established and understood by teachers, children, and parents?
> Is the emphasis on functional understanding rather than the acquisition of isolated facts and information?
> Is a variety of study and work materials available?
> Are there adequate provisions for the use of field experiences and community resources?
> Is sufficient attention given to the development of work skills in social studies and science?
> Are the content areas being correlated and unified in a meaningful way?
> Is there a rich stock of library and audio-visual resources available?
> Does the program have both continuity and flexibility?
> Is the spirit of experimentation being encouraged?
> Are there opportunities for children to develop reasonable proficiency in research skills?
> Is emphasis placed on the applied phases of social understandings?
> Are varied methods of evaluation of growth employed?

Evaluating Growth in Creativity.—Much of the value of the creative arts is derived from the process involved rather than from the product created. In other words, what happens to the child as a result of

[3] National Society for the Study of Education, *The Measurement of Understanding: Forty-Fifth Yearbook,* Part I (Chicago: The University of Chicago Press, 1946).

creative activity is more important than the rendition of a song, the painting of a picture, or the telling of a story. This philosophy has resulted in evaluative processes which shift the emphasis from the sole method of rating the product of the creative effort of the child.

Several elements of creativity should be considered in the attempt to appraise growth in this area of human activity. Some of them are: (1) understanding of relationships between human ideals and experience and creative activity, (2) imagination, (3) self-expression, (4) appreciation or enjoyment, and (5) self-direction.

Some of the criteria for judging growth in the area of creative activity are:

Does personal *enjoyment* result from this activity?

Does personal *enrichment* result from this activity?

Does the child gain from this activity added *appreciation* for the efforts of others?

Does this activity help the child develop the *powers of choice and discrimination?*

Is the child growing in *self-direction* and *self-reliance* through this activity?

Is the child developing *responsible habits of work* and *persistence* through this activity?

Is the child growing in the *development of broader interests* and *better taste?*

As a result of creative activity is the child growing in the *constructive use of his leisure time?*

Is the child growing in *independence* and *individuality* of thought?

Such avenues of creative expression as art, music, construction work, dramatics, and creative writing are increasingly occupying a more important place in the modern elementary school. Administrative leaders, supervisors, and teachers should give diligent effort to the development of varied and satisfactory means for appraising growth in these important areas.

TESTING PROGRAM IN THE ELEMENTARY SCHOOL

The importance of the use of varied measurement and evaluation devices has been emphasized in the preceding sections. This emphasis does not minimize, however, the desirability of a systematic program of standardized testing in the elementary school. While there is undoubtedly considerable disagreement among educators as to the specifics of such a program, most would agree that the following areas should be covered.

Ability Testing.—There is no basis for establishing educational expectations for a child until one has some reliable evidence of his ability.

While they are not infallible, by any means, so-called intelligence tests are the most useful instruments available for this purpose at the present time. Therefore, appropriate group tests should be given at least three or four times during the years a child spends in the elementary school. Many educators recommend that such tests be administered in grades two, four, six, and eight. This recommendation is based on the assumption that most educational aptitude tests are verbal in nature and thus unsuited for children younger than those in their second year of school. If, for any reason, the test results for a child are inconsistent with other observable factors of behavior, an individual test should be administered.

Some of the group tests of intelligence in wide use at the present time are:

The California Test of Mental Maturity	California Test Bureau
Henmon-Nelson Tests of Mental Ability	Psychological Corporation
Kuhlmann-Anderson Intelligence Tests	Educational Test Bureau
Otis Quick-Scoring Test of Mental Ability	World Book Company

Readiness Testing.—In many schools attempts are made to determine the readiness of children for a beginning reading program. This is usually done through the administration of a reading-readiness test to children who are either completing the year in the kindergarten or entering the first grade. In this way, some guidance is given in the adaptation or use of materials and methods as children enter the first grade.

Such tests as the following are often used for this purpose:

Gates Reading Readiness Test	Bureau of Publications, Teachers College, Columbia University
Lee-Clark Reading Readiness Test	California Test Bureau
Metropolitan Readiness Tests	World Book Company

Achievement Testing.—Standardized achievement tests are most useful when two forms are used—one near the beginning of the school year and the other near the end of the year. In this way, comparative judgments can be made regarding the indicated growth in whatever the tests measure.

At the primary levels achievement tests given are usually limited to the area of reading, and perhaps arithmetic and language in addition. While numerous schools administer such tests annually, this practice does not seem essential at the lower levels of the elementary school. At the upper grade levels, however, there appears to be considerable value in shortening the intervals between the times such tests are administered. With older children, it is often profitable to use a battery of tests covering most areas of the curriculum rather than selected tests in single areas. This, of course, is a matter that can well be decided on the basis of local circumstances.

Illustrations of test batteries, as well as specific achievement tests, were mentioned earlier in connection with the basic skills. Further listings can be examined in the catalogs of test publishers available to schools.

Diagnostic Testing.—Achievement tests can have considerable diagnostic value if the results are interpreted carefully and wisely. However, it is occasionally desirable to administer tests for the express purpose of identifying the learning difficulties of children. Commercial tests are available for this purpose and can be secured at a nominal cost. However, diagnostic tests constructed by teachers, if carefully prepared, often are found to be equally useful.

Evaluation of Teacher Performance and Growth

It is obvious that the most important evaluation in the elementary school is that related to the growth of children. However, desirable growth and achievement of children are not accomplished in an educational vacuum. Good education for children becomes a reality in terms of the presence and operation of other factors of the educational process. The most important of these factors is the teacher. Therefore, it seems unrealistic to think of evaluating the school program without due consideration for the performance and growth of the teachers who are largely responsible for the program.

Teachers are continuously subject to evaluative judgments from at least four sources: (1) children, (2) parents, (3) administrative and supervisory personnel, and (4) the teachers themselves. Cumulative appraisals of the teacher's competence are being formulated from day to day and it seems safe to say that, furthermore, teachers themselves tend to build with their experiences either increasing self-respect and confidence or self-depreciation and frustration. Each of these aspects of teacher evaluation will be considered briefly.

Evaluation of Teachers by Children.—The opinions of children regarding their teachers are extremely important. Good rapport is largely dependent upon a liking and respect for the teacher. A child tends to be motivated in his efforts by his opinion of his teacher. Moreover, classroom organization, management, and discipline all are related to the quality of teacher-pupil relationships.

There are many ways in the course of the school day in which a teacher may sample the opinions of pupils with regard to his performance. Of course, they will not be direct inquiries, but the skillful teacher who observes the reactions of children closely can obtain a fairly clear impression of the pupils' evaluation of him. The wise teacher will keep in mind the fact that he is undergoing a continuous evaluation by his pupils and will conduct himself accordingly.

Evaluation of Teachers by Parents.—Parents formulate their appraisals of teachers from direct contacts and from the reports and impressions brought home by children. Happy children are usually effective publicity agents for the teacher.

It is important that teachers recognize their continuous evaluation by the parents of children they teach. The greater importance of such evaluations lies in the fact that the teacher's performance at school is affected by the parent's opinion at home. A child whose parents have little respect for a teacher seldom responds to the teacher and to the school in the manner desired. For this reason, and many others, teachers should make a special effort to treat parents courteously and to show consideration for their ideas and opinions, even though they may be in error, and to show the kind of sympathetic regard for children that will encourage the respect of parents.

Administrative and Supervisory Evaluation of Teachers.—Many types of rating sheets and check lists have been devised for the use of administrators and supervisors in evaluating the work of teachers with whom they are associated. While such instruments have the advantage of focalizing attention on significant elements of good teaching, they are, at the same time, susceptible to many abuses. For this reason, those who make use of rating devices of this type should exercise certain precautions. Among them are: (1) avoid the use of the check list during a supervisory visit; (2) give the teacher an opportunity to compare her judgment with that of the supervisor with regard to the items on the check list or rating scale; (3) make sure the rated teacher has knowledge of the appraisal of the supervisor; and (4) emphasize possibilities for improvement rather than deficiencies.

Day-to-day association with teachers in the school will afford the administrative leader many opportunities to recognize the strengths and weaknesses of teachers. Supervisory visits to the classroom, followed by friendly conferences, often offer opportunities for evaluation and motivation at the same time. Observing the relationships which the teacher enjoys with children on the playground or in the cafeteria will tell the administrator a great deal about the teacher's over-all competence in working with children. Cheerfulness in meeting responsibilities, punctuality with reports and records, and comments of her teaching associates reveal a great deal about a teacher's character and personality.

Self-Evaluation by Teachers.—What a teacher actually thinks about himself is probably the most important aspect of his evaluation. His own evaluation of his teaching is more likely to lead to improvement than the evaluative judgments of others. For this reason, teachers should be encouraged to engage in the critical analysis of their own activities. This may be done in two ways: (1) through individual self-analysis by a teacher, and (2) through group discussion and study of teaching competence. While each may have considerable merit in particular situations, the latter is the more useful as a supervisory device because of its impersonal quality. A skillful administrative leader can accomplish a great deal toward the in-service improvement of the staff through judicious use of meetings devoted to discussion of the elements of good teaching.

The following is a condensed illustration of a check list that might be used by a teacher for self-evaluation.

I. *Personal qualities—to what extent:*
   Do I maintain a neat and well-groomed appearance at all times?
   Am I consistent in the example of behavior I demonstrate to children?
   Do I practice wholesome habits of living?
   Do I always demonstrate my interest in others?
   Am I considerate at all times?
   Do I maintain proper voice quality and pitch?

II. *Relationships with children—to what extent:*
   Do I value each individual in my classroom?
   Do I work to establish a good learning environment?
   Do I handle behavior problems in a positive manner?
   Do I provide for individual differences among children?
   Do I practice the Golden Rule in my relationships with children?

III. *Teaching effectiveness—to what extent:*
   Am I clear on teaching objectives and purposes?
   Do I utilize a variety of rich instructional materials?
   Do I utilize the ideas of children in planning?
   Am I able to motivate children?
   Do I integrate learning experiences?
   Do I adapt methods to particular needs or purposes?
   Do I evaluate learning in meaningful ways?

IV. *Relationships with associates—to what extent:*
   Do I cooperate with other teachers for the good of the child?
   Do I assume my share of routine responsibilities?
   Do I conduct myself ethically in my remarks and actions?
   Do I value my professional associations?

V. *Relationships with the community—to what extent:*
   Do I seek and utilize the cooperation of parents?

Do I participate cheerfully in community activities?
Do I utilize community resources in teaching?

Evaluating the Curriculum

The evaluation of the curriculum of the elementary school requires that answers be sought to a number of questions. Some of these questions are:

1. Are clear objectives developed and understood by all persons involved in the instructional program of the school?
2. Is the curriculum content emphasized in the school consistent with the objectives formulated?
3. Does the curriculum organization of the school functionalize and integrate the content into meaningful learning experiences?
4. Is there provision for flexibility in the curriculum so that each individual may progress with a desirable degree of continuity?
5. Is the teaching methodology employed by teachers consistent with the objectives of the school?
6. Are there provisions for a rich supply of instructional materials, varied both in nature and difficulty?
7. Do the organization and services of the school support the curriculum of the school?
8. Are there provisions for continuous evaluation of the instructional program?
9. Is curriculum study and experimentation encouraged in the school and are there provisions for group study of curriculum problems and improvement?

In evaluating the school curriculum with a view toward improvement there are at least seven points at which professional effort can result in a better program of instruction. They are: (1) purposes, (2) planning, (3) continuity, (4) individualization, (5) enrichment, (6) unity, and (7) evaluation.

As indicated earlier, it is important for purposes to be clear, as specific as possible, in terms of behavioral outcomes, and understood by those who are attempting to achieve them. Evaluative study by a staff often reveals considerable confusion as to the real purposes of the school.

One of the marks of a good modern school is the extent to which both children and parents are brought into the process of planning the activities which affect them. Careful study will reveal many ways in which children can participate in the planning of their groups, and in which teachers and parents can be involved in the development and planning of school policies and projects.

Continuous progress, according to the learning rate of each, is the goal of every good school for its children. Teachers, under effective leadership, can often discover ways in which they can make the progress of children much more continuous in nature. Evaluative study will help a group discover the means of pooling information and working together to help children learn at their own particular levels of maturity.

In a good school program, each child is considered as an individual as well as a member of the group. Both interests and abilities are considered in adapting materials and methods to the particular needs of each child. The staff of each school should attempt to determine, through evaluative study, just how well this is being done, followed by the exploration of means whereby individualization of instruction might be improved.

The evaluation of the curriculum of the elementary school should give some attention to the degree of enrichment present in the existing program of instruction. The extent to which textbooks are supplemented by other reading materials, audio-visual materials, and community resources is a rather reliable indication of the relative richness of the program; this aspect is concrete and can be studied and followed up with almost immediate results.

Much learning occurs through the association of ideas with previous experience. The curriculum cannot completely reach its potential level of quality unless there are provisions for relating and unifying the various experiences which combine to make up the program for each child. This type of integration may be achieved through various unitary approaches, but it is desirable for the staff of each school to explore means whereby it may locally be done more effectively.

Continuous evaluation is an integral part of curriculum development and implementation. The continuing tendency to apply critical judgments to the curriculum is one of the bases upon which rests the hope for keeping the curriculum alive and functional.

Action Suggestions for the Principal

1. Keep the educational objectives of the school clearly in mind in all evaluative processes of the school.
2. Strive to develop the tendency toward continuous evaluation.
3. Provide facilities for a variety of evaluative devices.
4. Include all major aspects of the program in evaluation.
5. Be able to distinguish measurement or testing from evaluation.
6. Keep evaluative data in useful and accessible form.
7. Include children in the evaluative process.

8. Evaluate the program in terms of local community needs and conditions.

9. Use all available data in the evaluative process.

10. Use only measurement instruments that are valid and reliable.

11. Develop a systematic and balanced testing program for the school.

12. Encourage the use of self-evaluation wherever possible.

13. Encourage teachers to use their resourcefulness in developing techniques for classroom evaluation.

14. Make cumulative records and evaluative data easily available to teachers.

15. Use faculty meetings to discuss evidences of growth in children.

16. Ask teachers to share the findings of research in child growth with other members of the staff.

17. Help teachers refine their use of anecdotal records.

18. Keep files of actual work of children as indications of growth and achievement.

19. Participate in cooperative curriculum evaluation.

20. Keep an up-to-date file of sample testing materials for teachers to examine.

21. Emphasize both individual and group evaluation.

SELECTED REFERENCES FOR EXTENDED READING

ADAMS, HAROLD P., and DICKEY, FRANK G. *Basic Principles of Supervision.* New York: American Book Co., 1953, chap. 12.

AYER, FRED C. *Fundamentals of Instructional Supervision.* New York: Harper & Bros., 1954, chaps. 21 and 22.

BEECHER, DWIGHT E. *The Evalution of Teaching.* Syracuse: Syracuse University Press, 1949.

COSWELL, HOLLIS, and FOSHAY, A. WELLESLEY. *Education in the Elementary School.* New York: American Book Co., 1950, chap. 3.

ELSBREE, WILLARD S., and McNALLY, HAROLD J. *Elementary School Administration and Supervision.* New York: American Book Co., 1951, chap. 28.

McNERNEY, CHESTER T. *Educational Supervision.* New York: McGraw-Hill Book Co., Inc., 1951, chap. 4.

MEHL, MARIE A., MILLS, HUBERT H., and DOUGLASS, HARL R. *Teaching in Elementary School.* New York: The Ronald Press Co., 1950, chap. 18.

NATIONAL SOCIETY FOR THE STUDY OF EDUCATION. *The Measurement of Understanding: Forty-Fifth Yearbook,* Part I. Chicago: University of Chicago Press, 1946.

RAGAN, WILLIAM B. *Modern Elementary Curriculum.* New York: The Dryden Press, 1953, chaps. 14 and 15.

SHANE, HAROLD G., and McSWAIN, E. T. *Evaluation and the Elementary Curriculum.* New York: Henry Holt & Co., 1951.

SHANE, HAROLD G., and YAUCH, WILBUR A. *Creative School Administration.* New York: Henry Holt & Co., 1954, chap. 5.

SPEARS, HAROLD. *Improving the Supervision of Instruction.* New York: Prentice-Hall, Inc., 1953, chaps. 20 and 21.

TORGERSON, THEODORE L., and ADAMS, GEORGIA SACKS. *Measurement and Evaluation.* New York: The Dryden Press, 1954.

WILES, KIMBALL. *Teaching for Better Schools.* New York: Prentice-Hall, Inc., 1952, chaps. 9 and 10.

Chapter 20

EVALUATING THE QUALITY OF EDUCATIONAL LEADERSHIP

We need little vision to see the distant sun; the greatest vision to see ourselves

It is extremely difficult to reduce the essence of leadership to concrete forms. Leadership is a matter of spirit as well as of techniques. It is much easier to observe and to feel the results of its operation than to describe it. It gets much of its meaning and most of its value not from what it does but from what it causes others to do. Leadership is the coordinating catalyst which enhances the efforts of individuals and makes them part of a process from which all contributors may derive mutual benefits. Leadership is sometimes most obvious when it is virtually absent and most powerful when it is difficult to detect. It is a source of inspiration and strength which causes people to want to do the best they can, and helps them do it. And in no human enterprise is leadership more vital than in education—and in no level of the educational effort is it more important than in the elementary school.

Chapter 19 was devoted to a discussion of the evaluation of the program of the elementary school. Presumably, the administrative leader is a substantial contributor to the quality of that program. As such, it is necessary, of course, for him to demonstrate an active interest in its evaluation as a basis for continuous improvement. But his professional obligation goes much beyond that point with reference to the process of evaluation. It is not enough for him to apply his energies and wisdom to the appraisal of the school program. He must also be sensitive to the need for evaluating the quality of his own leadership as one of the important elements of the existing school program. Only through turning the spotlight of critical evaluation on his own attitudes and activities can he hope for his own professional growth as a leader.

This chapter sets forth some of the conditions which indicate active educational leadership by the elementary school administrator and outlines some of the characteristics of effective supervisory leadership in action.

Earmarks of Constructive Leadership in the Elementary School

For the evaluation of the effectiveness of the administrative leader one must look at the attitudes and activities of persons other than the leader himself. It is in its effect on others that the impact of leadership is felt, and the nature and extent of this effect forms the chief basis for determining the qualitative level at which the leader is operating. The following statements reflect conditions that indicate good leadership.

1. *The quality of administrative leadership is indicated by the level of human relations that prevail in the school.* Effective leadership promotes the creation and maintenance of businesslike, yet cordial, working relations in the school. Teachers and pupils enjoy, rather than endure, each other and there is a minimum of conflict among the pupils and staff of the school. This is partly because, under the influence of constructive leadership, people are encouraged to differ in their professional ideas and opinions without the necessity for personal conflict. Another reason is that strong leadership contributes to the feeling of security possessed by staff members and children. Secure people are much less likely to be contentious in their relationships with others. A real test of leadership, then, is the degree to which all persons in the school work happily together.

2. *The quality of administrative leadership is indicated by the extent to which people other than the leader succeed.* It is the business of the school to help children succeed; it is the obligation of the administrative leader to help bring success to all persons involved in the educational program of the school. Under good leadership, a program of learning experiences is developed that permits children to advance at their own levels of maturity. In a similar manner, effective leadership aids individual staff members to move toward their potentials as rapidly as possible. When one visits an outstanding elementary school, he usually finds a situation in which children, teachers, parents, and administrators are deriving satisfactions from their efforts. In such cases, the whole tone of the school has a positive and hopeful ring to it. Genuine leadership helps people turn moderate successes into even greater achievements.

3. *The quality of administrative leadership is indicated by the extent to which people grow.* There is nothing static about a situation in which effective leadership is operating. This dynamism is shown by the growth of children and by the professional development of the staff. Parents desire genuine improvement in the program of learning experiences for the children, and they are willing to tolerate the change and help expend the effort of bringing about conditions which they sincerely believe will result in a better school for their children. Under this high level of leadership, teachers are willing to admit that they are still learners and

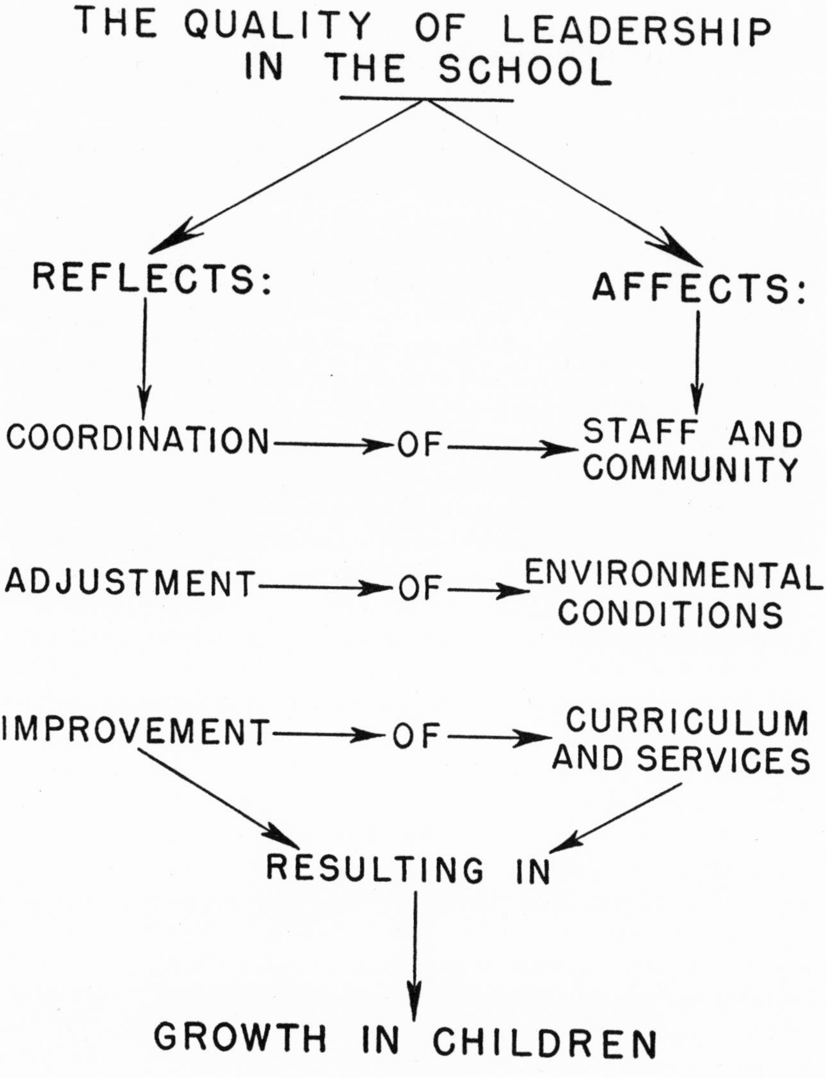

THE QUALITY OF LEADERSHIP
IN THE SCHOOL

REFLECTS:

AFFECTS:

COORDINATION ———→ OF ———→ STAFF AND
COMMUNITY

ADJUSTMENT ———→ OF ———→ ENVIRONMENTAL
CONDITIONS

IMPROVEMENT ———→ OF ———→ CURRICULUM
AND SERVICES

RESULTING IN

GROWTH IN CHILDREN

Figure 20

Focal Points of Administration Leadership

are seeking ways to grow in the profession. Under favorable conditions, even the more lethargic members of the professional staff catch the spirit of growth and begin to expand their educational horizons. Most important of all, emphasis is placed on the growing—including all aspects of growth—of boys and girls.

4. *The quality of educational leadership is indicated by the extent to which people exercise responsible freedom.* Complete freedom without a sense of responsibility leads to chaos, but freedom based on responsibility is one of the very basic tenets of the democratic process. In the modern elementary school children and staff alike are allowed to exercise as much individual freedom as they are able to use to advantage. They are not bound by unnecessary regulations and restrictions. Instead they are permitted to chart their own courses of behavior as long as they do not interfere with the basic rights of others.

The leadership which promotes this type of freedom is evident from the concepts of discipline which prevail in the school. Under this level of leadership, it is more important to give children guidance in becoming self-directive than it is to direct them. The same is true of the working relations between the administrative leader and the other members of the staff.

5. *The quality of administrative leadership is indicated by the extent to which people are encouraged to exercise originality and initiative.* The chance for individual accomplishment and recognition is a strong factor in motivating the efforts of either children or adults. Indeed, it would be most unfortunate if members of a professional staff were required to subscribe to exactly the same ideas and to teach in exactly the same manner. The different talents and abilities of people actually contribute to the composite strength of the group. If leadership operates in such a way that thinking is encouraged in individuals, the way is open for the pooling of the best ideas of all for the mutual advantage of all. Such opportunity for putting initiative to work is the very essence of educational experimentation from which much of our improvement has come. The leader who is interested in continuous improvement tries to maintain the conditions for the unrestricted operation of professional imagination on the part of the entire staff.

6. *The quality of administrative leadership is indicated by the extent to which people share their successes and problems.* If people are to improve as they pursue their educational tasks, they must be able to identify their problems and to share them with others. Dictatorial administrators sometimes create an atmosphere in which their associates are afraid to admit that they are having problems in the fear that such an admission is a sign of professional weakness that may be used against them. Really democratic leaders, on the other hand, recognize that an objective sensitivity to problems actually is often an indication of professional strength. Under such leadership, school personnel are encouraged to work together on problems and to share ideas regarding their possible solutions.

Sharing credit for educational successes is another mark of the modern school in which effective educational leadership is operating. Staff members are sufficiently secure in their positions that they are not forced to claim sole credit for school activities in order to bring recognition to themselves. They are more interested in bringing credit to the school than to themselves.

7. *The quality of educational leadership is indicated by the extent to which people are self-directive.* Someone has suggested that, if one wishes to judge the quality of leadership being exercised by the principal of a school, he should visit the school when the principal is away. This is to say that good leadership permeates the activities of people in such a way that its values persist even when the leader is not present. There seems to be a substantial basis for such an opinion. For example, the presence of self-discipline is not noted in a classroom as long as the teacher is present; the real quality of discipline is revealed when the teacher leaves a group of children on their own. When teachers and pupils are able to carry out their responsibilities without an undue amount of direction from someone else, there is a strong probability that the school is enjoying a high level of leadership. This does not suggest the desirability of an attitude of detachment on the part of the administrative leader; rather it means that leadership is not so much the direction of people as the ability to help them reach the stage where they can direct themselves.

8. *The quality of educational leadership is related to the location of authority and power.* Effective leaders are much more prone than others to share both responsibility and authority with others. If all the decisions and policies for a school are being made only by the administrator, the modern concept of leadership is not being applied. Wise leaders demonstrate their faith in their associates by sharing decisions and policy determination with them. This approach usually results in better decisions, easier implementation of them, and in the growth of the persons who contribute to the decisions.

Effective Supervisory Leadership in the Elementary School

Any comprehensive evaluation of educational leadership as applied to the elementary school must include a consideration of the supervisory role of the elementary school principal. The following outline is typical of numerous statements that have been formulated to serve as guiding criteria for judging supervisory leadership.[1]

[1] Adapted from a statement compiled by R. L. Springer and Hanne J. Hicks from materials developed by members of an In-service Workshop of Teachers, Supervisors, and Administrators of the Indianapolis Public Schools.

1. *Supervisory leadership is adaptable and flexible in terms of:*
   a) the local situation
   b) the experience of teachers
   c) the particular problems of teachers
   d) the personalities and attitudes of teachers
   e) available instructional materials.

2. *Supervisory leadership contributes to the improvement of instruction through:*
   a) making teachers and pupils feel comfortable
   b) encouraging teachers to consider newer methods and practices
   c) encouraging teachers to innovate
   d) making available and interpreting improved instructional materials and resources
   e) discovering and developing potential leadership
   f) discovering and encouraging special strengths of teachers
   g) encouraging self-evaluation on the part of the teacher
   h) helping teachers to see the value of immediate and long range planning

3. *Supervisory leadership stimulates good human relations through:*
   a) creating mutual respect and confidence
   b) recognition of individual differences among teachers
   c) tolerance of opposing viewpoints
   d) cooperative thinking, planning, and evaluating
   e) encouraging maximum growth in areas of greatest strength

4. *Supervisory leadership develops the power of self-confidence and a feeling of security through:*
   a) providing adequate materials
   b) providing recognition and commendation for constructive efforts
   c) providing opportunity for rotating leadership responsibilities
   d) contributing to a sense of personal achievement and pride
   e) creating situations that foster a feeling of mutual respect among teachers and co-workers
   f) sharing of knowledge of current school policies
   g) encouraging teachers to share common problems

5. *Supervisory leadership develops the power of self-evaluation through:*
   a) freedom in seeking help
   b) cooperative planning of objectives
   c) stimulating the desire for growth on the job
   d) cultivating an objective attitude
   e) providing knowledge of total school situation and conditions

6. *Supervisory leadership promotes the growth of both pupils and teachers through:*
   a) providing a continuous challenge
   b) exhibiting attributes of growth themselves

    c) providing recognition for evidences of growth
    d) encouraging self-evaluation
    e) providing resources of all types
    f) providing the experiences that make for growth
    g) encouraging teachers to accept responsibilities outside the classroom
    h) encouraging teachers to accept professional responsibilities outside the classroom
    i) encouraging of creative activities
    j) encouraging experimentation

7. *Supervisory leadership contributes to the building of high morale through:*
    a) teacher participation in formulation of building policy
    b) joint consideration of major physical changes such as audio-visual equipment, parking facilities, public address system, playground equipment, school uniforms, etc.
    c) adequate attention to physical well-being of teachers, e.g.,
       (1) teachers' lounge
       (2) adequate compensation for extracurricular duties
       (3) equitable teaching and curriculum load

8. *Supervisory leadership provides an effective and well planned in-service program through:*
    a) continuous series of meetings related to interpreting curriculum guides
    b) meetings designed to meet the felt needs of specific groups
    c) making use of instructional materials and techniques in demonstrations by successful teachers
    d) teacher participation in planning in-service programs

9. *Supervisory leadership stimulates and provides opportunities for all to reach their maximum potentialities through:*
    a) becoming acquainted with the teacher and knowing her background
    b) recognition of the teacher's talents
    c) conferences (outside the classroom) to determine:
       (1) educational philosophy
       (2) type of help desired
       (3) community orientation
       (4) building policies
       (5) consultant or supervisory services
       (6) explanation of services of professional organizations
       (7) constructive instructional practices
       (8) long and short term planning

10. *Supervisory leadership keeps abreast of present trends and shares knowledge of these trends through:*
    a) attendance at professional meetings
    b) recent publications of books and magazines
    c) attendance at clinics, seminars, and university classes
    d) visual aids

11. *Supervisory leadership promotes creative teaching through:*
    a) encouraging classroom experimentations
    b) recognizing special prospects of teachers
    c) assisting in locating stimulating professional references
    d) sharing noteworthy ideas of teachers

12. *Supervisory leadership contributes to a common understanding of objectives through:*
    a) cooperative efforts in formulating school purposes
    b) frequent opportunities to study and re-evaluate purposes and outcomes
    c) provisions for effective communication throughout the school system
    d) provisions for consistent interpretation of school policies throughout the system

13. *Supervisory leadership, in its evaluative processes:*
    a) considers the purposes of learning activities and instructional methods
    b) takes into account all attributes of strength or weakness on the part of the teacher as well as his total effectiveness
    c) considers evaluation as a point of departure for improvement
    d) utilizes self-evaluation by teachers as much as possible in the total evaluative process

14. *Supervisory leadership promotes the democratic way of life through:*
    a) demonstrated respect for individuals
    b) provisions for effective group decisions
    c) demonstrating democracy in all its processes

QUALITY OF ADMINISTRATIVE LEADERSHIP IN THE ELEMENTARY SCHOOL

Administrative leadership is not easily described in terms of precise mechanics. Neither can its results always be tabulated in concrete and terminal forms. However, certain types of evidence seem to suggest the presence of effective democratic leadership in the elementary school. Most of these indicative conditions are related to the attitudes and actions of the individuals—teachers, nonprofessional staff, pupils, and parents—who make up the educational team and who are involved in the program of the school.

In the modern elementary school blessed with competent administrative leadership, one is likely to find that:

A. *Individuals concerned with the educational process*
    1. enjoy a comfortable degree of security
    2. see purpose in their activities
    3. are deriving satisfactions from their work
    4. feel the pride of co-ownership in the school
    5. attach importance to their distinctive educational roles
    6. remain imaginative and creative in performing day-to-day tasks

7. are positive in their attitudes toward and comments about the school
8. assume leadership roles when the occasion demands
9. are straightforward, honest, and objective in discussing their own weaknesses and mistakes of judgment
10. demonstrate faith in their fellows
11. understand how to pool resources effectively
12. exercise initiative but do not hesitate to seek assistance when it is needed
13. practice continuous self-evaluation
14. are continuously seeking opportunities for growth and improvement
15. appreciate, respect, and demonstrate basic democratic tenets in their own activities and relationships

B. *Conditions surrounding and supporting the educational process are*
1. safe and wholesome
2. rich and stimulating to growth
3. flexible in terms of changing school purposes and needs
4. balanced in terms of the total program of the school
5. organized sufficiently to promote efficient action
6. consistent with basic educational purposes
7. continuously evaluated in terms of the best that is known
8. related to life as it exists
9. cooperatively developed
10. developed and maintained in terms of the human values involved

SELF-EVALUATION OF THE ADMINISTRATIVE LEADER

One of the chief characteristics of the effective administrative leader is the strong desire for self-improvement at the same time he is working to bring about improvement in others. Such leaders possess the vision to see opportunities for growth and are sufficiently alert to avail themselves of such opportunities. An earnest approach to self-improvement really can be made only by administrators who have enough competence and confidence to be reasonably secure in their jobs. Otherwise they are likely to fear that any evaluative analysis of their characteristics and professional activities may be construed as indications of weaknesses which may be used against them.

In spite of the reluctance of some educational personnel to accept any responsibility for self-evaluation, serious and systematic self-analysis has become one of the vital professional processes of modern education. The fact that the elementary principal may enjoy an official status which exempts him from the necessity of legally justifying the quality of his performance does not excuse him from the professional and moral obligation of demonstrated competence and growth on the job. Indeed, his

Characteristic	Yes	No	Improving
I Do I demonstrate			
faith in education as a process for human improvement?			
faith in my associates?			
an active belief in the group process?			
a devotion to the welfare of children as the prime purpose of the school?			
a respect for educational research and experiment as a basis for educational improvement?			
an interest in the successes and problems of children and members of the staff?			
active commitment to American ideals?			
II Do I encourage			
teachers to use intelligent initiative?			
children to exercise responsible freedom?			
cooperative pooling of the best ideas of all concerned?			
constructive participation of parents and citizens in developing school purposes and policies?			
creative thinking?			
flexibility of operation in selecting and organizing learning experiences?			
constructive criticism and honest difference of opinion?			
III Do I assist			
in the personal problems of children and staff members?			
teachers in exploring new materials and methods?			
both parents and citizens in developing an understanding of the school program?			
in the organization of in-service activities of a profitable nature?			
IV Do I use			
all possible human resources in the development of the school program and in the solution of school problems?			
the best knowledge available as a basis for my actions?			

Characteristic	Yes	No	Improving
a personalized approach to the individual differences of children and staff members?			
my time to best advantage?			
V Do I provide			
all possible types of instructional materials needed for good teaching and effective learning?			
administrative procedures that are consistent with the objectives and instructional procedures of the school?			
clerical help and other services necessary to free teachers for their main obligation of teaching?			
opportunities for others to assume leadership roles in various aspects of the school program?			
VI Am I exercising leadership in helping to develop a school in which			
objectives are sound and clear?			
people work together effectively?			
each child is important?			
the curriculum is rich but flexible?			
the organization is efficient in terms of its relation to learning?			
the plant is comfortable and safe?			
instructional resources are varied and stimulating?			
self-direction and initiative are encouraged?			
evaluation is thorough and continuous?			
human values come first?			
VII Am I growing			
in my understanding of children?			
in my human relations skills?			
through extended knowledge of educational literature and research?			
in the ability to utilize group processes effectively?			
through broadening professional associations?			
in community participation?			
in the technical skills of administration?			
in cultural and spiritual resources?			
in my understanding of the role of leadership?			

position of leadership should serve as an additional reason for his interest in improvement.

It is generally agreed that the first step toward self-improvement is self-evaluation. In the case of the elementary principal this evaluation should include such things as personal characteristics, professional skills, breadth of information and understanding, and human relations. The following illustrative check list of questions may serve as a basic type of guide a principal might use to develop a self-evaluative scale for himself.

Even in this modern age, buildings can be no grander than the visions of their architects; machines can travel no faster than the imagination of their engineers; and nations of mankind will continue to be relegated to despair, doomed to continuing mediocrity, or inspired to new heights of civilization by the aspirations and the competencies of their leaders.

In America the public school has become a mighty force for the preservation and improvement of our society. Because it touches the lives of virtually all the people, the elementary school is on the front line of this notable effort. Its contribution to date is so great and far-reaching that it cannot be measured; its potentiality for the future is infinite. A genuine leader in the modern elementary school can exert an influence that will enrich the lives of innumerable children and persist for generations to come. Such is the challenge—and the privilege—of the elementary school principalship.

ACTION SUGGESTIONS FOR THE PRINCIPAL

1. Analyze and study the qualities of great educational leaders to identify factors related to their success.

2. Learn and practice the techniques for becoming an effective group member.

3. Compare the year's professional successes with those of previous years to detect areas of growth.

4. Welcome recognition for all members of the staff.

5. Give *direction* to the efforts of associates rather than *directions*.

6. Cherish and protect the professional confidence of staff members and children.

7. When others are asked to assume responsibilities, give them also enough freedom and authority to accomplish the task.

8. Relinquish regulations and controls when they are unnecessary.

9. Respect individual opinions of staff members.

10. Search for specialized talents and leadership ability on the part of staff members and provide opportunities for their constructive use.

11. Become a participating community leader.

12. Give full support to appropriate professional organizations at the local, state, and national levels.

13. Keep abreast of literature and research in the field of educational leadership.

14. Arrange informal sessions with fellow principals to exchange views on current issues and problems.

15. Keep in contact with recognized leaders in the field of elementary school administration and supervision.

16. Develop the ability to engage in self-analysis.

17. Search for opportunities to get stimulating advanced training.

18. Attend and help organize workshops on community leadership.

19. Strive to exemplify wholesome and well-balanced living.

20. Try something experimental occasionally in administering the school.

21. Develop a well-rounded personal library.

22. Strive to make each new experience educative.

23. Improve the art of public speaking.

24. Develop the power to remember names.

25. Keep a strong faith and an active sense of humor.

SELECTED REFERENCES FOR EXTENDED READING

ADAMS, HAROLD P., and DICKEY, FRANK G. *Basic Principles of Supervision.* New York: American Book Co., 1953, chap. 3.

ASSOCIATION FOR SUPERVISION AND CURRICULUM DEVELOPMENT. *Leadership Through Supervision: 1946 Yearbook.* Washington, D. C.: National Education Association, 1946.

AYER, FRED C. *Fundamentals of Instructional Supervision.* New York: Harper & Bros., 1954, chaps. 3 and 4.

CAMPBELL, CLYDE (ed.). *Practical Applications of Democratic Administration.* New York: Harper & Bros., 1952.

DEPARTMENT OF ELEMENTARY SCHOOL PRINCIPALS. *Bases for Effective Learning: Thirty-First Yearbook.* Washington, D. C.: National Education Association, 1952.

OTTO, HENRY J. *Elementary-School Organization and Administration.* New York: Prentice-Hall, Inc., 1953, chap. 12.

SHANE, HAROLD G., and YAUCH, WILBUR A. *Creative School Administration.* New York: Henry Holt & Co., 1954.

SPEARS, HAROLD. *Improving the Supervision of Instruction.* New York: Prentice-Hall, Inc., 1953, chap. 10.

WILES, KIMBALL. *Supervision for Better Schools.* New York: Prentice-Hall, Inc., 1950.

NAME INDEX

SUBJECT INDEX